ASCENDANCE OF A BOOKWORM

I'll do anything to become a librarian!

Part 1 If there aren't any books, I'll just have to make some!

Volume 4

Author: **Miya Kazuki** / Artist: **Suzuka**
Character Designer: **You Shiina**

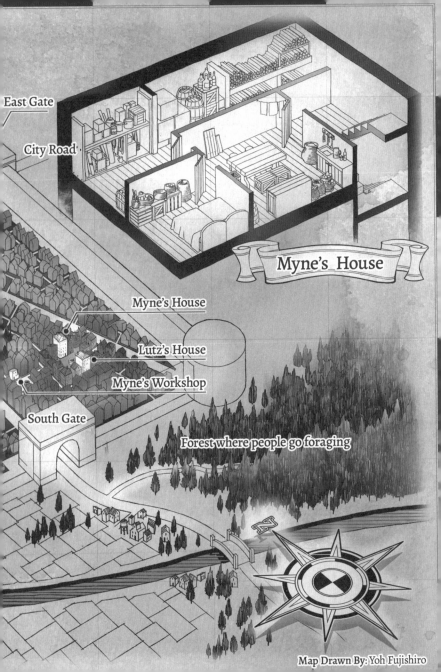

East Gate

City Road

Myne's House

Myne's House

Lutz's House

Myne's Workshop

South Gate

Forest where people go foraging

Map Drawn By: Yoh Fujishiro

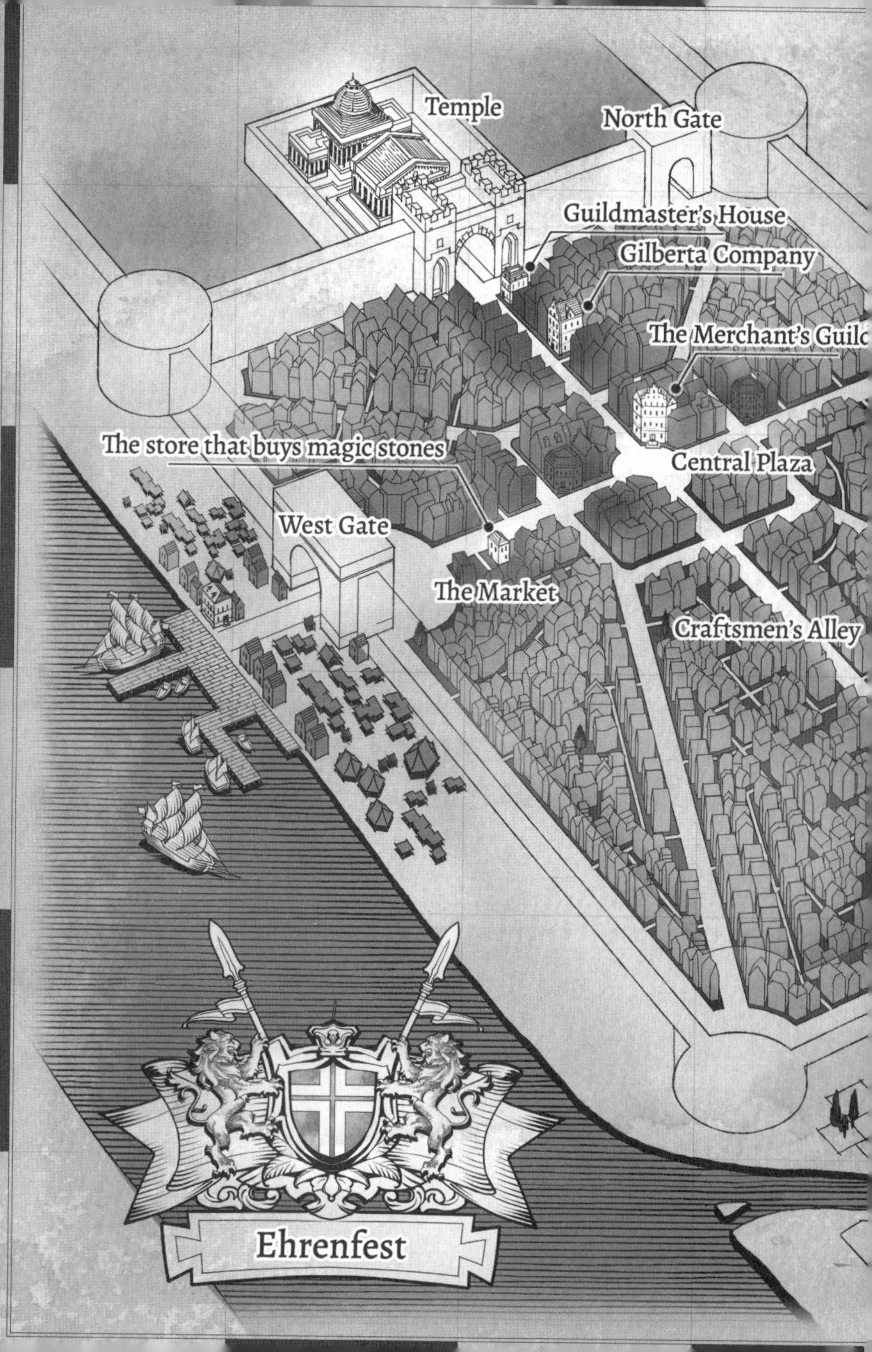
Temple
North Gate
Guildmaster's House
Gilberta Company
The Merchant's Guild
The store that buys magic stones
Central Plaza
West Gate
The Market
Craftsmen's Alley
Ehrenfest

ASCENDANCE OF A BOOKWORM
I'll do anything to become a librarian!
Part 1 If there aren't any books,
I'll just have to make some!

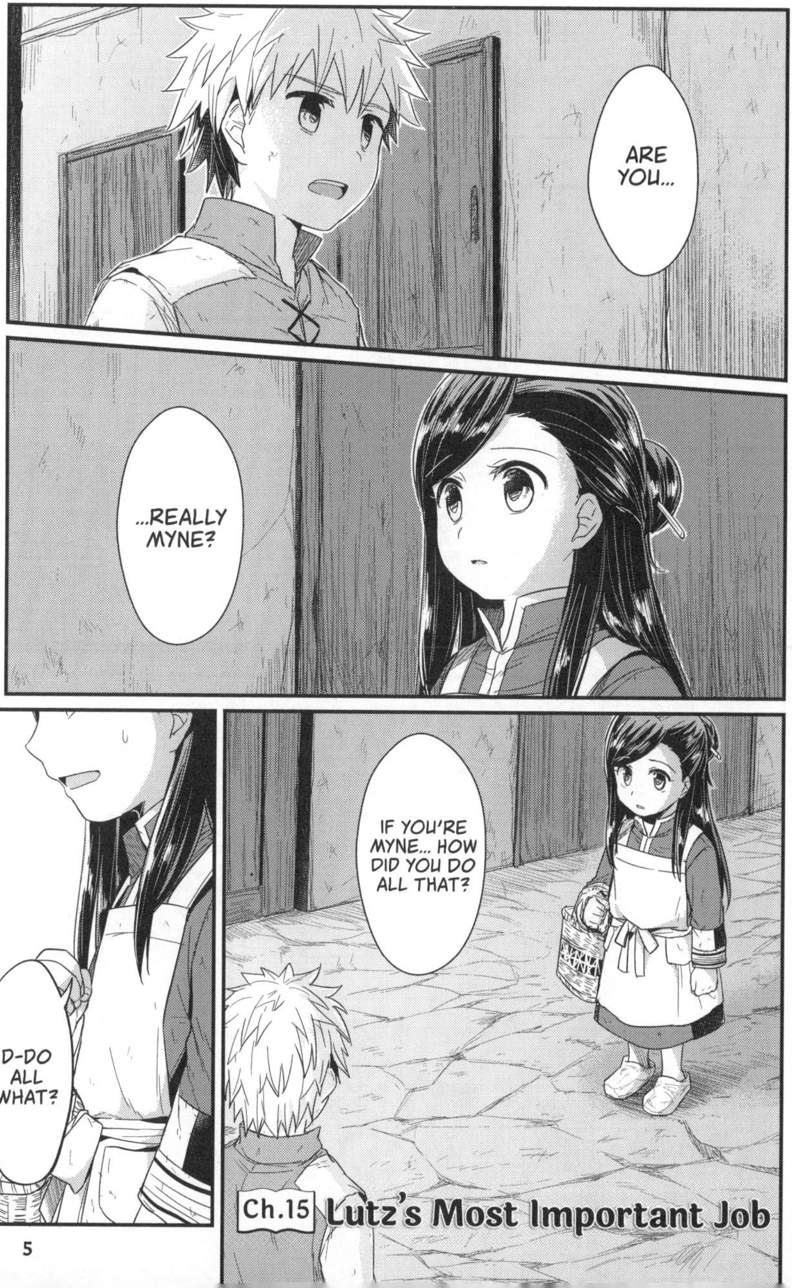
ARE YOU...
...REALLY MYNE?
IF YOU'RE MYNE... HOW DID YOU DO ALL THAT?
Ch.15 Lutz's Most Important Job
D-DO ALL WHAT?

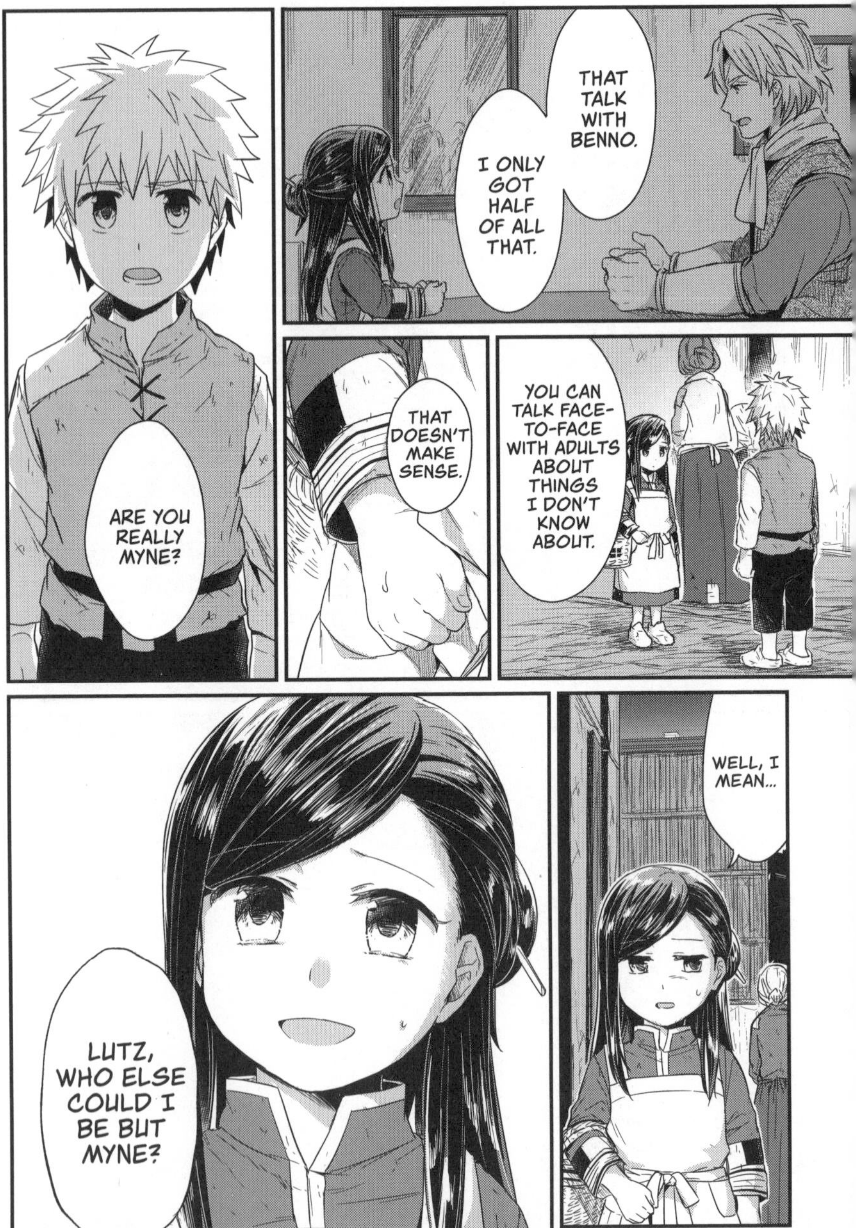
THAT TALK WITH BENNO.
I ONLY GOT HALF OF ALL THAT.
YOU CAN TALK FACE-TO-FACE WITH ADULTS ABOUT THINGS I DON'T KNOW ABOUT.
THAT DOESN'T MAKE SENSE.
ARE YOU REALLY MYNE?
WELL, I MEAN...
LUTZ, WHO ELSE COULD I BE BUT MYNE?

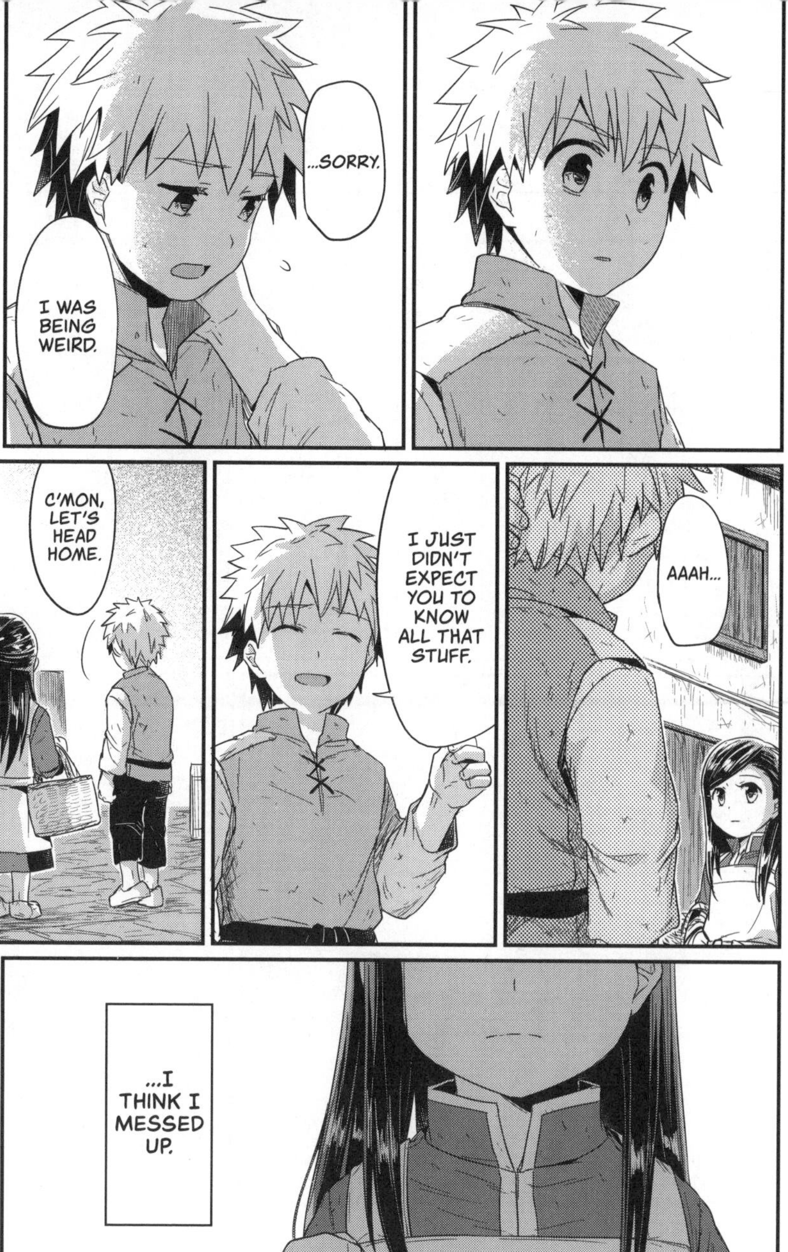
...SORRY.
I WAS BEING WEIRD.
AAAH...
I JUST DIDN'T EXPECT YOU TO KNOW ALL THAT STUFF.
C'MON, LET'S HEAD HOME.
...I THINK I MESSED UP.

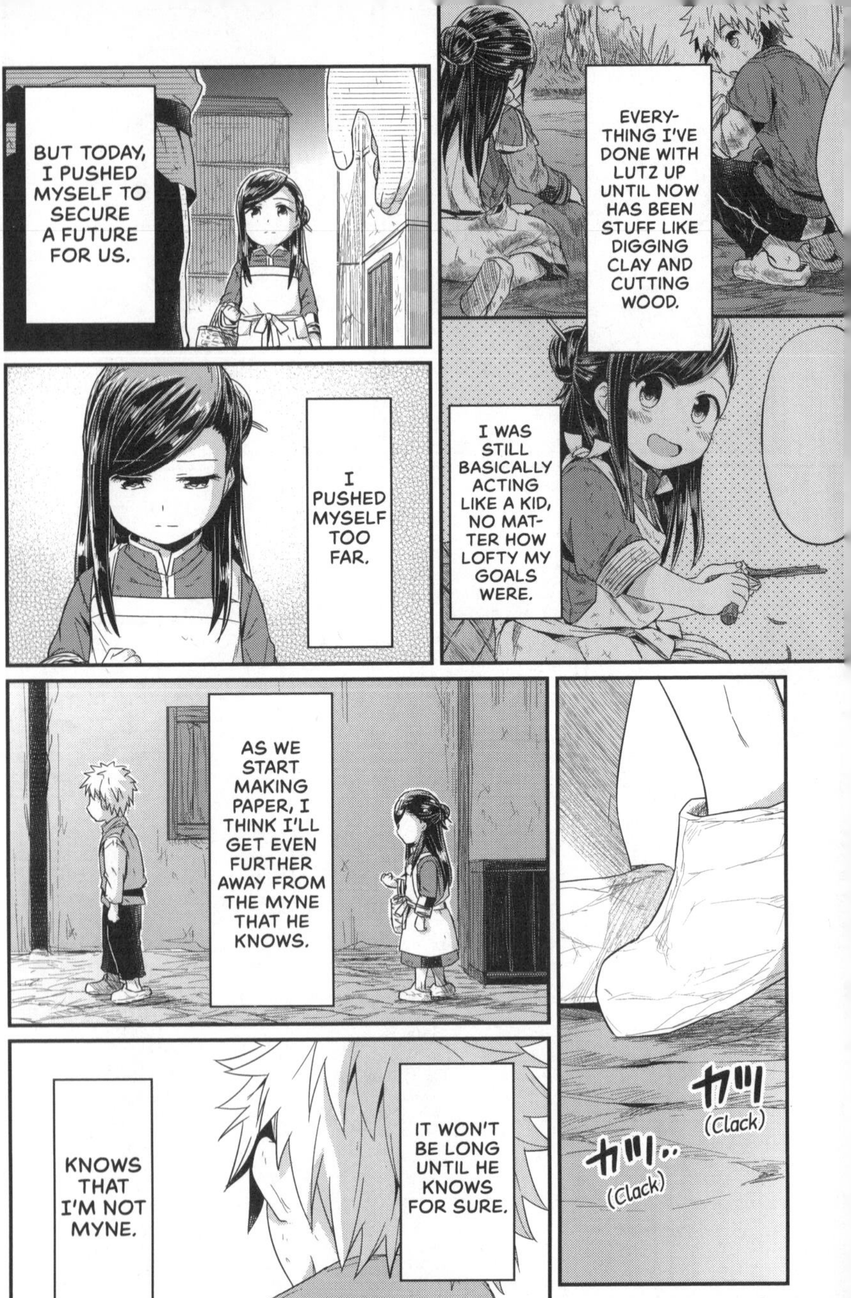
EVERY-THING I'VE DONE WITH LUTZ UP UNTIL NOW HAS BEEN STUFF LIKE DIGGING CLAY AND CUTTING WOOD.
BUT TODAY, I PUSHED MYSELF TO SECURE A FUTURE FOR US.
I WAS STILL BASICALLY ACTING LIKE A KID, NO MAT-TER HOW LOFTY MY GOALS WERE.
I PUSHED MYSELF TOO FAR.
カツ
(Clack)
カツ..
(Clack)
AS WE START MAKING PAPER, I THINK I'LL GET EVEN FURTHER AWAY FROM THE MYNE THAT HE KNOWS.
IT WON'T BE LONG UNTIL HE KNOWS FOR SURE.
KNOWS THAT I'M NOT MYNE.

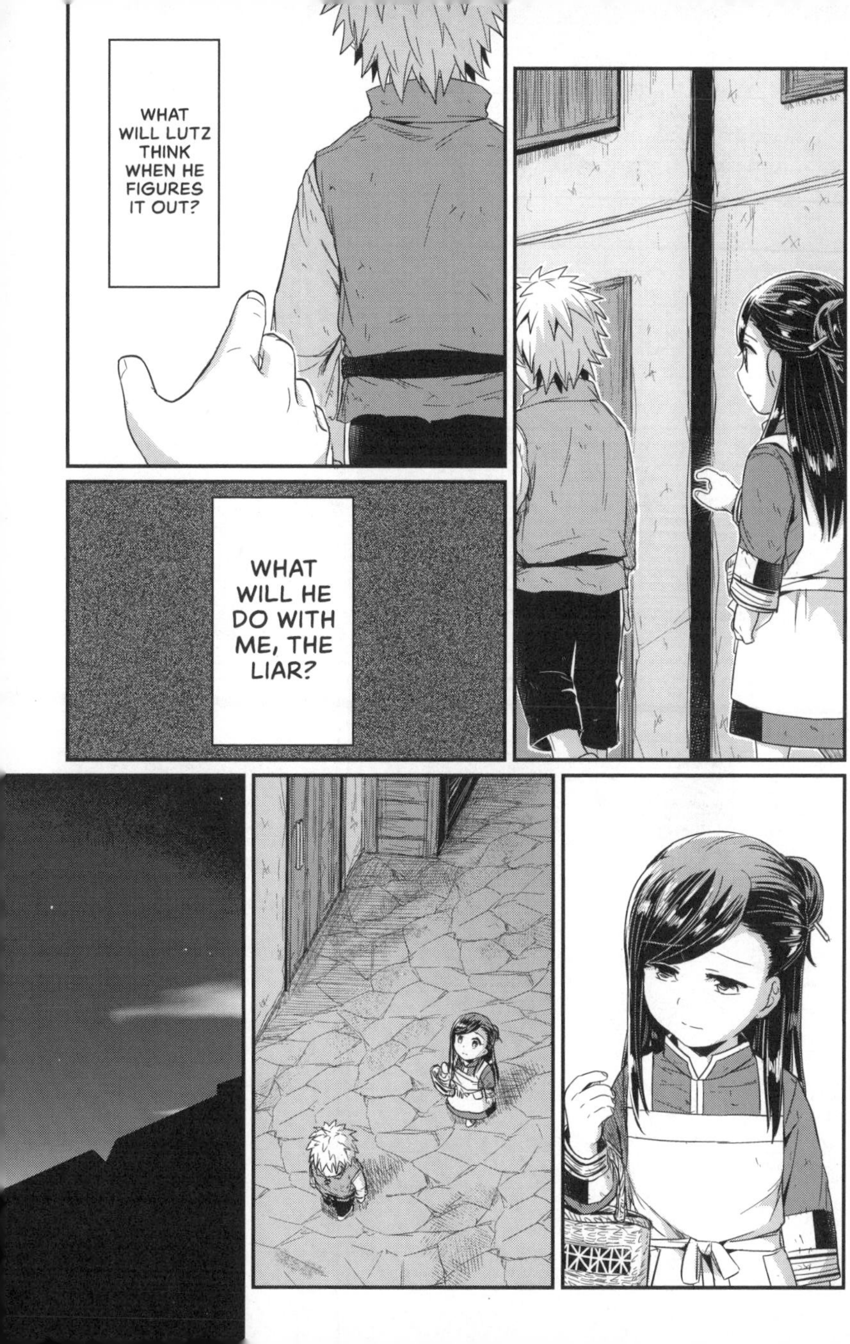
WHAT WILL LUTZ THINK WHEN HE FIGURES IT OUT?
WHAT WILL HE DO WITH ME, THE LIAR?

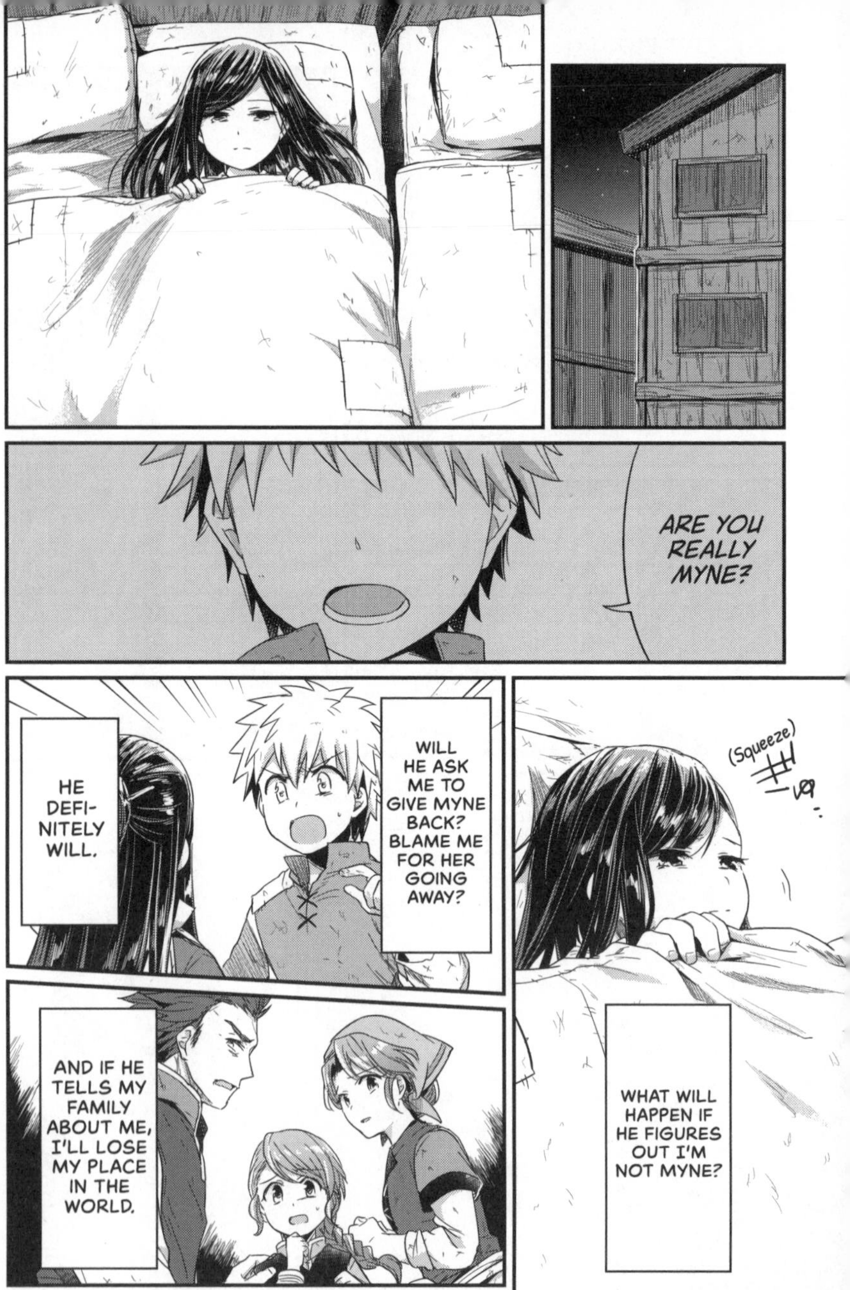
ARE YOU REALLY MYNE?
(Squeeze)
WHAT WILL HAPPEN IF HE FIGURES OUT I'M NOT MYNE?
WILL HE ASK ME TO GIVE MYNE BACK? BLAME ME FOR HER GOING AWAY?
HE DEFINITELY WILL.
AND IF HE TELLS MY FAMILY ABOUT ME, I'LL LOSE MY PLACE IN THE WORLD.

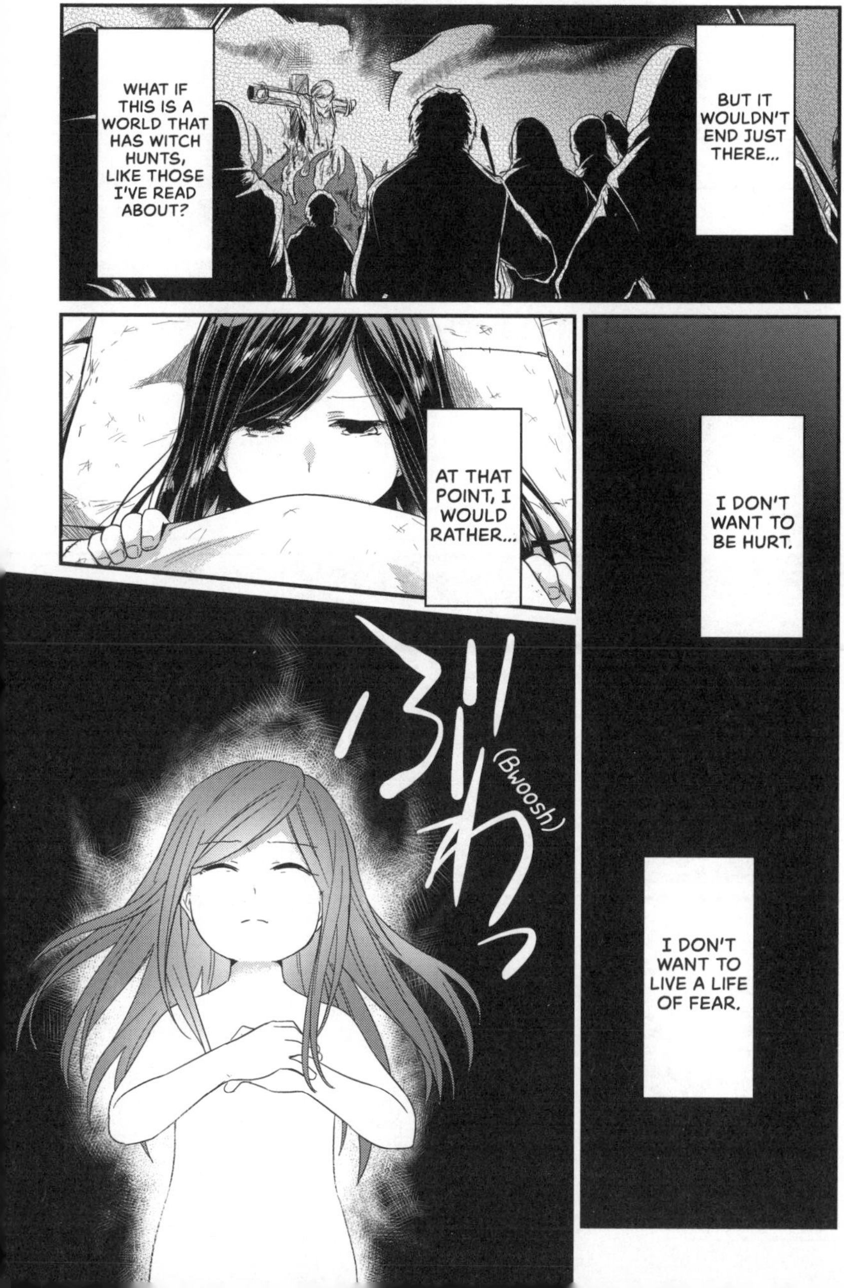
BUT IT WOULDN'T END JUST THERE...
WHAT IF THIS IS A WORLD THAT HAS WITCH HUNTS, LIKE THOSE I'VE READ ABOUT?
I DON'T WANT TO BE HURT.
I DON'T WANT TO LIVE A LIFE OF FEAR.
AT THAT POINT, I WOULD RATHER...
ふぃわっ
(Bwoosh)

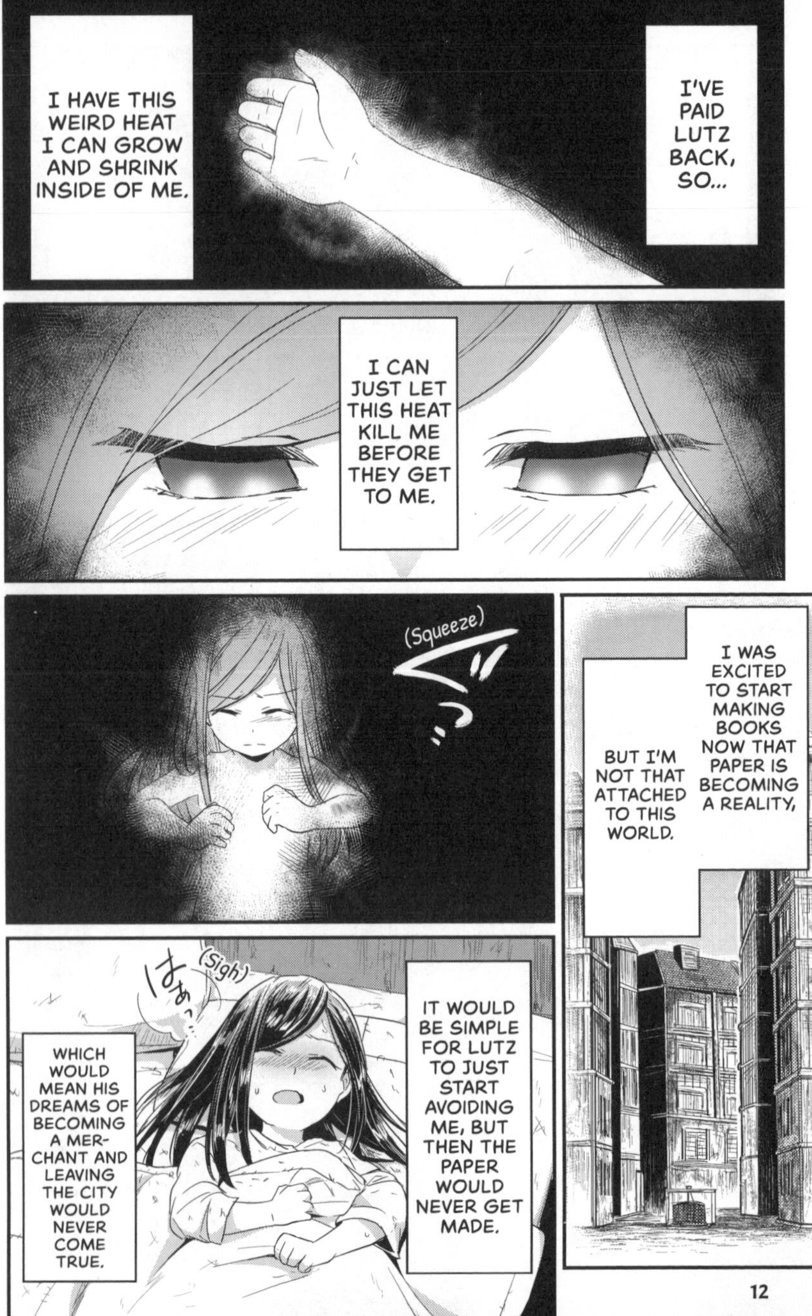
I'VE PAID LUTZ BACK, SO...
I HAVE THIS WEIRD HEAT I CAN GROW AND SHRINK INSIDE OF ME.
I CAN JUST LET THIS HEAT KILL ME BEFORE THEY GET TO ME.
I WAS EXCITED TO START MAKING BOOKS NOW THAT PAPER IS BECOMING A REALITY,
BUT I'M NOT THAT ATTACHED TO THIS WORLD.
(Squeeze)
(Sigh)
IT WOULD BE SIMPLE FOR LUTZ TO JUST START AVOIDING ME, BUT THEN THE PAPER WOULD NEVER GET MADE.
WHICH WOULD MEAN HIS DREAMS OF BECOMING A MER-CHANT AND LEAVING THE CITY WOULD NEVER COME TRUE.

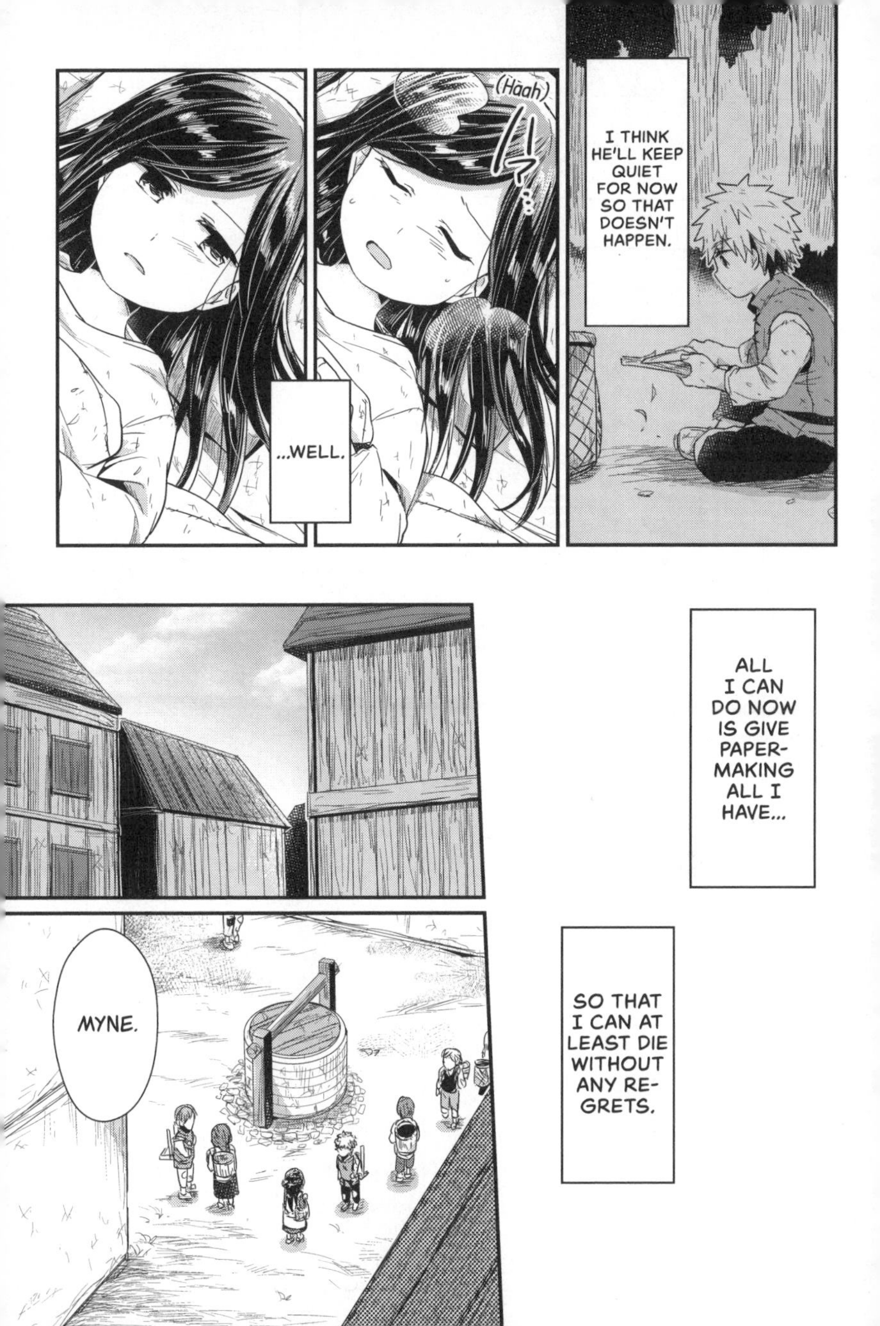
I THINK HE'LL KEEP QUIET FOR NOW SO THAT DOESN'T HAPPEN.
(Hàah)
...WELL.
ALL I CAN DO NOW IS GIVE PAPER-MAKING ALL I HAVE...
SO THAT I CAN AT LEAST DIE WITHOUT ANY RE-GRETS.
MYNE.

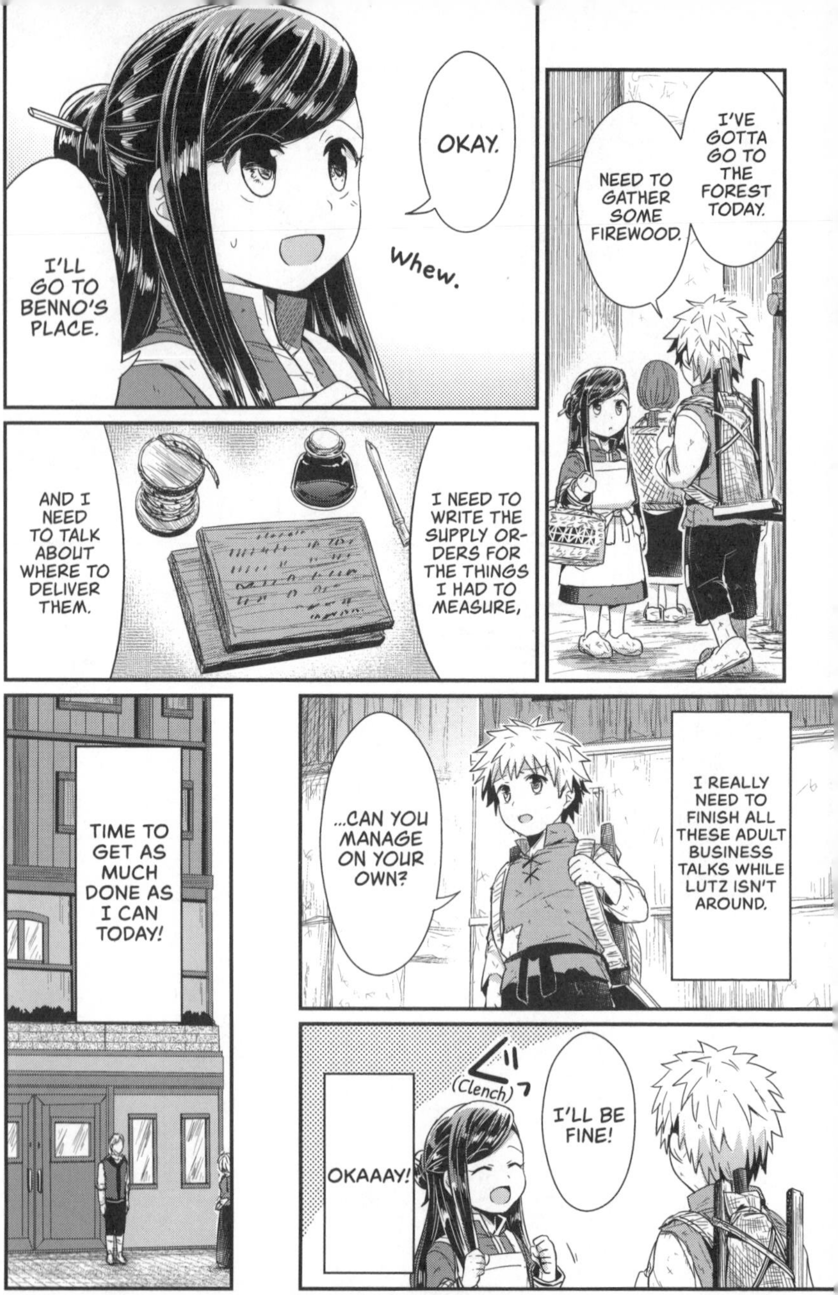
I'VE GOTTA GO TO THE FOREST TODAY.
NEED TO GATHER SOME FIREWOOD.
OKAY.
Whew.
I'LL GO TO BENNO'S PLACE.
I NEED TO WRITE THE SUPPLY OR-DERS FOR THE THINGS I HAD TO MEASURE,
AND I NEED TO TALK ABOUT WHERE TO DELIVER THEM.
I REALLY NEED TO FINISH ALL THESE ADULT BUSINESS TALKS WHILE LUTZ ISN'T AROUND.
...CAN YOU MANAGE ON YOUR OWN?
I'LL BE FINE!
(Clench)
OKAAAY!
TIME TO GET AS MUCH DONE AS I CAN TODAY!

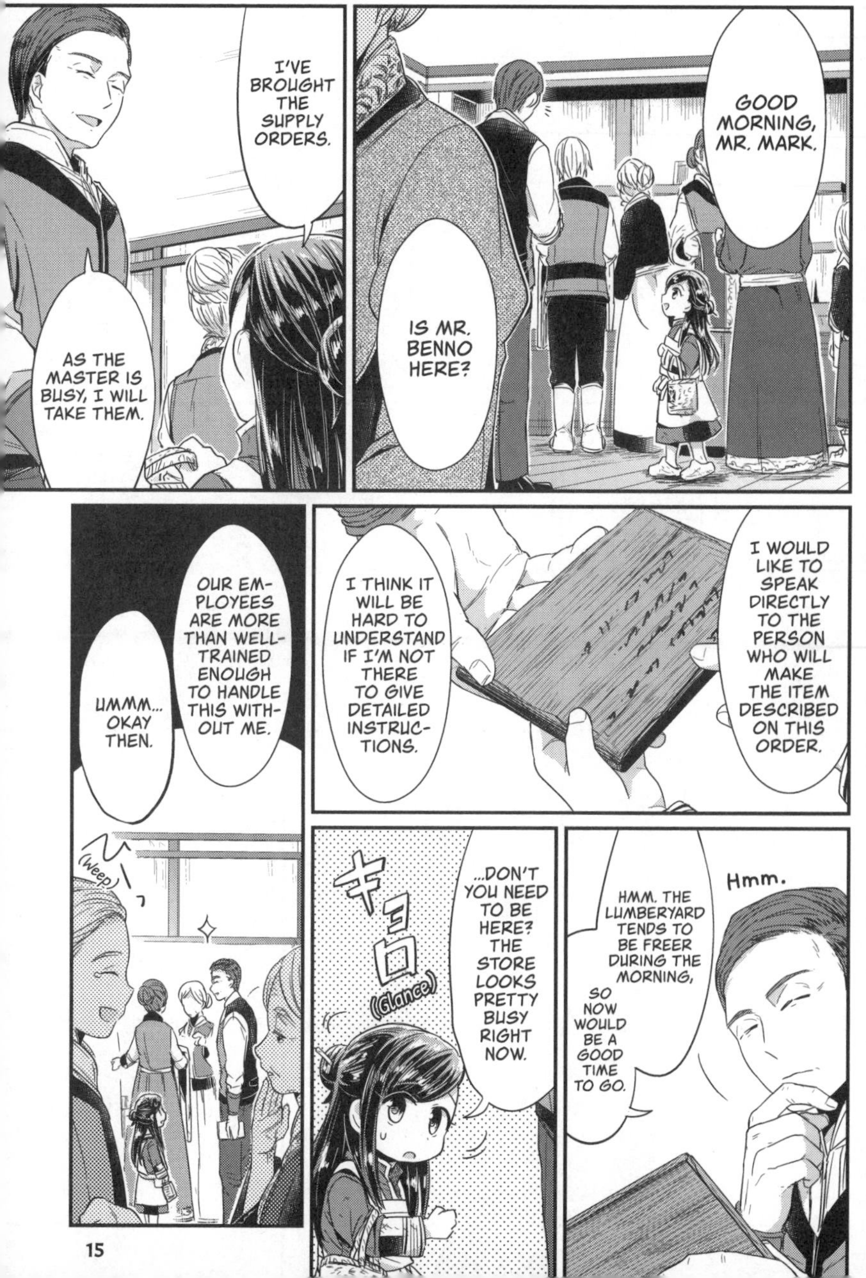
GOOD MORNING, MR. MARK.
IS MR. BENNO HERE?
I'VE BROUGHT THE SUPPLY ORDERS.
AS THE MASTER IS BUSY, I WILL TAKE THEM.
I WOULD LIKE TO SPEAK DIRECTLY TO THE PERSON WHO WILL MAKE THE ITEM DESCRIBED ON THIS ORDER.
I THINK IT WILL BE HARD TO UNDERSTAND IF I'M NOT THERE TO GIVE DETAILED INSTRUCTIONS.
Hmm.
HMM. THE LUMBERYARD TENDS TO BE FREER DURING THE MORNING,
SO NOW WOULD BE A GOOD TIME TO GO.
(Glance)
...DON'T YOU NEED TO BE HERE? THE STORE LOOKS PRETTY BUSY RIGHT NOW.
OUR EMPLOYEES ARE MORE THAN WELL-TRAINED ENOUGH TO HANDLE THIS WITHOUT ME.
UMMM... OKAY THEN.
(Weep)

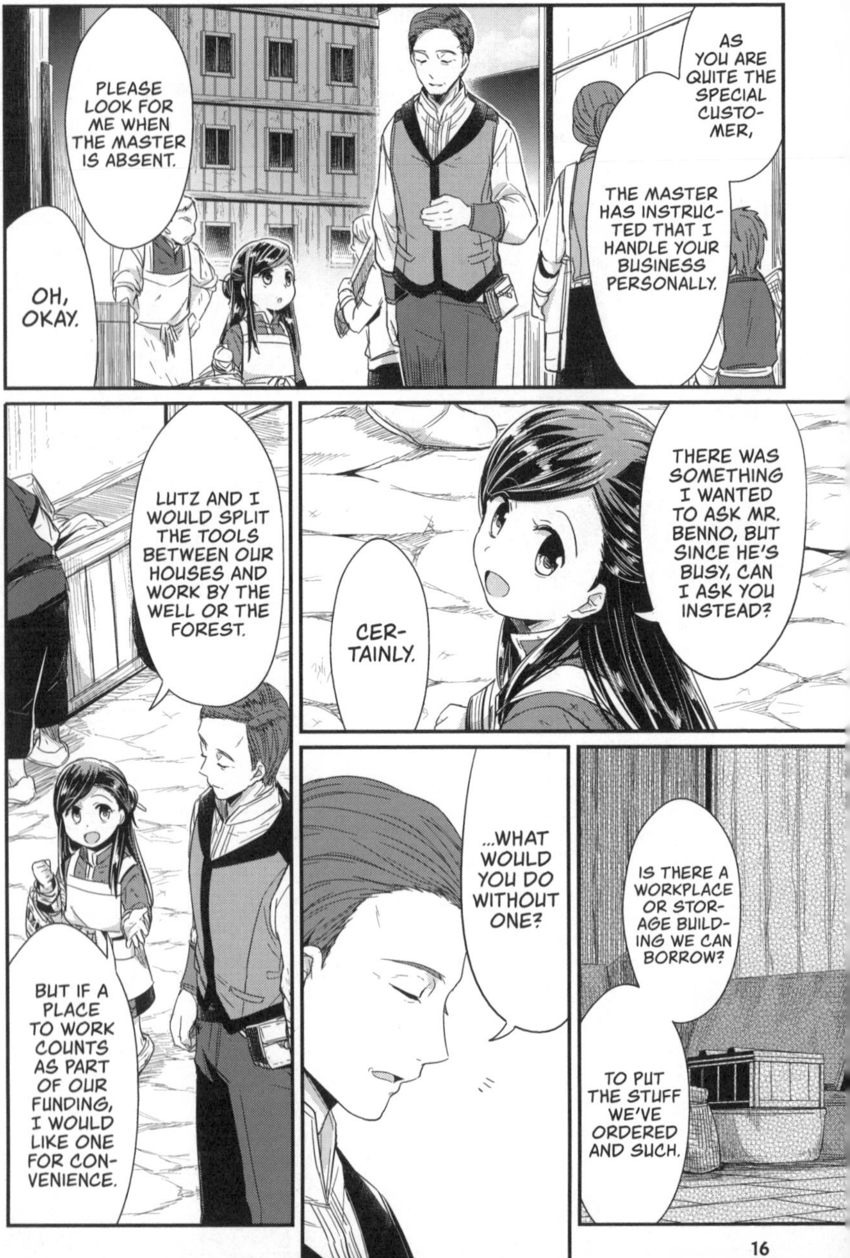

AS YOU ARE QUITE THE SPECIAL CUSTO-MER,
THE MASTER HAS INSTRUC-TED THAT I HANDLE YOUR BUSINESS PERSONALLY.
PLEASE LOOK FOR ME WHEN THE MASTER IS ABSENT.
OH, OKAY.
THERE WAS SOMETHING I WANTED TO ASK MR. BENNO, BUT SINCE HE'S BUSY, CAN I ASK YOU INSTEAD?
CER-TAINLY.
IS THERE A WORKPLACE OR STOR-AGE BUILD-ING WE CAN BORROW?
TO PUT THE STUFF WE'VE ORDERED AND SUCH.
...WHAT WOULD YOU DO WITHOUT ONE?
...
LUTZ AND I WOULD SPLIT THE TOOLS BETWEEN OUR HOUSES AND WORK BY THE WELL OR THE FOREST.
BUT IF A PLACE TO WORK COUNTS AS PART OF OUR FUNDING, I WOULD LIKE ONE FOR CON-VENIENCE.

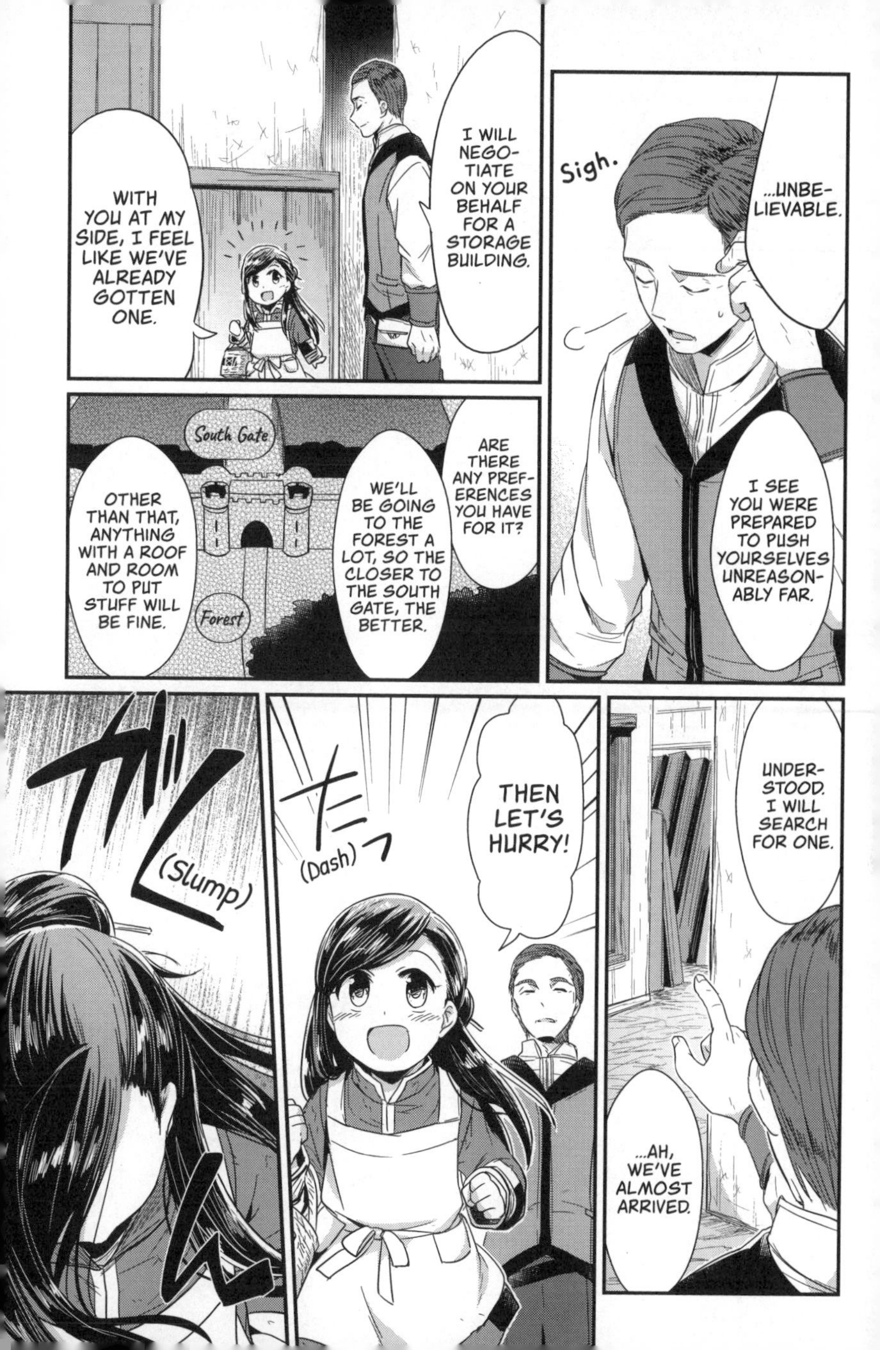
Sigh.
...UNBELIEVABLE.
I SEE YOU WERE PREPARED TO PUSH YOURSELVES UNREASONABLY FAR.
I WILL NEGOTIATE ON YOUR BEHALF FOR A STORAGE BUILDING.
WITH YOU AT MY SIDE, I FEEL LIKE WE'VE ALREADY GOTTEN ONE.
ARE THERE ANY PREFERENCES YOU HAVE FOR IT?
WE'LL BE GOING TO THE FOREST A LOT, SO THE CLOSER TO THE SOUTH GATE, THE BETTER.
South Gate
Forest
OTHER THAN THAT, ANYTHING WITH A ROOF AND ROOM TO PUT STUFF WILL BE FINE.
UNDERSTOOD. I WILL SEARCH FOR ONE.
...AH, WE'VE ALMOST ARRIVED.
THEN LET'S HURRY!
(Dash)
(Slump)

WHAT?

(Collapse)

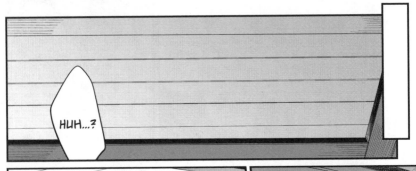

HUH...?

YOU'RE AWAKE, MYNE?

MRS. CORINNA...

WHERE AM I...?

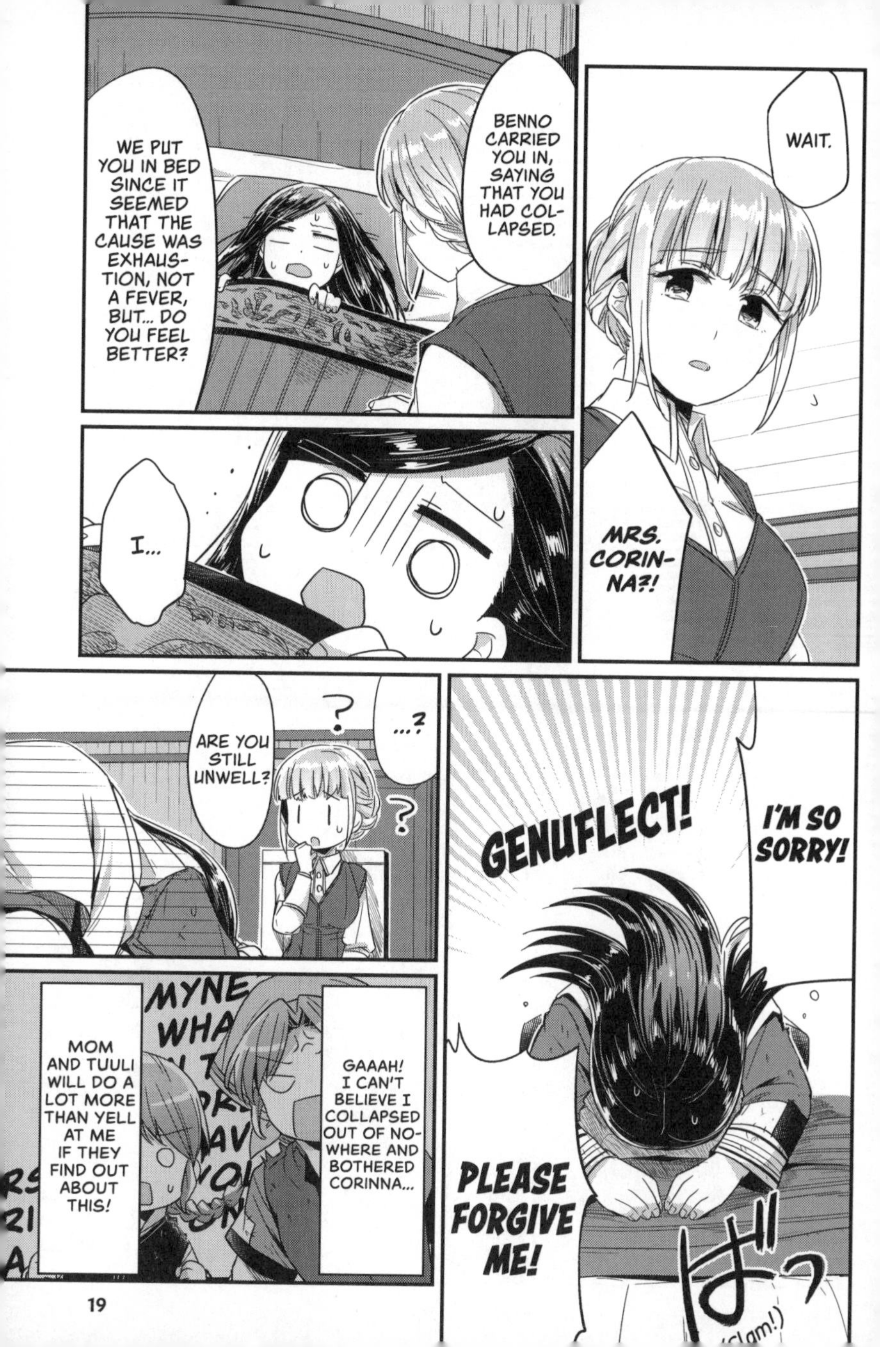
WAIT.
MRS. CORINNA?!
BENNO CARRIED YOU IN, SAYING THAT YOU HAD COL-LAPSED.
WE PUT YOU IN BED SINCE IT SEEMED THAT THE CAUSE WAS EXHAUS-TION, NOT A FEVER, BUT... DO YOU FEEL BETTER?
I...
GENUFLECT!
I'M SO SORRY!
PLEASE FORGIVE ME!
(Slam!)
...?
ARE YOU STILL UNWELL?
GAAAH! I CAN'T BELIEVE I COLLAPSED OUT OF NO-WHERE AND BOTHERED CORINNA...
MOM AND TUULI WILL DO A LOT MORE THAN YELL AT ME IF THEY FIND OUT ABOUT THIS!

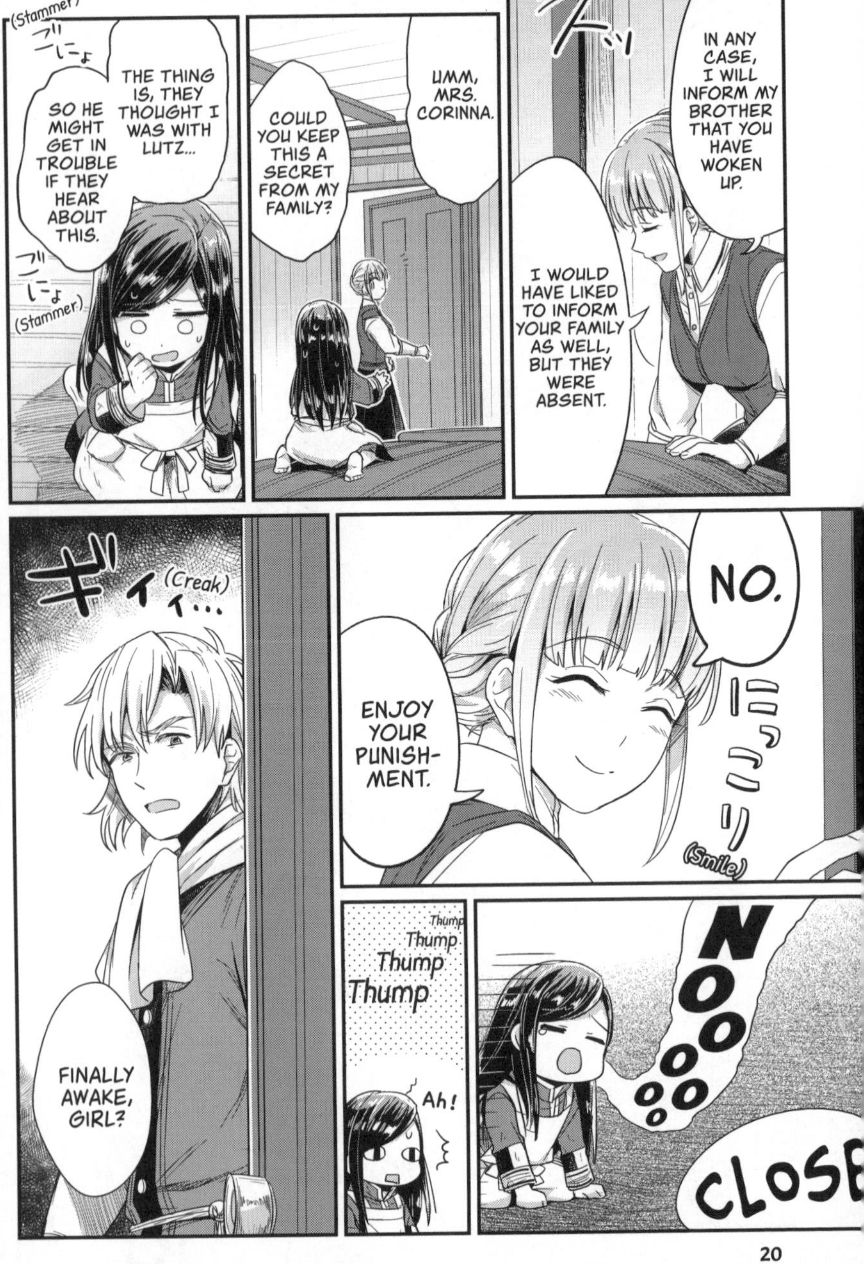
(Stand)
ズッ
IN ANY CASE, I WILL INFORM MY BROTHER THAT YOU HAVE WOKEN UP.
I WOULD HAVE LIKED TO INFORM YOUR FAMILY AS WELL, BUT THEY WERE ABSENT.
UMM, MRS. CORINNA.
COULD YOU KEEP THIS A SECRET FROM MY FAMILY?
(Stammer)
ゴにょ
THE THING IS, THEY THOUGHT I WAS WITH LUTZ...
SO HE MIGHT GET IN TROUBLE IF THEY HEAR ABOUT THIS.
ゴにょ
(Stammer.)
NO.
ENJOY YOUR PUNISHMENT.
ニッコリ
(Smile)
NOOOOOOOO
CLOSE
Thump
Thump
Thump
Thump
Ah!
ギィィ…
(Creak)
FINALLY AWAKE, GIRL?

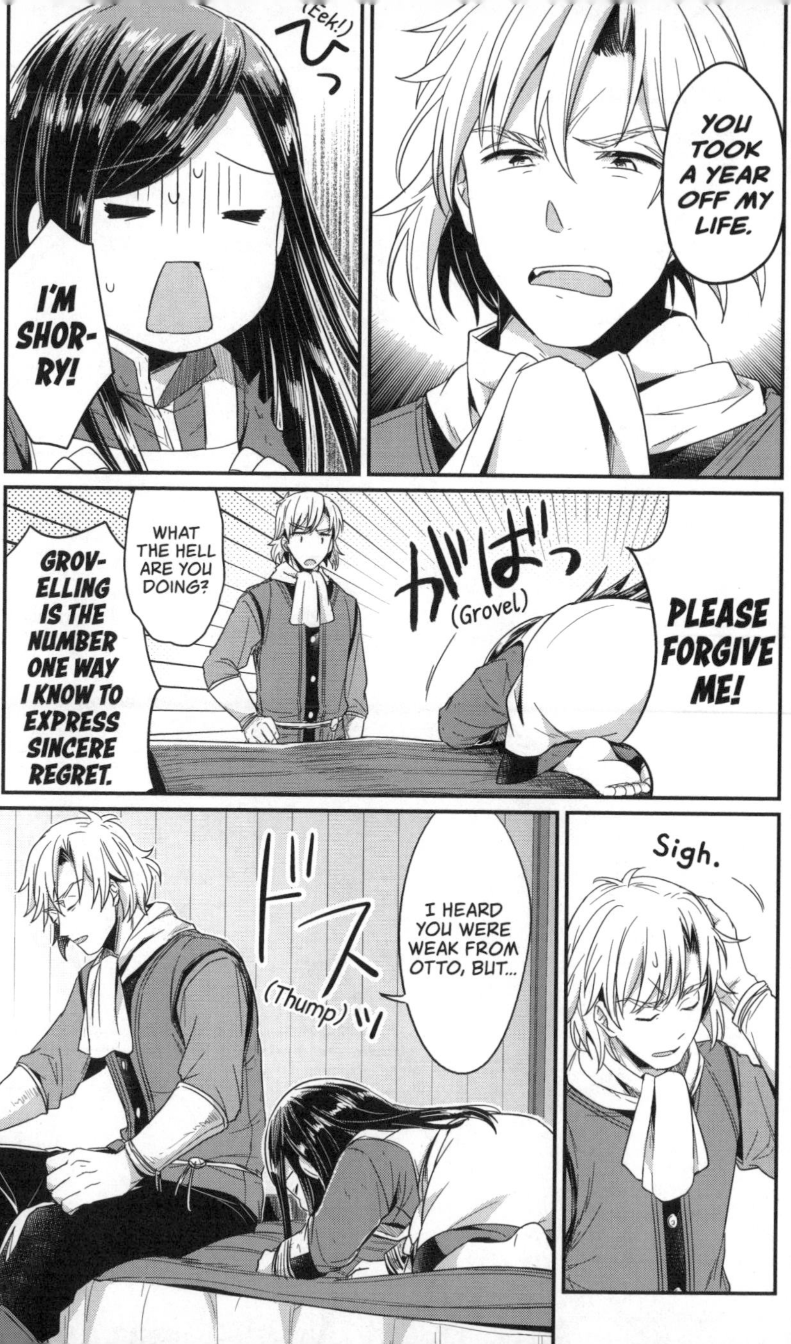
YOU TOOK A YEAR OFF MY LIFE.
ひっ
(Eek!)
I'M SHORRY!
PLEASE FORGIVE ME!
がばっ
(Grovel)
WHAT THE HELL ARE YOU DOING?
GROVELLING IS THE NUMBER ONE WAY I KNOW TO EXPRESS SINCERE REGRET.
Sigh.
I HEARD YOU WERE WEAK FROM OTTO, BUT...
ドスッ
(Thump)

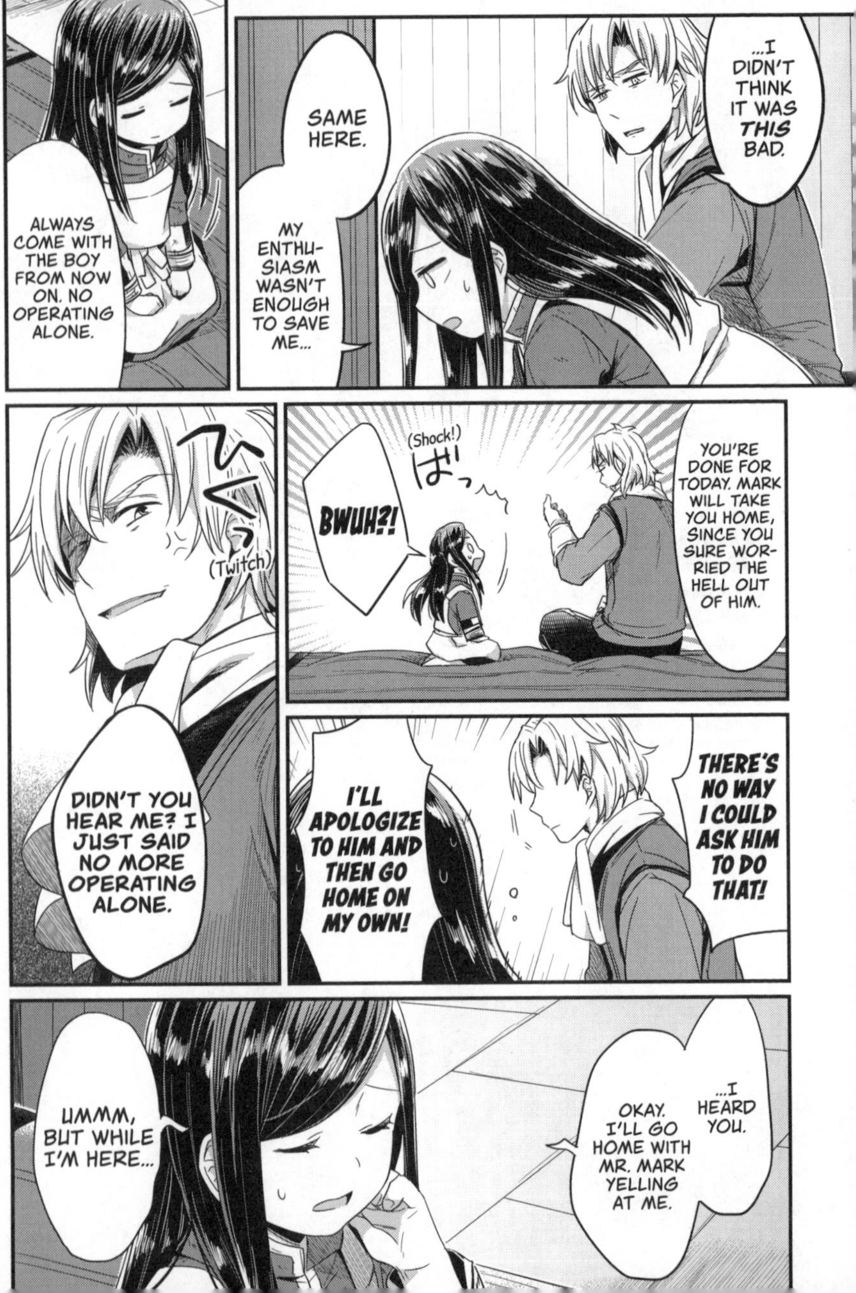
...I DIDN'T THINK IT WAS *THIS* BAD.
SAME HERE.
MY ENTHU-SIASM WASN'T ENOUGH TO SAVE ME...
ALWAYS COME WITH THE BOY FROM NOW ON. NO OPERATING ALONE.
YOU'RE DONE FOR TODAY. MARK WILL TAKE YOU HOME, SINCE YOU SURE WOR-RIED THE HELL OUT OF HIM.
(Shock!)
BWUH?!
THERE'S NO WAY I COULD ASK HIM TO DO THAT!
I'LL APOLOGIZE TO HIM AND THEN GO HOME ON MY OWN!
(Twitch)
DIDN'T YOU HEAR ME? I JUST SAID NO MORE OPERATING ALONE.
...I HEARD YOU.
OKAY. I'LL GO HOME WITH MR. MARK YELLING AT ME.
UMMM, BUT WHILE I'M HERE...

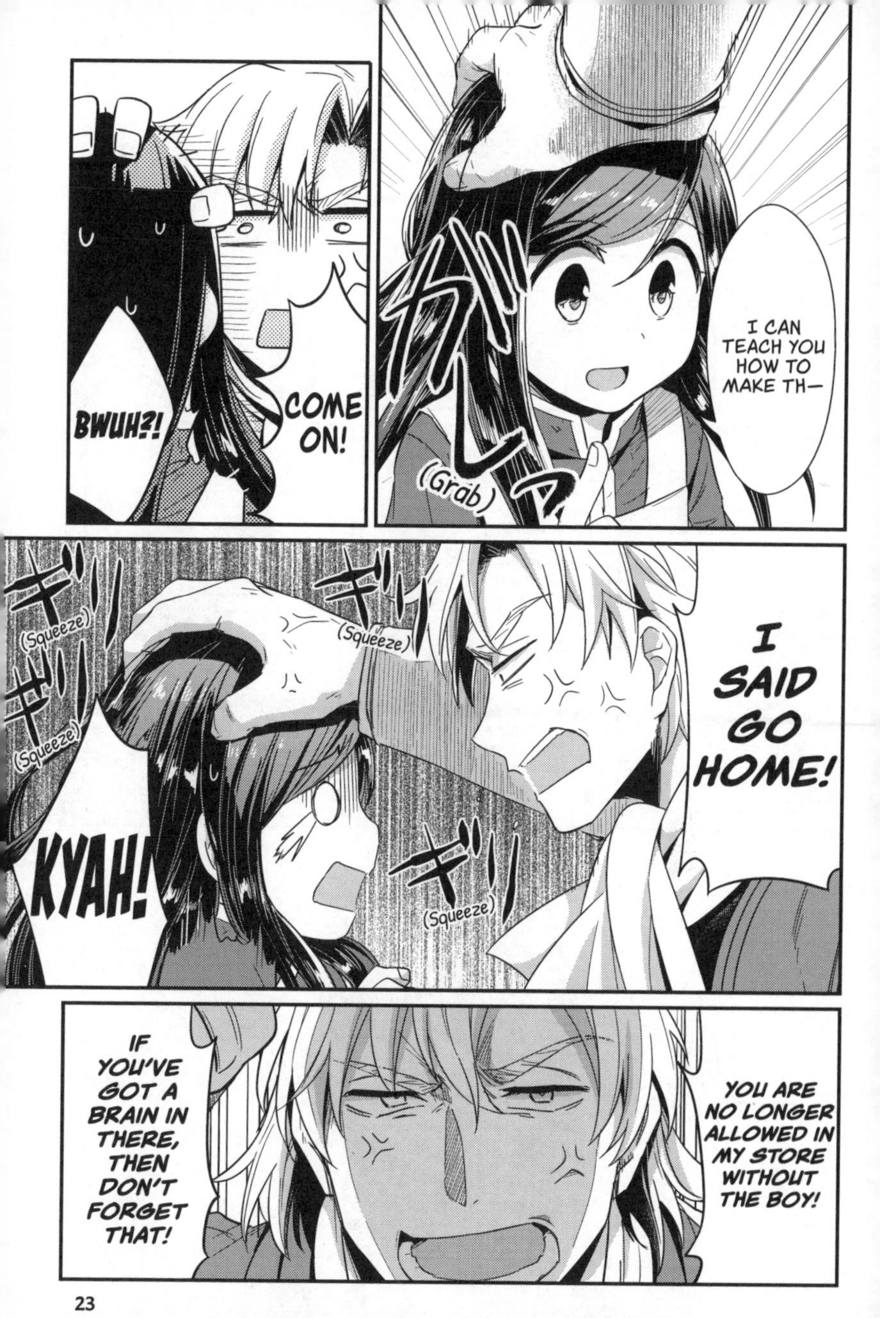
I CAN TEACH YOU HOW TO MAKE TH—
(Grab)
COME ON!
BWUH?!
I SAID GO HOME!
(Squeeze)
(Squeeze)
(Squeeze)
(Squeeze)
KYAH!
YOU ARE NO LONGER ALLOWED IN MY STORE WITHOUT THE BOY!
IF YOU'VE GOT A BRAIN IN THERE, THEN DON'T FORGET THAT!

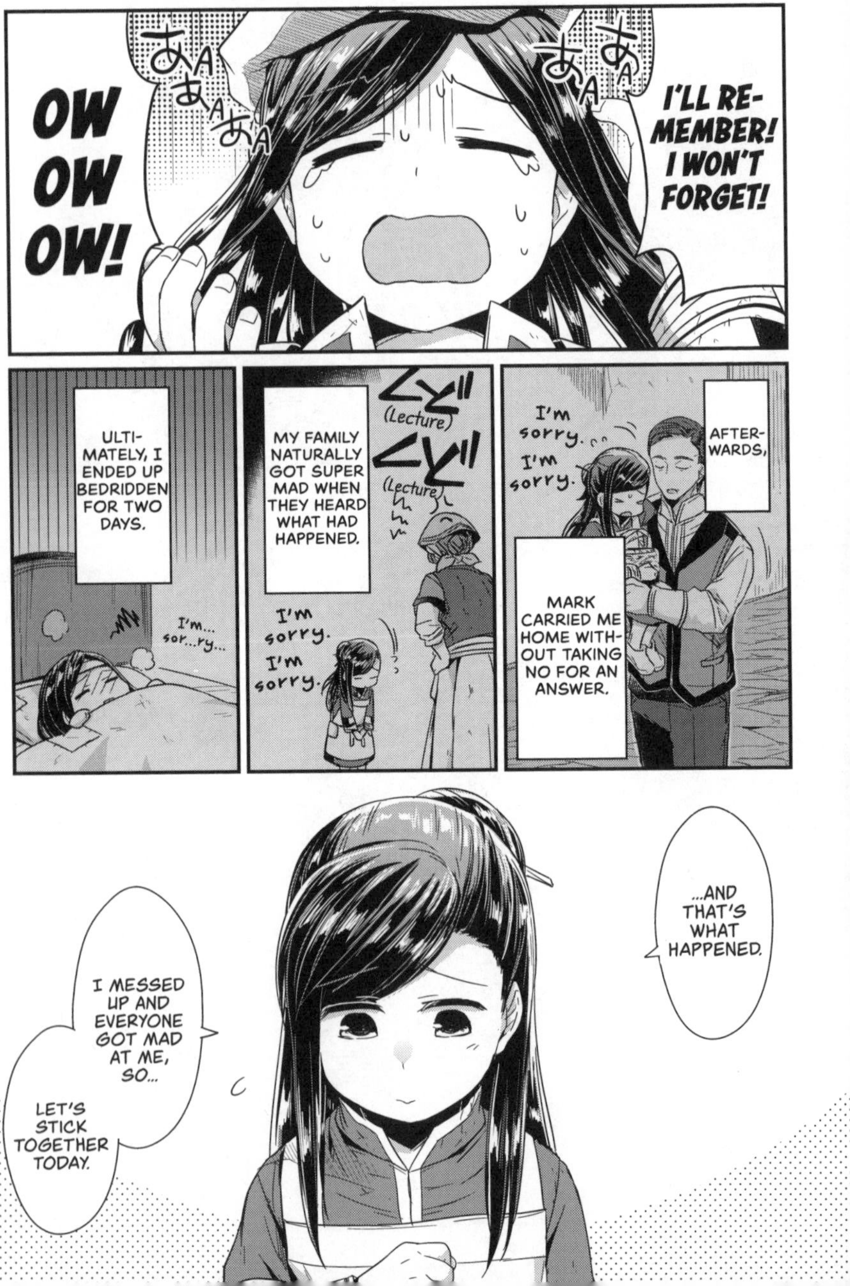
あAあA
I'LL RE-MEMBER! I WON'T FORGET!
あAあAあA
OW OW OW!
AFTER-WARDS,
I'm sorry. I'm sorry.
MARK CARRIED ME HOME WITH-OUT TAKING NO FOR AN ANSWER.
くど (Lecture)
くど (Lecture)
MY FAMILY NATURALLY GOT SUPER MAD WHEN THEY HEARD WHAT HAD HAPPENED.
I'm sorry. I'm sorry.
ULTI-MATELY, I ENDED UP BEDRIDDEN FOR TWO DAYS.
I'm... sor...ry...
...AND THAT'S WHAT HAPPENED.
I MESSED UP AND EVERYONE GOT MAD AT ME, SO...
LET'S STICK TOGETHER TODAY.

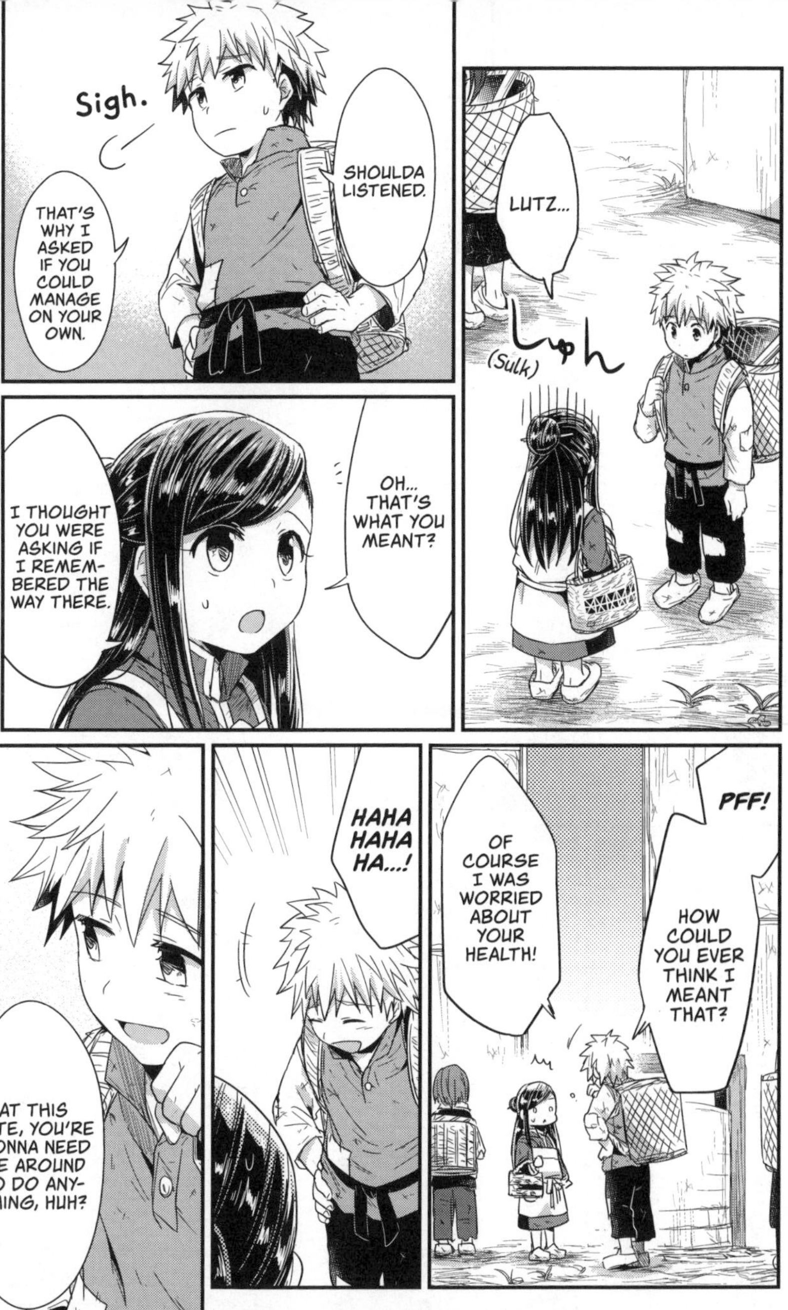
LUTZ...
しゅん
(Sulk)
SHOULDA LISTENED.
Sigh.
THAT'S WHY I ASKED IF YOU COULD MANAGE ON YOUR OWN.
OH... THAT'S WHAT YOU MEANT?
I THOUGHT YOU WERE ASKING IF I REMEMBERED THE WAY THERE.
PFF!
HOW COULD YOU EVER THINK I MEANT THAT?
OF COURSE I WAS WORRIED ABOUT YOUR HEALTH!
HAHA HAHA HA...!
AT THIS RATE, YOU'RE GONNA NEED ME AROUND TO DO ANYTHING, HUH?

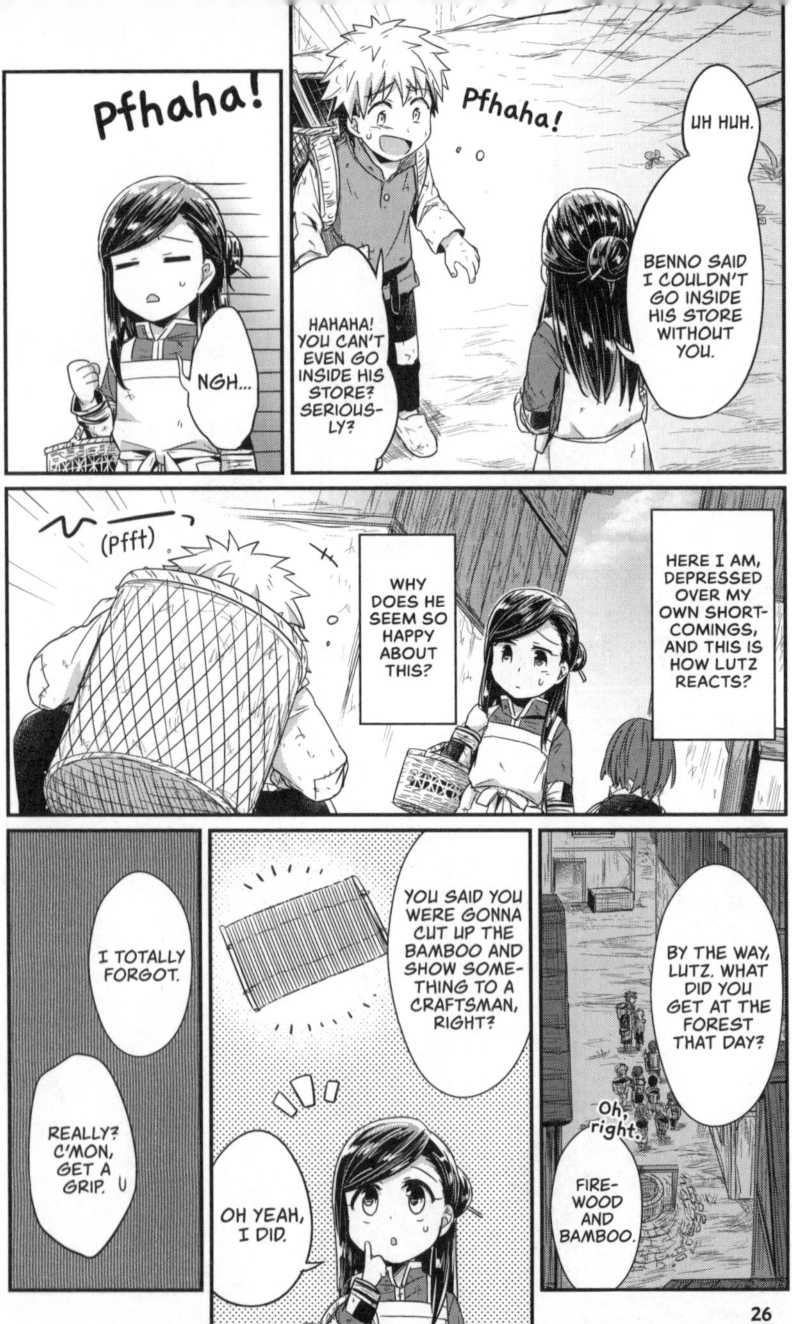
UH HUH.
Pfhaha!
BENNO SAID I COULDN'T GO INSIDE HIS STORE WITHOUT YOU.
HAHAHA! YOU CAN'T EVEN GO INSIDE HIS STORE? SERIOUS-LY?
Pfhaha!
NGH...
HERE I AM, DEPRESSED OVER MY OWN SHORT-COMINGS, AND THIS IS HOW LUTZ REACTS?
WHY DOES HE SEEM SO HAPPY ABOUT THIS?
(pfft)
BY THE WAY, LUTZ. WHAT DID YOU GET AT THE FOREST THAT DAY?
Oh, right.
FIRE-WOOD AND BAMBOO.
YOU SAID YOU WERE GONNA CUT UP THE BAMBOO AND SHOW SOME-THING TO A CRAFTSMAN, RIGHT?
OH YEAH, I DID.
I TOTALLY FORGOT.
REALLY? C'MON, GET A GRIP.

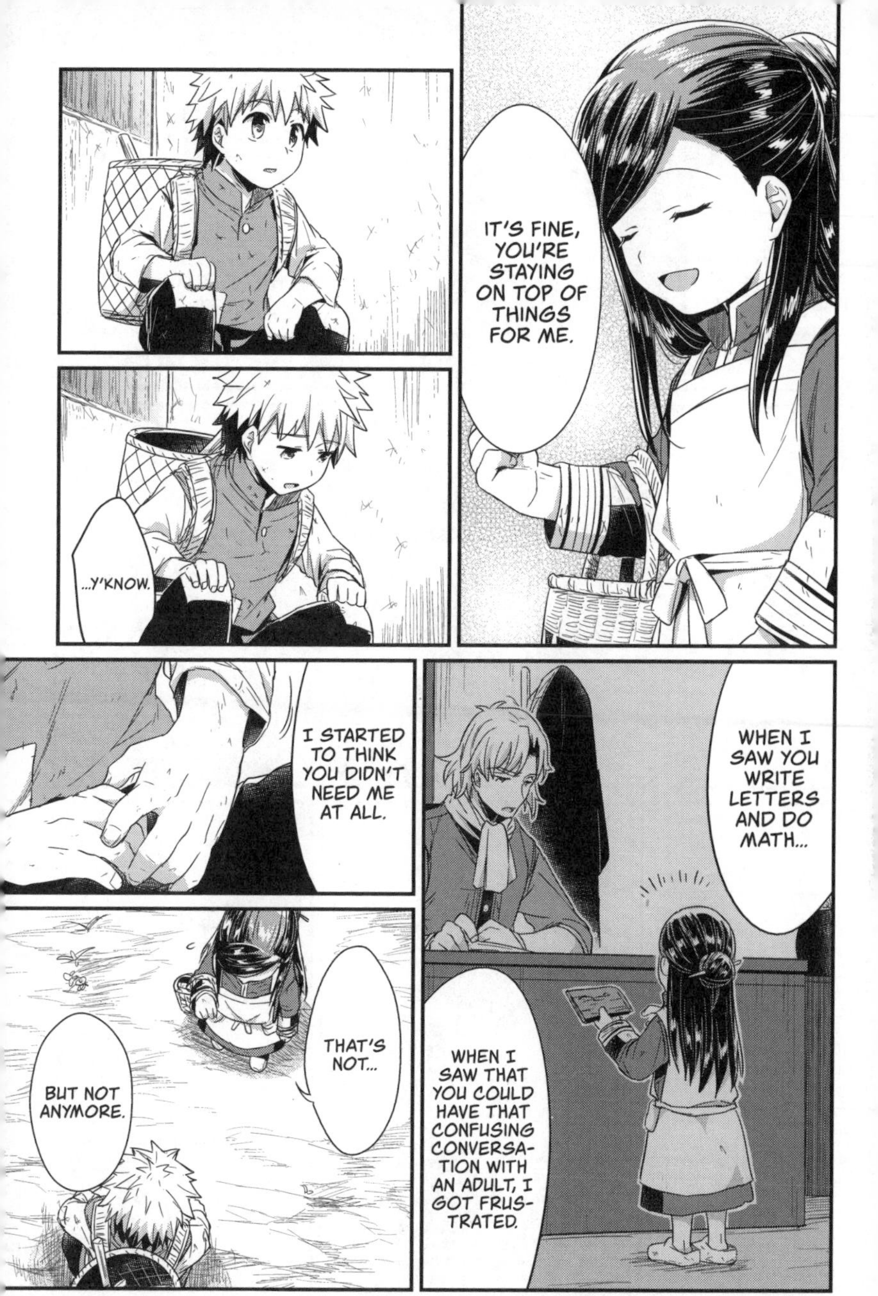
IT'S FINE, YOU'RE STAYING ON TOP OF THINGS FOR ME.
...Y'KNOW.
WHEN I SAW YOU WRITE LETTERS AND DO MATH...
WHEN I SAW THAT YOU COULD HAVE THAT CONFUSING CONVERSA-TION WITH AN ADULT, I GOT FRUS-TRATED.
I STARTED TO THINK YOU DIDN'T NEED ME AT ALL.
THAT'S NOT...
BUT NOT ANYMORE.

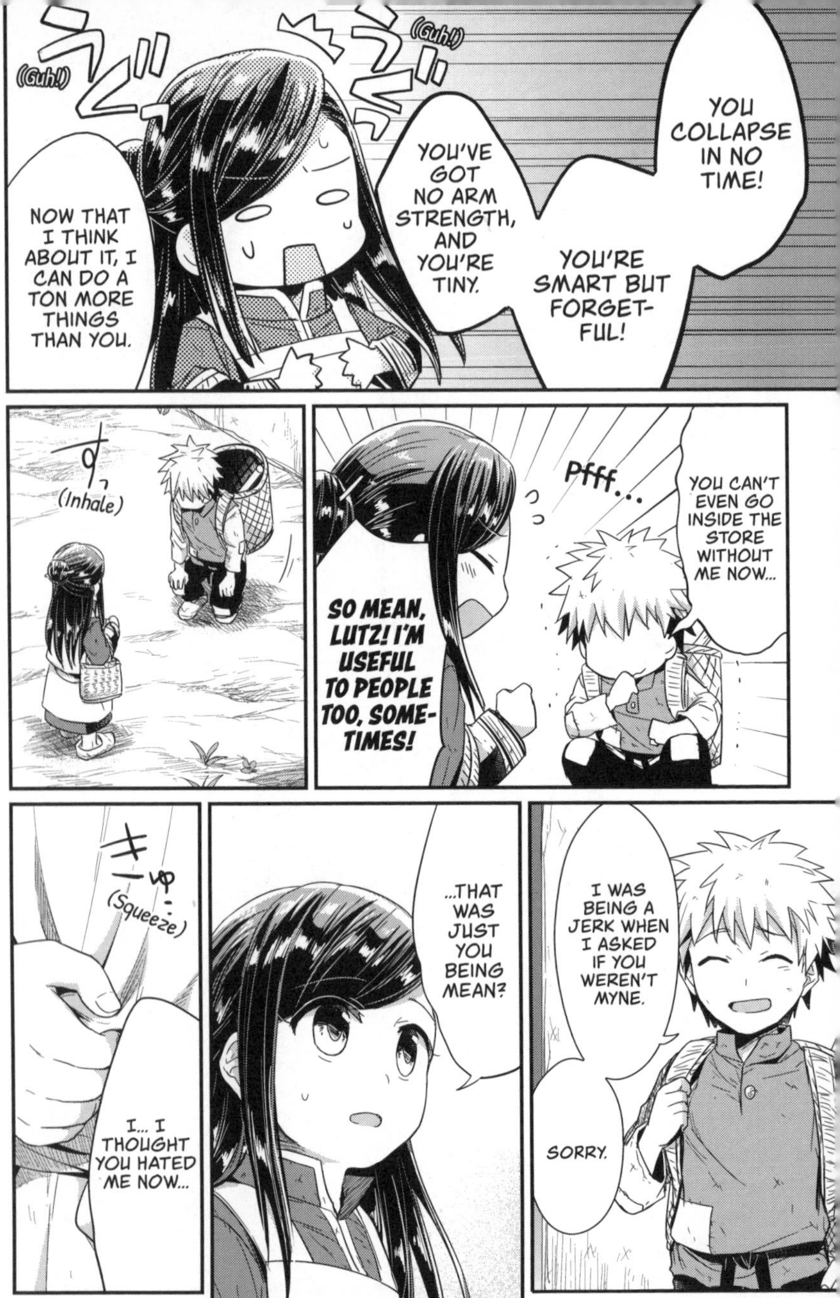
YOU COLLAPSE IN NO TIME!
YOU'VE GOT NO ARM STRENGTH, AND YOU'RE TINY.
YOU'RE SMART BUT FORGET-FUL!
(Guh!)
(Guh!)
NOW THAT I THINK ABOUT IT, I CAN DO A TON MORE THINGS THAN YOU.
YOU CAN'T EVEN GO INSIDE THE STORE WITHOUT ME NOW...
Pfff...
SO MEAN, LUTZ! I'M USEFUL TO PEOPLE TOO, SOME-TIMES!
(Inhale)
I WAS BEING A JERK WHEN I ASKED IF YOU WEREN'T MYNE.
SORRY.
...THAT WAS JUST YOU BEING MEAN?
(Squeeze)
I... I THOUGHT YOU HATED ME NOW...

Lutz, we're leaviiing.

DEFINITE-LY NOT.

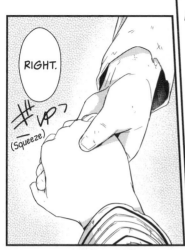

RIGHT.

#ッ
(Squeeze)

Ah.

C'MON, LET'S GO.

LISTEN UP, KID.

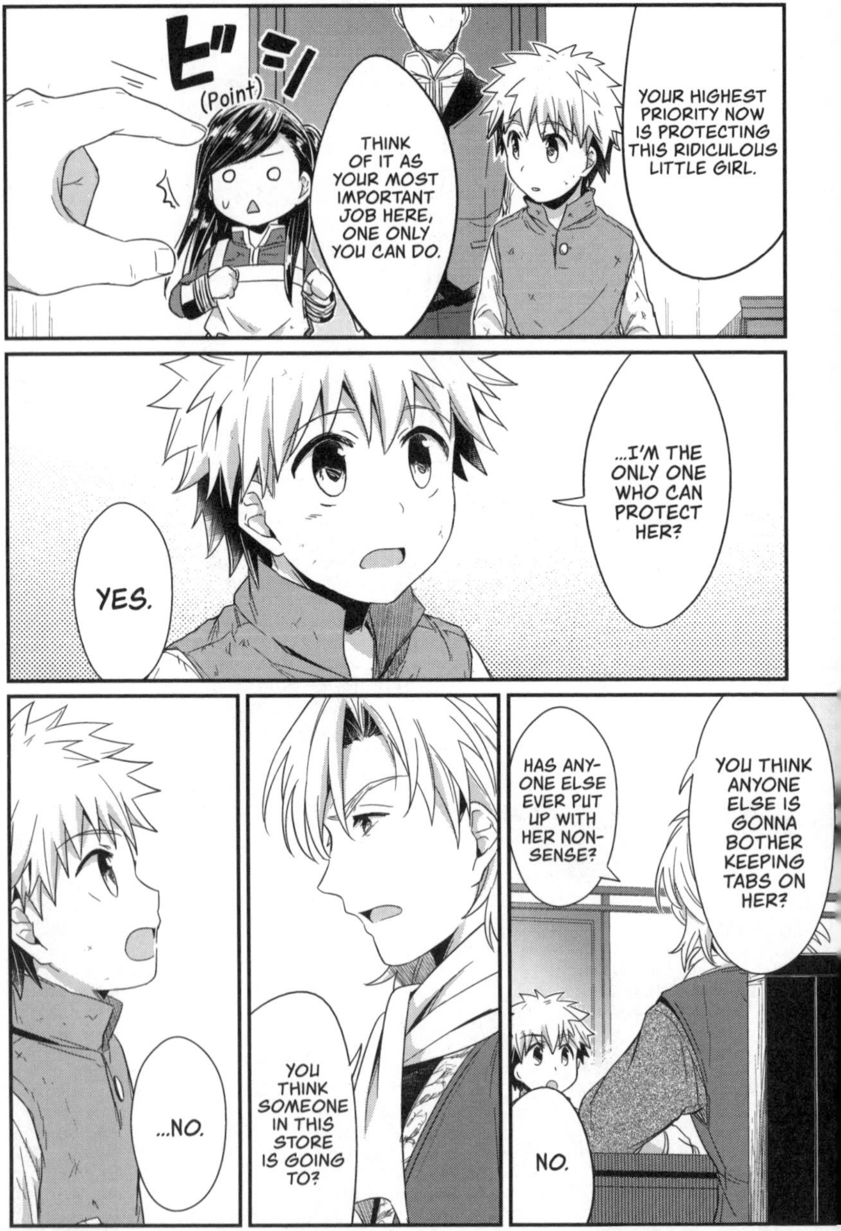
YOUR HIGHEST PRIORITY NOW IS PROTECTING THIS RIDICULOUS LITTLE GIRL.
THINK OF IT AS YOUR MOST IMPORTANT JOB HERE, ONE ONLY YOU CAN DO.
(Point)
...I'M THE ONLY ONE WHO CAN PROTECT HER?
YES.
YOU THINK ANYONE ELSE IS GONNA BOTHER KEEPING TABS ON HER?
HAS ANY-ONE ELSE EVER PUT UP WITH HER NON-SENSE?
NO.
YOU THINK SOMEONE IN THIS STORE IS GOING TO?
...NO.

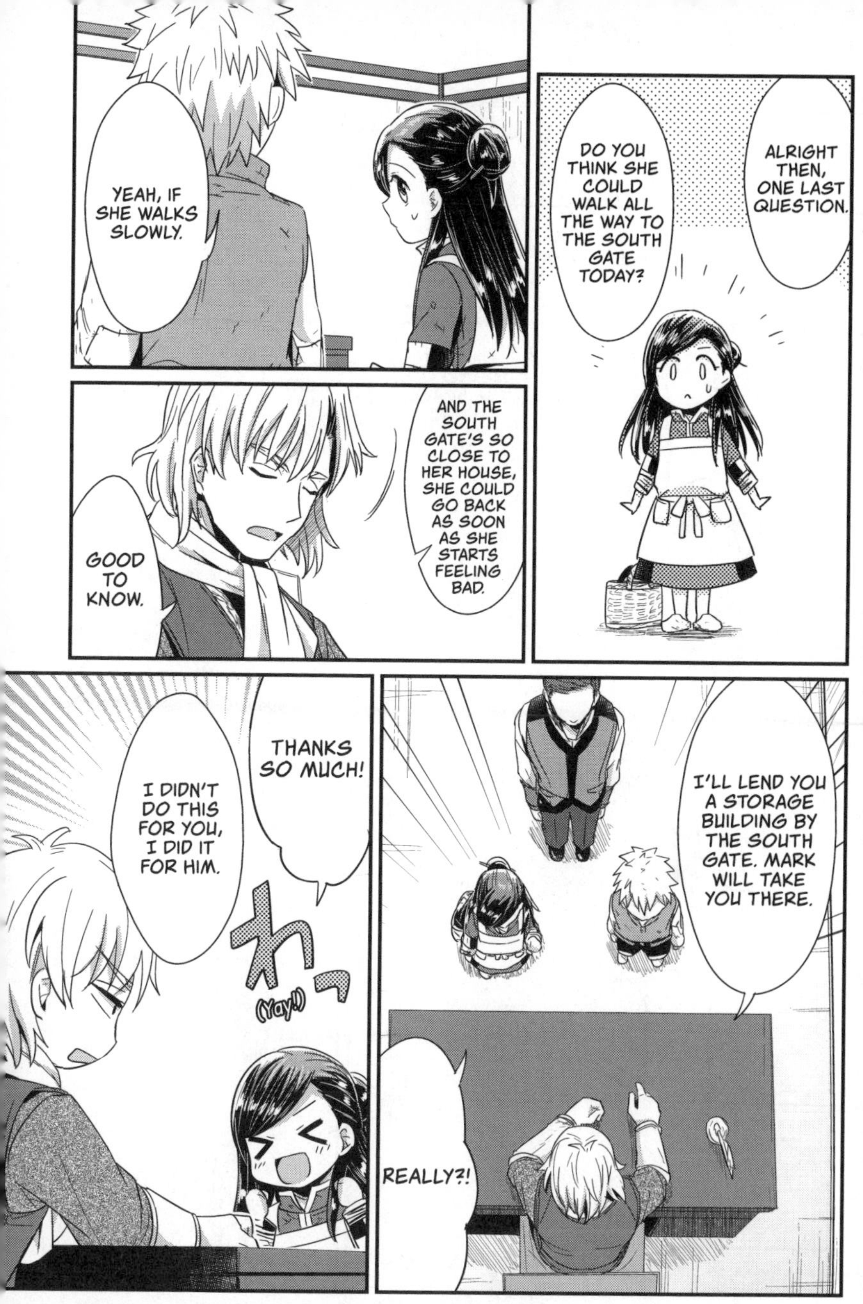
ALRIGHT THEN, ONE LAST QUESTION.
DO YOU THINK SHE COULD WALK ALL THE WAY TO THE SOUTH GATE TODAY?
YEAH, IF SHE WALKS SLOWLY.
AND THE SOUTH GATE'S SO CLOSE TO HER HOUSE, SHE COULD GO BACK AS SOON AS SHE STARTS FEELING BAD.
GOOD TO KNOW.
I'LL LEND YOU A STORAGE BUILDING BY THE SOUTH GATE. MARK WILL TAKE YOU THERE.
REALLY?!
THANKS SO MUCH!
(Yay!)
I DIDN'T DO THIS FOR YOU, I DID IT FOR HIM.

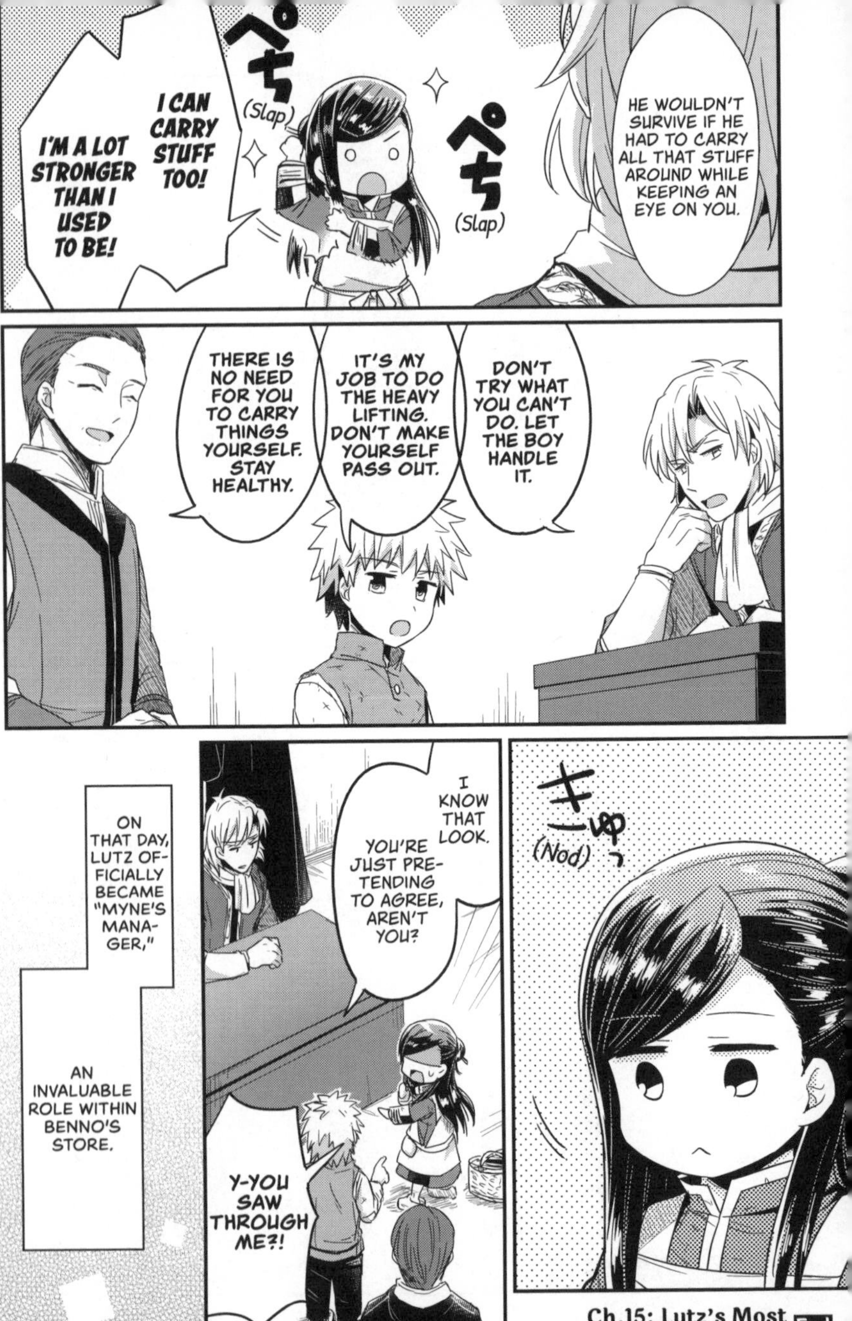
HE WOULDN'T SURVIVE IF HE HAD TO CARRY ALL THAT STUFF AROUND WHILE KEEPING AN EYE ON YOU.
ぺち
(Slap)
ぺち
(Slap)
I CAN CARRY STUFF TOO!
I'M A LOT STRONGER THAN I USED TO BE!
DON'T TRY WHAT YOU CAN'T DO. LET THE BOY HANDLE IT.
IT'S MY JOB TO DO THE HEAVY LIFTING. DON'T MAKE YOURSELF PASS OUT.
THERE IS NO NEED FOR YOU TO CARRY THINGS YOURSELF. STAY HEALTHY.
(Nod)
I KNOW THAT LOOK.
YOU'RE JUST PRETENDING TO AGREE, AREN'T YOU?
Y-YOU SAW THROUGH ME?!
ON THAT DAY, LUTZ OFFICIALLY BECAME "MYNE'S MANAGER,"
AN INVALUABLE ROLE WITHIN BENNO'S STORE.

Ch.15: Lutz's Most Important Job End

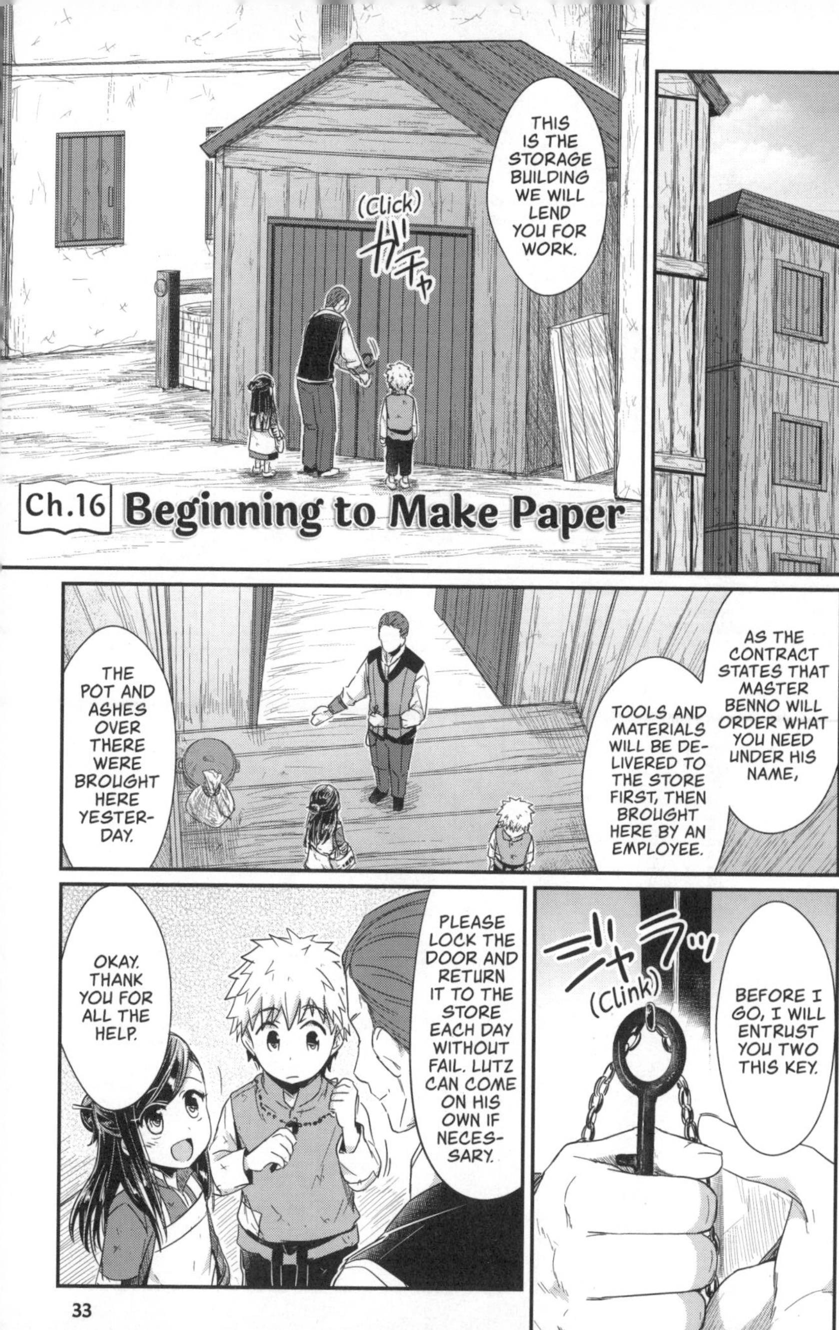
THIS IS THE STORAGE BUILDING WE WILL LEND YOU FOR WORK.
(Click)
Ch.16 Beginning to Make Paper
AS THE CONTRACT STATES THAT MASTER BENNO WILL ORDER WHAT YOU NEED UNDER HIS NAME,
TOOLS AND MATERIALS WILL BE DE-LIVERED TO THE STORE FIRST, THEN BROUGHT HERE BY AN EMPLOYEE.
THE POT AND ASHES OVER THERE WERE BROUGHT HERE YESTER-DAY.
(Clink)
BEFORE I GO, I WILL ENTRUST YOU TWO THIS KEY.
PLEASE LOCK THE DOOR AND RETURN IT TO THE STORE EACH DAY WITHOUT FAIL. LUTZ CAN COME ON HIS OWN IF NECES-SARY.
OKAY. THANK YOU FOR ALL THE HELP.

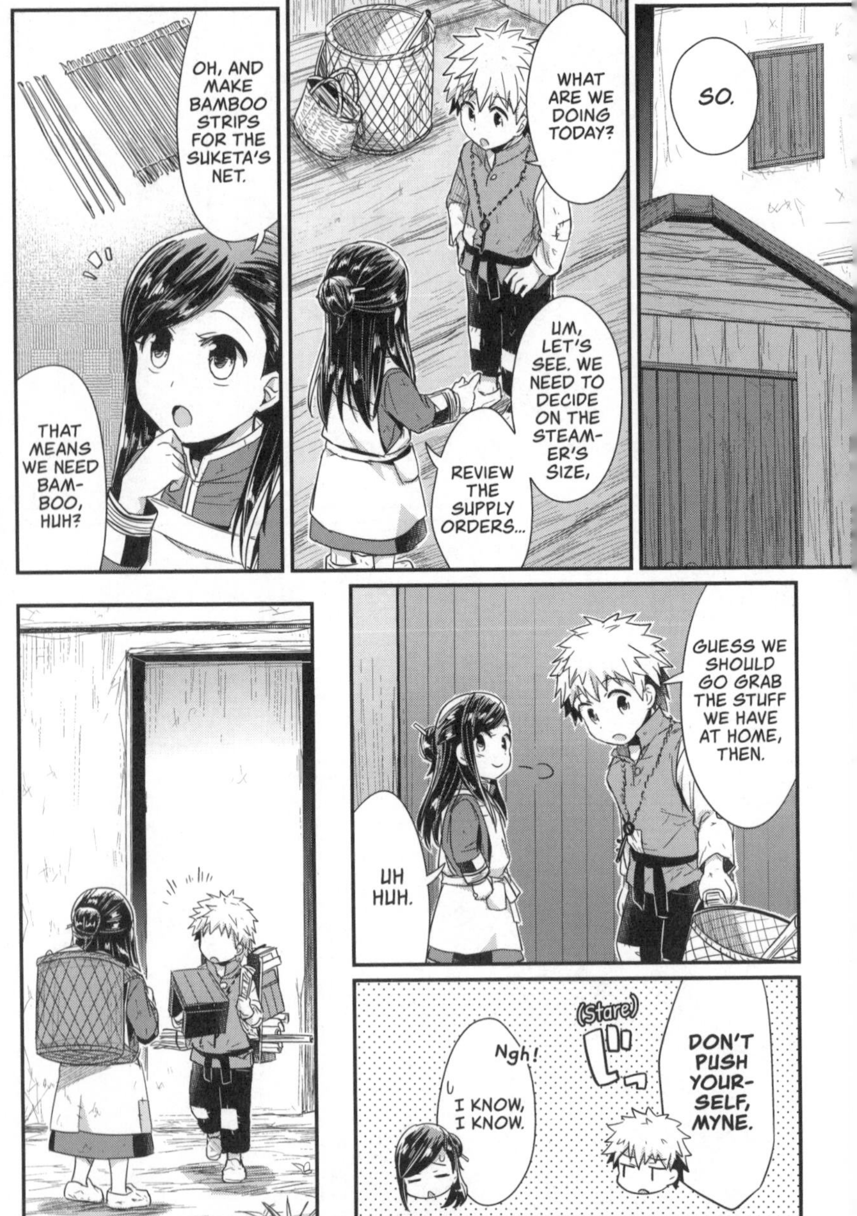
SO.
WHAT ARE WE DOING TODAY?
UM, LET'S SEE. WE NEED TO DECIDE ON THE STEAMER'S SIZE,
REVIEW THE SUPPLY ORDERS...
OH, AND MAKE BAMBOO STRIPS FOR THE SUKETA'S NET.
THAT MEANS WE NEED BAMBOO, HUH?
GUESS WE SHOULD GO GRAB THE STUFF WE HAVE AT HOME, THEN.
UH HUH.
DON'T PUSH YOURSELF, MYNE.
(Stare)
Ngh!
I KNOW, I KNOW.

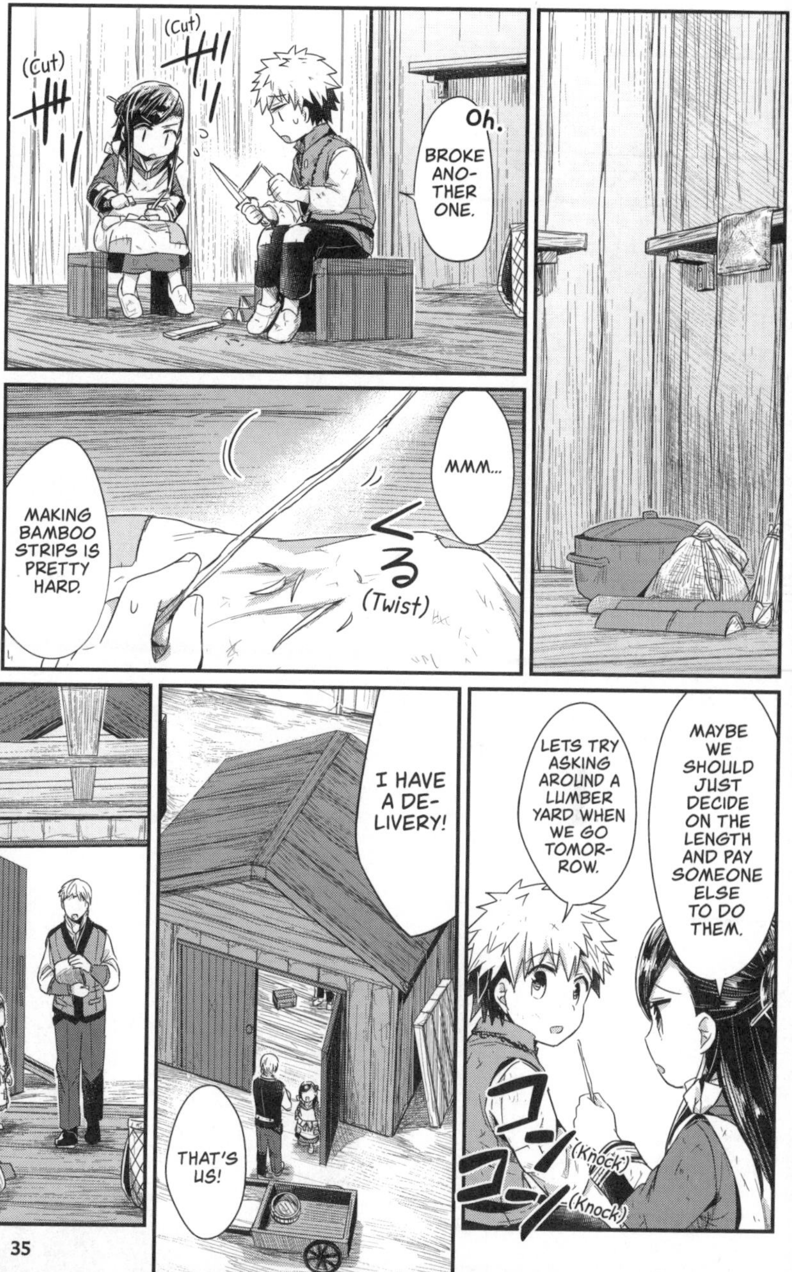
Oh.
BROKE ANOTHER ONE.
(Cut)
(Cut)
MMM...
くる
(Twist)
MAKING BAMBOO STRIPS IS PRETTY HARD.
MAYBE WE SHOULD JUST DECIDE ON THE LENGTH AND PAY SOMEONE ELSE TO DO THEM.
LETS TRY ASKING AROUND A LUMBER YARD WHEN WE GO TOMORROW.
(Knock)
(Knock)
I HAVE A DELIVERY!
THAT'S US!

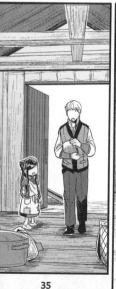

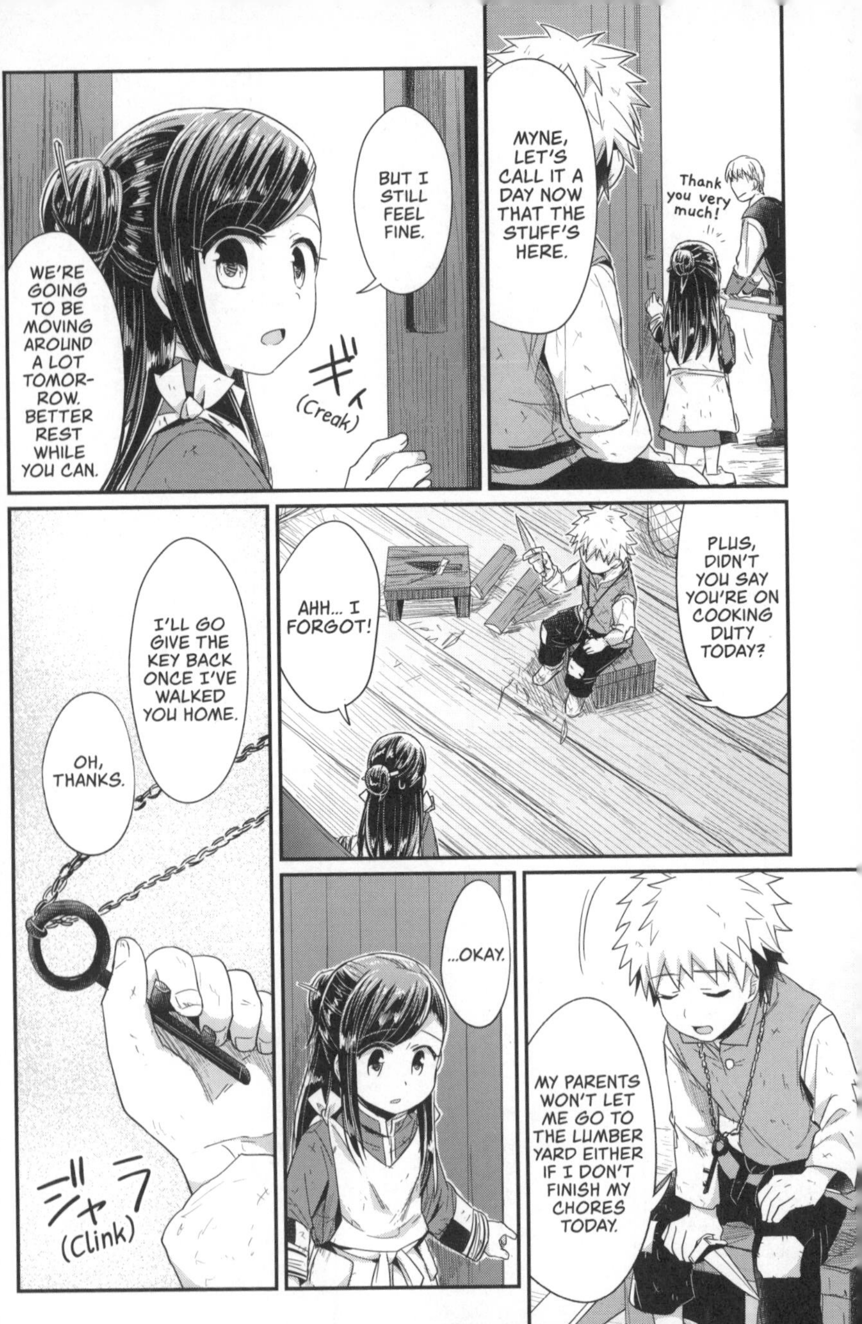
Thank you very much!
MYNE, LET'S CALL IT A DAY NOW THAT THE STUFF'S HERE.
BUT I STILL FEEL FINE.
ギイ
(Creak)
WE'RE GOING TO BE MOVING AROUND A LOT TOMOR-ROW. BETTER REST WHILE YOU CAN.
PLUS, DIDN'T YOU SAY YOU'RE ON COOKING DUTY TODAY?
AHH... I FORGOT!
MY PARENTS WON'T LET ME GO TO THE LUMBER YARD EITHER IF I DON'T FINISH MY CHORES TODAY.
...OKAY.
I'LL GO GIVE THE KEY BACK ONCE I'VE WALKED YOU HOME.
OH, THANKS.
ジャラ
(Clink)

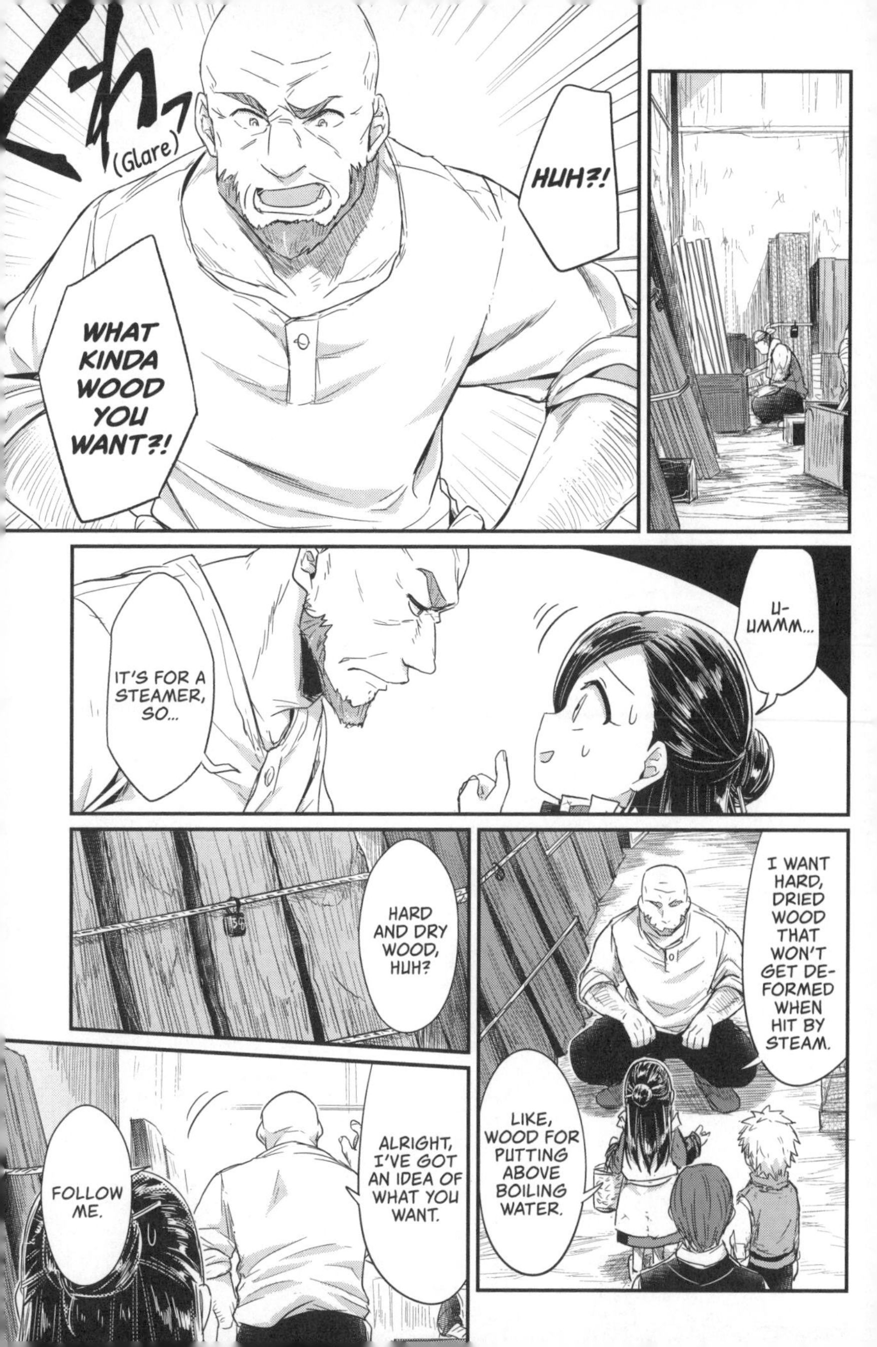
HUH?!
(Glare)
WHAT KINDA WOOD YOU WANT?!
U-UMMM...
IT'S FOR A STEAMER, SO...
I WANT HARD, DRIED WOOD THAT WON'T GET DE-FORMED WHEN HIT BY STEAM.
LIKE, WOOD FOR PUTTING ABOVE BOILING WATER.
HARD AND DRY WOOD, HUH?
ALRIGHT, I'VE GOT AN IDEA OF WHAT YOU WANT.
FOLLOW ME.

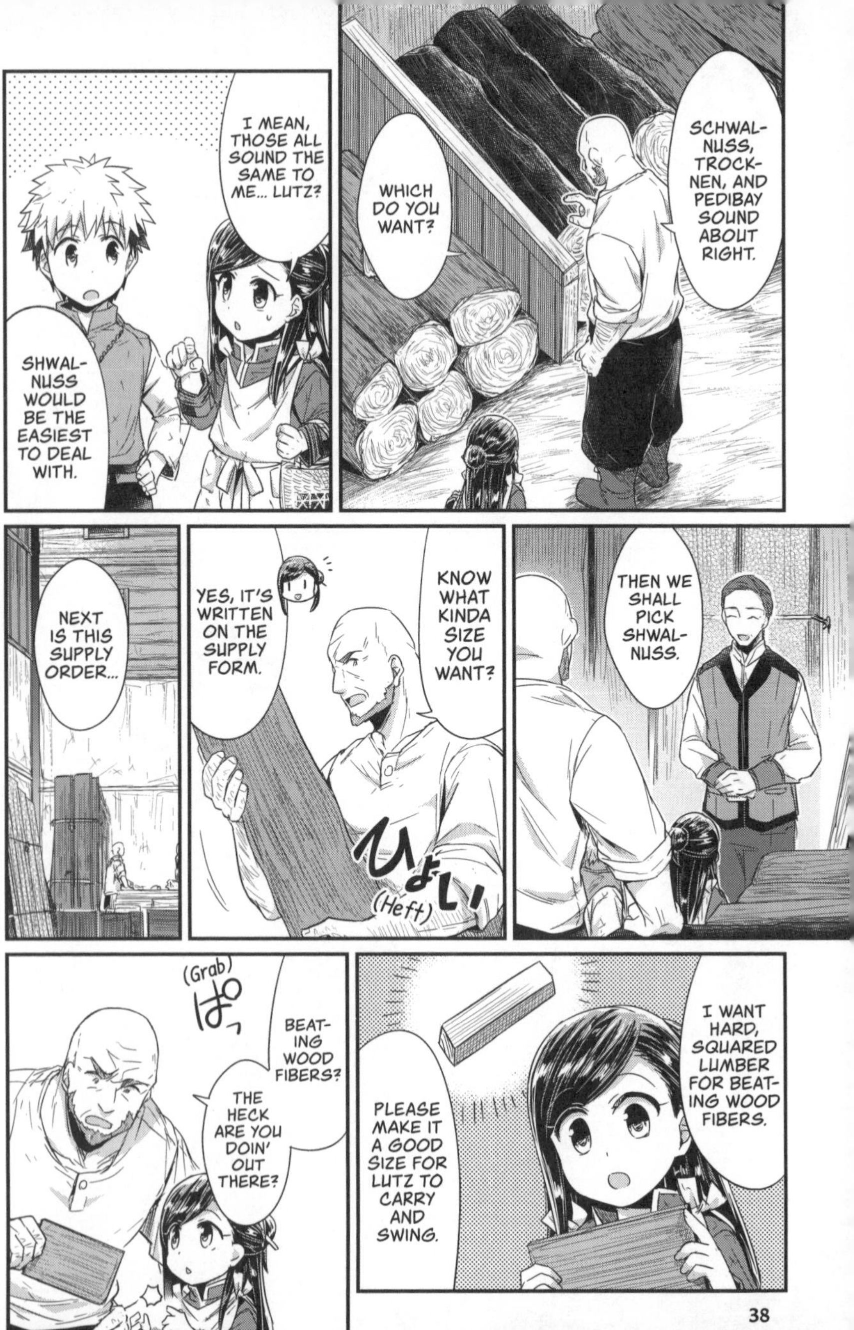
SCHWALNUSS, TROCKNEN, AND PEDIBAY SOUND ABOUT RIGHT.
WHICH DO YOU WANT?
I MEAN, THOSE ALL SOUND THE SAME TO ME... LUTZ?
SHWALNUSS WOULD BE THE EASIEST TO DEAL WITH.
THEN WE SHALL PICK SHWALNUSS.
KNOW WHAT KINDA SIZE YOU WANT?
YES, IT'S WRITTEN ON THE SUPPLY FORM.
ひょい
(Heft)
NEXT IS THIS SUPPLY ORDER...
I WANT HARD, SQUARED LUMBER FOR BEATING WOOD FIBERS.
PLEASE MAKE IT A GOOD SIZE FOR LUTZ TO CARRY AND SWING.
BEATING WOOD FIBERS?
ぱっ
(Grab)
THE HECK ARE YOU DOIN' OUT THERE?

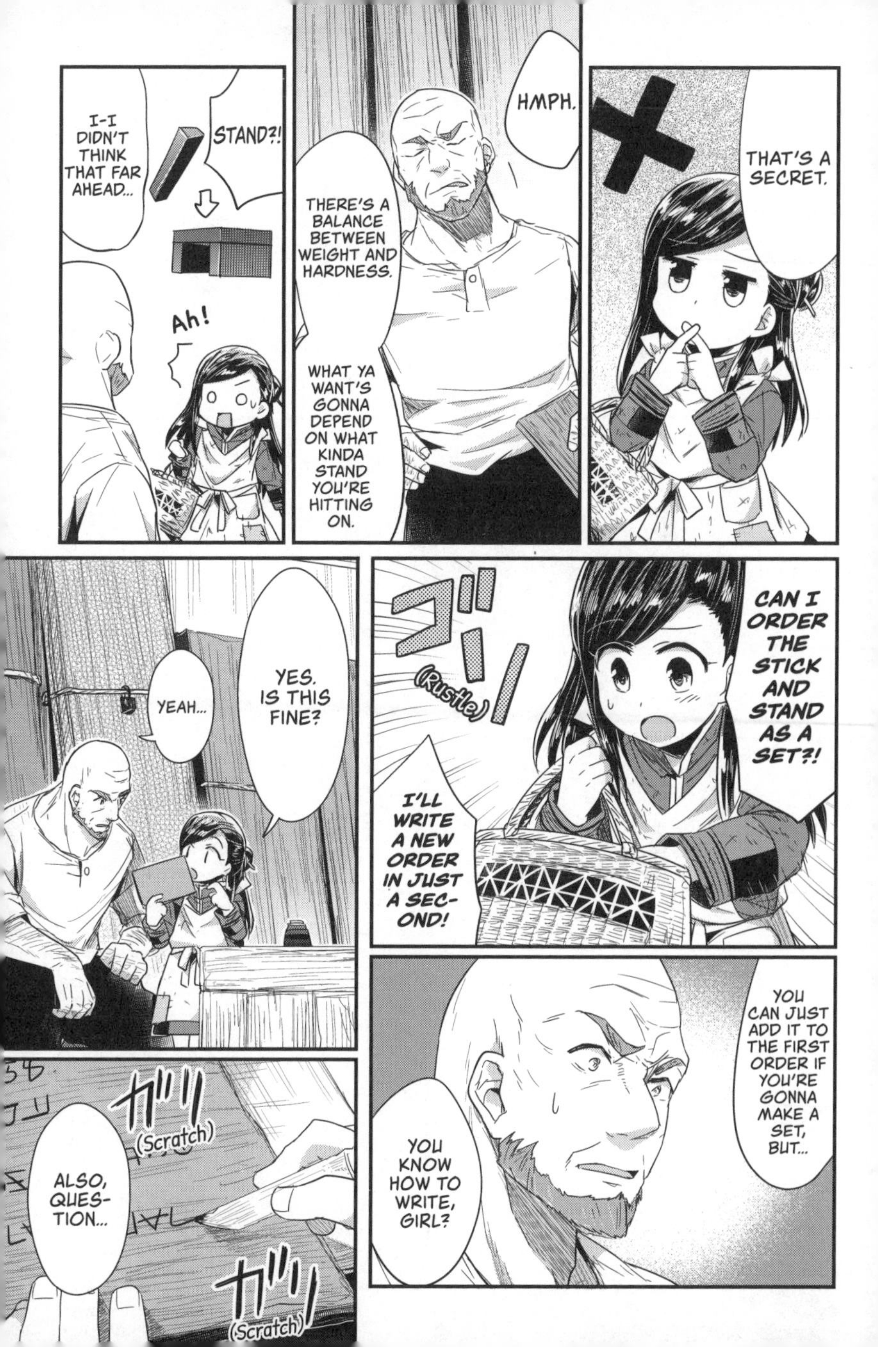
THAT'S A SECRET.
HMPH.
THERE'S A BALANCE BETWEEN WEIGHT AND HARDNESS.
WHAT YA WANT'S GONNA DEPEND ON WHAT KINDA STAND YOU'RE HITTING ON.
STAND?!
I-I DIDN'T THINK THAT FAR AHEAD...
Ah!
CAN I ORDER THE STICK AND STAND AS A SET?!
ゴソ
(Rustle)
I'LL WRITE A NEW ORDER IN JUST A SEC-OND!
YES. IS THIS FINE?
YEAH...
YOU CAN JUST ADD IT TO THE FIRST ORDER IF YOU'RE GONNA MAKE A SET, BUT...
YOU KNOW HOW TO WRITE, GIRL?
ガリ
(Scratch)
ALSO, QUES-TION...
ガリ
(Scratch)

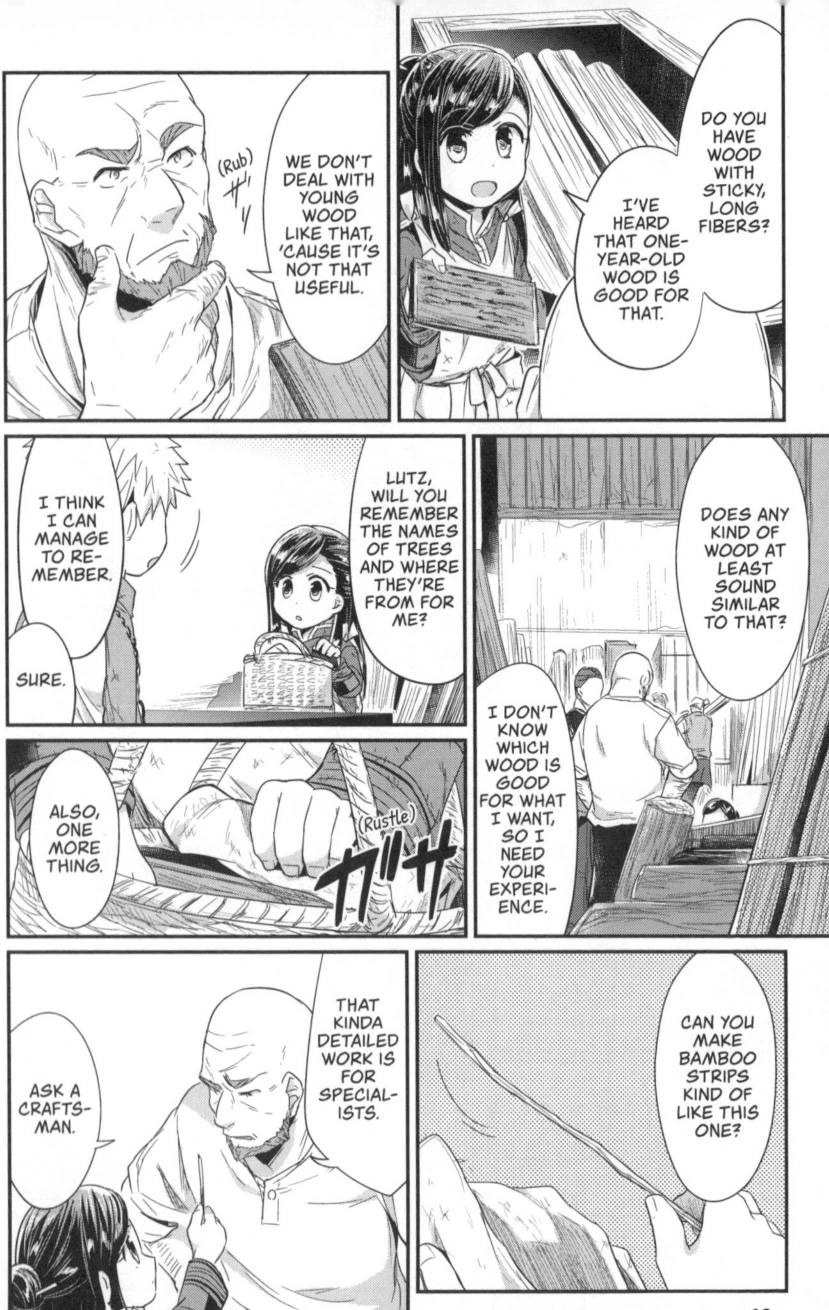
DO YOU HAVE WOOD WITH STICKY, LONG FIBERS?
I'VE HEARD THAT ONE-YEAR-OLD WOOD IS GOOD FOR THAT.
(Rub)
WE DON'T DEAL WITH YOUNG WOOD LIKE THAT, 'CAUSE IT'S NOT THAT USEFUL.
DOES ANY KIND OF WOOD AT LEAST SOUND SIMILAR TO THAT?
I DON'T KNOW WHICH WOOD IS GOOD FOR WHAT I WANT, SO I NEED YOUR EXPERIENCE.
LUTZ, WILL YOU REMEMBER THE NAMES OF TREES AND WHERE THEY'RE FROM FOR ME?
I THINK I CAN MANAGE TO REMEMBER.
SURE.
(Rustle)
ALSO, ONE MORE THING.
CAN YOU MAKE BAMBOO STRIPS KIND OF LIKE THIS ONE?
THAT KINDA DETAILED WORK IS FOR SPECIALISTS.
ASK A CRAFTSMAN.

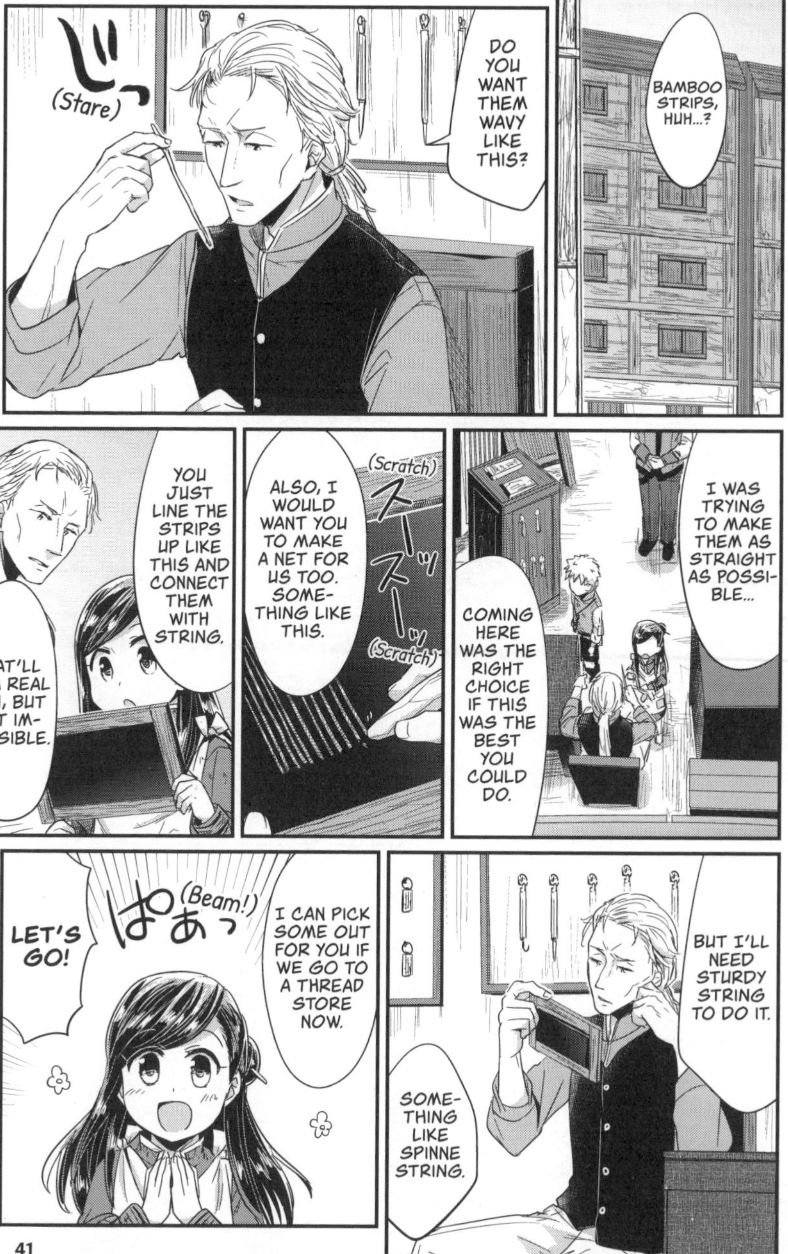

BAMBOO STRIPS, HUH...?
DO YOU WANT THEM WAVY LIKE THIS?
(Stare)
I WAS TRYING TO MAKE THEM AS STRAIGHT AS POSSIBLE...
COMING HERE WAS THE RIGHT CHOICE IF THIS WAS THE BEST YOU COULD DO.
ALSO, I WOULD WANT YOU TO MAKE A NET FOR US TOO. SOMETHING LIKE THIS.
(Scratch)
(Scratch)
YOU JUST LINE THE STRIPS UP LIKE THIS AND CONNECT THEM WITH STRING.
THAT'LL BE A REAL PAIN, BUT NOT IMPOSSIBLE.
BUT I'LL NEED STURDY STRING TO DO IT.
SOMETHING LIKE SPINNE STRING.
I CAN PICK SOME OUT FOR YOU IF WE GO TO A THREAD STORE NOW.
(Beam!)
LET'S GO!

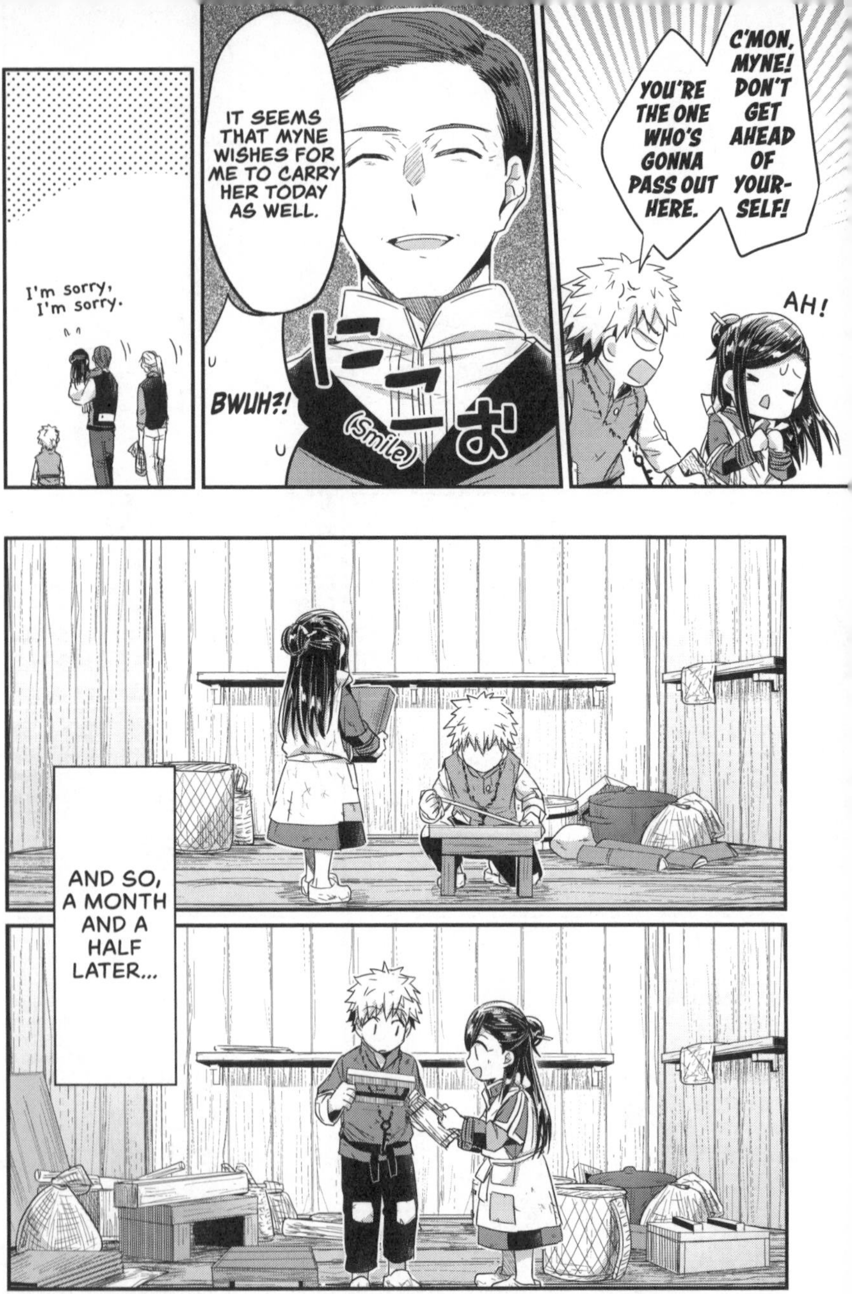
C'MON, MYNE! DON'T GET AHEAD OF YOURSELF!
YOU'RE THE ONE WHO'S GONNA PASS OUT HERE.
AH!
IT SEEMS THAT MYNE WISHES FOR ME TO CARRY HER TODAY AS WELL.
BWUH?!
(Smile)
I'm sorry, I'm sorry.
AND SO, A MONTH AND A HALF LATER...

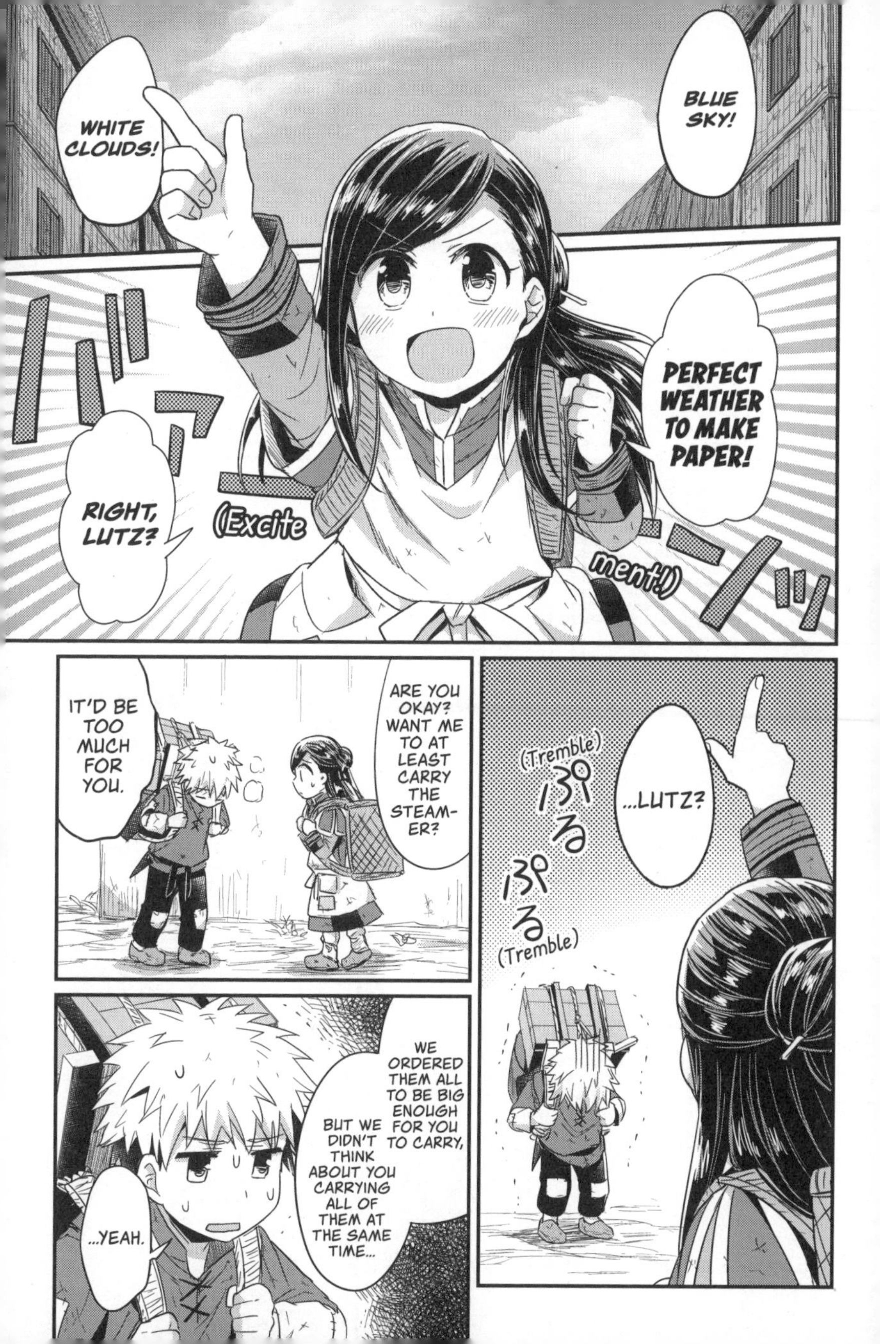
BLUE SKY!
WHITE CLOUDS!
PERFECT WEATHER TO MAKE PAPER!
RIGHT, LUTZ?
(Excite
ment!)
...LUTZ?
(Tremble)
ぷる
ぷる
(Tremble)
ARE YOU OKAY? WANT ME TO AT LEAST CARRY THE STEAMER?
IT'D BE TOO MUCH FOR YOU.
WE ORDERED THEM ALL TO BE BIG ENOUGH FOR YOU TO CARRY,
BUT WE DIDN'T THINK ABOUT YOU CARRYING ALL OF THEM AT THE SAME TIME...
...YEAH.

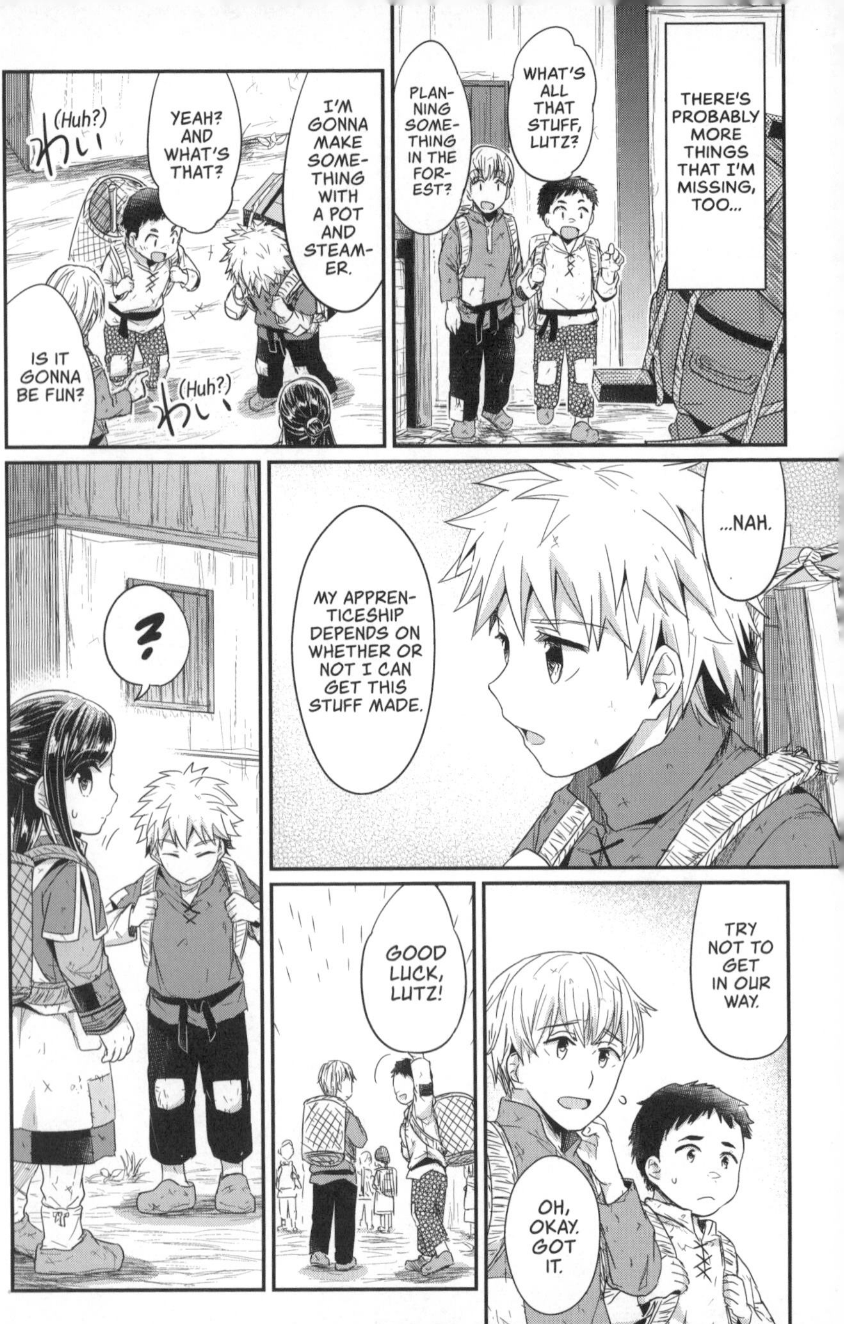

THERE'S PROBABLY MORE THINGS THAT I'M MISSING, TOO...
WHAT'S ALL THAT STUFF, LUTZ?
PLANNING SOMETHING IN THE FOREST?
I'M GONNA MAKE SOMETHING WITH A POT AND STEAMER.
YEAH? AND WHAT'S THAT?
(Huh?) わい
IS IT GONNA BE FUN?
(Huh?) わい
...NAH.
MY APPRENTICESHIP DEPENDS ON WHETHER OR NOT I CAN GET THIS STUFF MADE.
TRY NOT TO GET IN OUR WAY.
OH, OKAY. GOT IT.
GOOD LUCK, LUTZ!
?

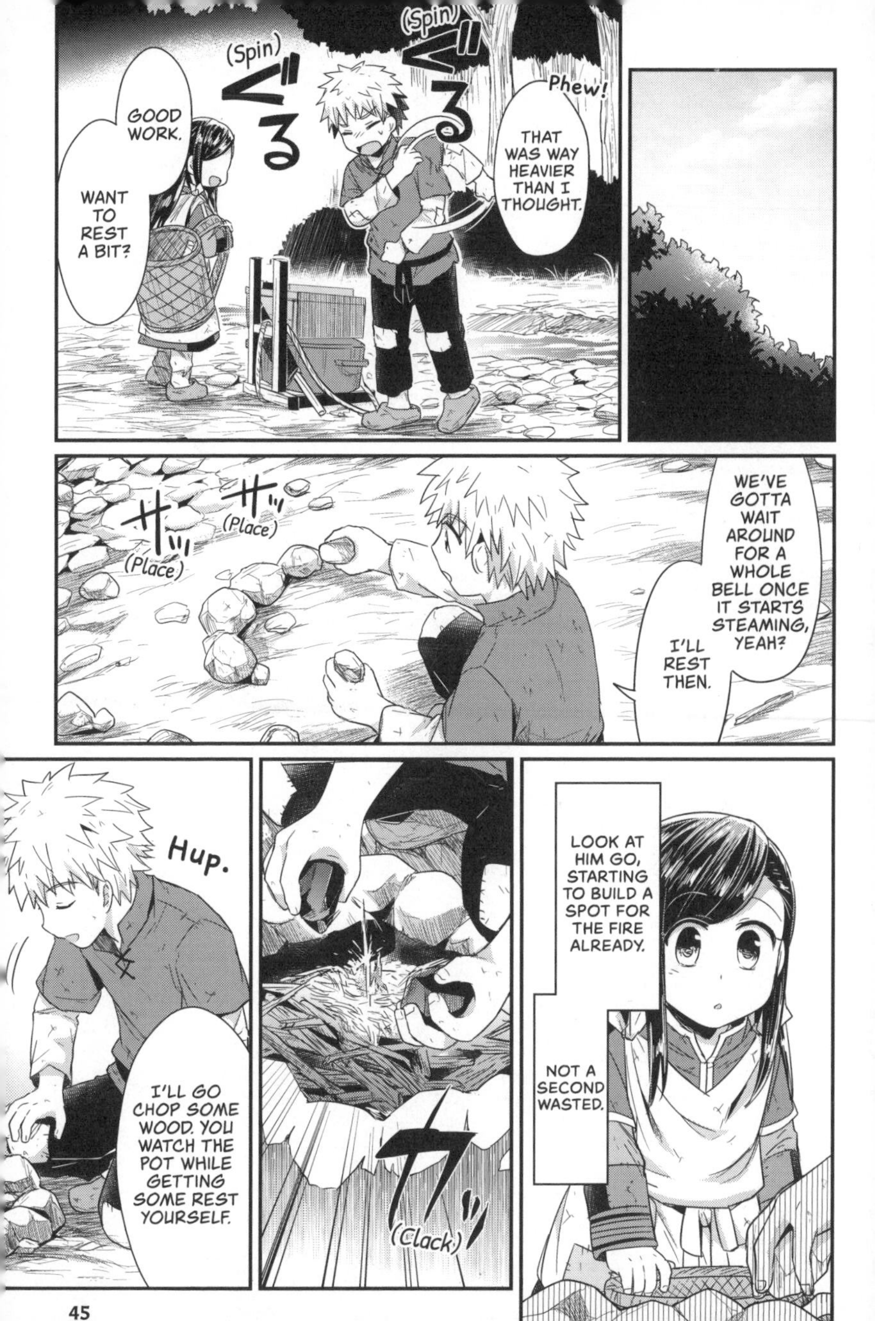
ぐる
(Spin)
Phew!
THAT WAS WAY HEAVIER THAN I THOUGHT.
ぐる
(Spin)
GOOD WORK.
WANT TO REST A BIT?
WE'VE GOTTA WAIT AROUND FOR A WHOLE BELL ONCE IT STARTS STEAMING, YEAH?
I'LL REST THEN.
ザッ
(Place)
ザッ
(Place)
LOOK AT HIM GO, STARTING TO BUILD A SPOT FOR THE FIRE ALREADY.
NOT A SECOND WASTED.
カッ
(Clack)
Hup.
I'LL GO CHOP SOME WOOD. YOU WATCH THE POT WHILE GETTING SOME REST YOURSELF.

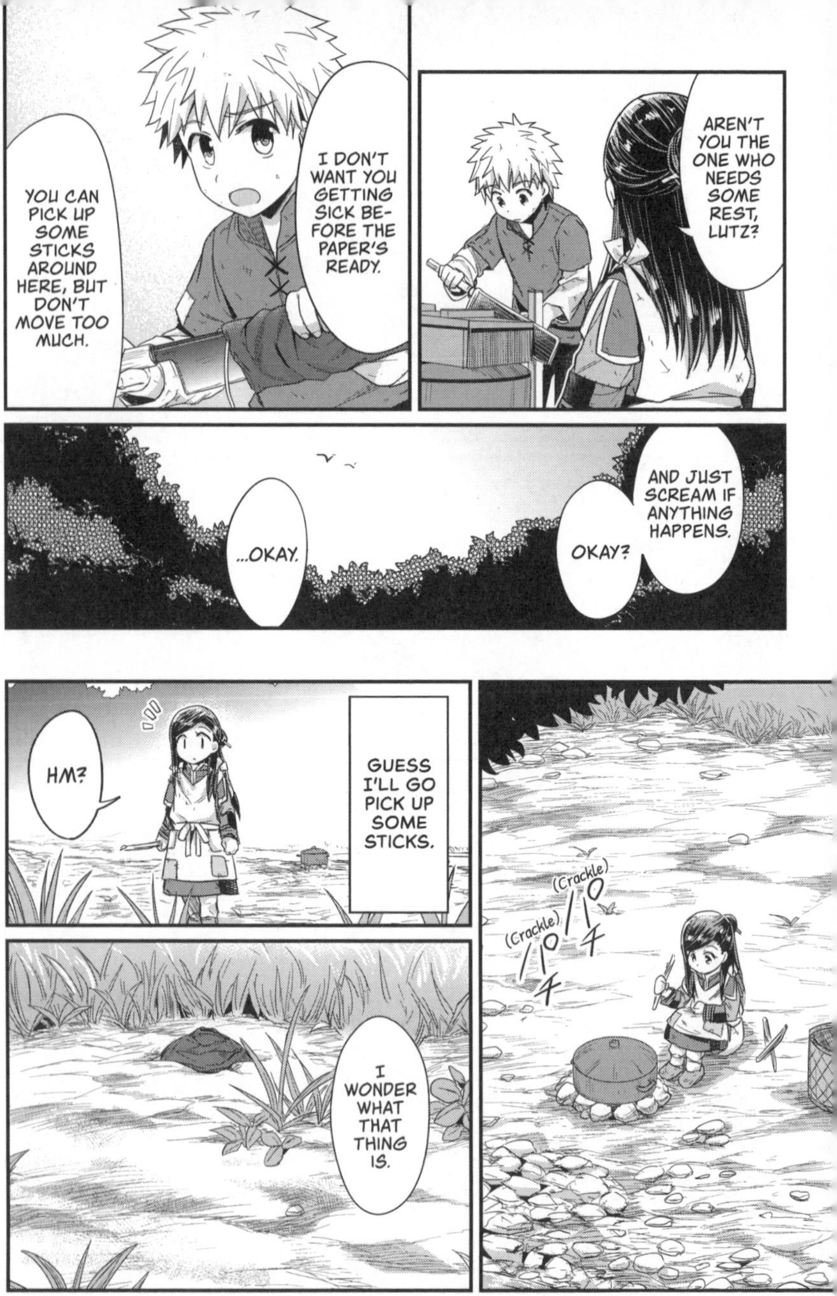
AREN'T YOU THE ONE WHO NEEDS SOME REST, LUTZ?
I DON'T WANT YOU GETTING SICK BE-FORE THE PAPER'S READY.
YOU CAN PICK UP SOME STICKS AROUND HERE, BUT DON'T MOVE TOO MUCH.
AND JUST SCREAM IF ANYTHING HAPPENS.
OKAY?
...OKAY.
パチ (Crackle)
パチ (Crackle)
GUESS I'LL GO PICK UP SOME STICKS.
HM?
I WONDER WHAT THAT THING IS.

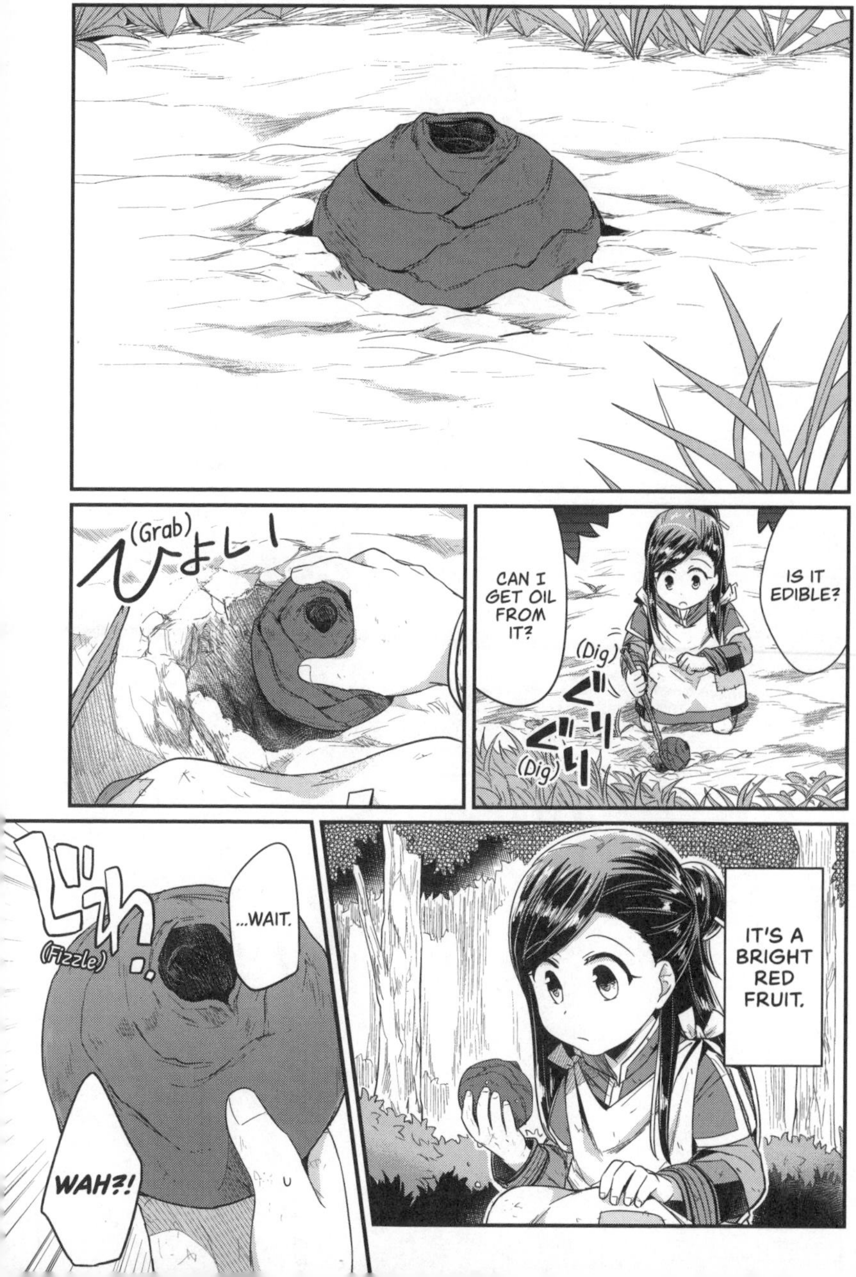
IS IT EDIBLE?
CAN I GET OIL FROM IT?
(Dig)
(Dig)
(Grab)
IT'S A BRIGHT RED FRUIT.
...WAIT.
(Fizzle)
WAH?!

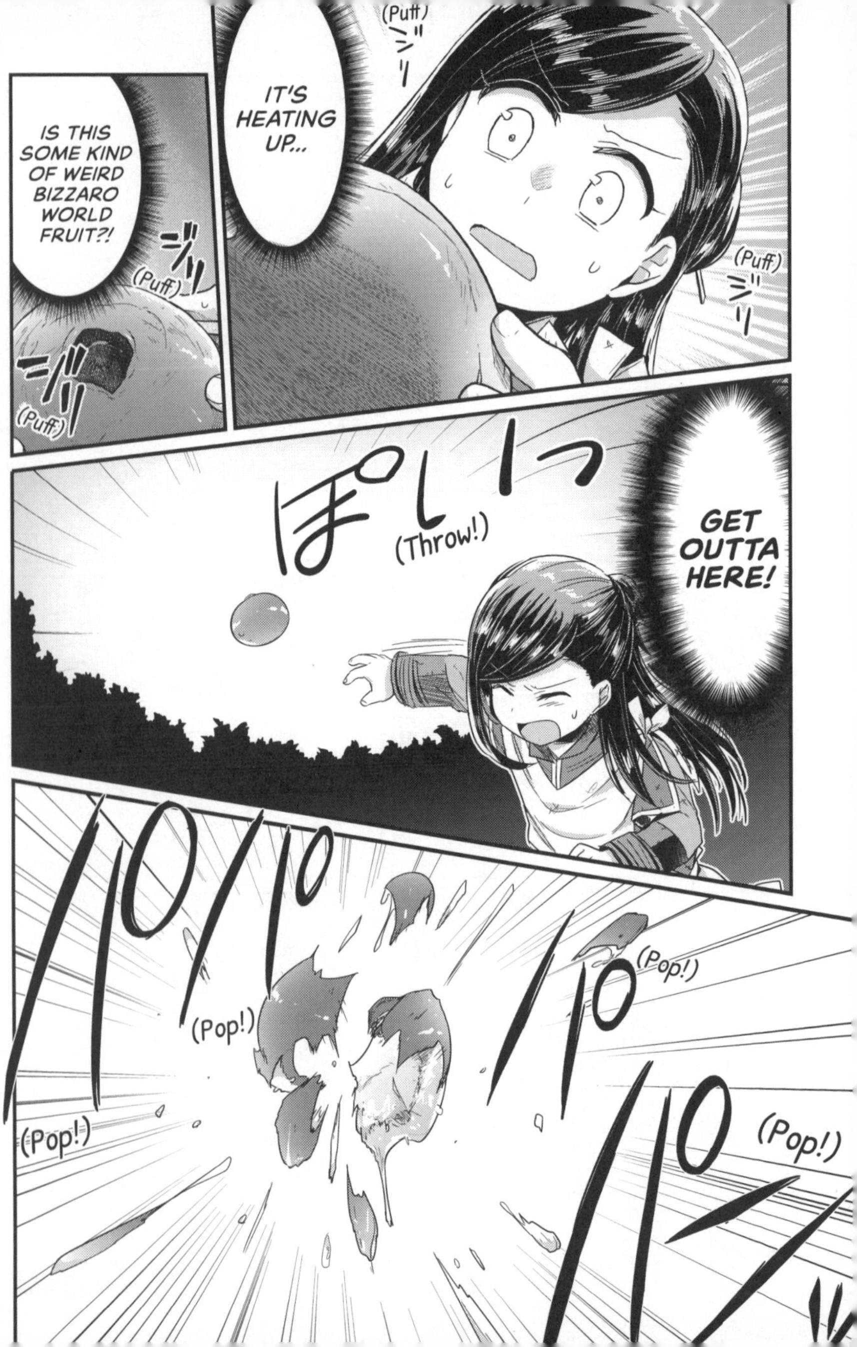
(Puff)
IT'S HEATING UP...
(Puff)
IS THIS SOME KIND OF WEIRD BIZZARO WORLD FRUIT?!
(Puff)
(Puff)
GET OUTTA HERE!
ぽいっ
(Throw!)
(Pop!)
(Pop!)
(Pop!)
(Pop!)

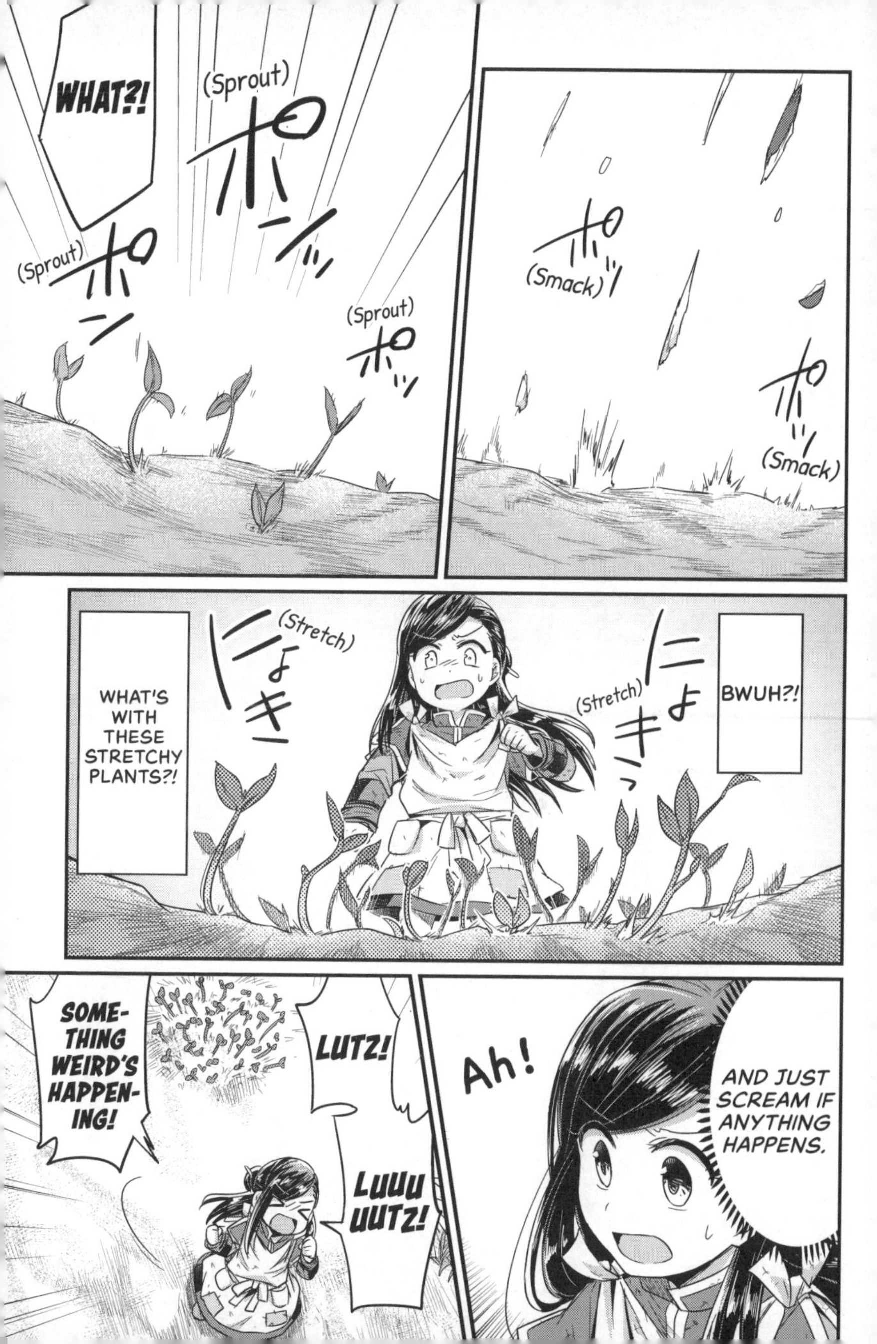

ポッ
(Smack)
ポッ
(Smack)
(Sprout)
ポンッ
WHAT?!
(Sprout)
ポン
(Sprout)
ポッ
BWUH?!
(Stretch)
ニョキッ
(Stretch)
ニョキ
WHAT'S WITH THESE STRETCHY PLANTS?!
Ah!
AND JUST SCREAM IF ANYTHING HAPPENS.
LUTZ!
LUUUUUTZ!
SOMETHING WEIRD'S HAPPENING!

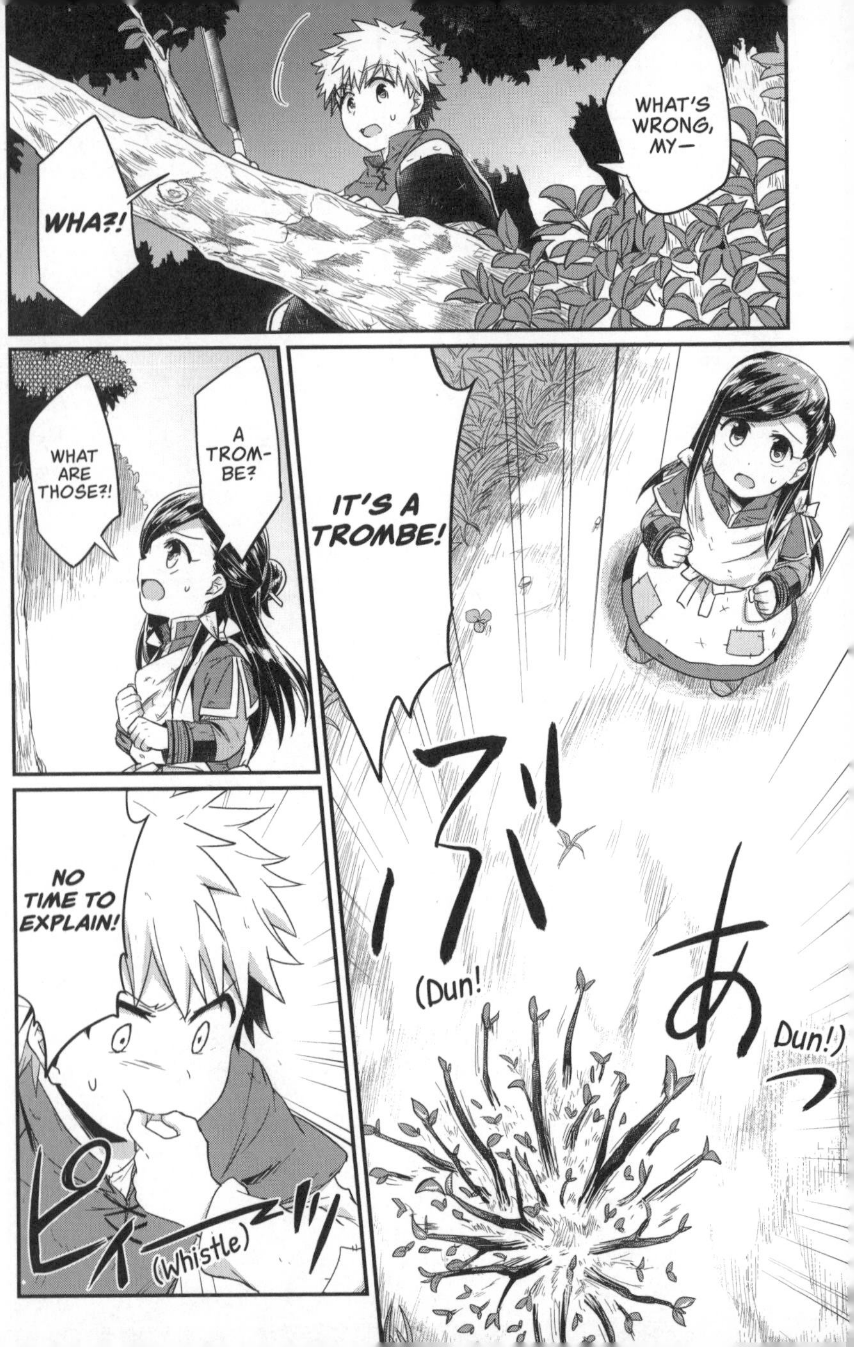
WHAT'S WRONG, MY—
WHA?!
IT'S A TROMBE!
(Dun!
Dun!)
A TROMBE?
WHAT ARE THOSE?!
NO TIME TO EXPLAIN!
(Whistle)

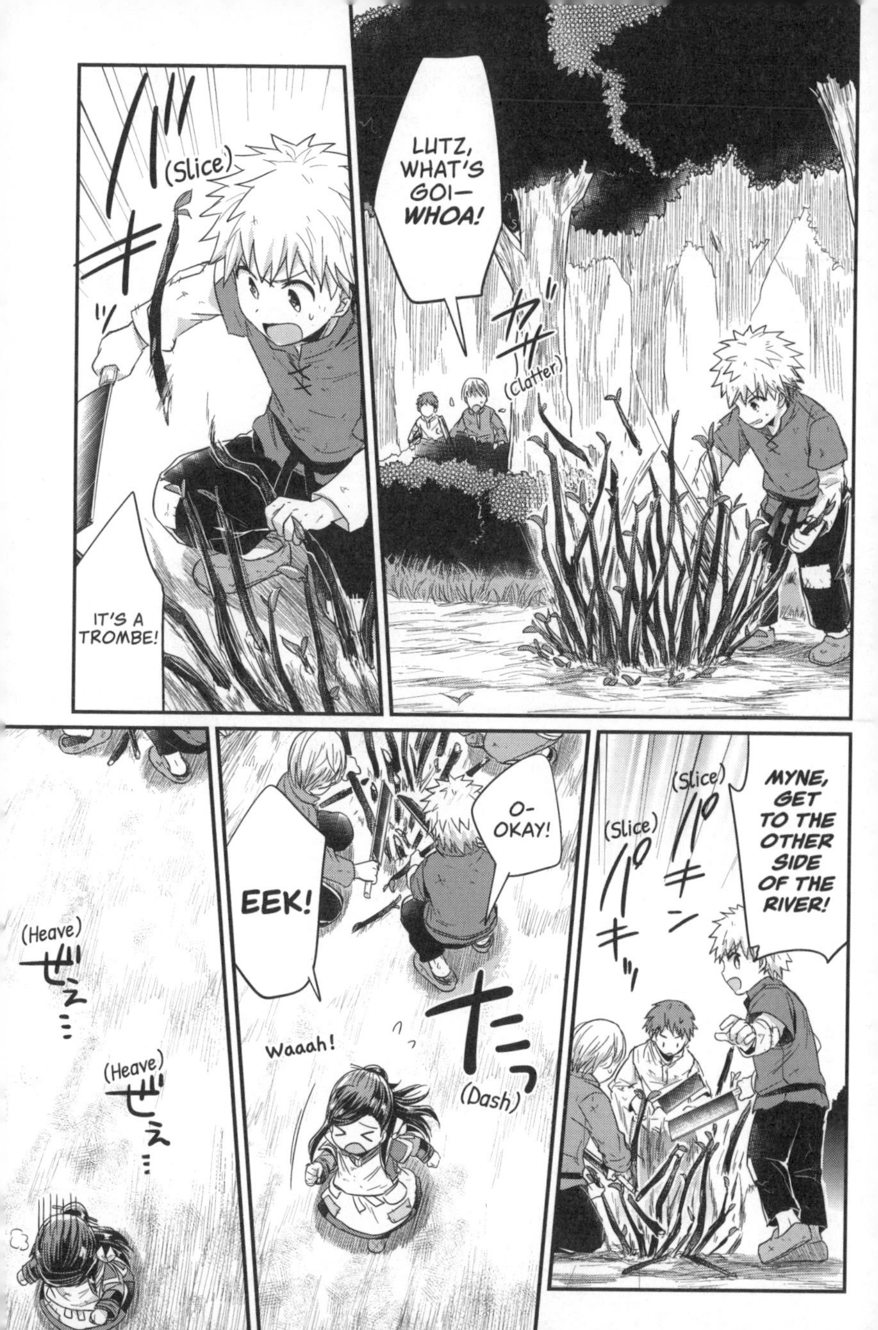
LUTZ, WHAT'S GOI— WHOA!
(Clatter)
(Slice)
IT'S A TROMBE!
MYNE, GET TO THE OTHER SIDE OF THE RIVER!
(Slice)
(Slice)
O-OKAY!
EEK!
Waaah!
(Dash)
(Heave)
(Heave)

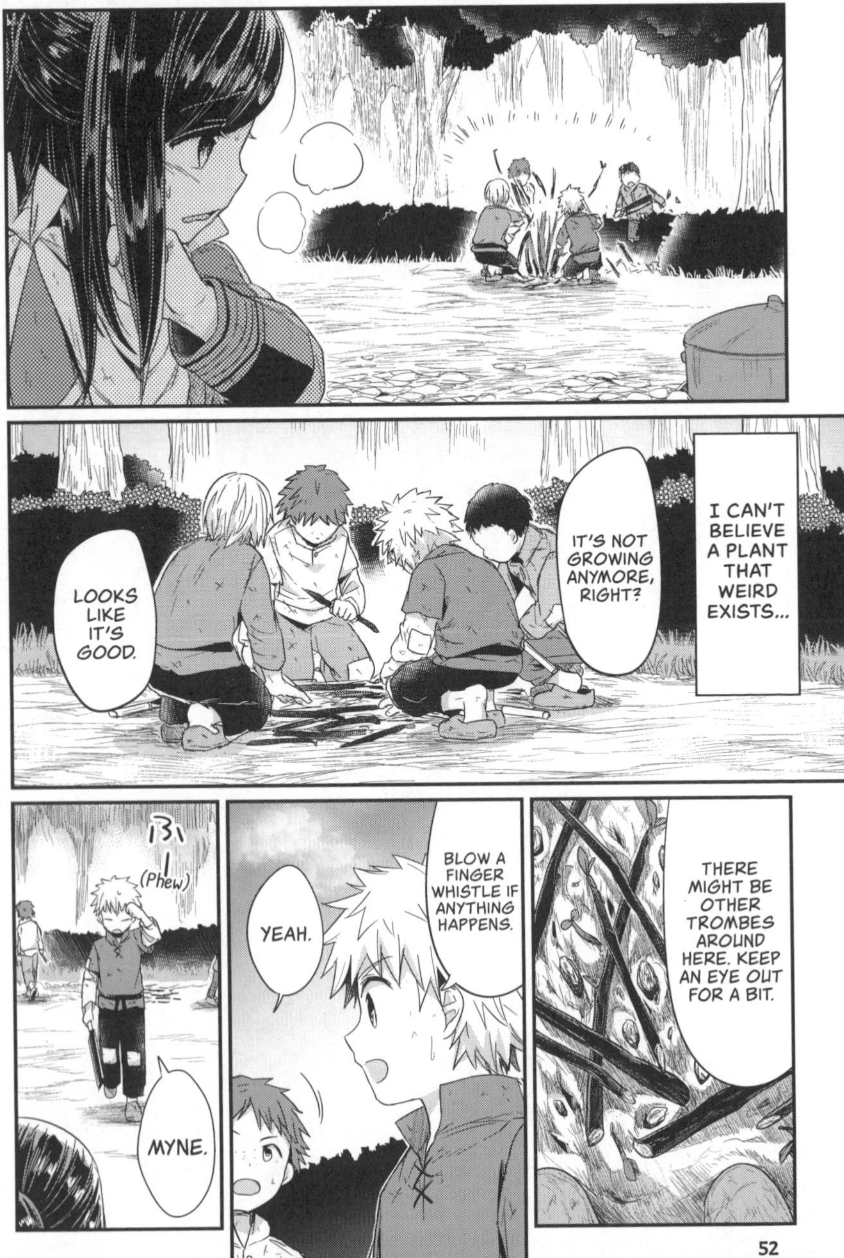
I CAN'T BELIEVE A PLANT THAT WEIRD EXISTS...
IT'S NOT GROWING ANYMORE, RIGHT?
LOOKS LIKE IT'S GOOD.
THERE MIGHT BE OTHER TROMBES AROUND HERE. KEEP AN EYE OUT FOR A BIT.
BLOW A FINGER WHISTLE IF ANYTHING HAPPENS.
YEAH.
ふぃー
(Phew)
MYNE.

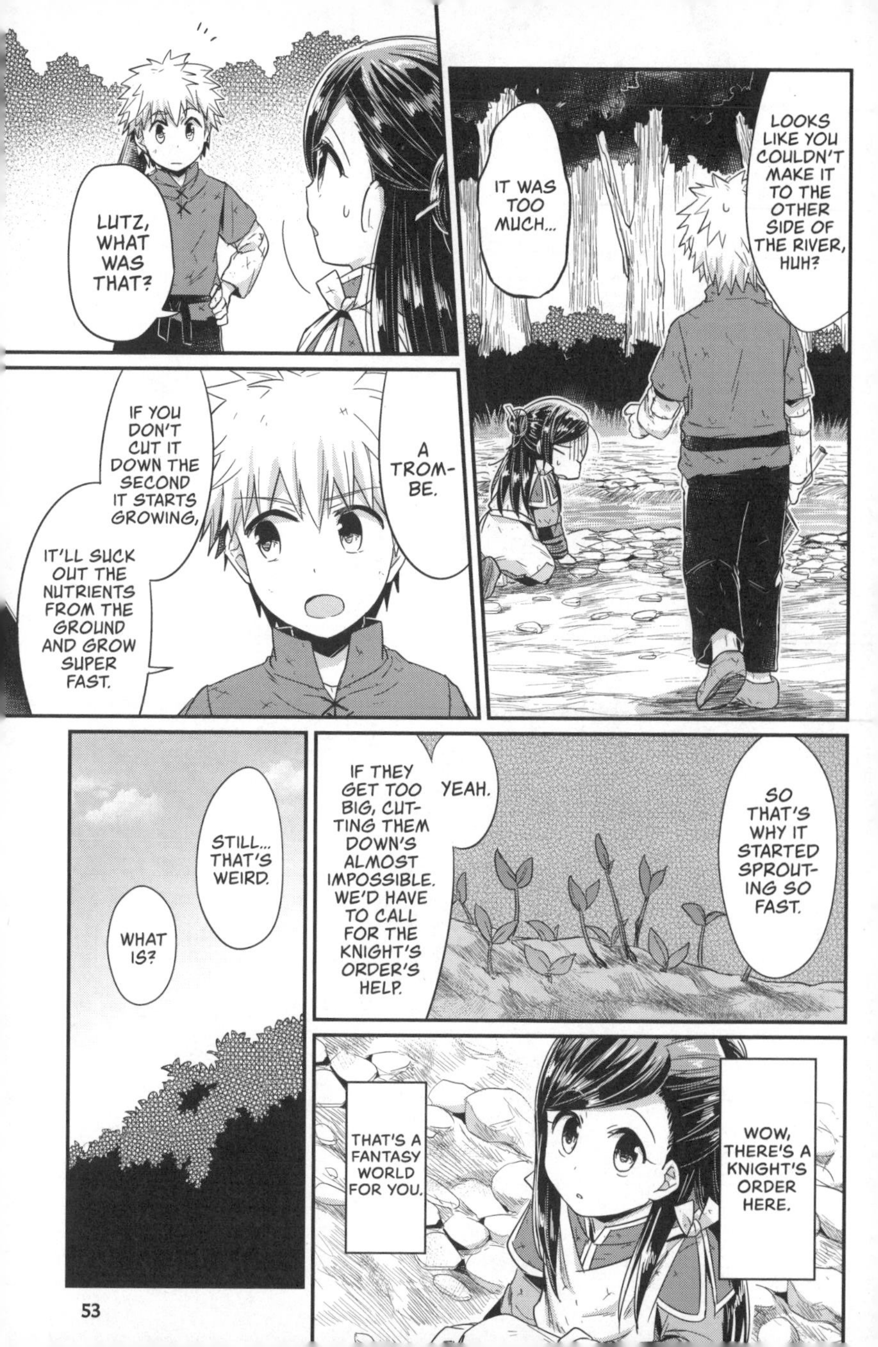
LOOKS LIKE YOU COULDN'T MAKE IT TO THE OTHER SIDE OF THE RIVER, HUH?
IT WAS TOO MUCH...
LUTZ, WHAT WAS THAT?
A TROM-BE.
IF YOU DON'T CUT IT DOWN THE SECOND IT STARTS GROWING,
IT'LL SUCK OUT THE NUTRIENTS FROM THE GROUND AND GROW SUPER FAST.
SO THAT'S WHY IT STARTED SPROUT-ING SO FAST.
YEAH.
IF THEY GET TOO BIG, CUT-TING THEM DOWN'S ALMOST IMPOSSIBLE. WE'D HAVE TO CALL FOR THE KNIGHT'S ORDER'S HELP.
WOW, THERE'S A KNIGHT'S ORDER HERE.
THAT'S A FANTASY WORLD FOR YOU.
STILL... THAT'S WEIRD.
WHAT IS?

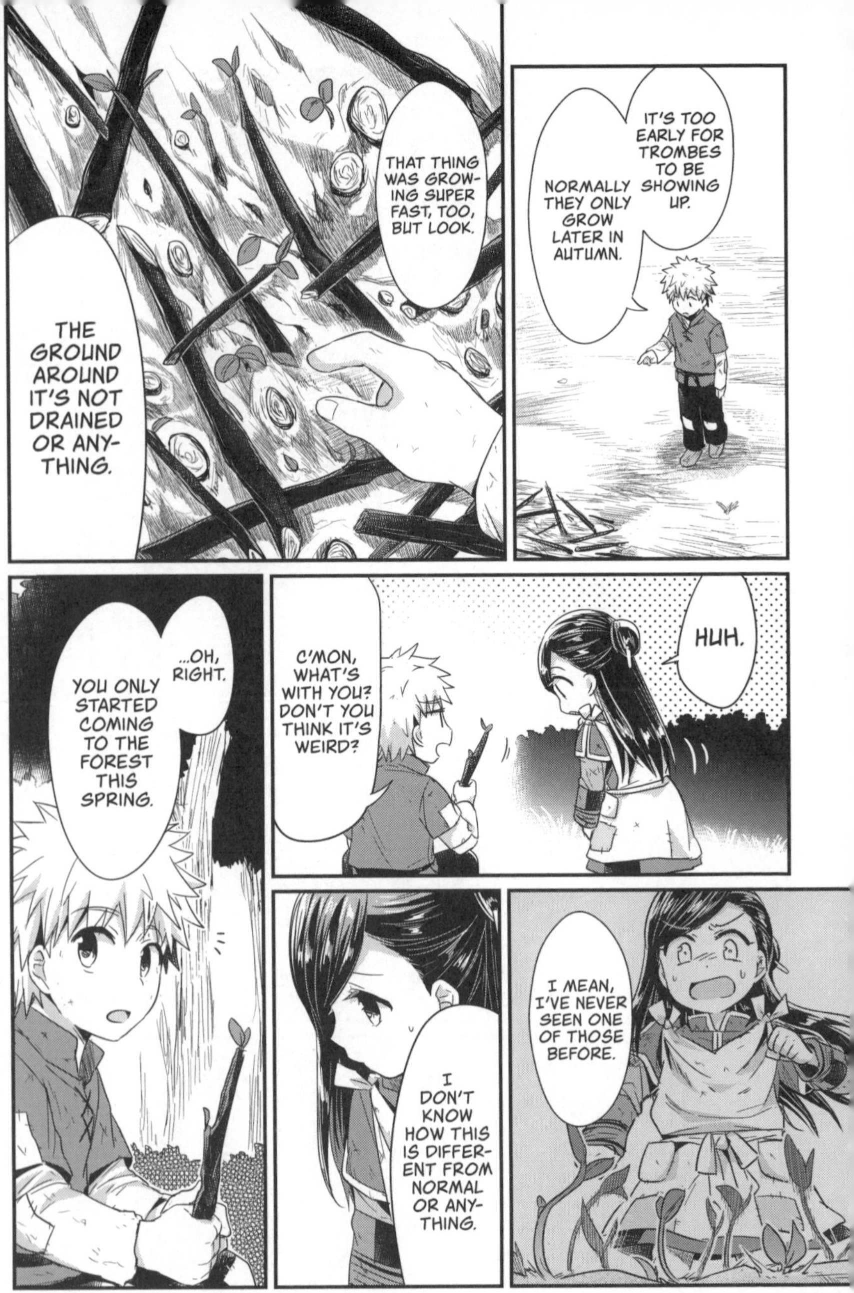
IT'S TOO EARLY FOR TROMBES TO BE SHOWING UP.
NORMALLY THEY ONLY GROW LATER IN AUTUMN.
THAT THING WAS GROWING SUPER FAST, TOO, BUT LOOK.
THE GROUND AROUND IT'S NOT DRAINED OR ANYTHING.
HUH.
C'MON, WHAT'S WITH YOU? DON'T YOU THINK IT'S WEIRD?
I MEAN, I'VE NEVER SEEN ONE OF THOSE BEFORE.
I DON'T KNOW HOW THIS IS DIFFERENT FROM NORMAL OR ANYTHING.
...OH, RIGHT.
YOU ONLY STARTED COMING TO THE FOREST THIS SPRING.

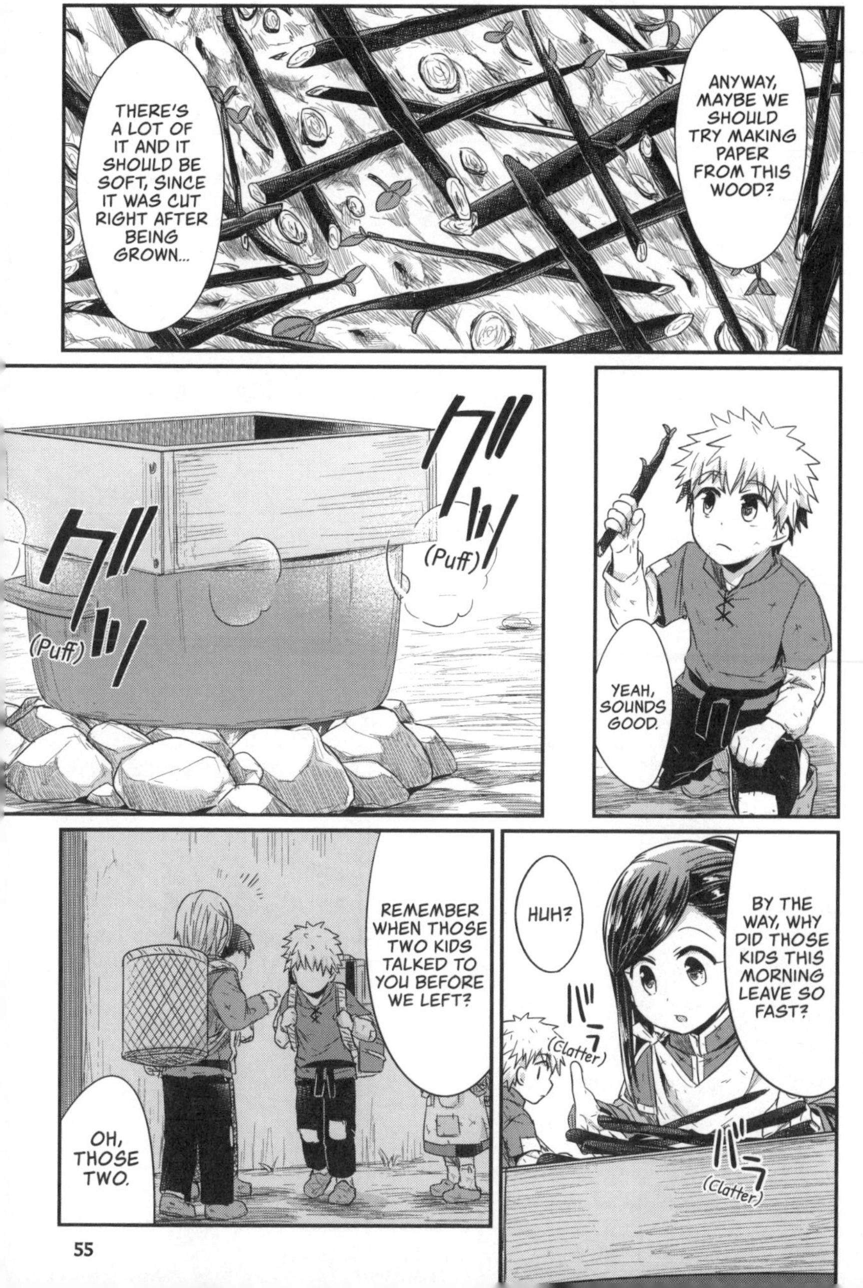
ANYWAY, MAYBE WE SHOULD TRY MAKING PAPER FROM THIS WOOD?
THERE'S A LOT OF IT AND IT SHOULD BE SOFT, SINCE IT WAS CUT RIGHT AFTER BEING GROWN...
YEAH, SOUNDS GOOD.
(Puff)
(Puff)
BY THE WAY, WHY DID THOSE KIDS THIS MORNING LEAVE SO FAST?
HUH?
(Clatter)
(Clatter)
REMEMBER WHEN THOSE TWO KIDS TALKED TO YOU BEFORE WE LEFT?
OH, THOSE TWO.

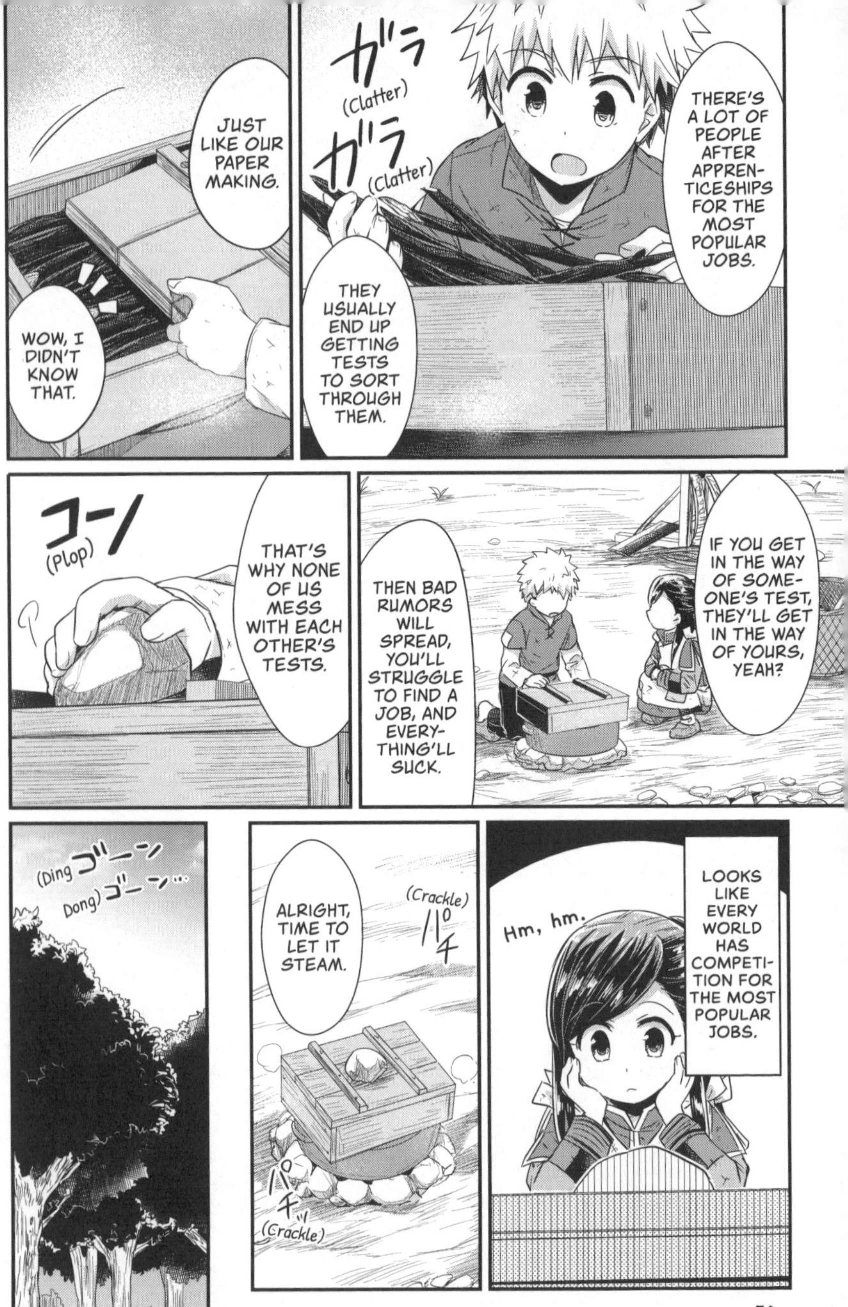
ガラ (Clatter)
ガラ (Clatter)
THERE'S A LOT OF PEOPLE AFTER APPREN-TICESHIPS FOR THE MOST POPULAR JOBS.
THEY USUALLY END UP GETTING TESTS TO SORT THROUGH THEM.
JUST LIKE OUR PAPER MAKING.
WOW, I DIDN'T KNOW THAT.
IF YOU GET IN THE WAY OF SOME-ONE'S TEST, THEY'LL GET IN THE WAY OF YOURS, YEAH?
THEN BAD RUMORS WILL SPREAD, YOU'LL STRUGGLE TO FIND A JOB, AND EVERY-THING'LL SUCK.
THAT'S WHY NONE OF US MESS WITH EACH OTHER'S TESTS.
コーン (Plop)
LOOKS LIKE EVERY WORLD HAS COMPETI-TION FOR THE MOST POPULAR JOBS.
Hm, hm.
ALRIGHT, TIME TO LET IT STEAM.
パチ (Crackle)
パチッ (Crackle)
(Ding ゴーン
Dong) ゴーン…

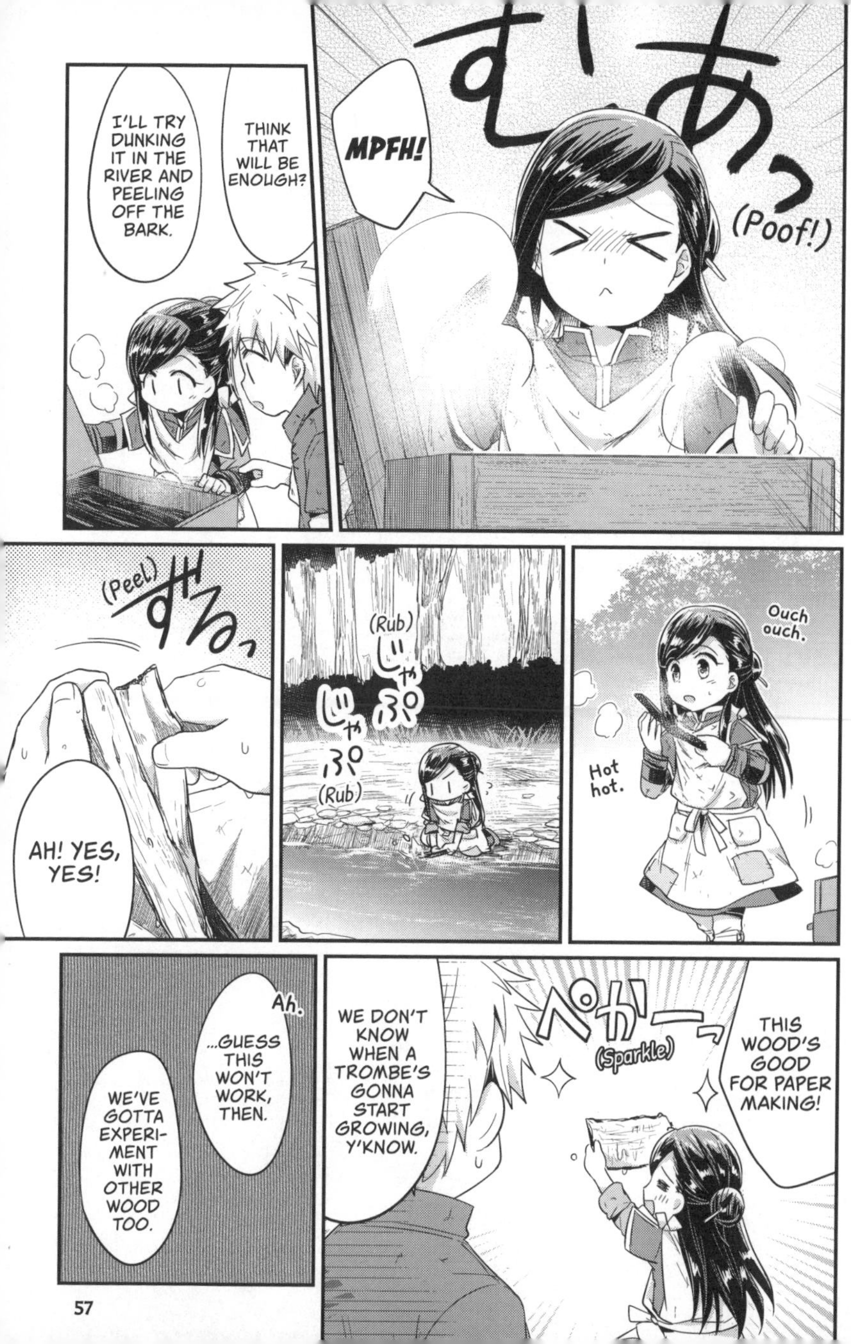

(Poof!)
MPFH!
THINK THAT WILL BE ENOUGH?
I'LL TRY DUNKING IT IN THE RIVER AND PEELING OFF THE BARK.
Ouch ouch.
Hot hot.
(Rub)
じゃぶ
じゃぶ
(Rub)
(Peel)
ずるっ
AH! YES, YES!
THIS WOOD'S GOOD FOR PAPER MAKING!
ぺかーっ
(Sparkle)
WE DON'T KNOW WHEN A TROMBE'S GONNA START GROWING, Y'KNOW.
Ah.
...GUESS THIS WON'T WORK, THEN.
WE'VE GOTTA EXPERIMENT WITH OTHER WOOD TOO.

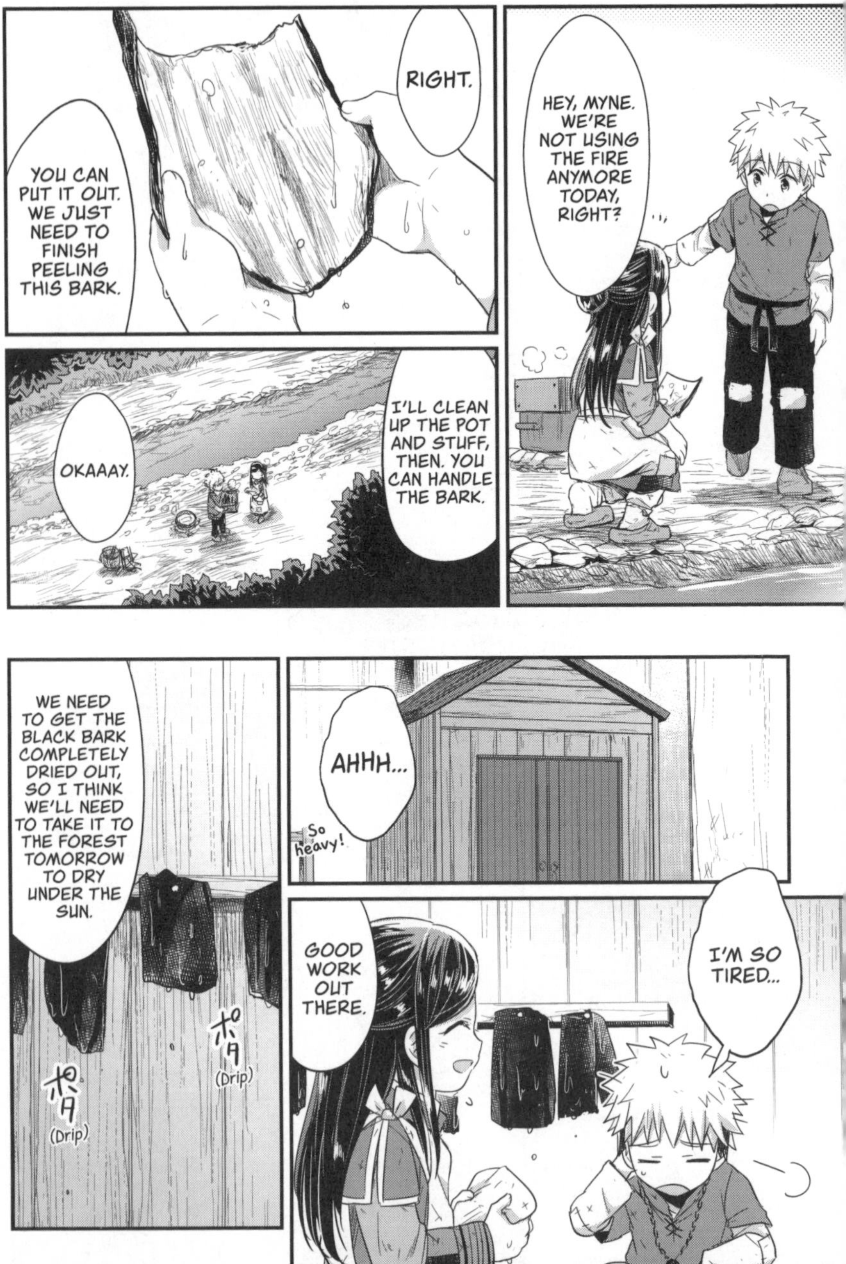
HEY, MYNE. WE'RE NOT USING THE FIRE ANYMORE TODAY, RIGHT?
RIGHT.
YOU CAN PUT IT OUT. WE JUST NEED TO FINISH PEELING THIS BARK.
I'LL CLEAN UP THE POT AND STUFF, THEN. YOU CAN HANDLE THE BARK.
OKAAAY.
AHHH...
So heavy!
I'M SO TIRED...
GOOD WORK OUT THERE.
WE NEED TO GET THE BLACK BARK COMPLETELY DRIED OUT, SO I THINK WE'LL NEED TO TAKE IT TO THE FOREST TOMORROW TO DRY UNDER THE SUN.
ポタ
(Drip)
ポタ
(Drip)

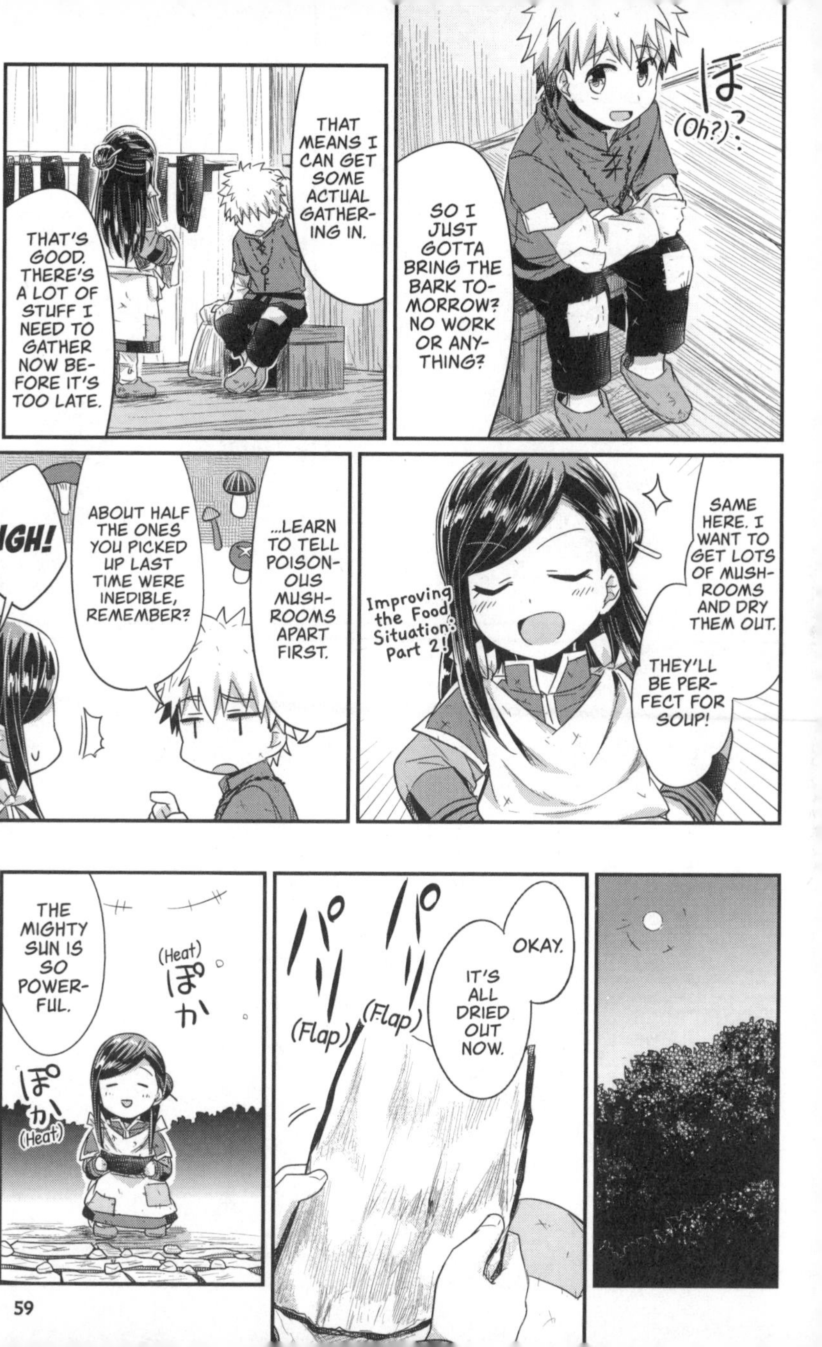
ほっ
(Oh?)
SO I JUST GOTTA BRING THE BARK TOMORROW? NO WORK OR ANYTHING?
THAT MEANS I CAN GET SOME ACTUAL GATHERING IN.
THAT'S GOOD. THERE'S A LOT OF STUFF I NEED TO GATHER NOW BEFORE IT'S TOO LATE.
SAME HERE. I WANT TO GET LOTS OF MUSHROOMS AND DRY THEM OUT.
Improving the Food Situation: Part 2!
THEY'LL BE PERFECT FOR SOUP!
...LEARN TO TELL POISONOUS MUSHROOMS APART FIRST.
ABOUT HALF THE ONES YOU PICKED UP LAST TIME WERE INEDIBLE, REMEMBER?
NGH!
パリ
(Flap)
パリ
(Flap)
OKAY.
IT'S ALL DRIED OUT NOW.
THE MIGHTY SUN IS SO POWERFUL.
ぽか
(Heat)
ぽか
(Heat)

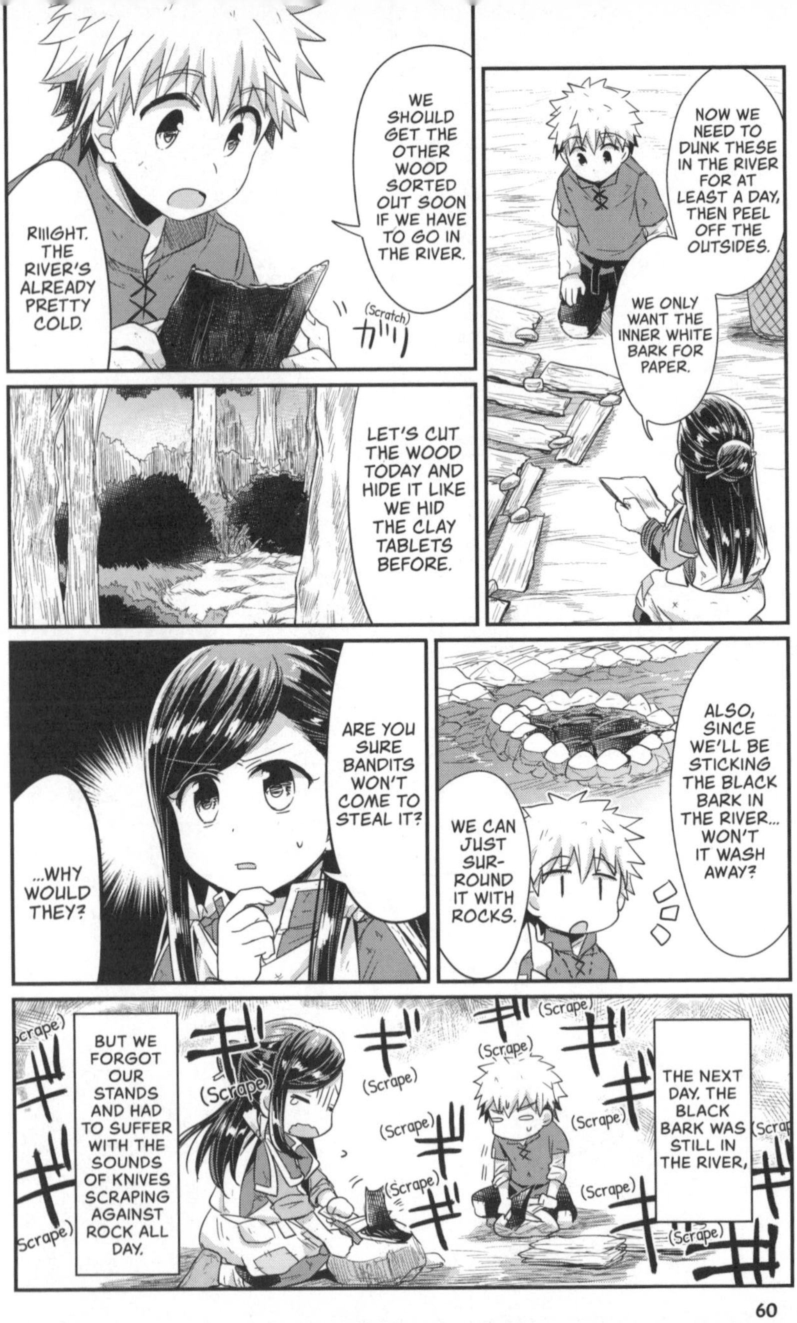
NOW WE NEED TO DUNK THESE IN THE RIVER FOR AT LEAST A DAY, THEN PEEL OFF THE OUTSIDES.
WE ONLY WANT THE INNER WHITE BARK FOR PAPER.
WE SHOULD GET THE OTHER WOOD SORTED OUT SOON IF WE HAVE TO GO IN THE RIVER.
RIIIGHT. THE RIVER'S ALREADY PRETTY COLD.
(Scratch)
ガリ
LET'S CUT THE WOOD TODAY AND HIDE IT LIKE WE HID THE CLAY TABLETS BEFORE.
ALSO, SINCE WE'LL BE STICKING THE BLACK BARK IN THE RIVER... WON'T IT WASH AWAY?
WE CAN JUST SUR-ROUND IT WITH ROCKS.
ARE YOU SURE BANDITS WON'T COME TO STEAL IT?
...WHY WOULD THEY?
THE NEXT DAY, THE BLACK BARK WAS STILL IN THE RIVER,
BUT WE FORGOT OUR STANDS AND HAD TO SUFFER WITH THE SOUNDS OF KNIVES SCRAPING AGAINST ROCK ALL DAY.
(Scrape)
ギ

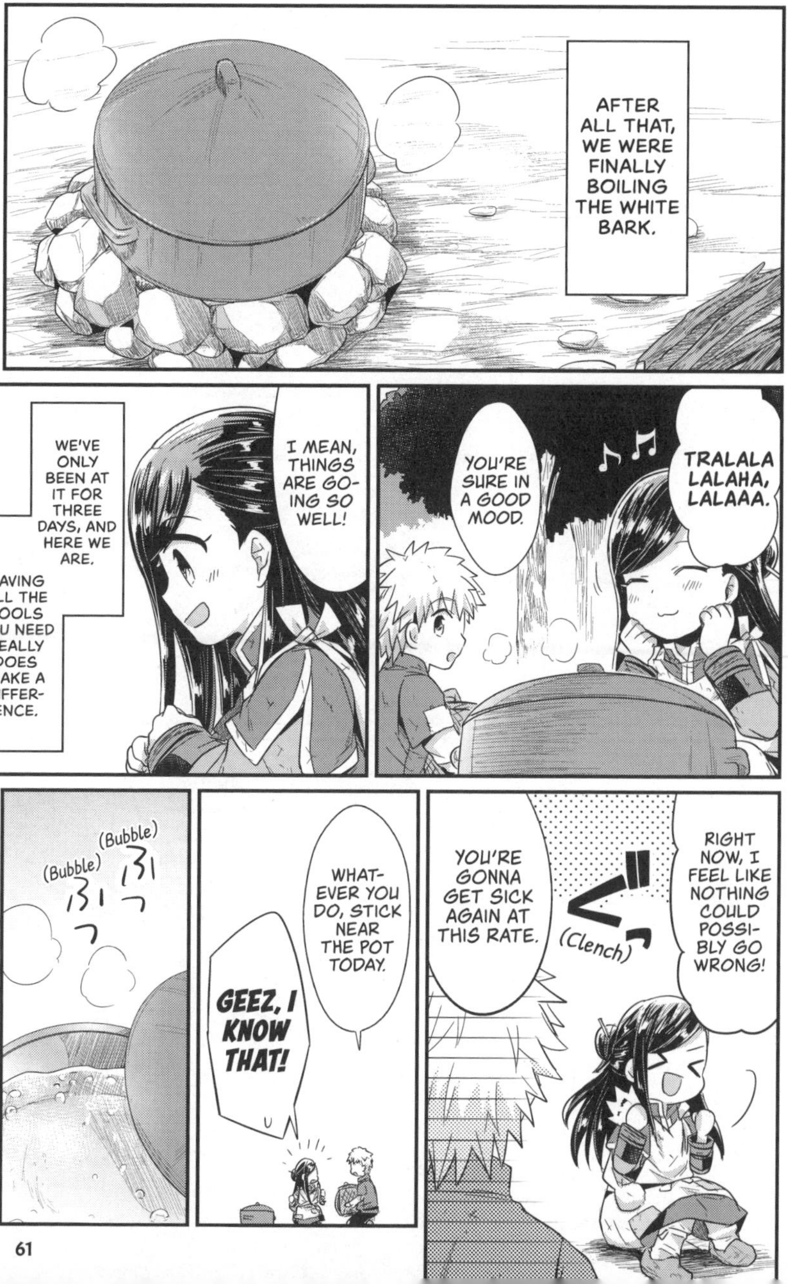
AFTER ALL THAT, WE WERE FINALLY BOILING THE WHITE BARK.
TRALALA LALAHA, LALAAA.
YOU'RE SURE IN A GOOD MOOD.
I MEAN, THINGS ARE GOING SO WELL!
WE'VE ONLY BEEN AT IT FOR THREE DAYS, AND HERE WE ARE.
HAVING ALL THE TOOLS YOU NEED REALLY DOES MAKE A DIFFERENCE.
RIGHT NOW, I FEEL LIKE NOTHING COULD POSSIBLY GO WRONG!
(Clench)
YOU'RE GONNA GET SICK AGAIN AT THIS RATE.
WHATEVER YOU DO, STICK NEAR THE POT TODAY.
GEEZ, I KNOW THAT!
(Bubble)
(Bubble)

� (Pour)
アアア

BOIL THE WHITE BARK WITH ASHES UNTIL THEY'RE SOFT...

WE NEED TO STIR IT TOO, SO...

WAIT.

WE JUST GOTTA WAIT A BELL'S WORTH, YEAH?

UH HUH.

(Puff)
(Puff)

THEN WAIT ABOUT TWO TO THREE HOURS, I THINK?

SO BASICALLY, MAKE TWO STICKS OUT OF BAMBOO?

NORMAL WOOD STICKS WOULD HAVE THEIR BARK PEEL OFF INSIDE, SO MAYBE USE BAMBOO.

I WANT TWO STICKS OF THE SAME LENGTH TO STIR UP WHAT'S IN THE POT.

NOOO! I REMEMBERED SOMETHING ELSE I FORGOT!

ビクッ
(Twitch)

62

(Slice)

GUESS THAT SHOULD DO IT?

(Stir)

(Stir)

♪

HERE.

THANKS, LUTZ!

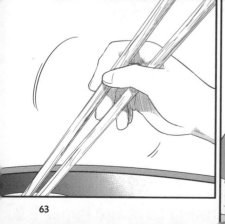

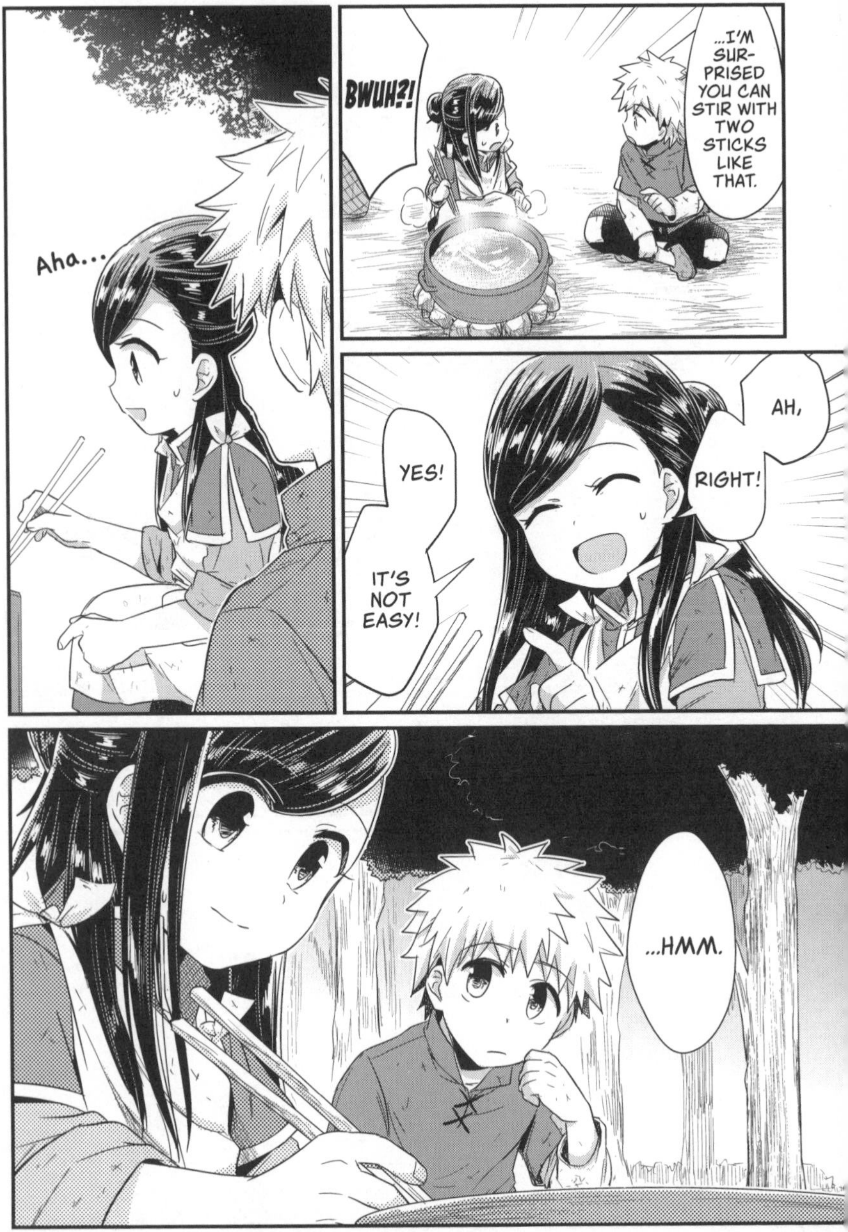
...I'M SUR-PRISED YOU CAN STIR WITH TWO STICKS LIKE THAT.
BWUH?!
AH, RIGHT!
YES! IT'S NOT EASY!
Aha...
...HMM.

Ch.16: Beginning to Make Paper End

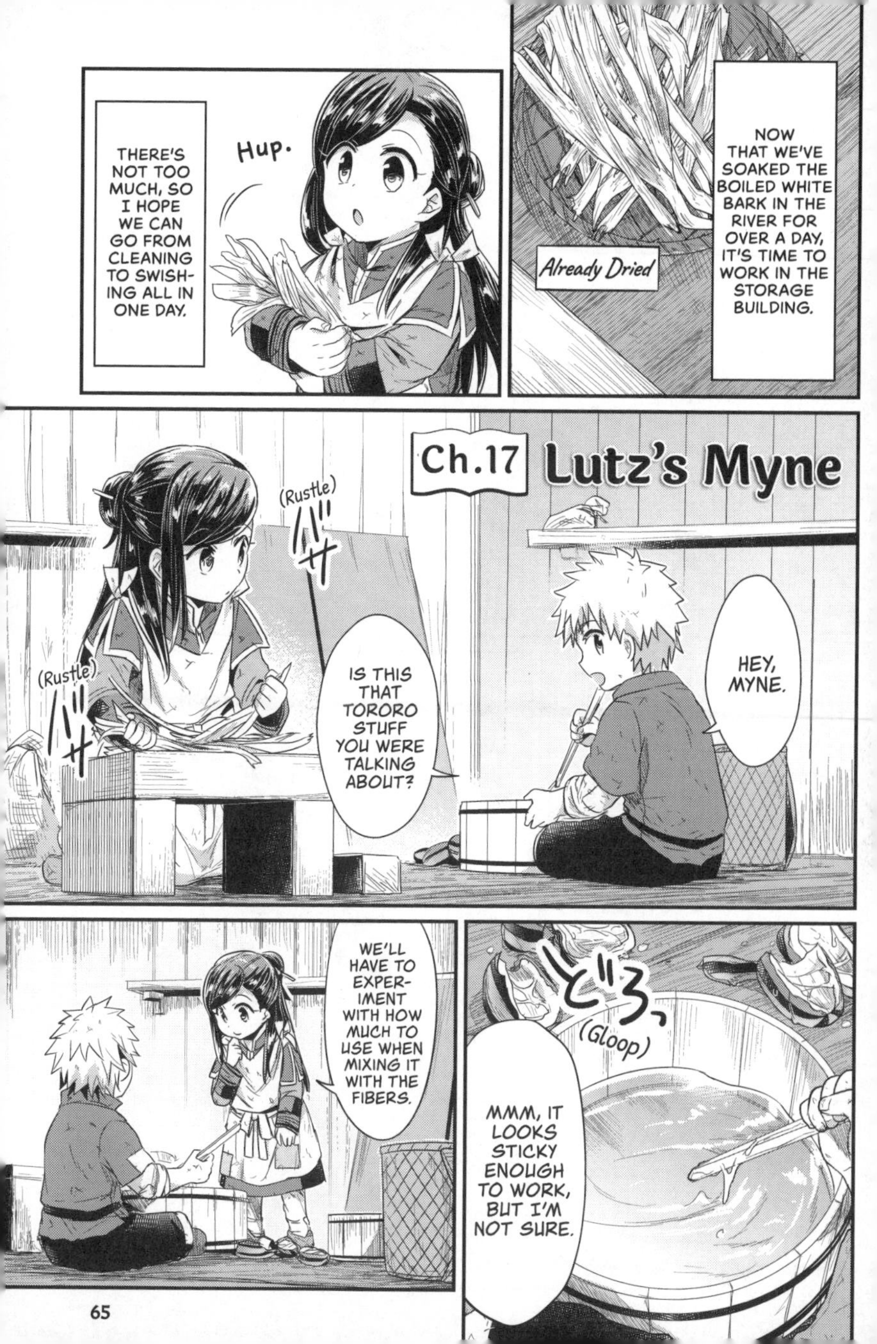
NOW THAT WE'VE SOAKED THE BOILED WHITE BARK IN THE RIVER FOR OVER A DAY, IT'S TIME TO WORK IN THE STORAGE BUILDING.
Already Dried
Hup.
THERE'S NOT TOO MUCH, SO I HOPE WE CAN GO FROM CLEANING TO SWISHING ALL IN ONE DAY.
Ch.17 Lutz's Myne
HEY, MYNE.
(Rustle)
IS THIS THAT TORORO STUFF YOU WERE TALKING ABOUT?
(Rustle)
(Gloop)
MMM, IT LOOKS STICKY ENOUGH TO WORK, BUT I'M NOT SURE.
WE'LL HAVE TO EXPERIMENT WITH HOW MUCH TO USE WHEN MIXING IT WITH THE FIBERS.

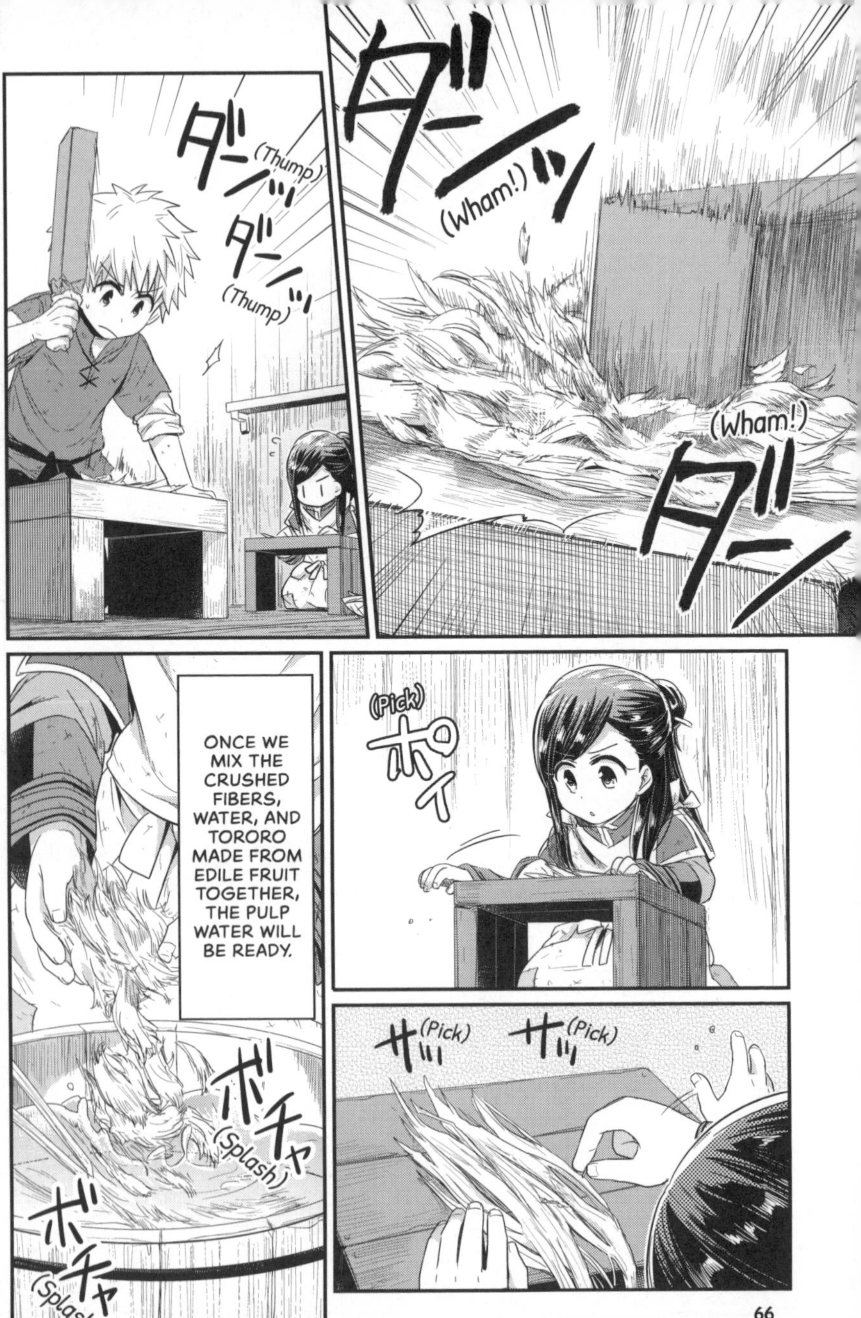
ダーンッ
(Wham!)
(Wham!)
ダーン
ダーンッ
(Thump)
ダーンッ
(Thump)
(Pick)
ポイ
ザッ
(Pick)
ザッ
(Pick)
ONCE WE MIX THE CRUSHED FIBERS, WATER, AND TORORO MADE FROM EDILE FRUIT TOGETHER, THE PULP WATER WILL BE READY.
ボチャ
(Splash)
ボチャ
(Splash)

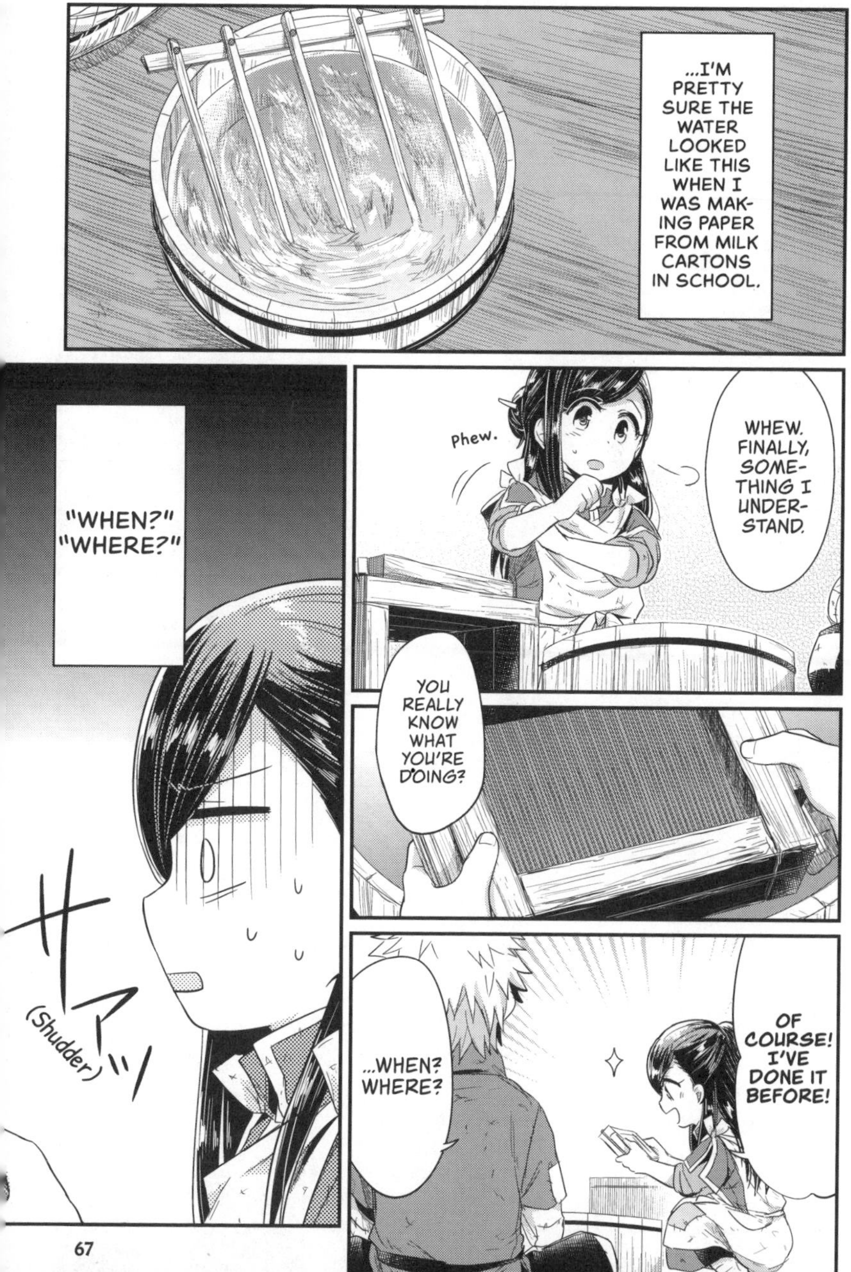
...I'M PRETTY SURE THE WATER LOOKED LIKE THIS WHEN I WAS MAKING PAPER FROM MILK CARTONS IN SCHOOL.
Phew.
WHEW. FINALLY, SOMETHING I UNDERSTAND.
YOU REALLY KNOW WHAT YOU'RE DOING?
OF COURSE! I'VE DONE IT BEFORE!
...WHEN? WHERE?
"WHEN?" "WHERE?"
(Shudder)

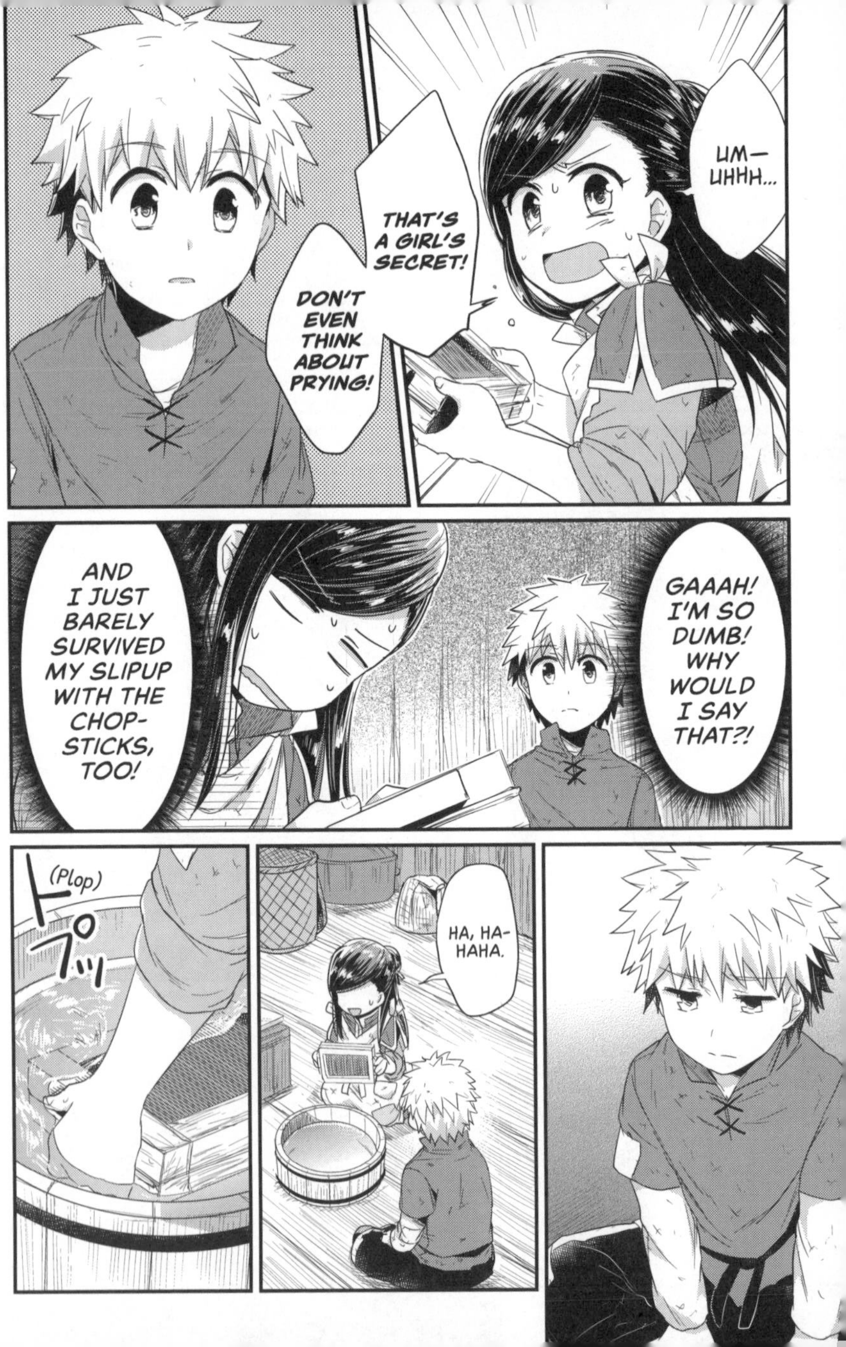
UM—UHHH...
THAT'S A GIRL'S SECRET!
DON'T EVEN THINK ABOUT PRYING!
GAAAH! I'M SO DUMB! WHY WOULD I SAY THAT?!
AND I JUST BARELY SURVIVED MY SLIPUP WITH THE CHOP-STICKS, TOO!
HA, HA-HAHA.
トプッ
(Plop)

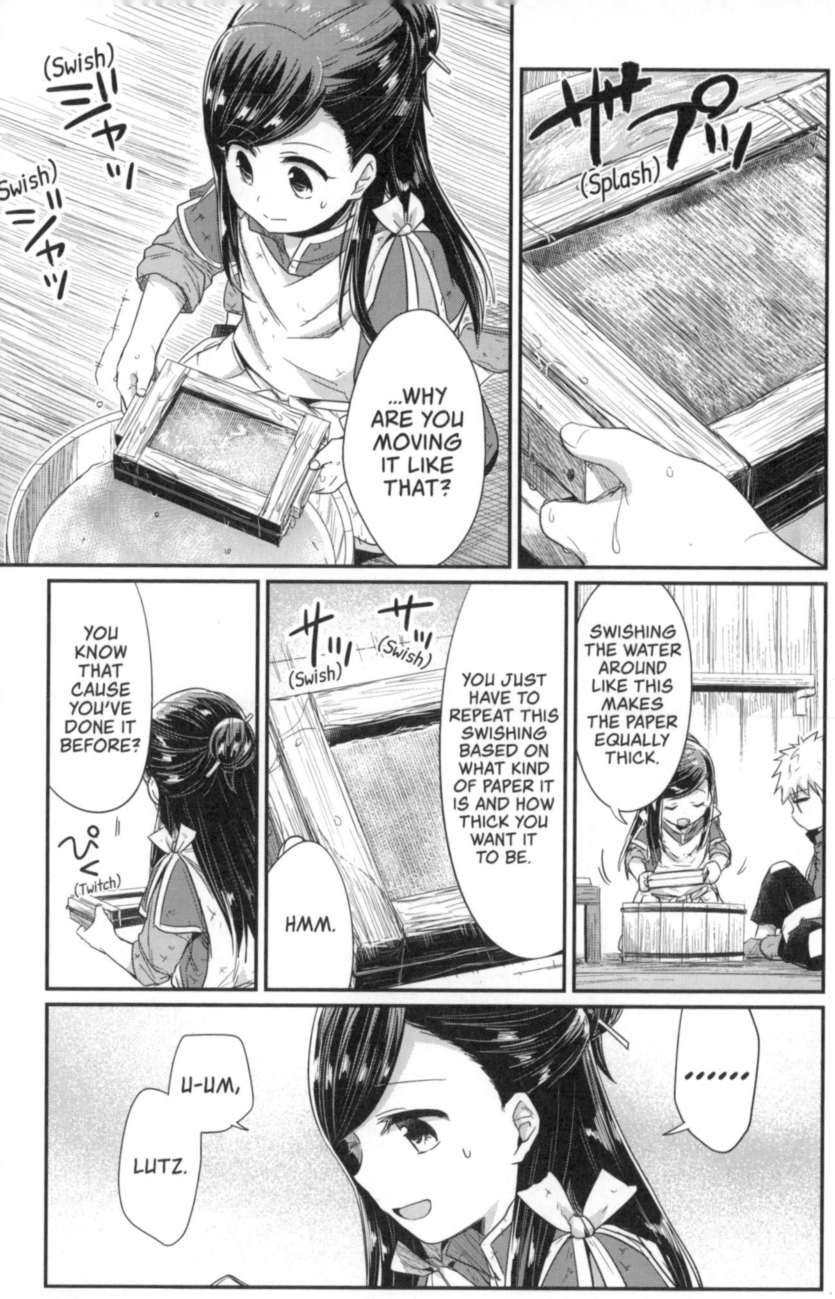
ザプッ
(Splash)
(Swish)
ジャッ
(Swish)
ジャッ
...WHY ARE YOU MOVING IT LIKE THAT?
SWISHING THE WATER AROUND LIKE THIS MAKES THE PAPER EQUALLY THICK.
サッ
(Swish)
サッ
(Swish)
YOU JUST HAVE TO REPEAT THIS SWISHING BASED ON WHAT KIND OF PAPER IT IS AND HOW THICK YOU WANT IT TO BE.
HMM.
YOU KNOW THAT CAUSE YOU'VE DONE IT BEFORE?
ぴく
(Twitch)
......
U-UM,
LUTZ.

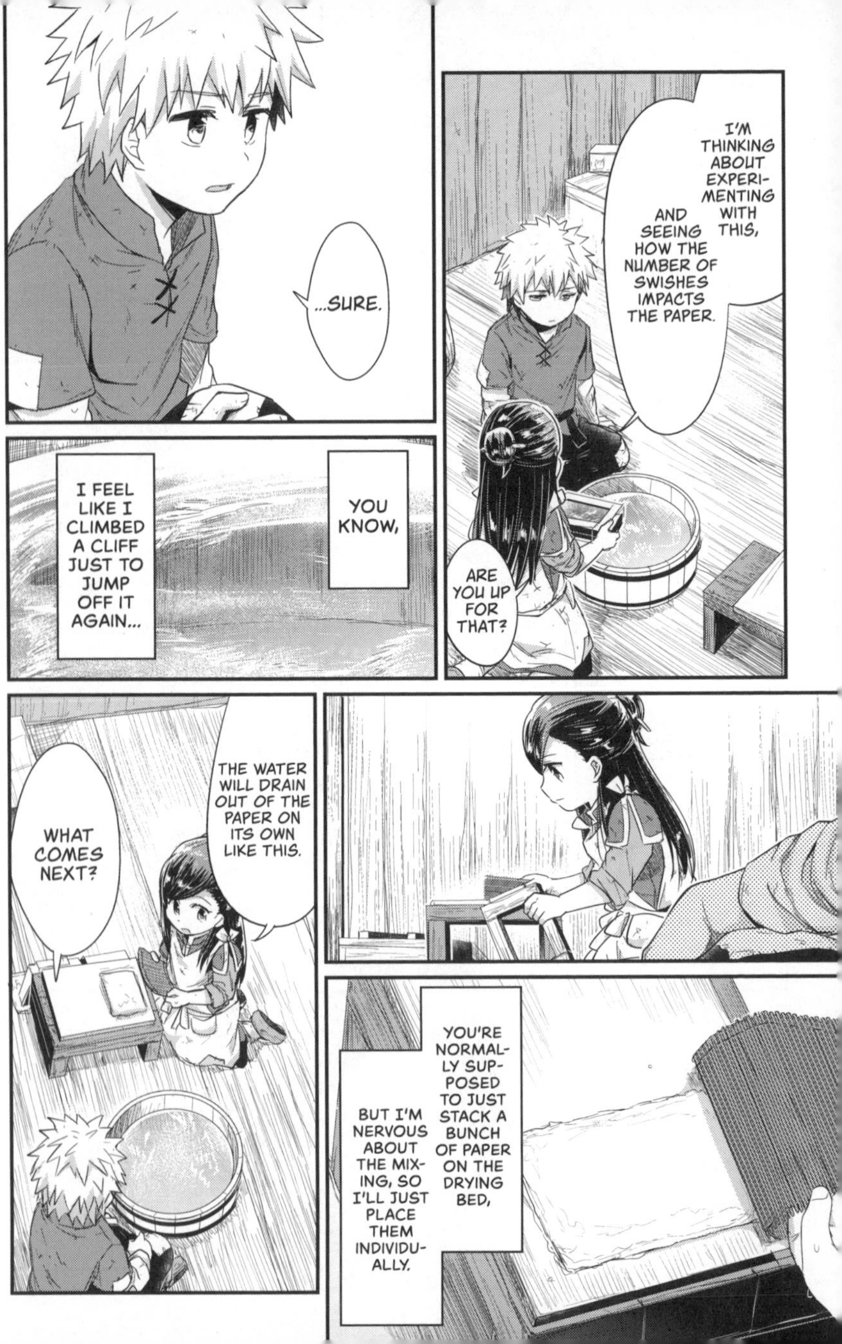
I'M THINKING ABOUT EXPERIMENTING WITH THIS,
AND SEEING HOW THE NUMBER OF SWISHES IMPACTS THE PAPER.
ARE YOU UP FOR THAT?
...SURE.
YOU KNOW,
I FEEL LIKE I CLIMBED A CLIFF JUST TO JUMP OFF IT AGAIN...
YOU'RE NORMALLY SUPPOSED TO JUST STACK A BUNCH OF PAPER ON THE DRYING BED,
BUT I'M NERVOUS ABOUT THE MIXING, SO I'LL JUST PLACE THEM INDIVIDUALLY.
THE WATER WILL DRAIN OUT OF THE PAPER ON ITS OWN LIKE THIS.
WHAT COMES NEXT?

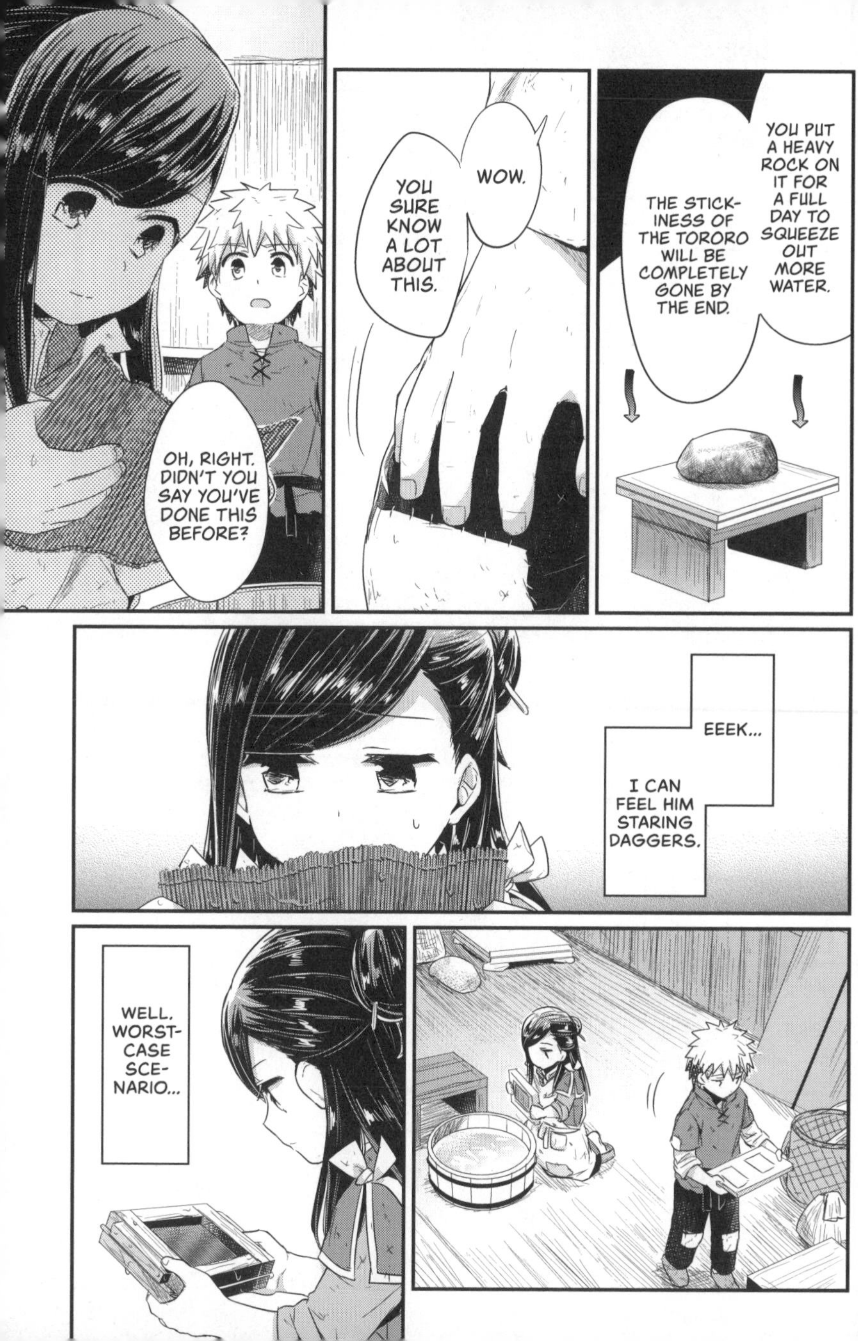
YOU PUT A HEAVY ROCK ON IT FOR A FULL DAY TO SQUEEZE OUT MORE WATER.
THE STICKINESS OF THE TORORO WILL BE COMPLETELY GONE BY THE END.
WOW.
YOU SURE KNOW A LOT ABOUT THIS.
OH, RIGHT. DIDN'T YOU SAY YOU'VE DONE THIS BEFORE?
EEEK...
I CAN FEEL HIM STARING DAGGERS.
WELL, WORST-CASE SCENARIO...

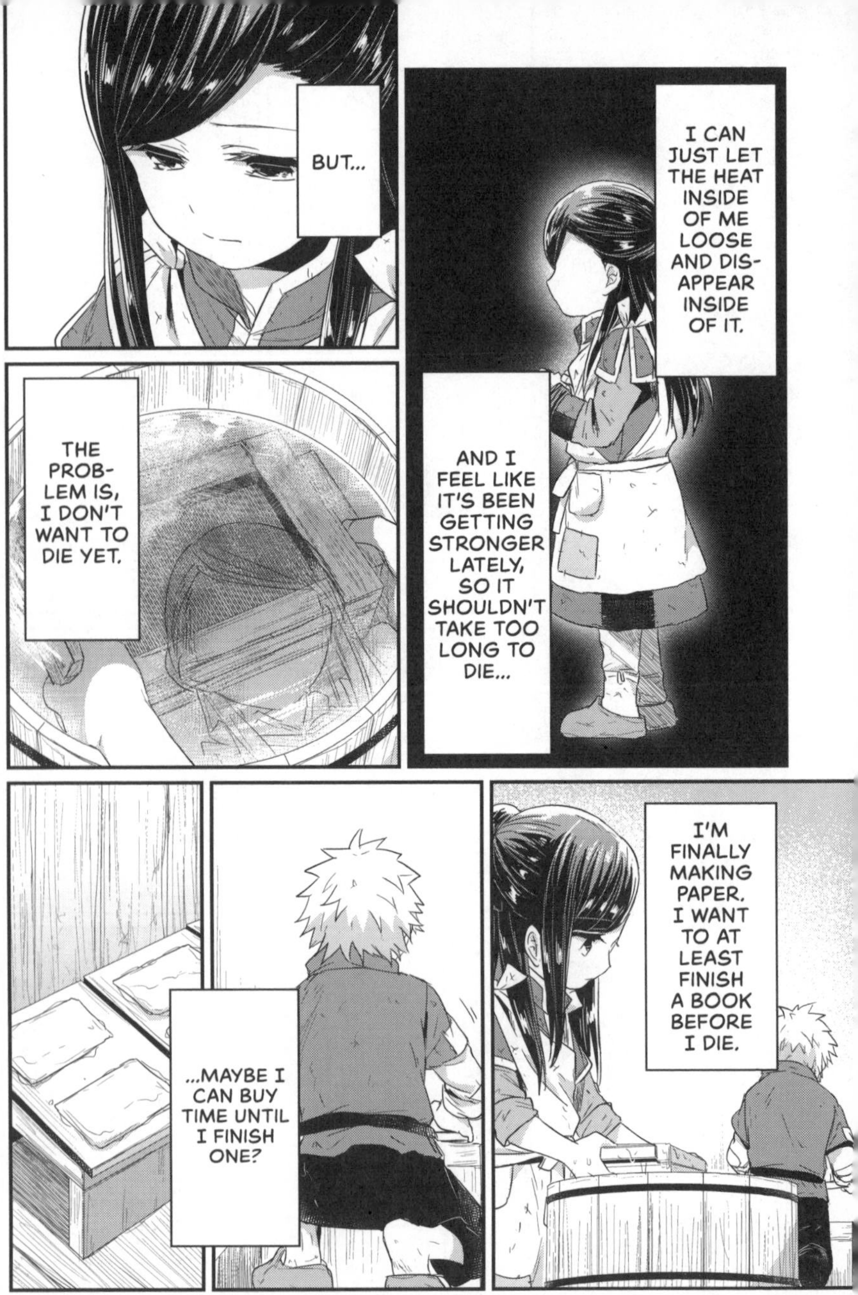
I CAN JUST LET THE HEAT INSIDE OF ME LOOSE AND DIS-APPEAR INSIDE OF IT.
AND I FEEL LIKE IT'S BEEN GETTING STRONGER LATELY, SO IT SHOULDN'T TAKE TOO LONG TO DIE...
BUT...
THE PROB-LEM IS, I DON'T WANT TO DIE YET.
I'M FINALLY MAKING PAPER. I WANT TO AT LEAST FINISH A BOOK BEFORE I DIE.
...MAYBE I CAN BUY TIME UNTIL I FINISH ONE?

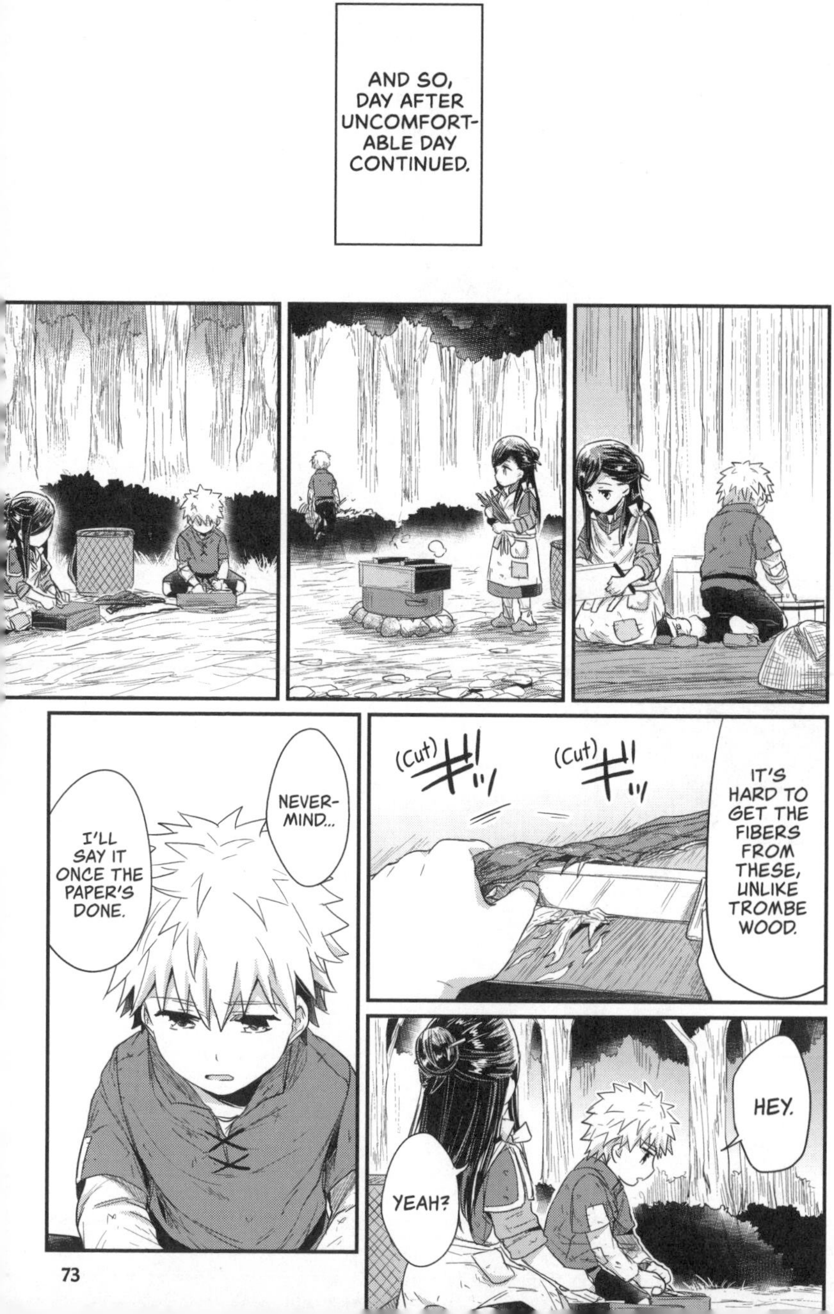
AND SO, DAY AFTER UNCOMFORTABLE DAY CONTINUED.
(Cut) ギッ
(Cut) ギッ
IT'S HARD TO GET THE FIBERS FROM THESE, UNLIKE TROMBE WOOD.
HEY.
YEAH?
NEVER-MIND...
I'LL SAY IT ONCE THE PAPER'S DONE.

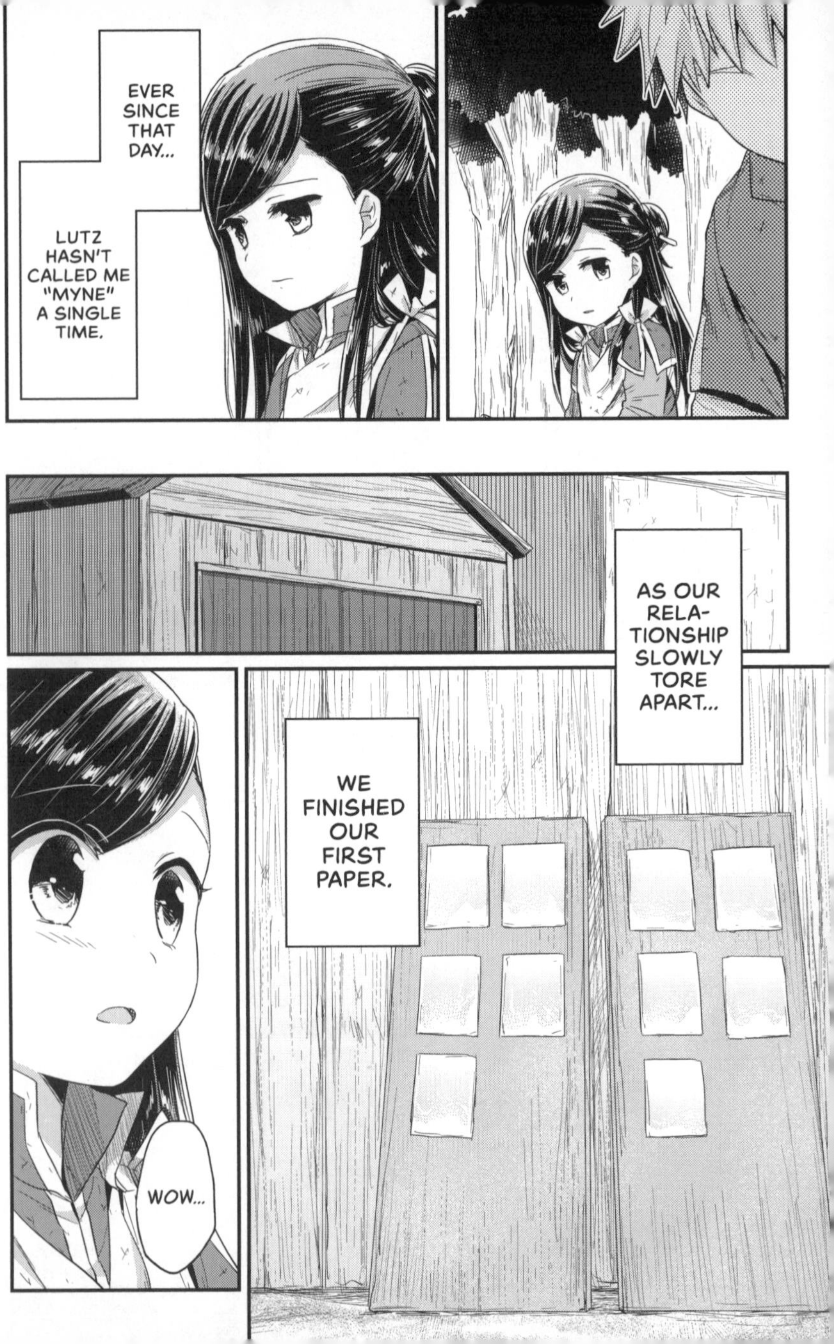
EVER SINCE THAT DAY...
LUTZ HASN'T CALLED ME "MYNE" A SINGLE TIME.
AS OUR RELA-TIONSHIP SLOWLY TORE APART...
WE FINISHED OUR FIRST PAPER.
WOW...

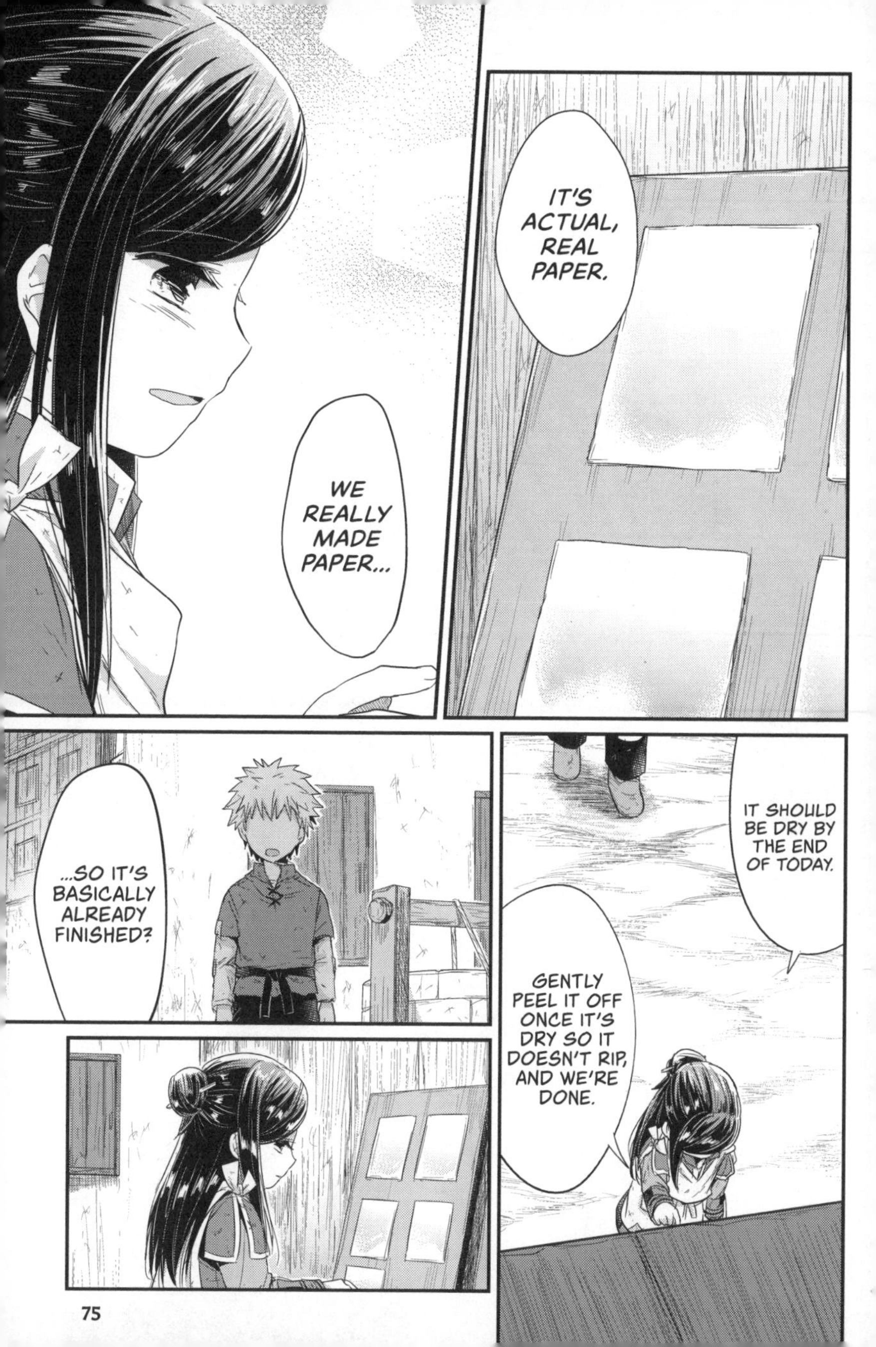
IT'S ACTUAL, REAL PAPER.
WE REALLY MADE PAPER...
IT SHOULD BE DRY BY THE END OF TODAY.
GENTLY PEEL IT OFF ONCE IT'S DRY SO IT DOESN'T RIP, AND WE'RE DONE.
...SO IT'S BASICALLY ALREADY FINISHED?

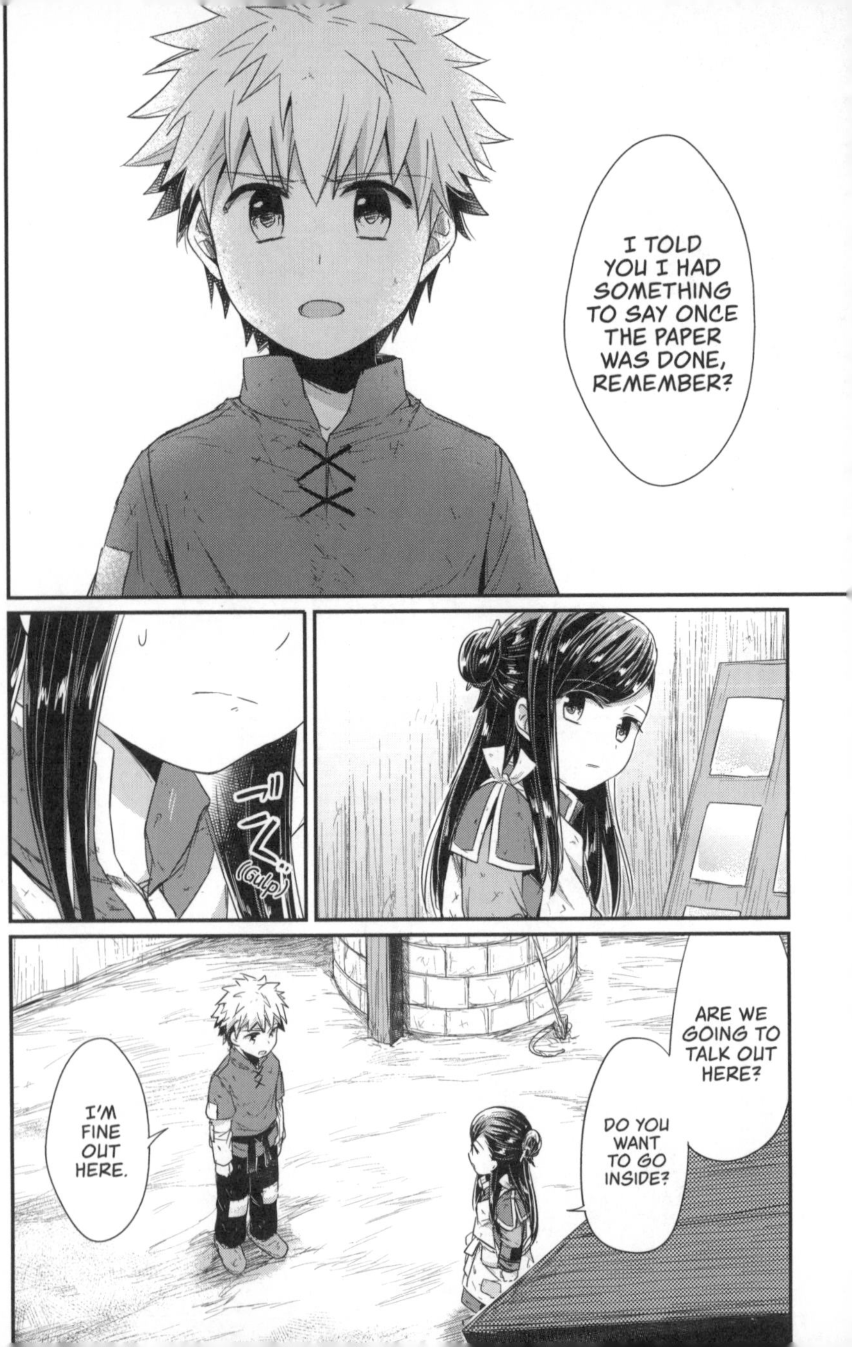
I TOLD YOU I HAD SOMETHING TO SAY ONCE THE PAPER WAS DONE, REMEMBER?
(Gulp)
ARE WE GOING TO TALK OUT HERE?
DO YOU WANT TO GO INSIDE?
I'M FINE OUT HERE.

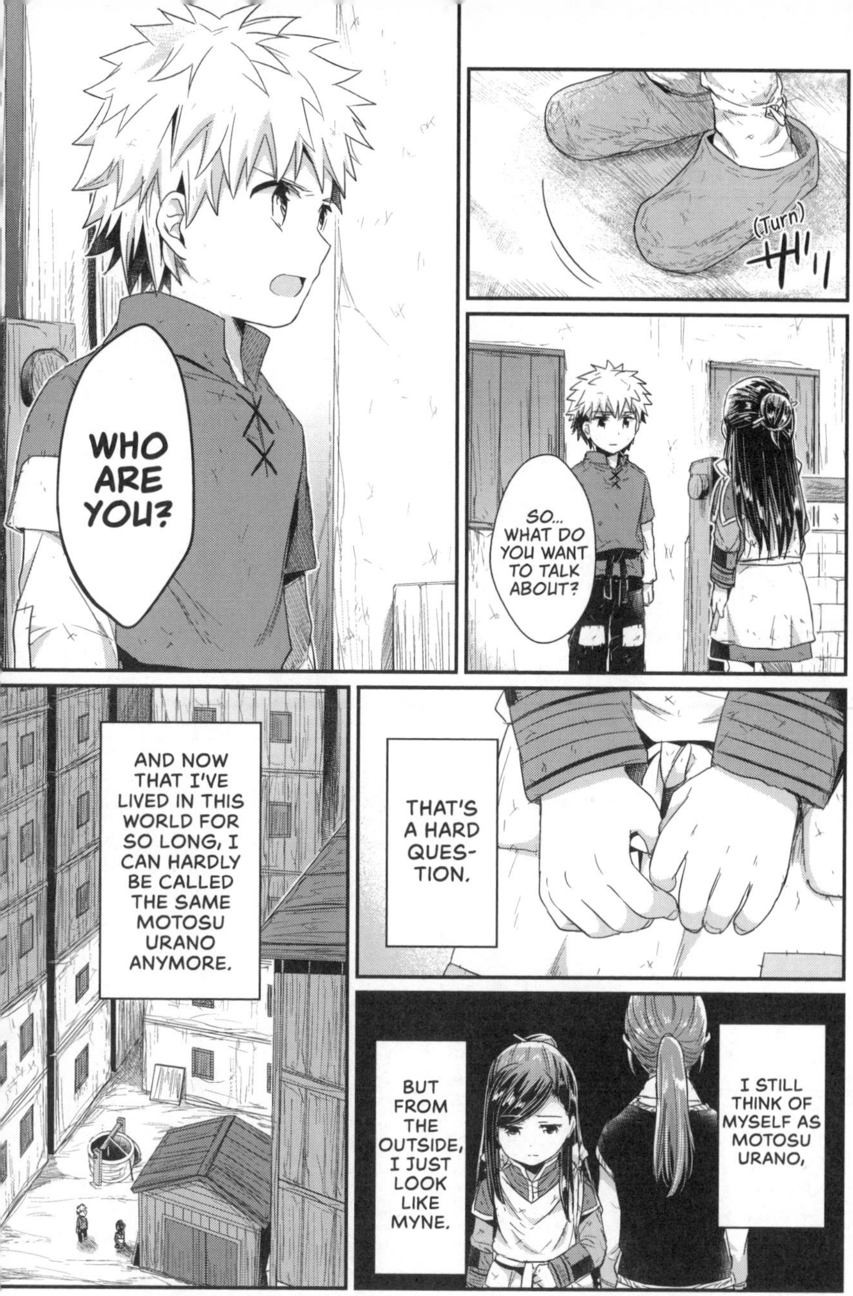
(Turn)
ザリ
SO... WHAT DO YOU WANT TO TALK ABOUT?
WHO ARE YOU?
THAT'S A HARD QUES- TION.
I STILL THINK OF MYSELF AS MOTOSU URANO,
BUT FROM THE OUTSIDE, I JUST LOOK LIKE MYNE.
AND NOW THAT I'VE LIVED IN THIS WORLD FOR SO LONG, I CAN HARDLY BE CALLED THE SAME MOTOSU URANO ANYMORE.

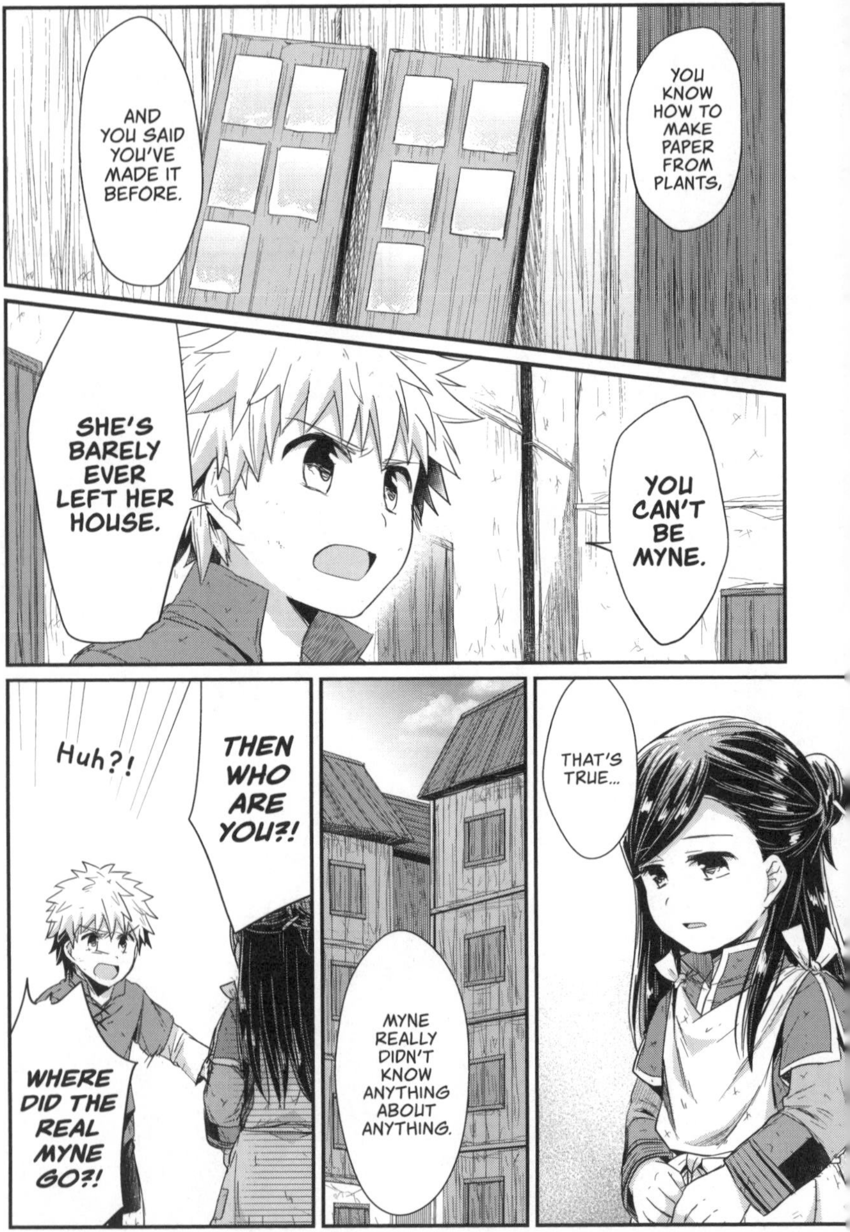
YOU KNOW HOW TO MAKE PAPER FROM PLANTS,
AND YOU SAID YOU'VE MADE IT BEFORE.
YOU CAN'T BE MYNE.
SHE'S BARELY EVER LEFT HER HOUSE.
THAT'S TRUE...
MYNE REALLY DIDN'T KNOW ANYTHING ABOUT ANYTHING.
THEN WHO ARE YOU?!
Huh?!
WHERE DID THE REAL MYNE GO?!

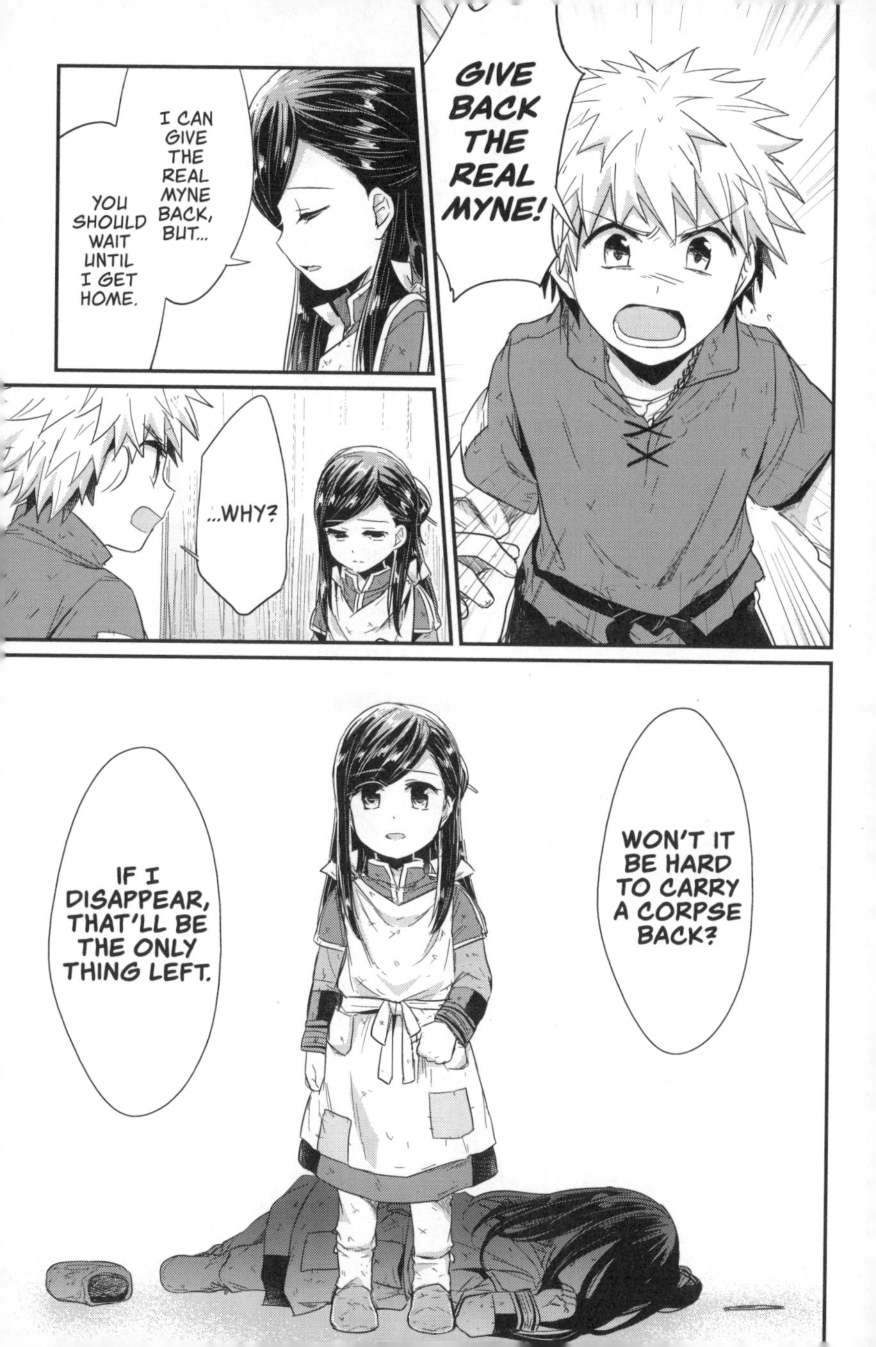
GIVE BACK THE REAL MYNE!
I CAN GIVE THE REAL MYNE BACK, BUT...
YOU SHOULD WAIT UNTIL I GET HOME.
...WHY?
WON'T IT BE HARD TO CARRY A CORPSE BACK?
IF I DISAPPEAR, THAT'LL BE THE ONLY THING LEFT.

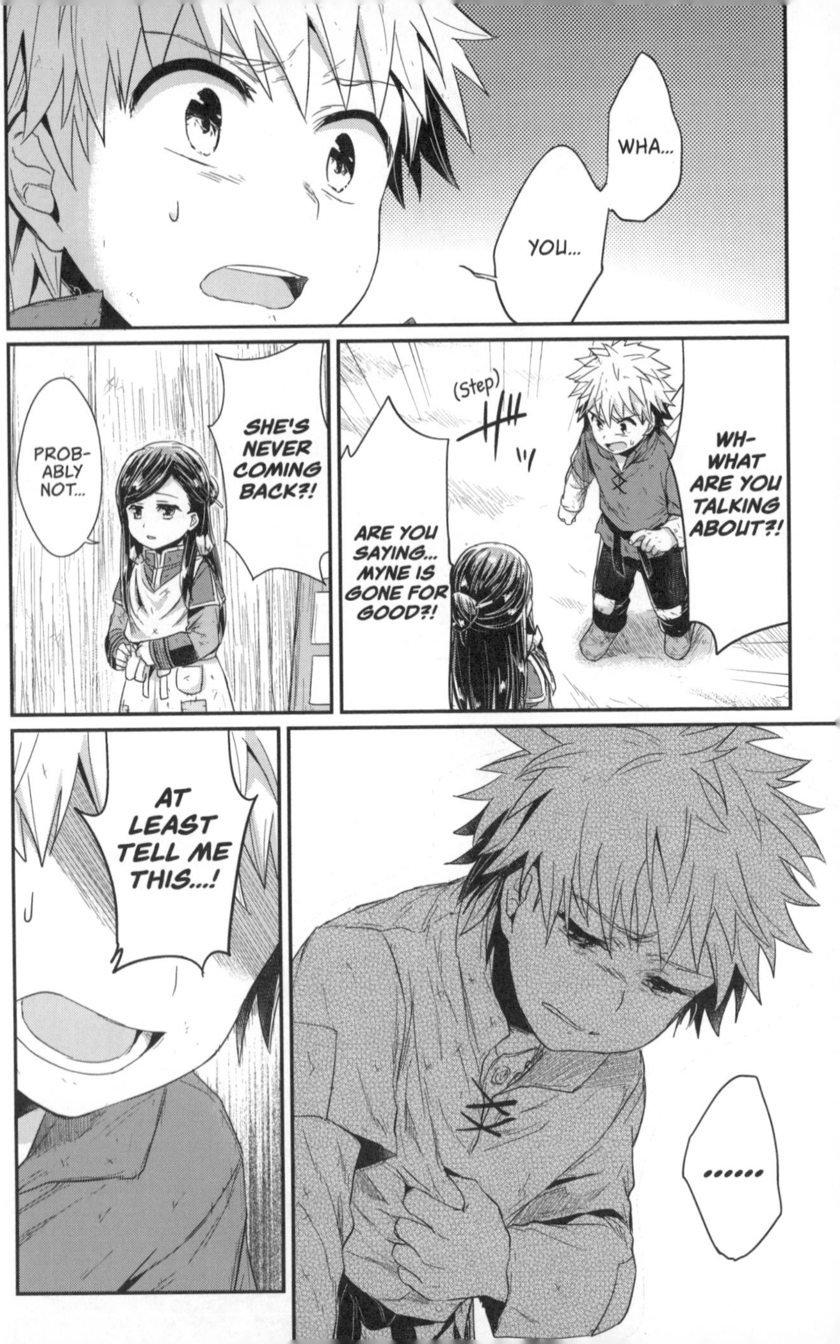
WHA...
YOU...
(Step)
WH-WHAT ARE YOU TALKING ABOUT?!
ARE YOU SAYING... MYNE IS GONE FOR GOOD?!
SHE'S NEVER COMING BACK?!
PROB-ABLY NOT...
......
AT LEAST TELL ME THIS...!

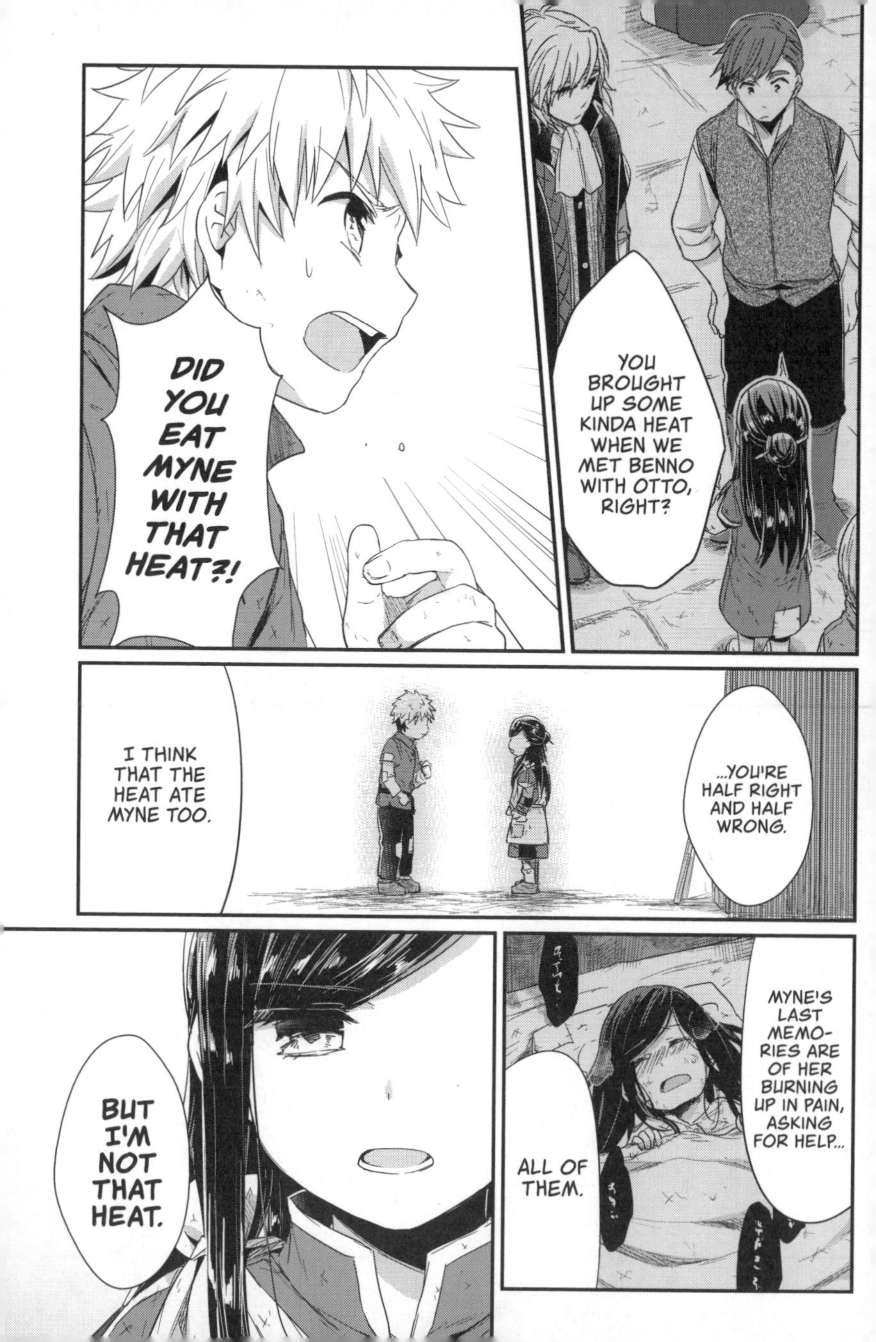
YOU BROUGHT UP SOME KINDA HEAT WHEN WE MET BENNO WITH OTTO, RIGHT?
DID YOU EAT MYNE WITH THAT HEAT?!
...YOU'RE HALF RIGHT AND HALF WRONG.
I THINK THAT THE HEAT ATE MYNE TOO.
MYNE'S LAST MEMORIES ARE OF HER BURNING UP IN PAIN, ASKING FOR HELP...
ALL OF THEM.
BUT I'M NOT THAT HEAT.

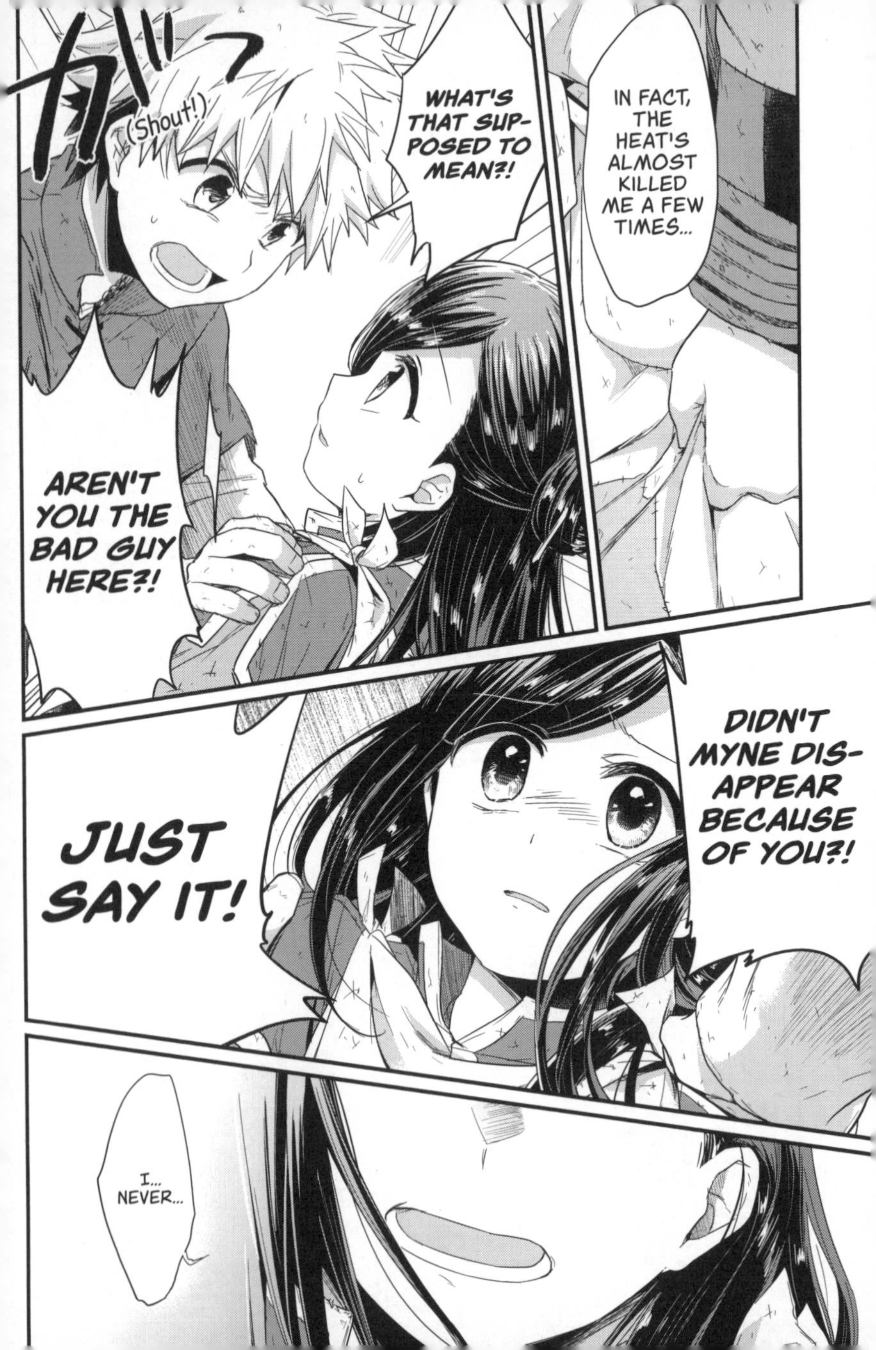
IN FACT, THE HEAT'S ALMOST KILLED ME A FEW TIMES...
カッ
(Shout!)
WHAT'S THAT SUPPOSED TO MEAN?!
AREN'T YOU THE BAD GUY HERE?!
DIDN'T MYNE DISAPPEAR BECAUSE OF YOU?!
JUST SAY IT!
I... NEVER...

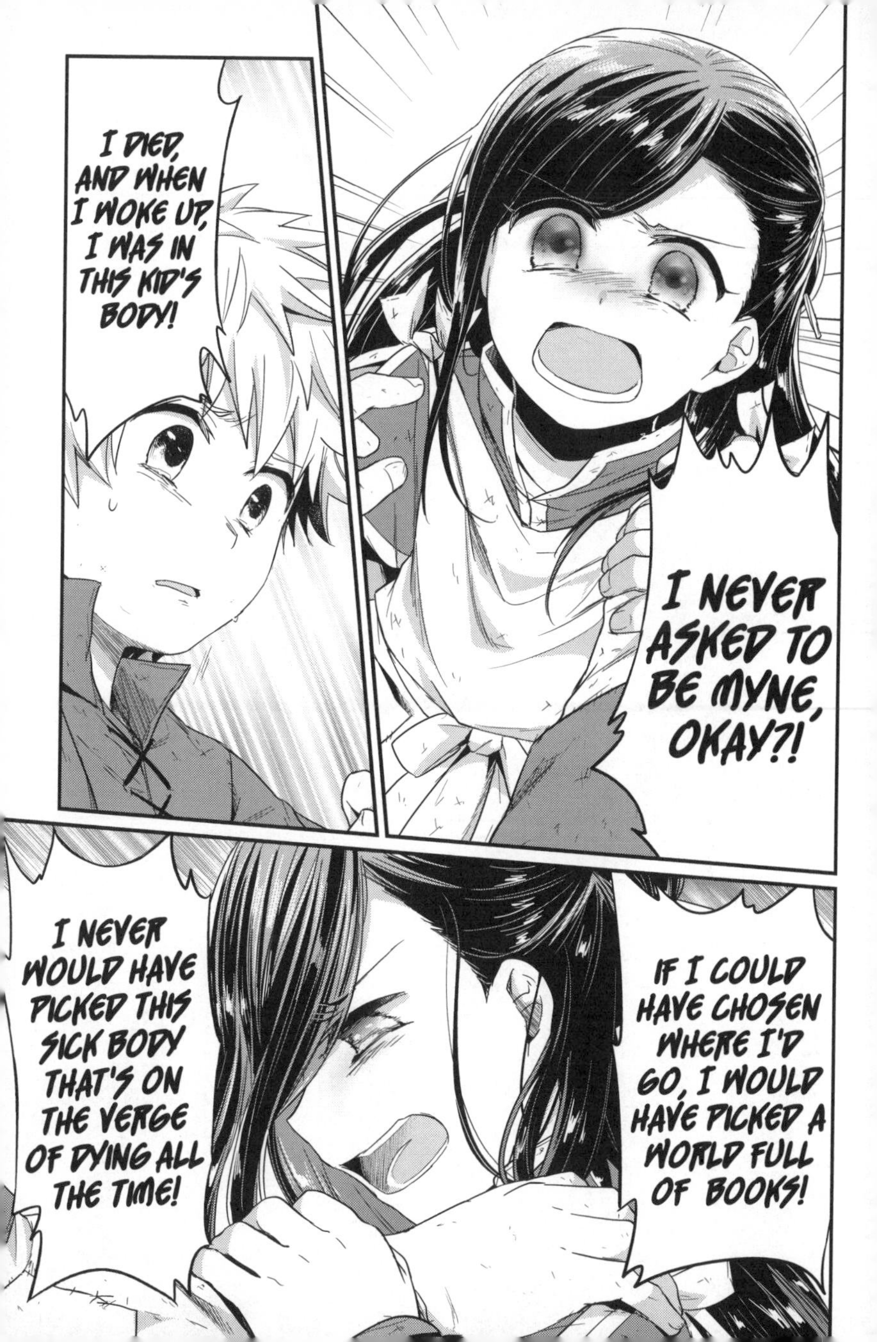
I NEVER ASKED TO BE MYNE, OKAY?!
I DIED, AND WHEN I WOKE UP, I WAS IN THIS KID'S BODY!
IF I COULD HAVE CHOSEN WHERE I'D GO, I WOULD HAVE PICKED A WORLD FULL OF BOOKS!
I NEVER WOULD HAVE PICKED THIS SICK BODY THAT'S ON THE VERGE OF DYING ALL THE TIME!

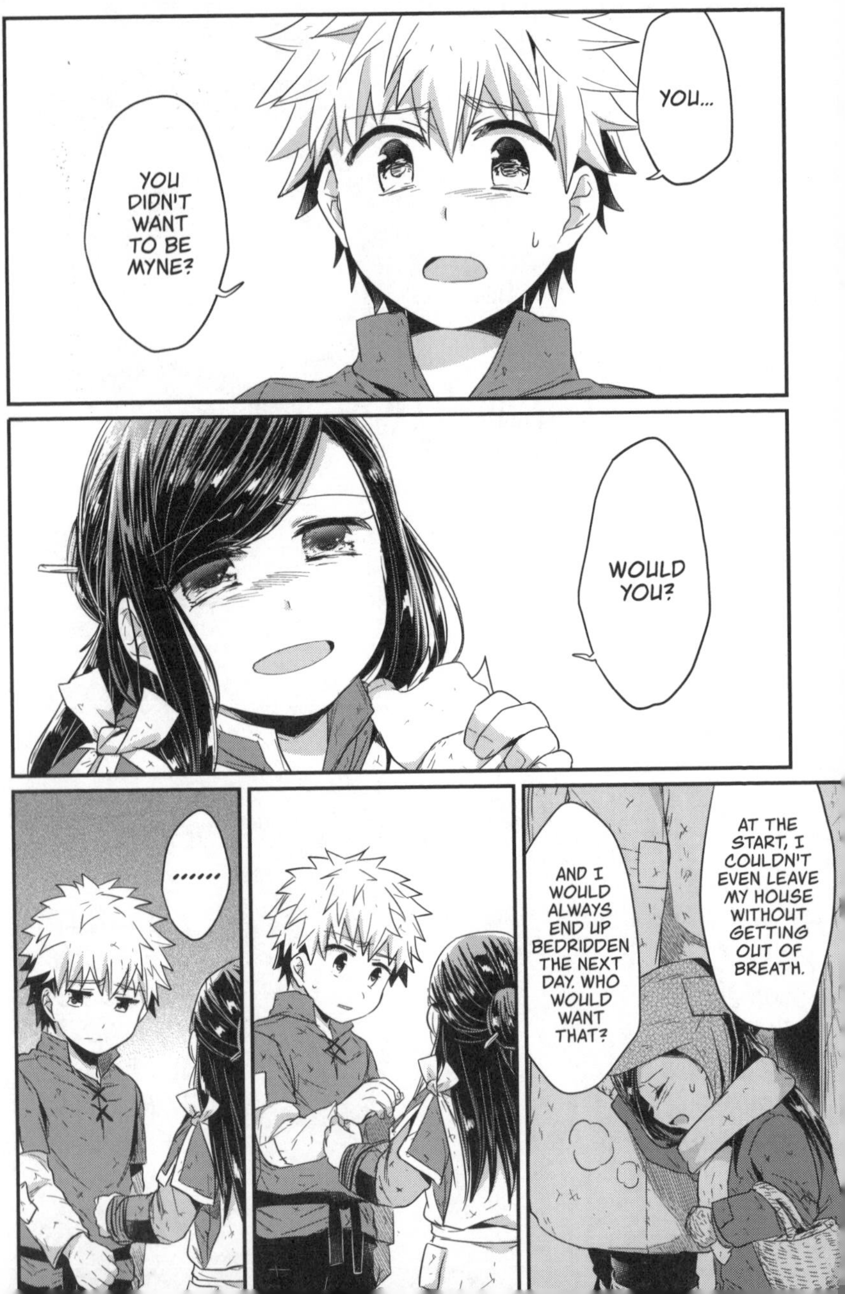
YOU...
YOU DIDN'T WANT TO BE MYNE?
WOULD YOU?
AT THE START, I COULDN'T EVEN LEAVE MY HOUSE WITHOUT GETTING OUT OF BREATH.
AND I WOULD ALWAYS END UP BEDRIDDEN THE NEXT DAY. WHO WOULD WANT THAT?
......

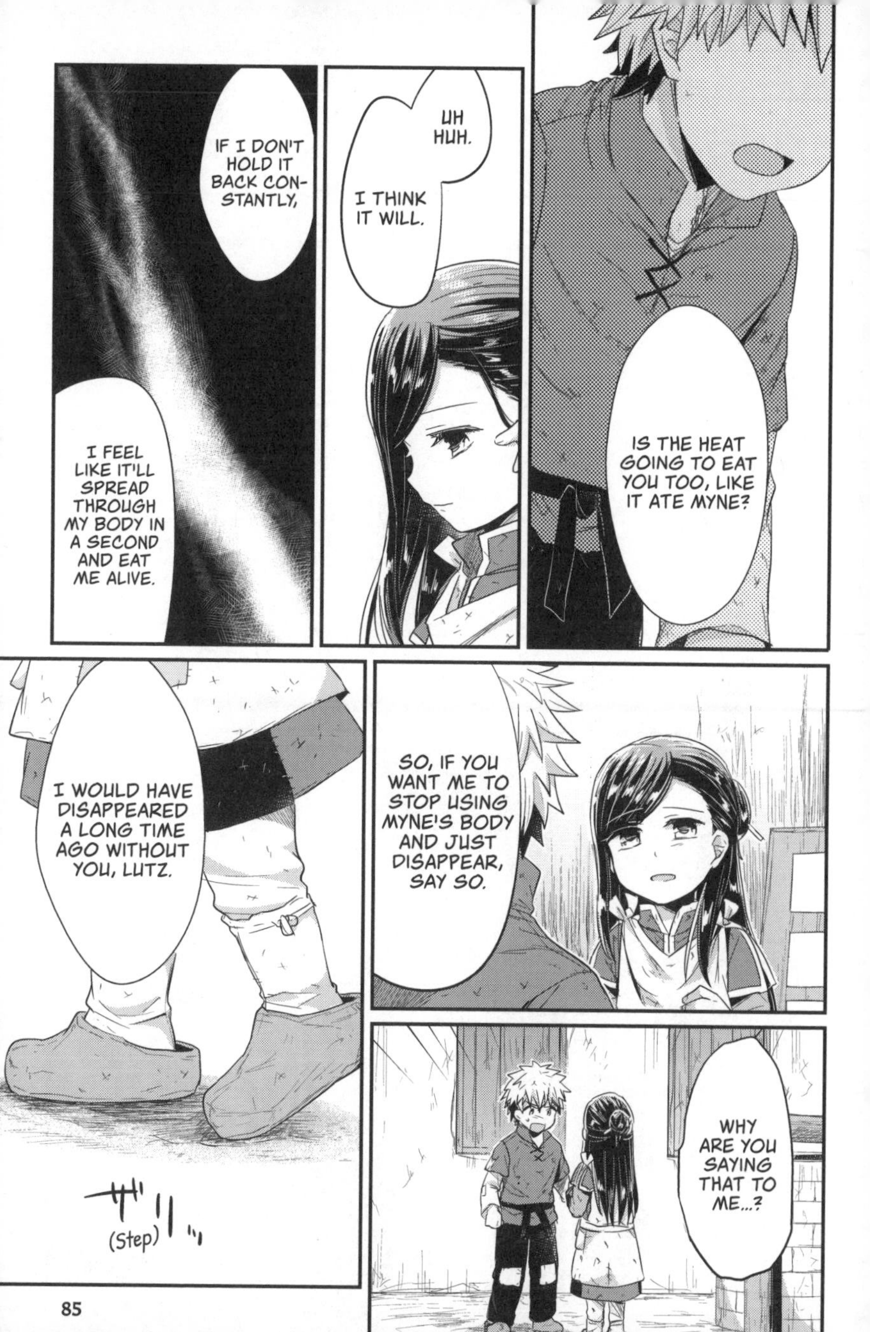
IS THE HEAT GOING TO EAT YOU TOO, LIKE IT ATE MYNE?
UH HUH.
I THINK IT WILL.
IF I DON'T HOLD IT BACK CON-STANTLY,
I FEEL LIKE IT'LL SPREAD THROUGH MY BODY IN A SECOND AND EAT ME ALIVE.
SO, IF YOU WANT ME TO STOP USING MYNE'S BODY AND JUST DISAPPEAR, SAY SO.
WHY ARE YOU SAYING THAT TO ME...?
I WOULD HAVE DISAPPEARED A LONG TIME AGO WITHOUT YOU, LUTZ.
ザリッ
(Step)

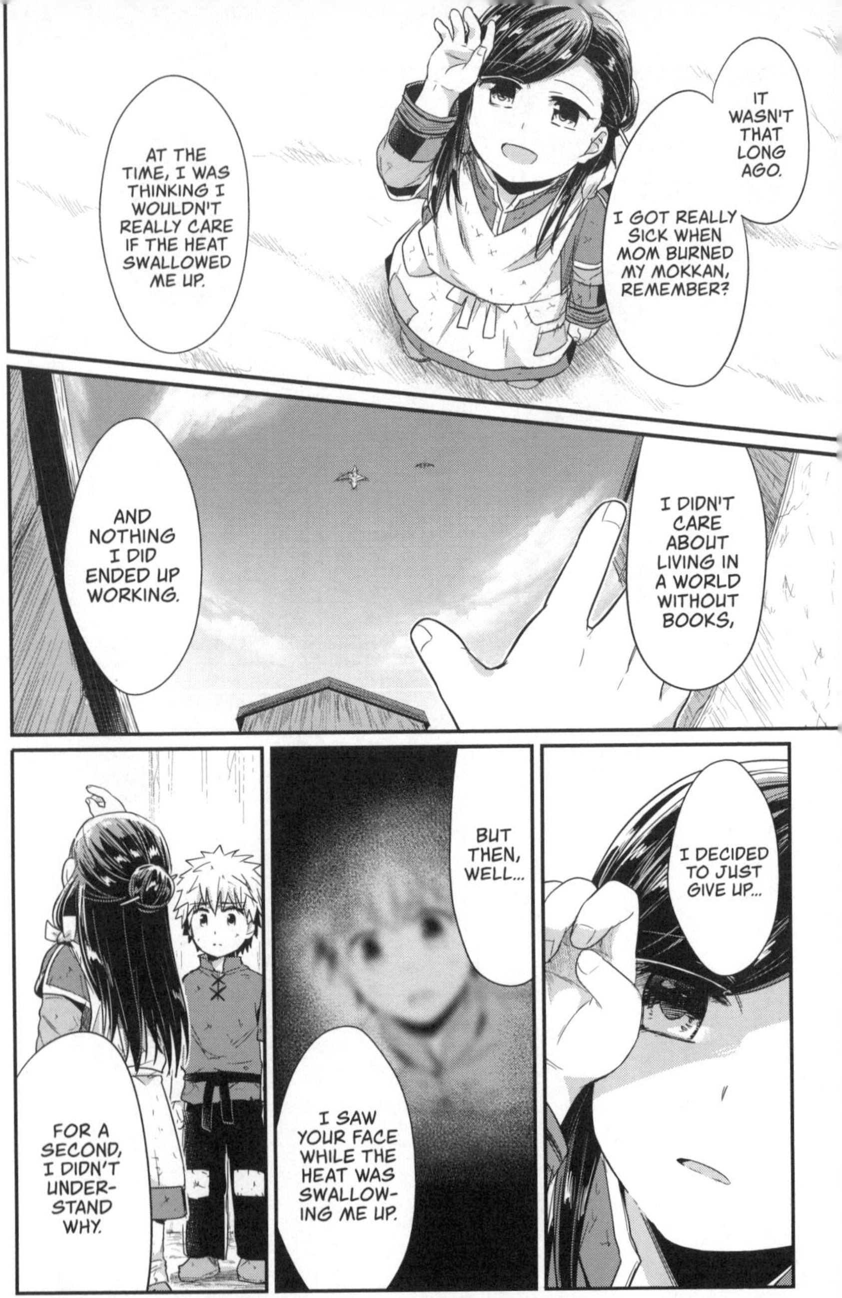
IT WASN'T THAT LONG AGO.
I GOT REALLY SICK WHEN MOM BURNED MY MOKKAN, REMEMBER?
AT THE TIME, I WAS THINKING I WOULDN'T REALLY CARE IF THE HEAT SWALLOWED ME UP.
I DIDN'T CARE ABOUT LIVING IN A WORLD WITHOUT BOOKS,
AND NOTHING I DID ENDED UP WORKING.
I DECIDED TO JUST GIVE UP...
BUT THEN, WELL...
I SAW YOUR FACE WHILE THE HEAT WAS SWALLOW-ING ME UP.
FOR A SECOND, I DIDN'T UNDER-STAND WHY.

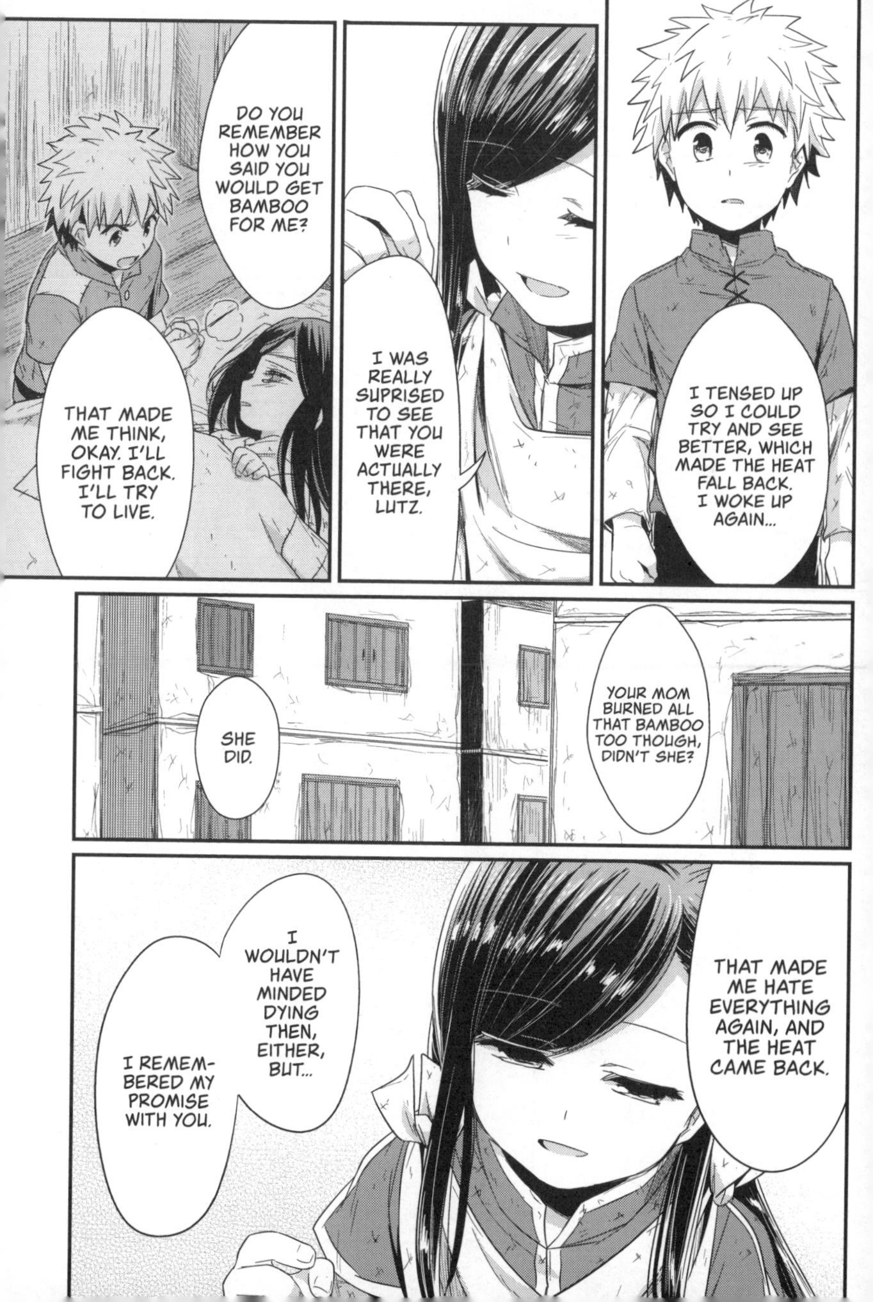
I TENSED UP SO I COULD TRY AND SEE BETTER, WHICH MADE THE HEAT FALL BACK. I WOKE UP AGAIN...
I WAS REALLY SUPRISED TO SEE THAT YOU WERE ACTUALLY THERE, LUTZ.
DO YOU REMEMBER HOW YOU SAID YOU WOULD GET BAMBOO FOR ME?
THAT MADE ME THINK, OKAY. I'LL FIGHT BACK. I'LL TRY TO LIVE.
YOUR MOM BURNED ALL THAT BAMBOO TOO THOUGH, DIDN'T SHE?
SHE DID.
THAT MADE ME HATE EVERYTHING AGAIN, AND THE HEAT CAME BACK.
I WOULDN'T HAVE MINDED DYING THEN, EITHER, BUT...
I REMEMBERED MY PROMISE WITH YOU.

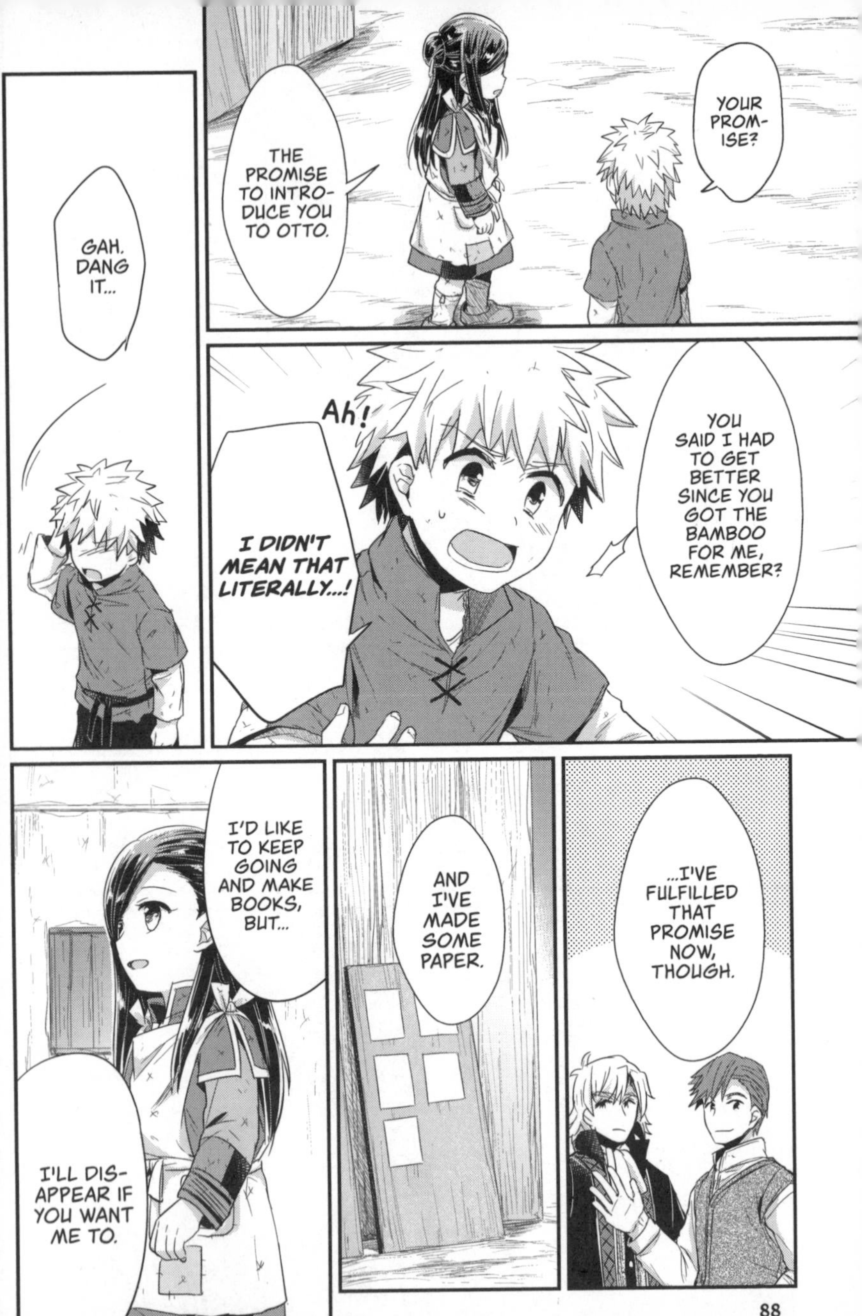
YOUR PROM-ISE?
THE PROMISE TO INTRO-DUCE YOU TO OTTO.
YOU SAID I HAD TO GET BETTER SINCE YOU GOT THE BAMBOO FOR ME, REMEMBER?
Ah!
I DIDN'T MEAN THAT LITERALLY...!
GAH. DANG IT...
...I'VE FULFILLED THAT PROMISE NOW, THOUGH.
AND I'VE MADE SOME PAPER.
I'D LIKE TO KEEP GOING AND MAKE BOOKS, BUT...
I'LL DIS-APPEAR IF YOU WANT ME TO.

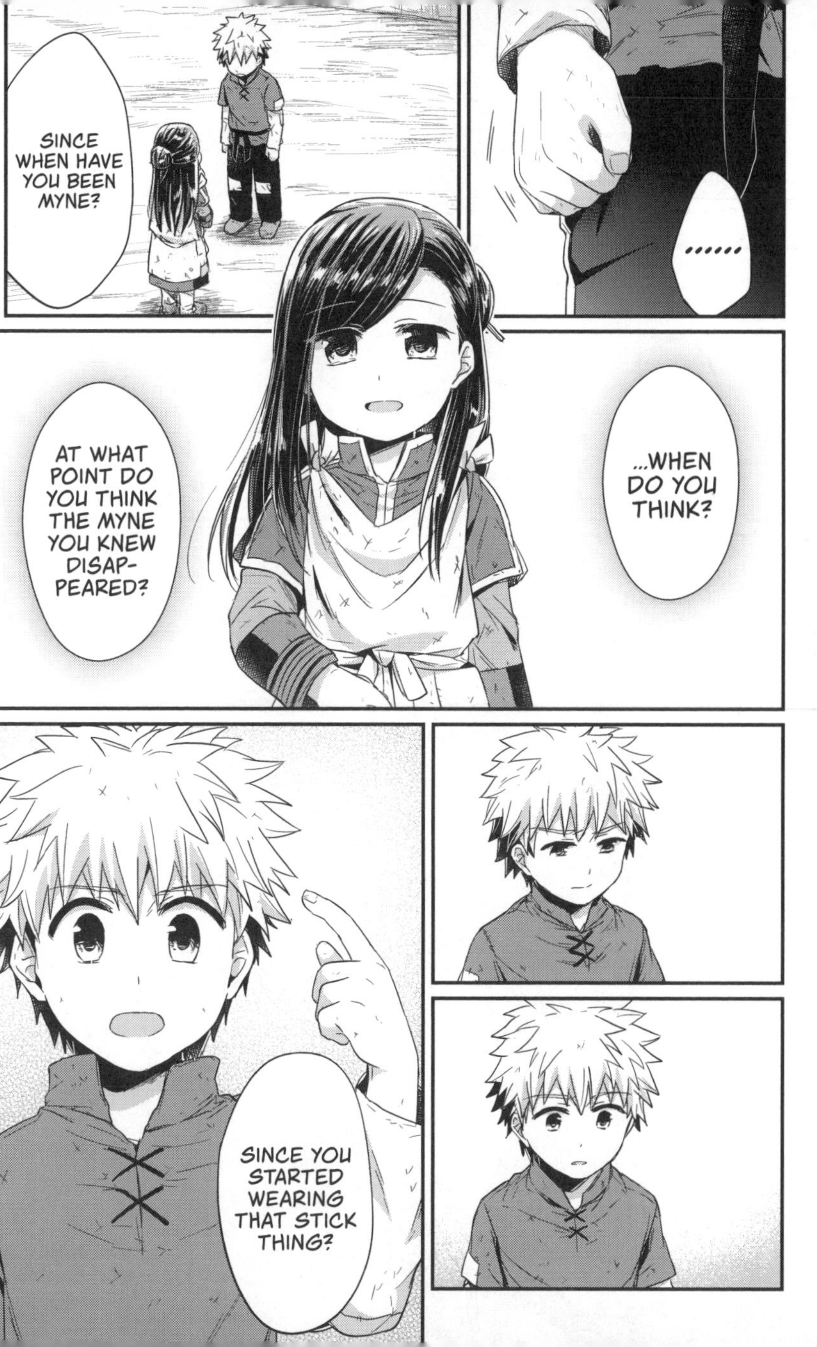
......
SINCE WHEN HAVE YOU BEEN MYNE?
...WHEN DO YOU THINK?
AT WHAT POINT DO YOU THINK THE MYNE YOU KNEW DISAP-PEARED?
SINCE YOU STARTED WEARING THAT STICK THING?

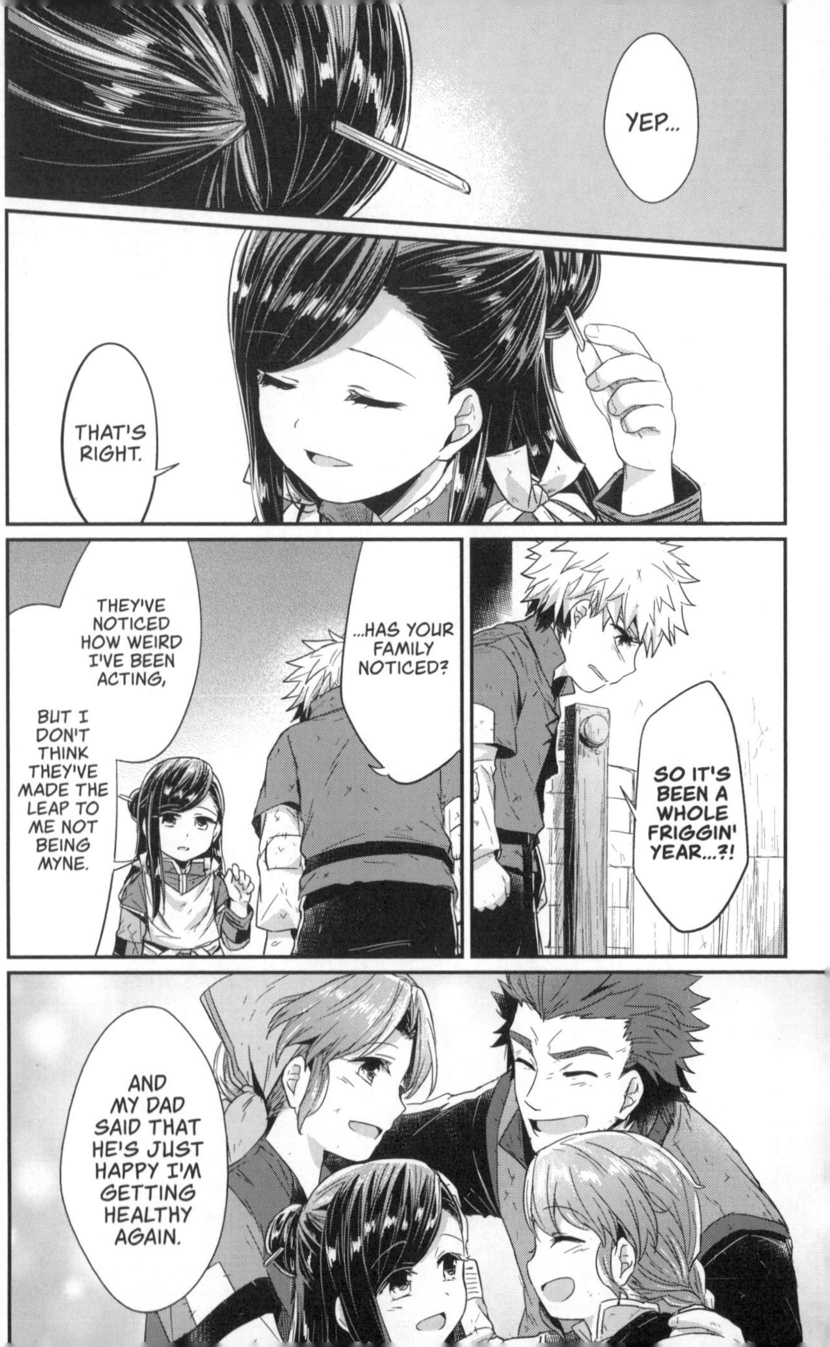
YEP...
THAT'S RIGHT.
SO IT'S BEEN A WHOLE FRIGGIN' YEAR...?!
...HAS YOUR FAMILY NOTICED?
THEY'VE NOTICED HOW WEIRD I'VE BEEN ACTING,
BUT I DON'T THINK THEY'VE MADE THE LEAP TO ME NOT BEING MYNE.
AND MY DAD SAID THAT HE'S JUST HAPPY I'M GETTING HEALTHY AGAIN.

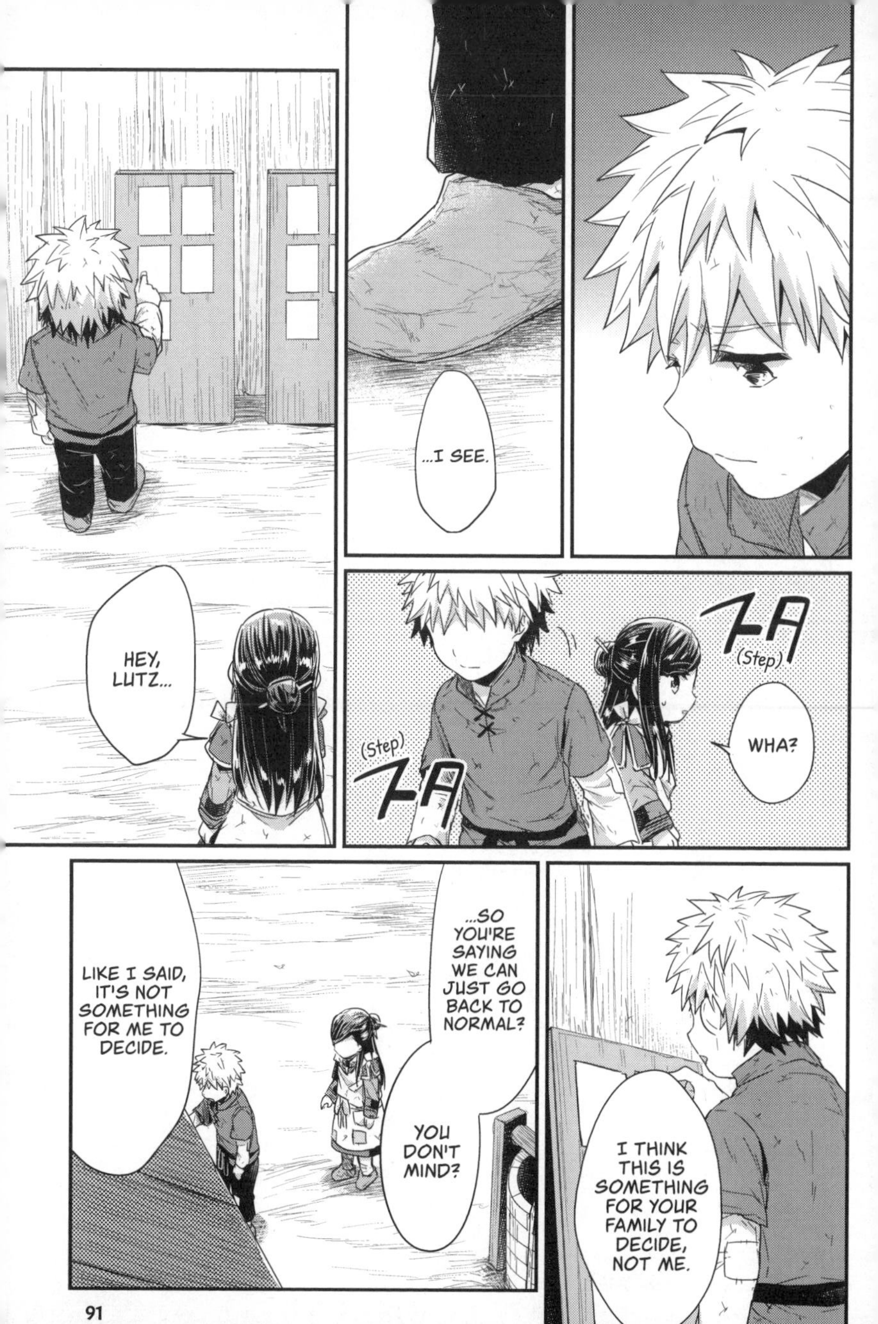

...I SEE.
(Step)
(Step)
WHA?
HEY, LUTZ...
I THINK THIS IS SOMETHING FOR YOUR FAMILY TO DECIDE, NOT ME.
...SO YOU'RE SAYING WE CAN JUST GO BACK TO NORMAL?
YOU DON'T MIND?
LIKE I SAID, IT'S NOT SOMETHING FOR ME TO DECIDE.

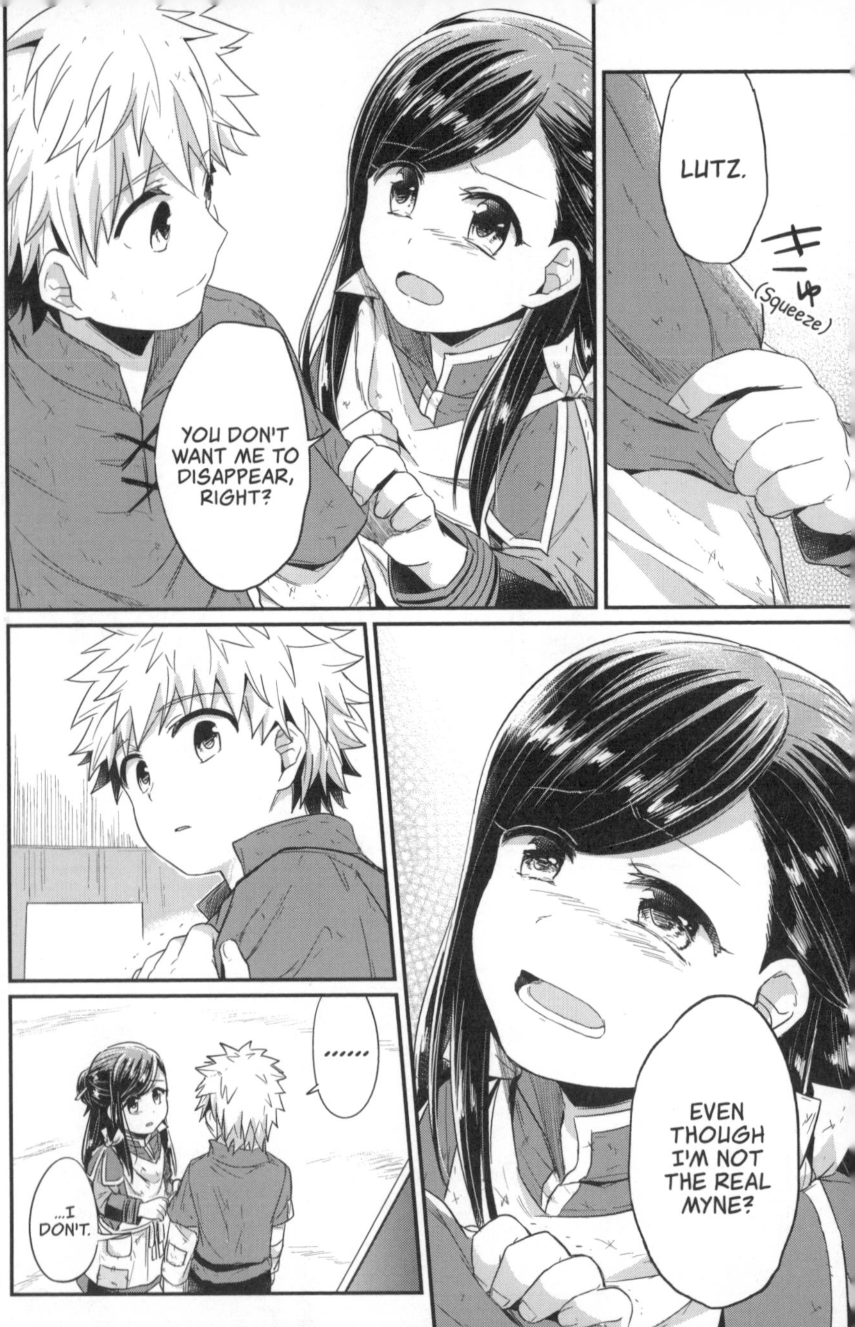
LUTZ.
(Squeeze)
YOU DON'T WANT ME TO DISAPPEAR, RIGHT?
EVEN THOUGH I'M NOT THE REAL MYNE?
......
...I DON'T.

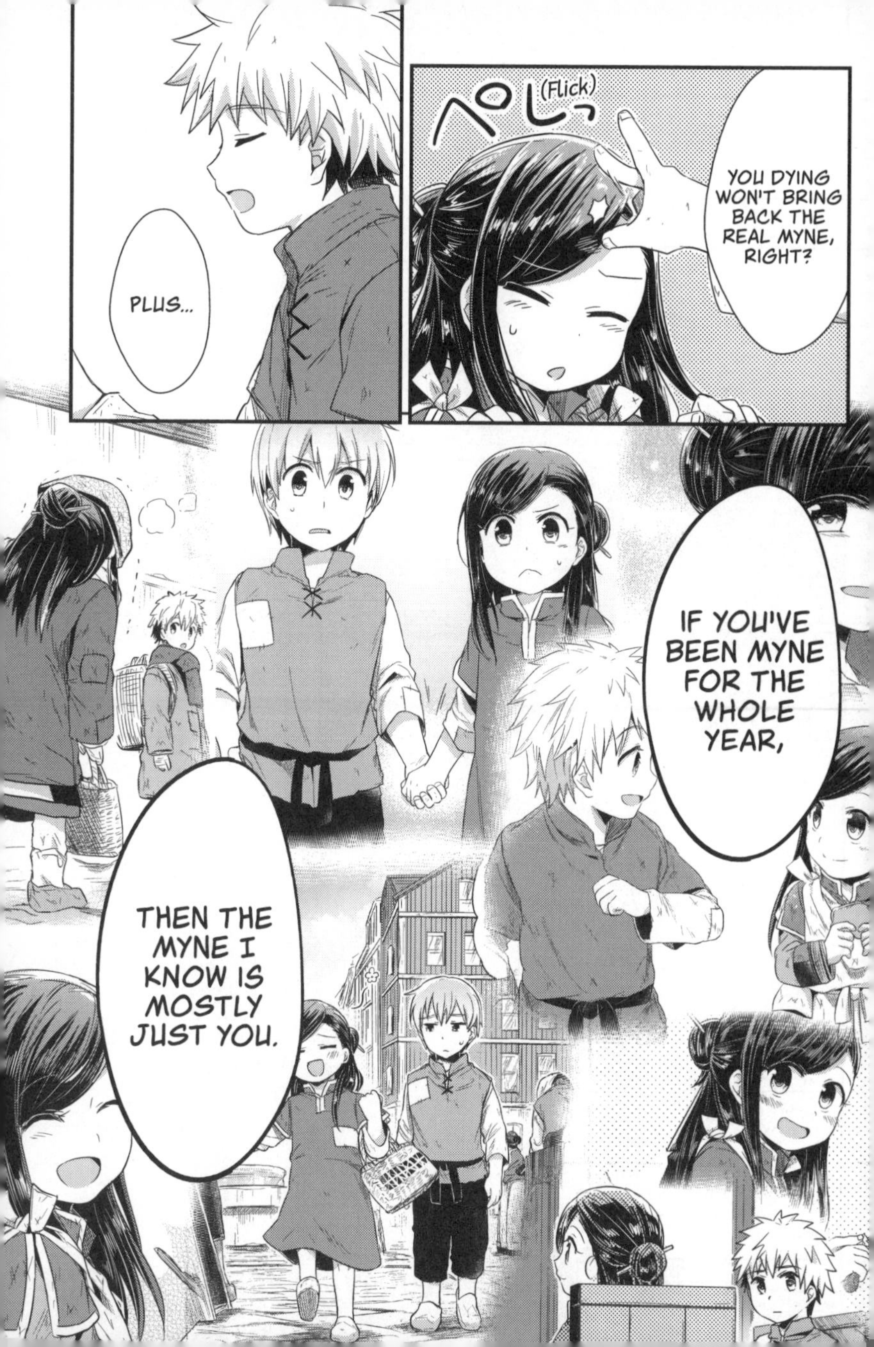
ぺしっ
(Flick)
YOU DYING WON'T BRING BACK THE REAL MYNE, RIGHT?
PLUS...
IF YOU'VE BEEN MYNE FOR THE WHOLE YEAR,
THEN THE MYNE I KNOW IS MOSTLY JUST YOU.

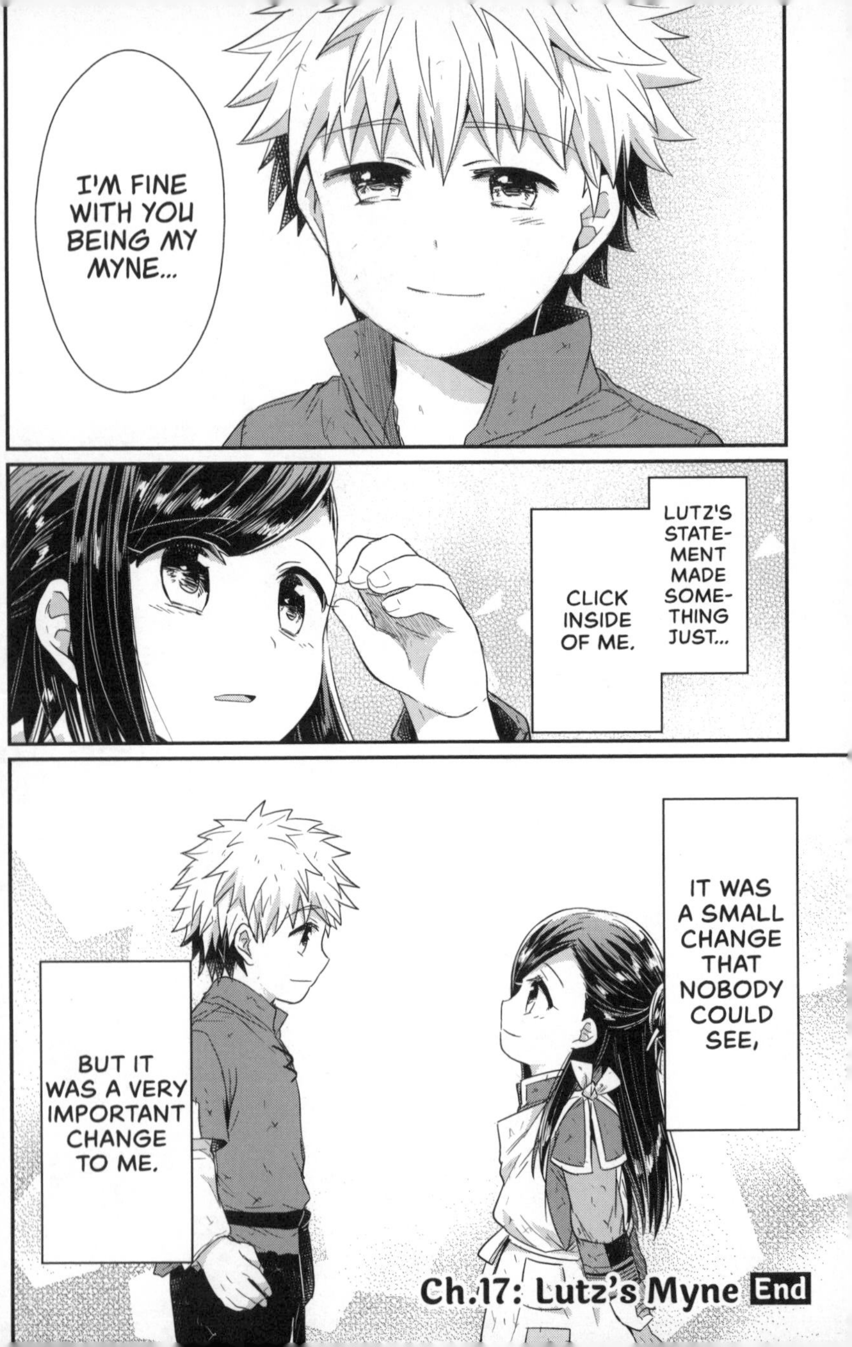
I'M FINE WITH YOU BEING MY MYNE...
LUTZ'S STATEMENT MADE SOMETHING JUST...
CLICK INSIDE OF ME.
IT WAS A SMALL CHANGE THAT NOBODY COULD SEE,
BUT IT WAS A VERY IMPORTANT CHANGE TO ME.
Ch.17: Lutz's Myne End

ASCENDANCE OF A BOOKWORM

OF A

BOOKWORM

I'll do anything to become a librarian!

Part 1 If there aren't any books, I'll just have to make some!

Put important things under your shirt.

Take them out when you need them.

(Rustle)

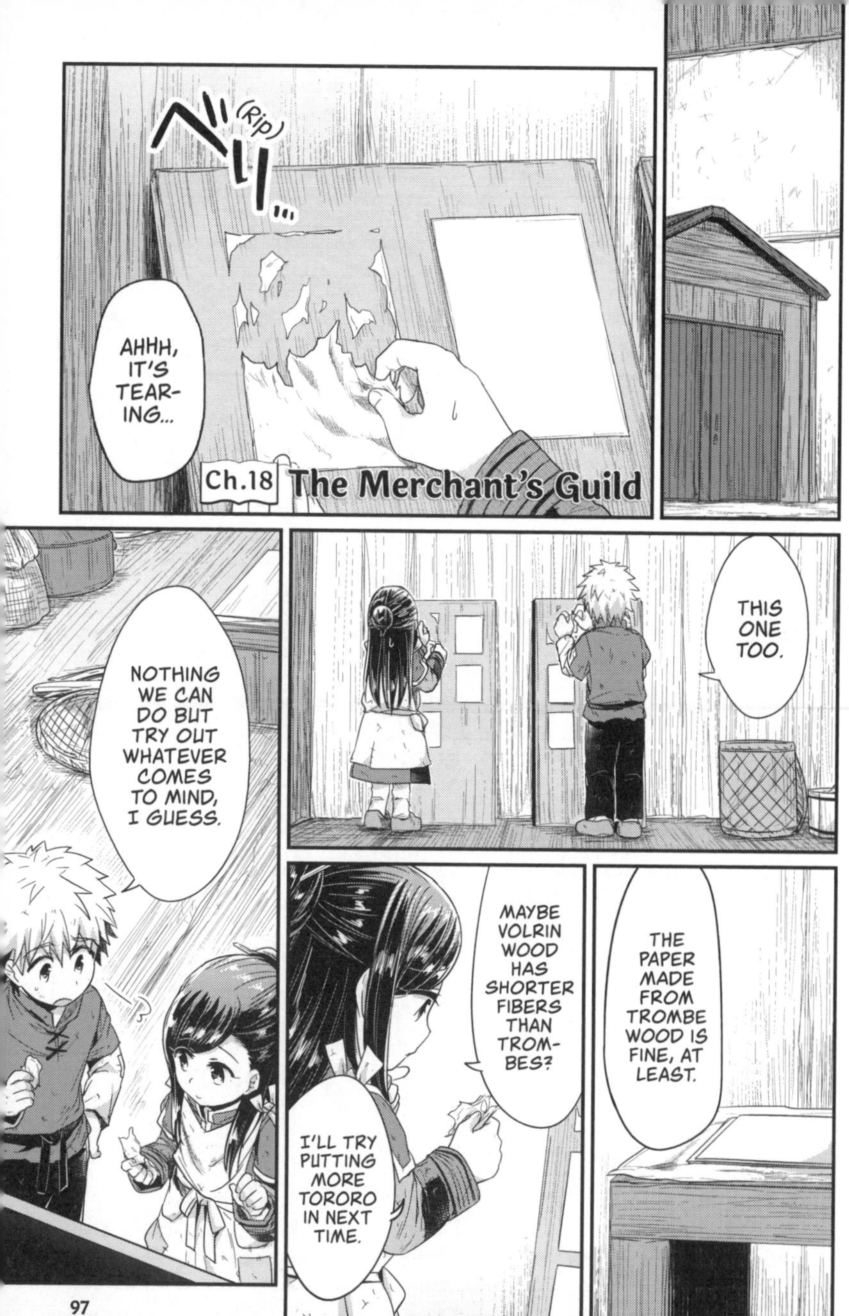

(Rip)
AHHH, IT'S TEARING...
Ch.18 The Merchant's Guild
THIS ONE TOO.
THE PAPER MADE FROM TROMBE WOOD IS FINE, AT LEAST.
MAYBE VOLRIN WOOD HAS SHORTER FIBERS THAN TROMBES?
I'LL TRY PUTTING MORE TORORO IN NEXT TIME.
NOTHING WE CAN DO BUT TRY OUT WHATEVER COMES TO MIND, I GUESS.

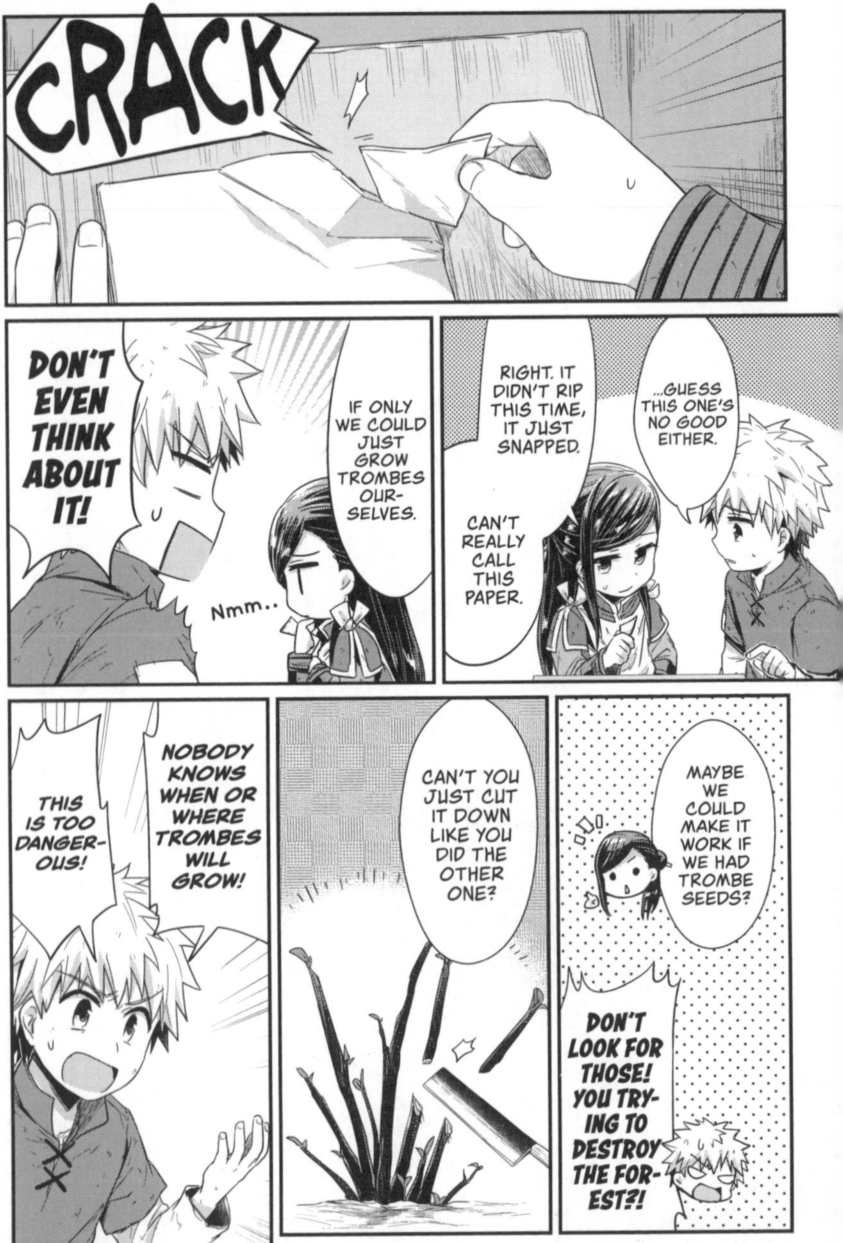
CRACK
...GUESS THIS ONE'S NO GOOD EITHER.
RIGHT. IT DIDN'T RIP THIS TIME, IT JUST SNAPPED.
CAN'T REALLY CALL THIS PAPER.
IF ONLY WE COULD JUST GROW TROMBES OURSELVES.
Nmm..
DON'T EVEN THINK ABOUT IT!
MAYBE WE COULD MAKE IT WORK IF WE HAD TROMBE SEEDS?
DON'T LOOK FOR THOSE! YOU TRYING TO DESTROY THE FOREST?!
CAN'T YOU JUST CUT IT DOWN LIKE YOU DID THE OTHER ONE?
NOBODY KNOWS WHEN OR WHERE TROMBES WILL GROW!
THIS IS TOO DANGEROUS!

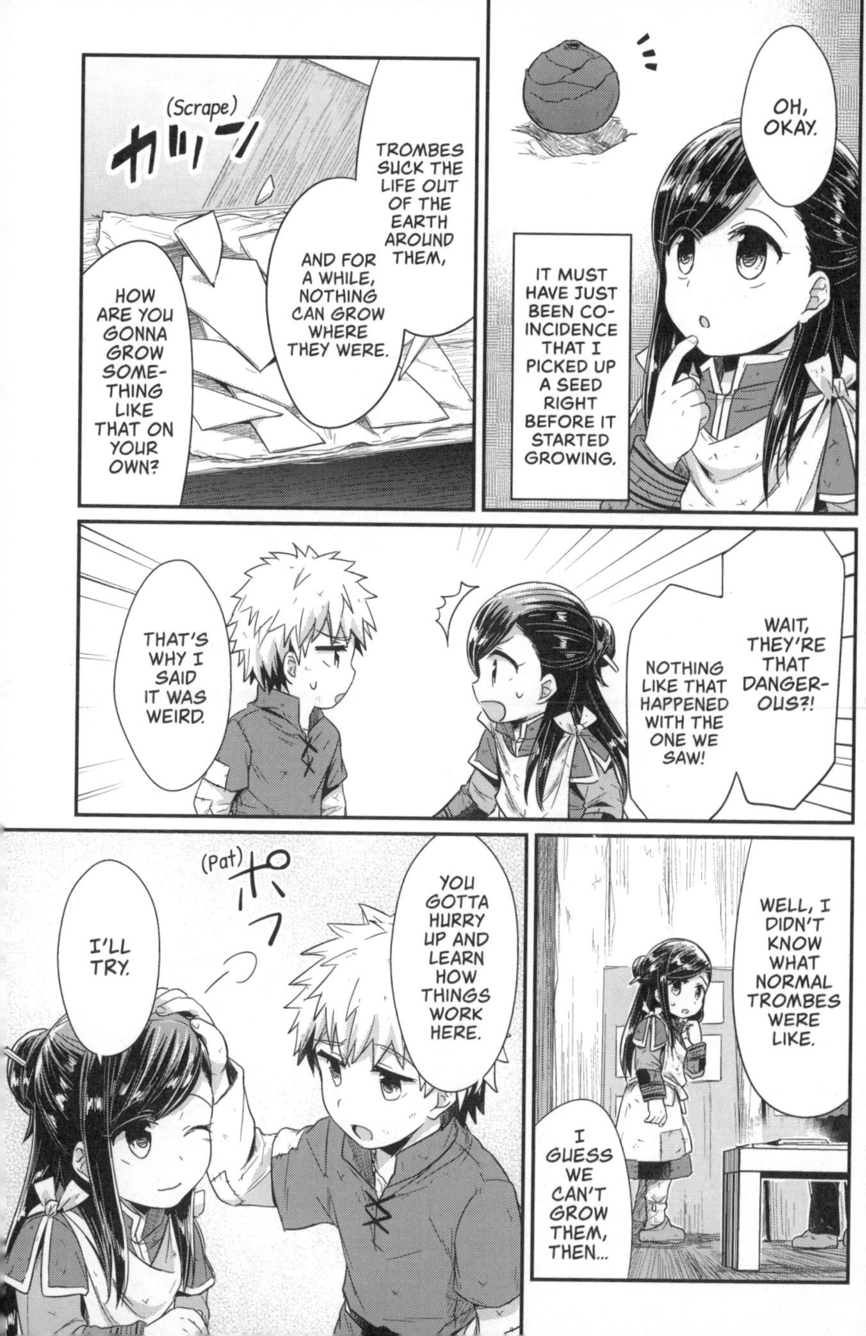
OH, OKAY.
IT MUST HAVE JUST BEEN CO-INCIDENCE THAT I PICKED UP A SEED RIGHT BEFORE IT STARTED GROWING.
(Scrape)
TROMBES SUCK THE LIFE OUT OF THE EARTH AROUND THEM,
AND FOR A WHILE, NOTHING CAN GROW WHERE THEY WERE.
HOW ARE YOU GONNA GROW SOME-THING LIKE THAT ON YOUR OWN?
WAIT, THEY'RE THAT DANGER-OUS?!
NOTHING LIKE THAT HAPPENED WITH THE ONE WE SAW!
THAT'S WHY I SAID IT WAS WEIRD.
WELL, I DIDN'T KNOW WHAT NORMAL TROMBES WERE LIKE.
I GUESS WE CAN'T GROW THEM, THEN...
(Pat)
YOU GOTTA HURRY UP AND LEARN HOW THINGS WORK HERE.
I'LL TRY.

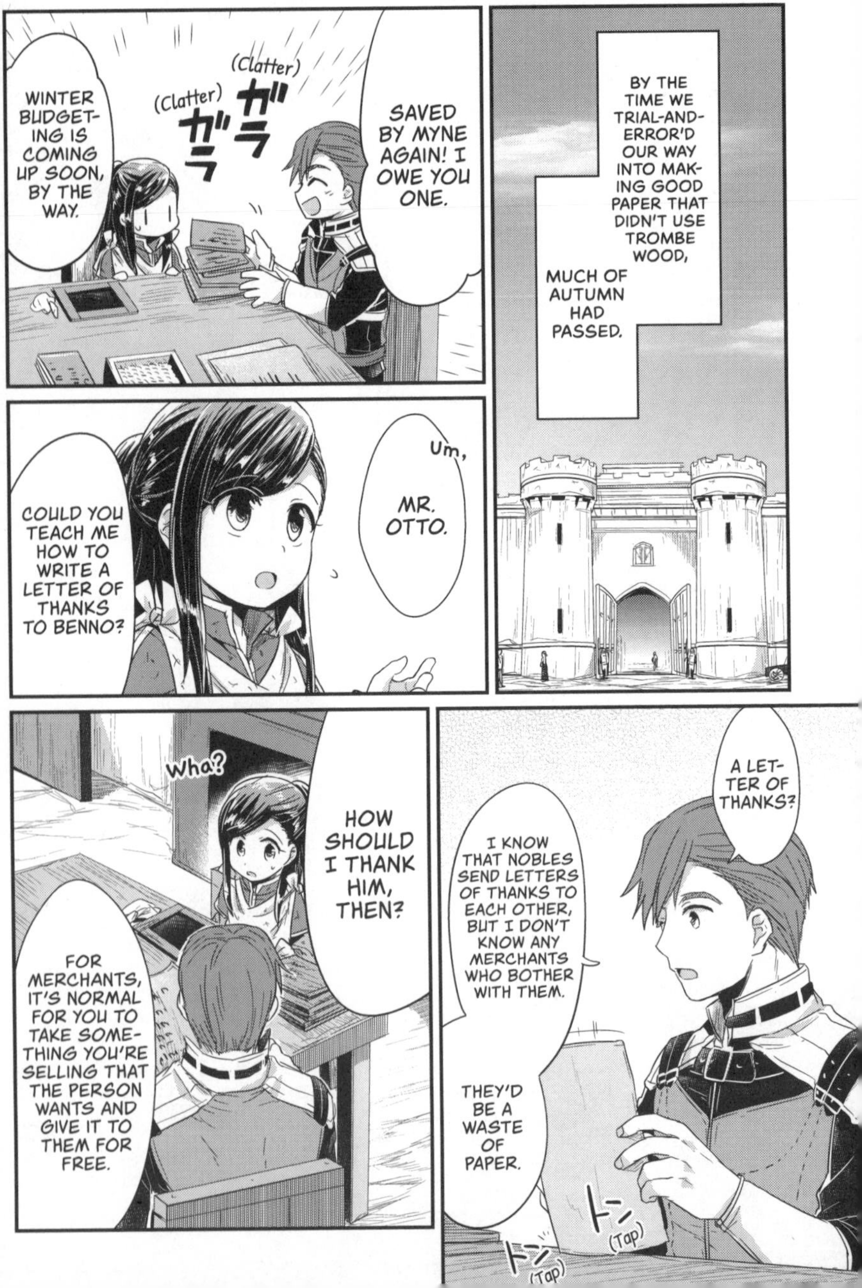
BY THE TIME WE TRIAL-AND-ERROR'D OUR WAY INTO MAKING GOOD PAPER THAT DIDN'T USE TROMBE WOOD,
MUCH OF AUTUMN HAD PASSED.
SAVED BY MYNE AGAIN! I OWE YOU ONE.
(Clatter) ガラ
(Clatter) ガラ
WINTER BUDGETING IS COMING UP SOON, BY THE WAY.
Um,
MR. OTTO.
COULD YOU TEACH ME HOW TO WRITE A LETTER OF THANKS TO BENNO?
A LETTER OF THANKS?
I KNOW THAT NOBLES SEND LETTERS OF THANKS TO EACH OTHER, BUT I DON'T KNOW ANY MERCHANTS WHO BOTHER WITH THEM.
THEY'D BE A WASTE OF PAPER.
(Tap)
(Tap)
HOW SHOULD I THANK HIM, THEN?
Wha?
FOR MERCHANTS, IT'S NORMAL FOR YOU TO TAKE SOMETHING YOU'RE SELLING THAT THE PERSON WANTS AND GIVE IT TO THEM FOR FREE.

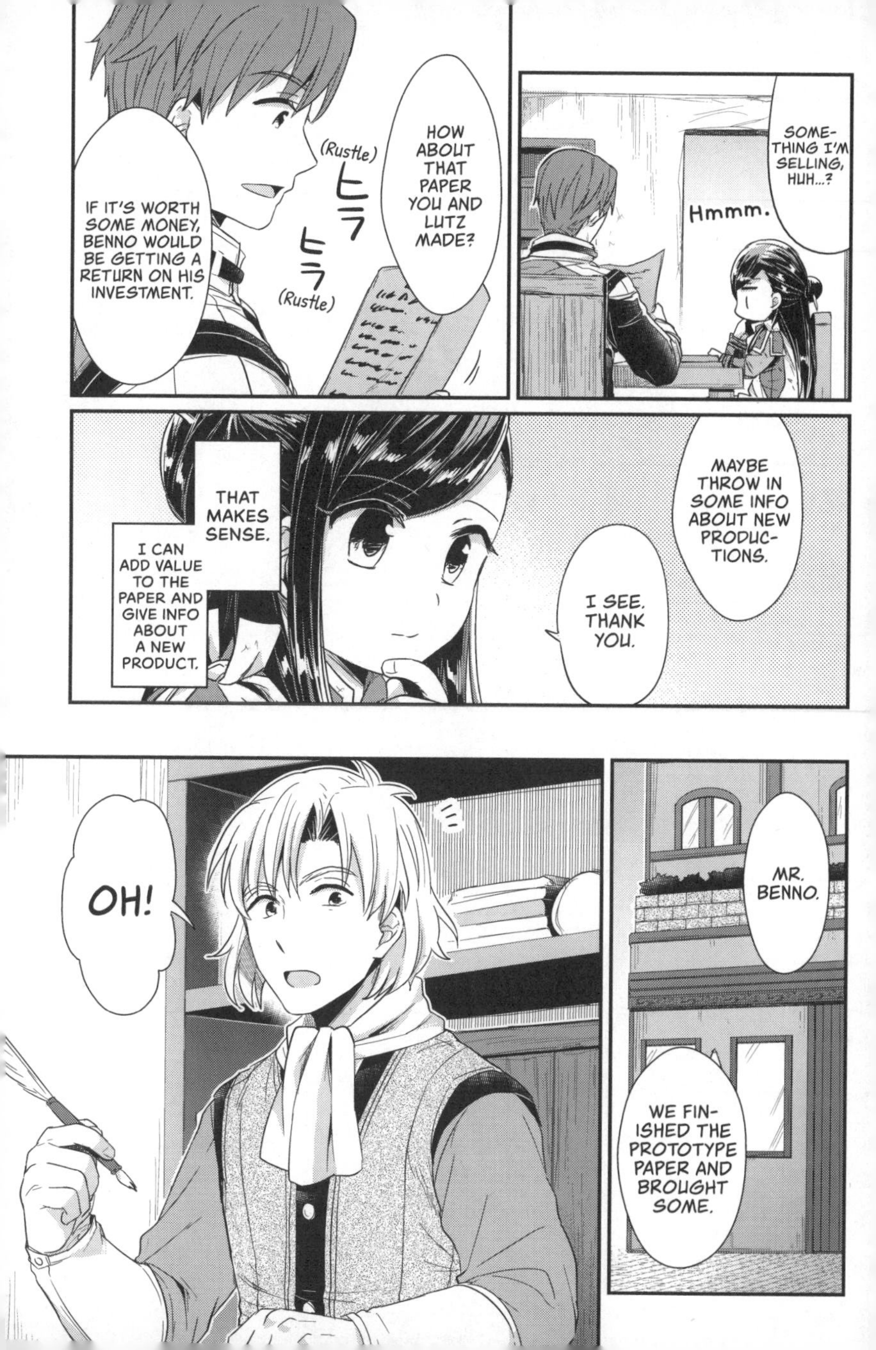
SOMETHING I'M SELLING, HUH...?
Hmmm.
HOW ABOUT THAT PAPER YOU AND LUTZ MADE?
(Rustle) ヒラ
ヒラ (Rustle)
IF IT'S WORTH SOME MONEY, BENNO WOULD BE GETTING A RETURN ON HIS INVESTMENT.
MAYBE THROW IN SOME INFO ABOUT NEW PRODUCTIONS.
I SEE. THANK YOU.
THAT MAKES SENSE.
I CAN ADD VALUE TO THE PAPER AND GIVE INFO ABOUT A NEW PRODUCT.
MR. BENNO.
WE FINISHED THE PROTOTYPE PAPER AND BROUGHT SOME.
OH!

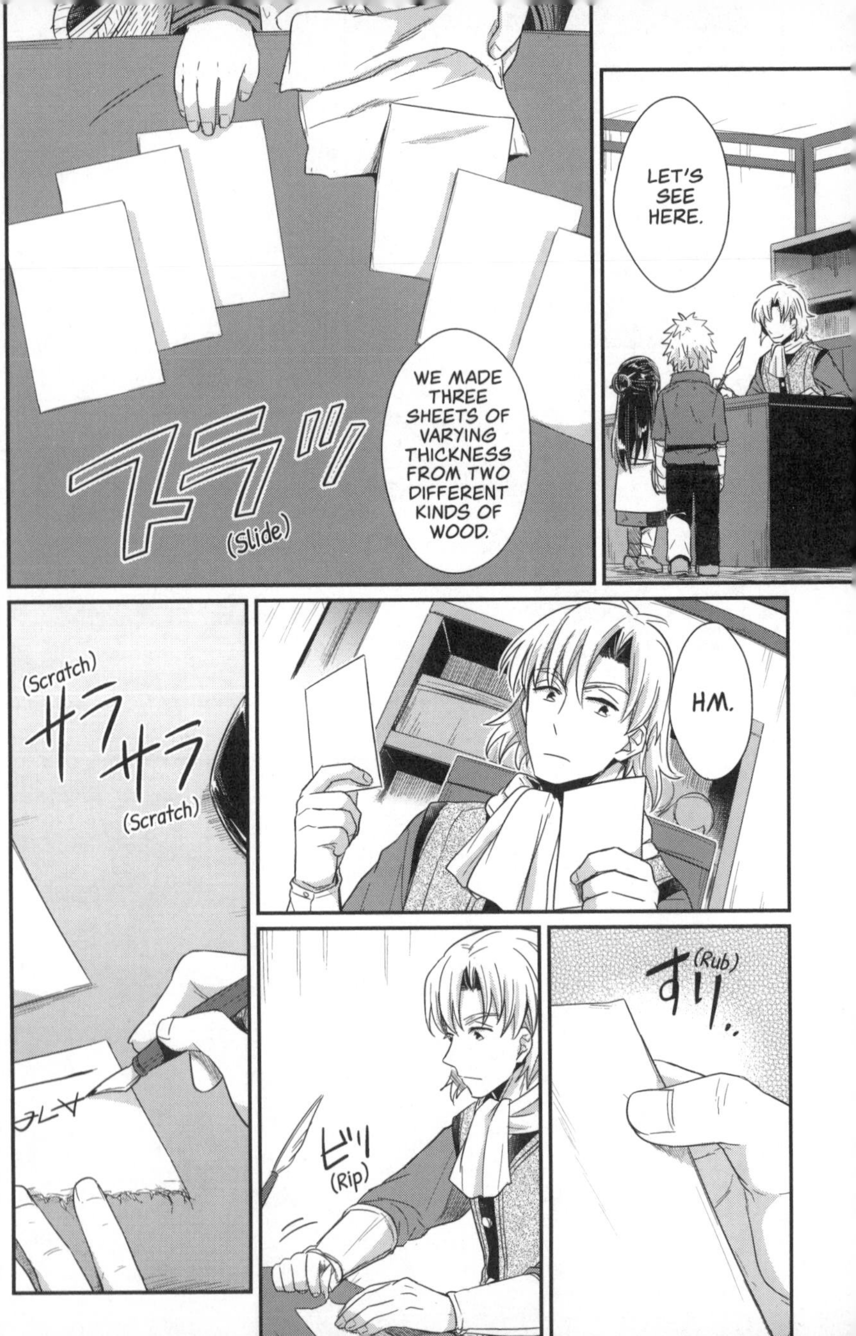
LET'S SEE HERE.
WE MADE THREE SHEETS OF VARYING THICKNESS FROM TWO DIFFERENT KINDS OF WOOD.
スラッ
(Slide)
HM.
すり..
(Rub)
ビリ
(Rip)
サラ
(Scratch)
サラ
(Scratch)

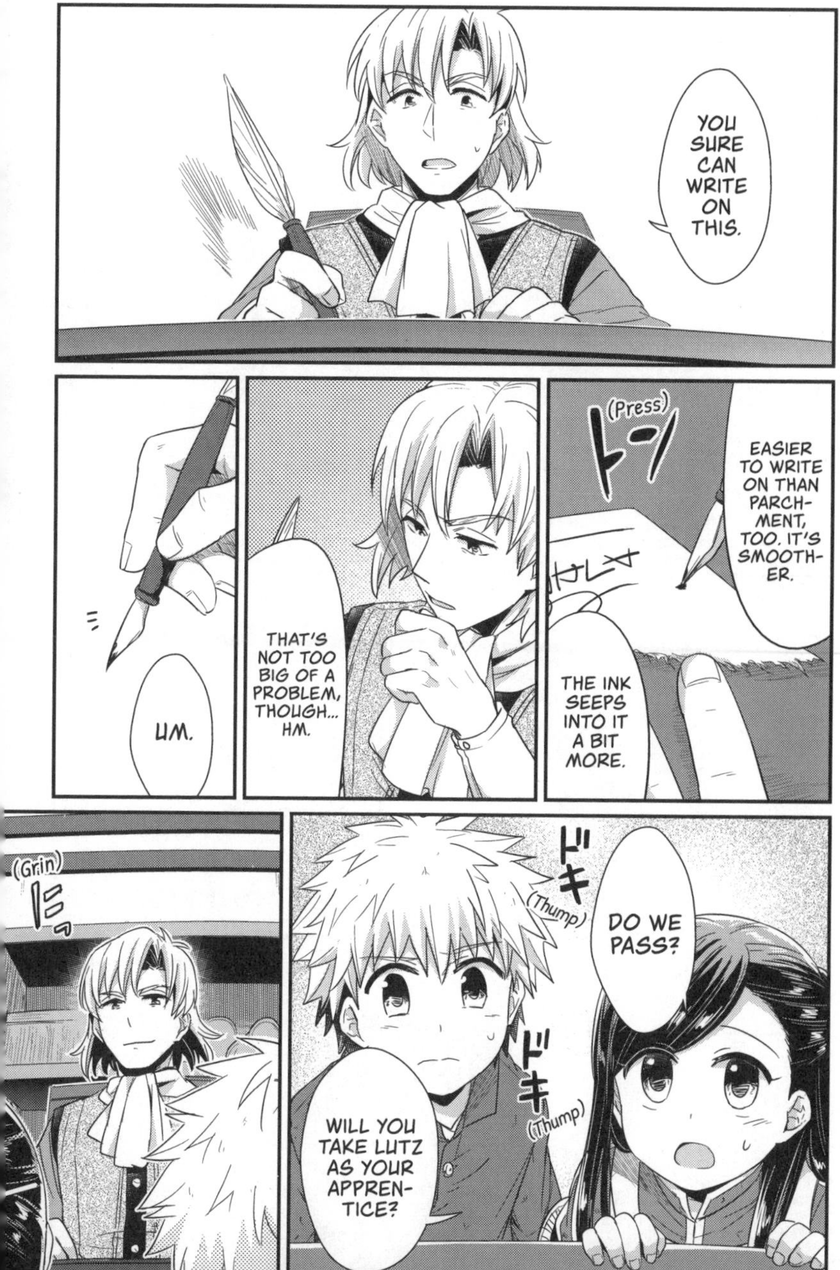
YOU SURE CAN WRITE ON THIS.
(Press)
EASIER TO WRITE ON THAN PARCH-MENT, TOO. IT'S SMOOTH-ER.
THE INK SEEPS INTO IT A BIT MORE.
THAT'S NOT TOO BIG OF A PROBLEM, THOUGH... HM.
UM.
ドキ
(Thump)
DO WE PASS?
ドキ
(Thump)
WILL YOU TAKE LUTZ AS YOUR APPREN-TICE?
(Grin)

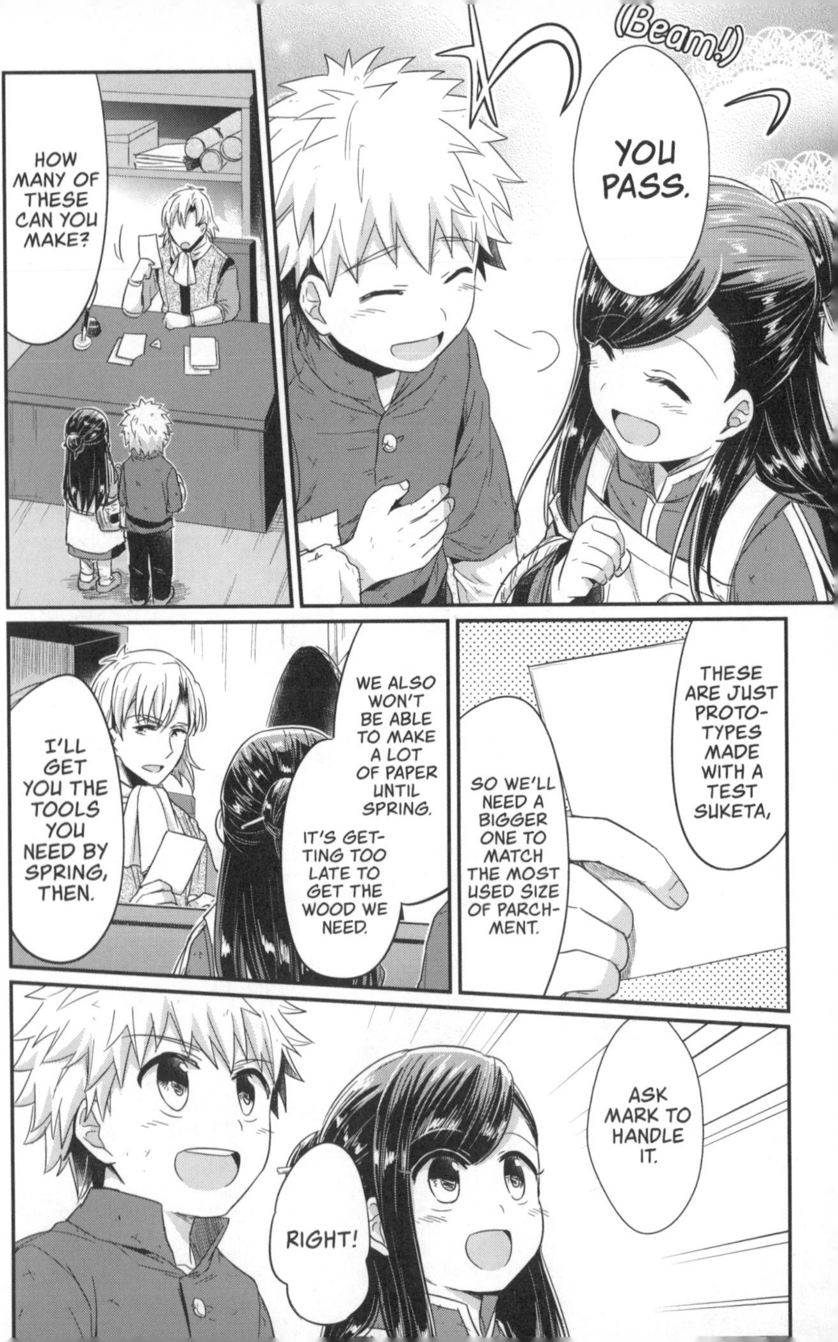
(Beam!)
YOU PASS.
HOW MANY OF THESE CAN YOU MAKE?
THESE ARE JUST PROTOTYPES MADE WITH A TEST SUKETA,
SO WE'LL NEED A BIGGER ONE TO MATCH THE MOST USED SIZE OF PARCHMENT.
WE ALSO WON'T BE ABLE TO MAKE A LOT OF PAPER UNTIL SPRING.
IT'S GETTING TOO LATE TO GET THE WOOD WE NEED.
I'LL GET YOU THE TOOLS YOU NEED BY SPRING, THEN.
ASK MARK TO HANDLE IT.
RIGHT!

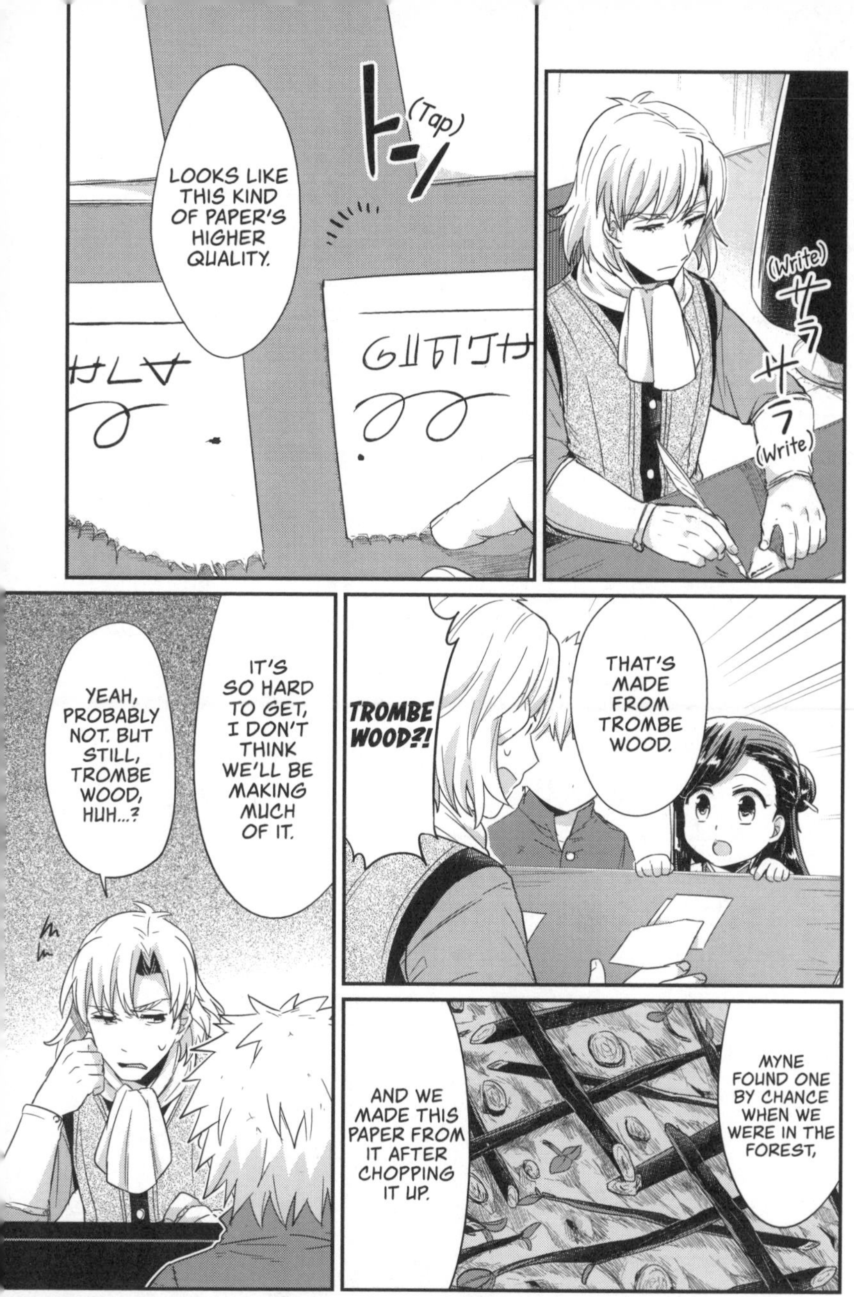
(Write)
サラ
サラ
(Write)
トーン
(Tap)
LOOKS LIKE THIS KIND OF PAPER'S HIGHER QUALITY.
THAT'S MADE FROM TROMBE WOOD.
TROMBE WOOD?!
MYNE FOUND ONE BY CHANCE WHEN WE WERE IN THE FOREST,
AND WE MADE THIS PAPER FROM IT AFTER CHOPPING IT UP.
IT'S SO HARD TO GET, I DON'T THINK WE'LL BE MAKING MUCH OF IT.
YEAH, PROBABLY NOT. BUT STILL, TROMBE WOOD, HUH...?

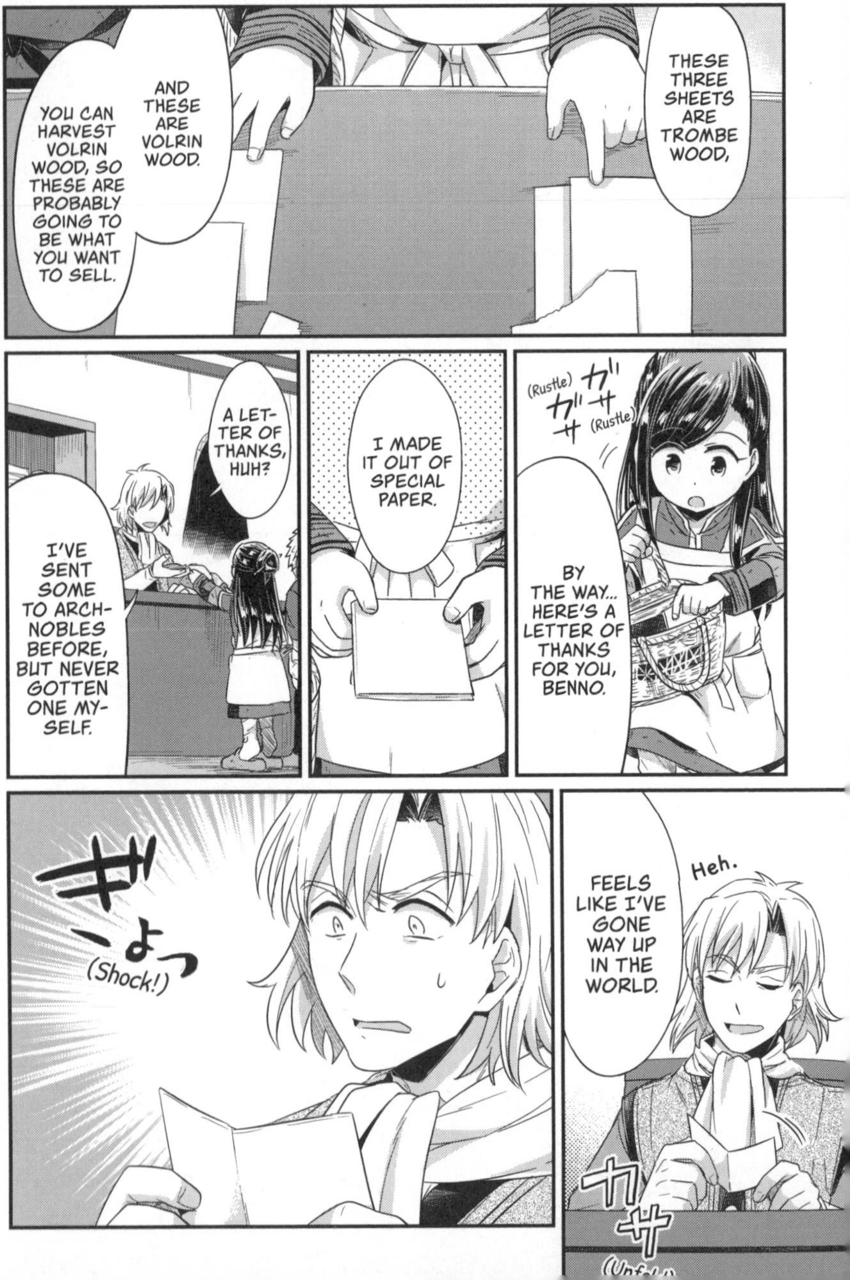
THESE THREE SHEETS ARE TROMBE WOOD,
AND THESE ARE VOLRIN WOOD.
YOU CAN HARVEST VOLRIN WOOD, SO THESE ARE PROBABLY GOING TO BE WHAT YOU WANT TO SELL.
(Rustle)
(Rustle)
BY THE WAY... HERE'S A LETTER OF THANKS FOR YOU, BENNO.
I MADE IT OUT OF SPECIAL PAPER.
A LETTER OF THANKS, HUH?
I'VE SENT SOME TO ARCHNOBLES BEFORE, BUT NEVER GOTTEN ONE MYSELF.
Heh.
FEELS LIKE I'VE GONE WAY UP IN THE WORLD.
(Shock!)

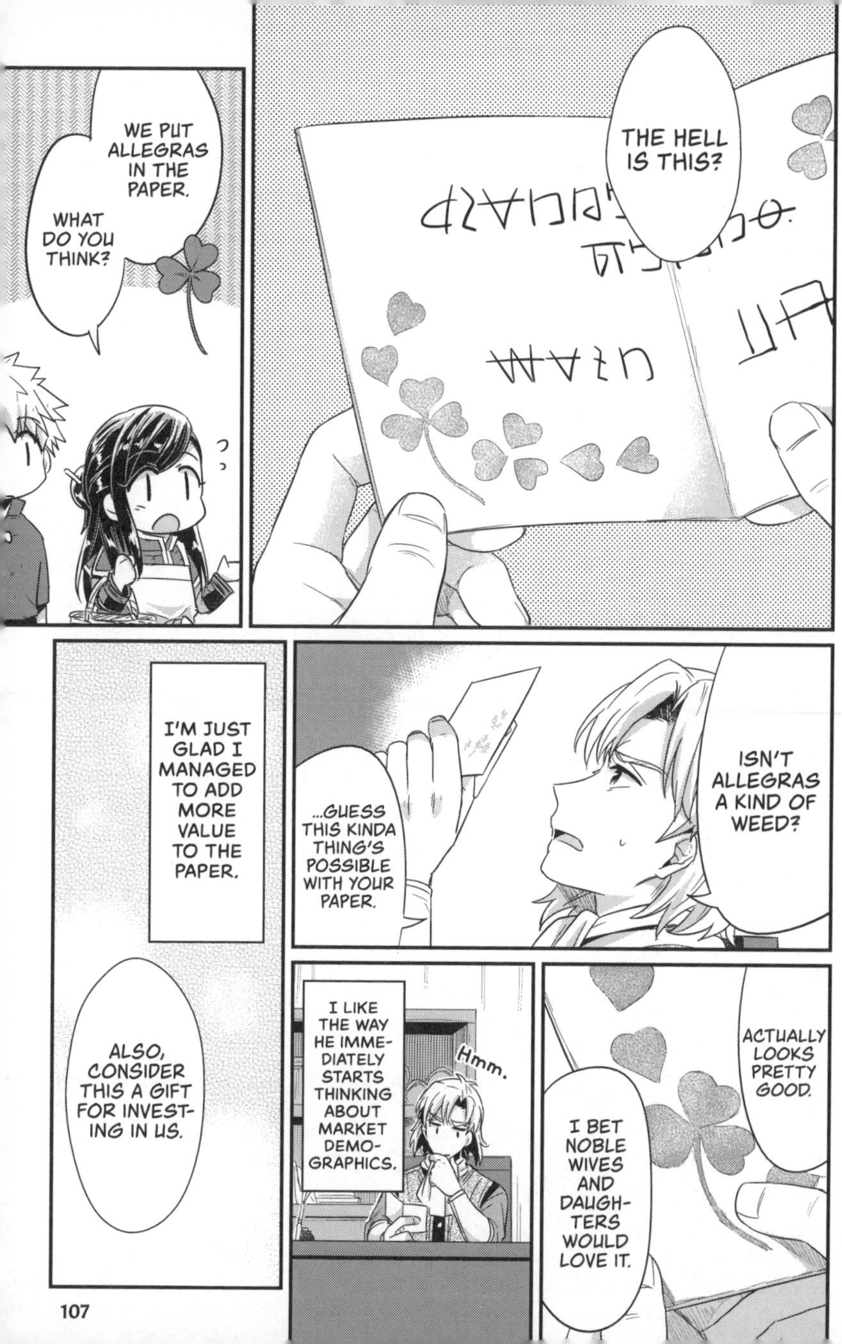
THE HELL IS THIS?
WE PUT ALLEGRAS IN THE PAPER.
WHAT DO YOU THINK?
ISN'T ALLEGRAS A KIND OF WEED?
...GUESS THIS KINDA THING'S POSSIBLE WITH YOUR PAPER.
ACTUALLY LOOKS PRETTY GOOD.
I BET NOBLE WIVES AND DAUGHTERS WOULD LOVE IT.
I LIKE THE WAY HE IMMEDIATELY STARTS THINKING ABOUT MARKET DEMOGRAPHICS.
Hmm.
I'M JUST GLAD I MANAGED TO ADD MORE VALUE TO THE PAPER.
ALSO, CONSIDER THIS A GIFT FOR INVESTING IN US.

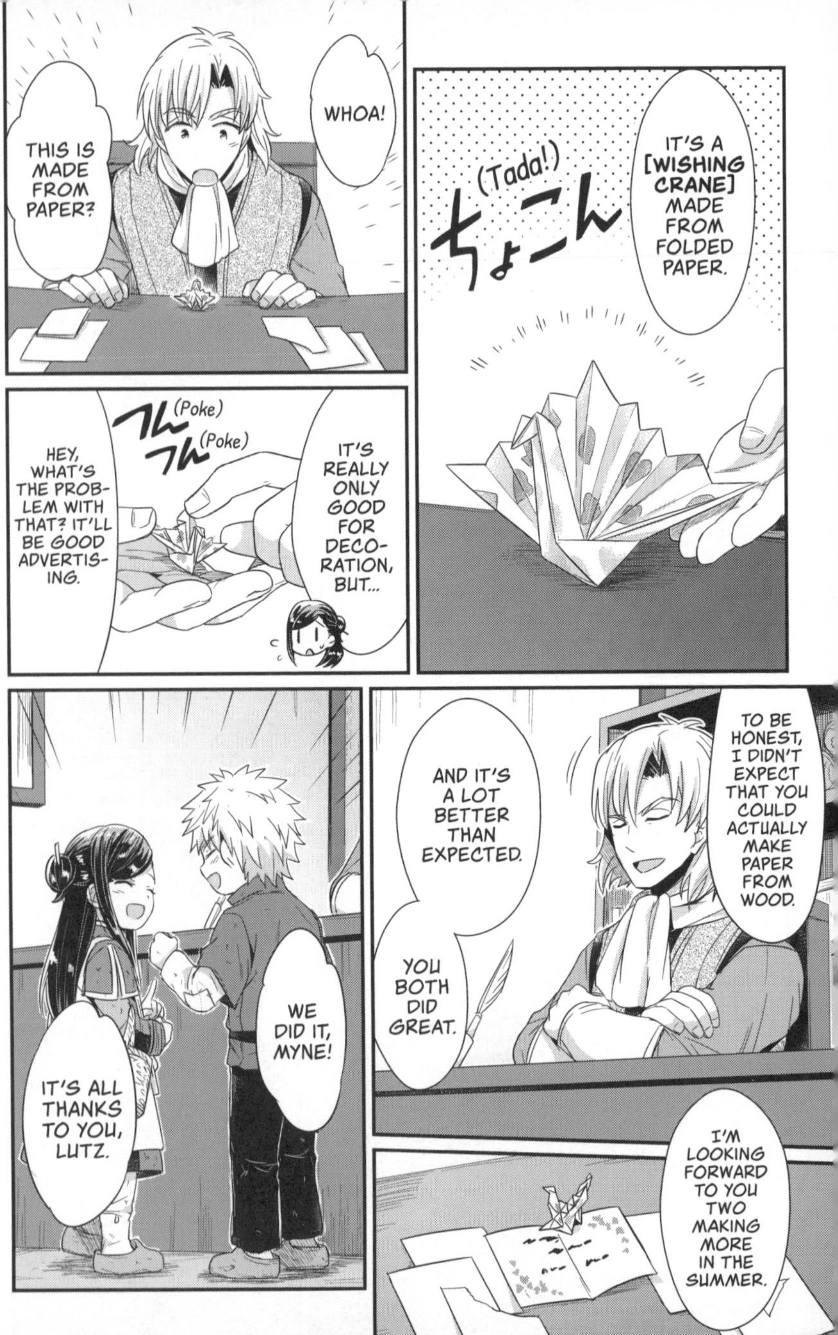

ちょこん
(Tada!)
IT'S A [WISHING CRANE] MADE FROM FOLDED PAPER.
WHOA!
THIS IS MADE FROM PAPER?
IT'S REALLY ONLY GOOD FOR DECO-RATION, BUT...
つん (Poke)
つん (Poke)
HEY, WHAT'S THE PROB-LEM WITH THAT? IT'LL BE GOOD ADVERTIS-ING.
TO BE HONEST, I DIDN'T EXPECT THAT YOU COULD ACTUALLY MAKE PAPER FROM WOOD.
AND IT'S A LOT BETTER THAN EXPECTED.
YOU BOTH DID GREAT.
I'M LOOKING FORWARD TO YOU TWO MAKING MORE IN THE SUMMER.
WE DID IT, MYNE!
IT'S ALL THANKS TO YOU, LUTZ.

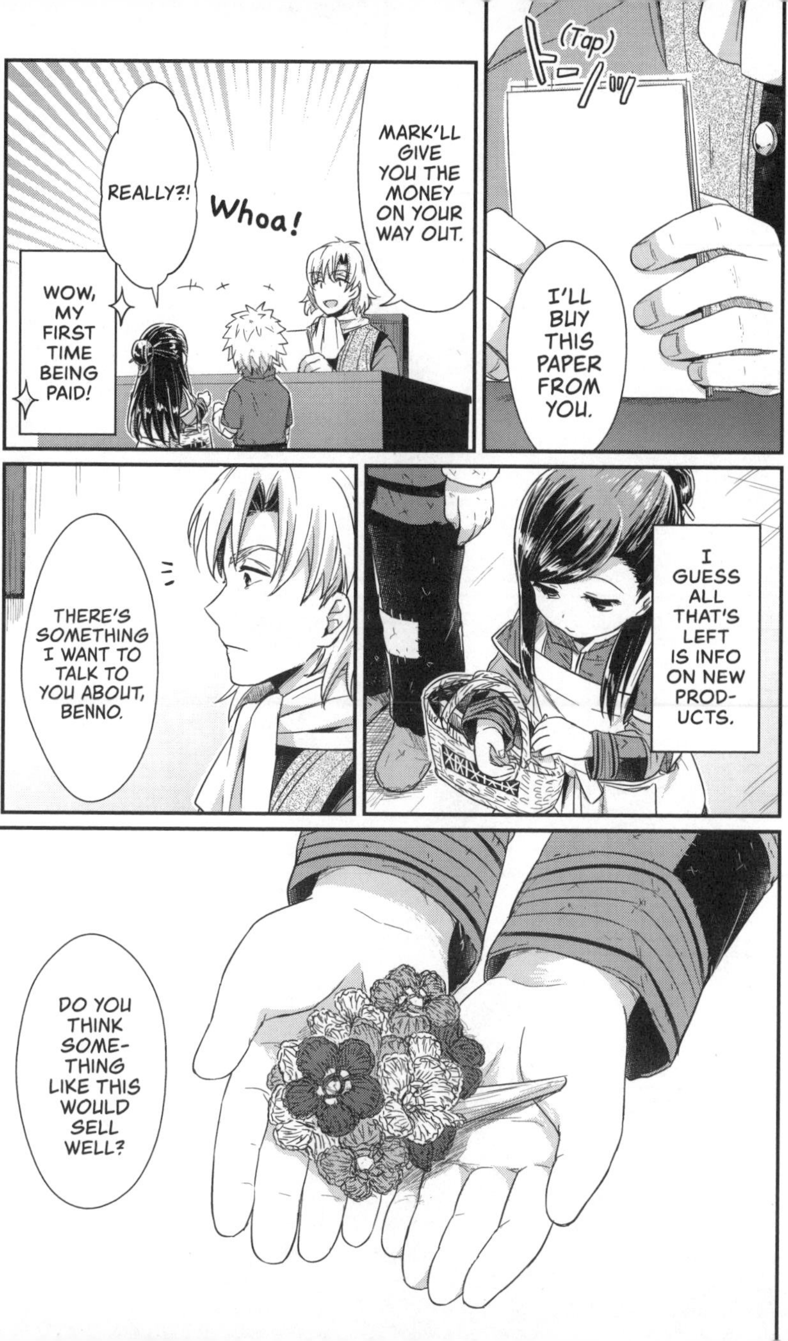
(Tap)
I'LL BUY THIS PAPER FROM YOU.
MARK'LL GIVE YOU THE MONEY ON YOUR WAY OUT.
REALLY?!
Whoa!
WOW, MY FIRST TIME BEING PAID!
I GUESS ALL THAT'S LEFT IS INFO ON NEW PROD-UCTS.
THERE'S SOMETHING I WANT TO TALK TO YOU ABOUT, BENNO.
DO YOU THINK SOME-THING LIKE THIS WOULD SELL WELL?

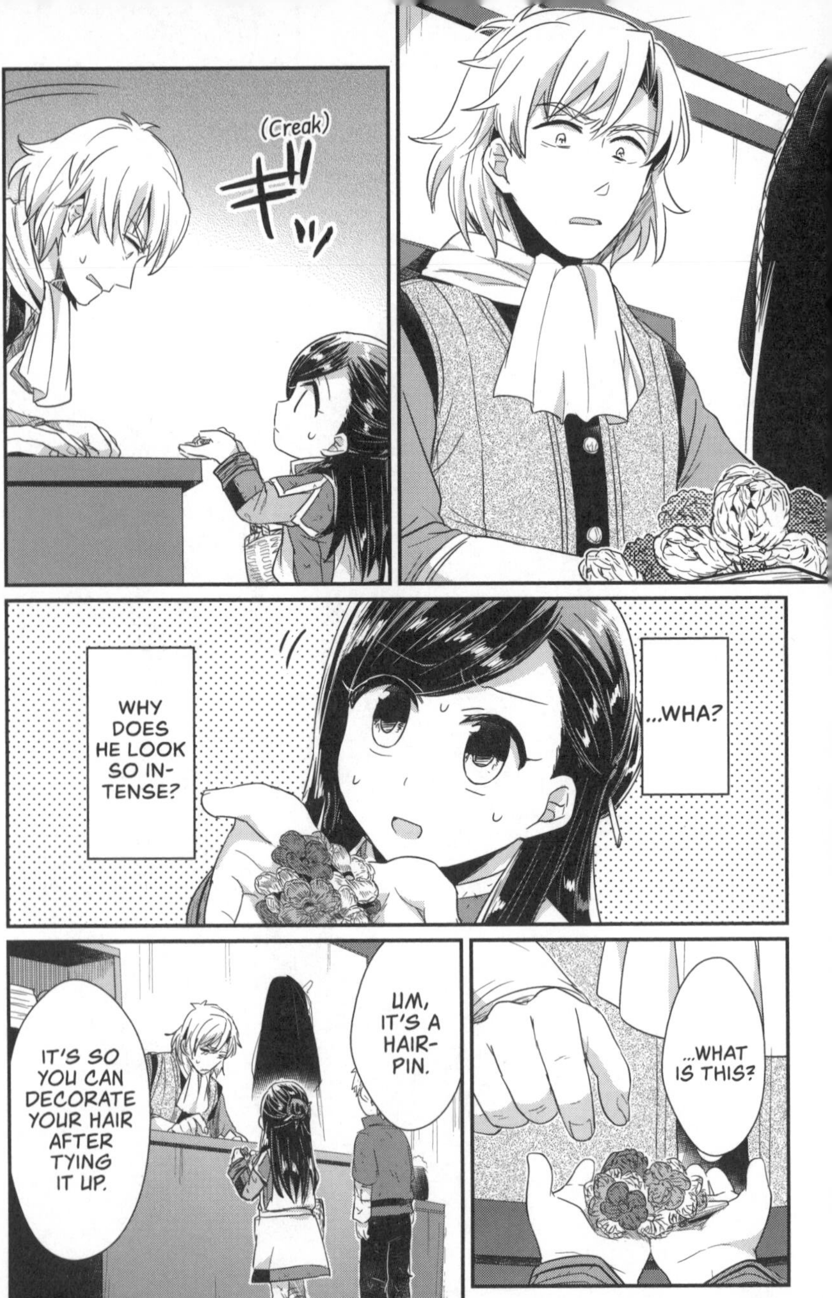
(Creak)
ギッ
...WHA?
WHY DOES HE LOOK SO IN-TENSE?
...WHAT IS THIS?
UM, IT'S A HAIR-PIN.
IT'S SO YOU CAN DECORATE YOUR HAIR AFTER TYING IT UP.

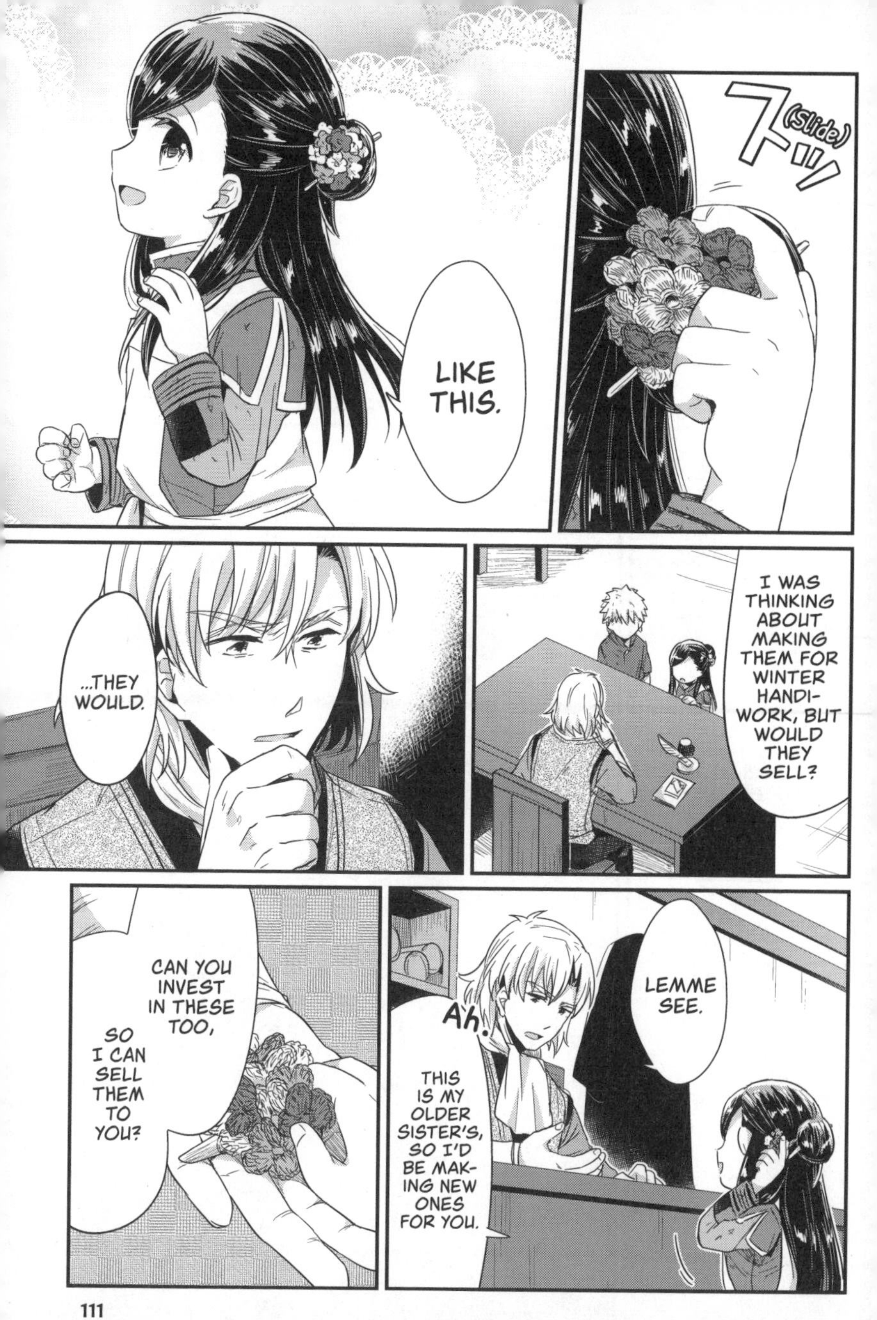
スッ
(Slide)
LIKE THIS.
I WAS THINKING ABOUT MAKING THEM FOR WINTER HANDI-WORK, BUT WOULD THEY SELL?
...THEY WOULD.
LEMME SEE.
Ah!
THIS IS MY OLDER SISTER'S, SO I'D BE MAK-ING NEW ONES FOR YOU.
CAN YOU INVEST IN THESE TOO,
SO I CAN SELL THEM TO YOU?

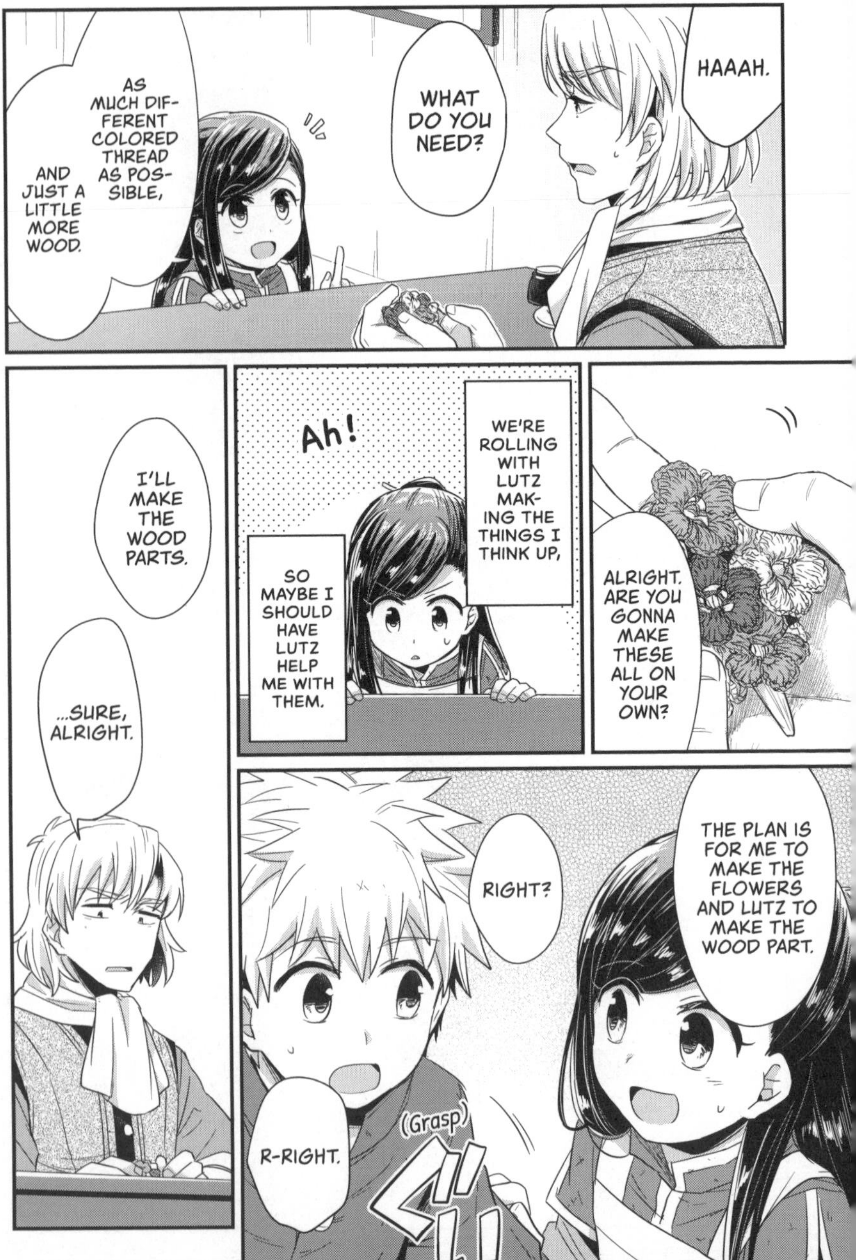
HAAAH.
WHAT DO YOU NEED?
AS MUCH DIFFERENT COLORED THREAD AS POSSIBLE,
AND JUST A LITTLE MORE WOOD.
ALRIGHT. ARE YOU GONNA MAKE THESE ALL ON YOUR OWN?
WE'RE ROLLING WITH LUTZ MAKING THE THINGS I THINK UP,
Ah!
SO MAYBE I SHOULD HAVE LUTZ HELP ME WITH THEM.
THE PLAN IS FOR ME TO MAKE THE FLOWERS AND LUTZ TO MAKE THE WOOD PART.
RIGHT?
(Grasp)
R-RIGHT.
I'LL MAKE THE WOOD PARTS.
...SURE, ALRIGHT.

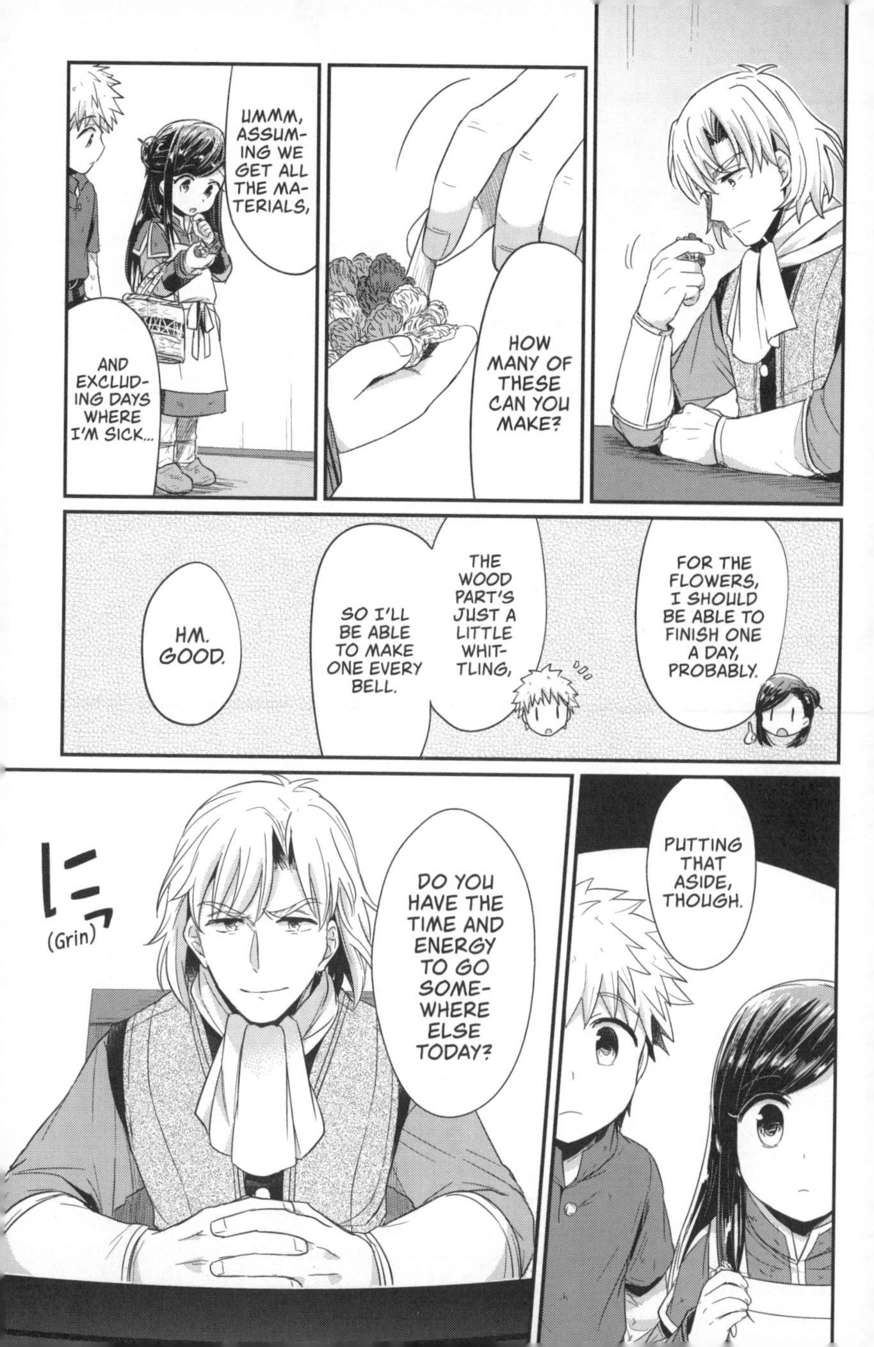
HOW MANY OF THESE CAN YOU MAKE?
UMMM, ASSUMING WE GET ALL THE MATERIALS,
AND EXCLUDING DAYS WHERE I'M SICK...
FOR THE FLOWERS, I SHOULD BE ABLE TO FINISH ONE A DAY, PROBABLY.
THE WOOD PART'S JUST A LITTLE WHITTLING,
SO I'LL BE ABLE TO MAKE ONE EVERY BELL.
HM. GOOD.
PUTTING THAT ASIDE, THOUGH.
DO YOU HAVE THE TIME AND ENERGY TO GO SOMEWHERE ELSE TODAY?
にっ
(Grin)

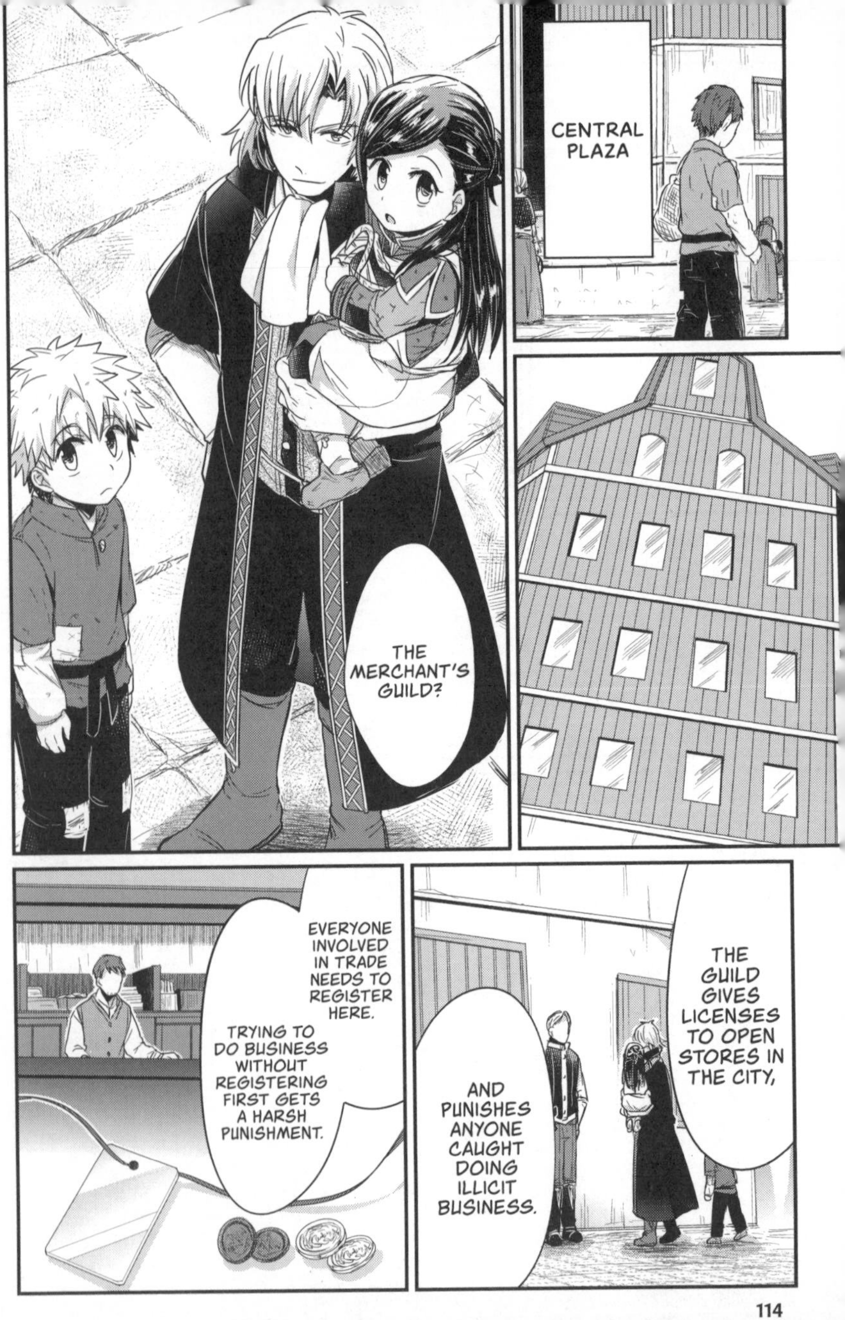
CENTRAL PLAZA
THE MERCHANT'S GUILD?
THE GUILD GIVES LICENSES TO OPEN STORES IN THE CITY,
AND PUNISHES ANYONE CAUGHT DOING ILLICIT BUSINESS.
EVERYONE INVOLVED IN TRADE NEEDS TO REGISTER HERE.
TRYING TO DO BUSINESS WITHOUT REGISTERING FIRST GETS A HARSH PUNISHMENT.

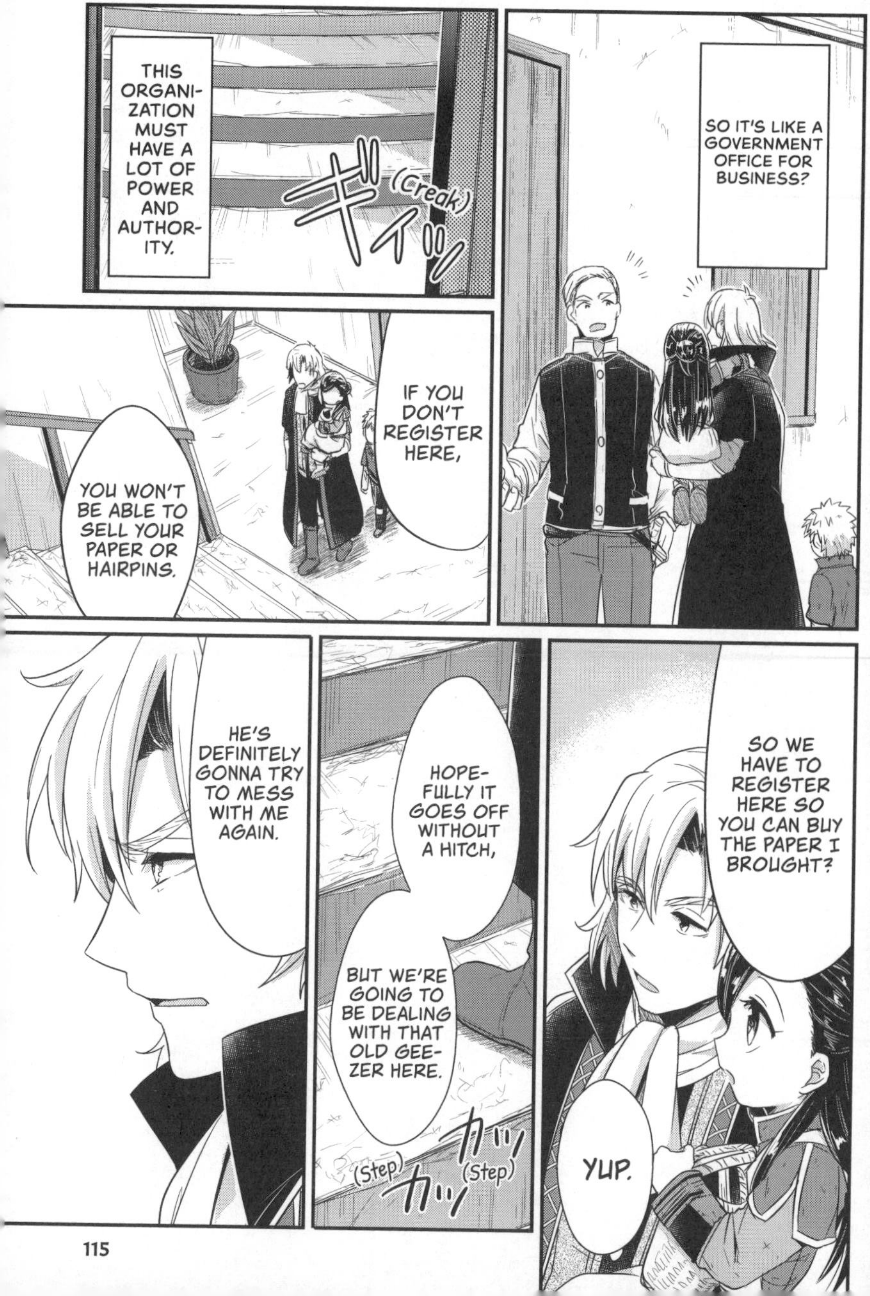
SO IT'S LIKE A GOVERNMENT OFFICE FOR BUSINESS?
THIS ORGANIZATION MUST HAVE A LOT OF POWER AND AUTHORITY.
(Creak)
IF YOU DON'T REGISTER HERE,
YOU WON'T BE ABLE TO SELL YOUR PAPER OR HAIRPINS.
SO WE HAVE TO REGISTER HERE SO YOU CAN BUY THE PAPER I BROUGHT?
YUP.
HOPEFULLY IT GOES OFF WITHOUT A HITCH,
BUT WE'RE GOING TO BE DEALING WITH THAT OLD GEEZER HERE.
(Step)
(Step)
HE'S DEFINITELY GONNA TRY TO MESS WITH ME AGAIN.

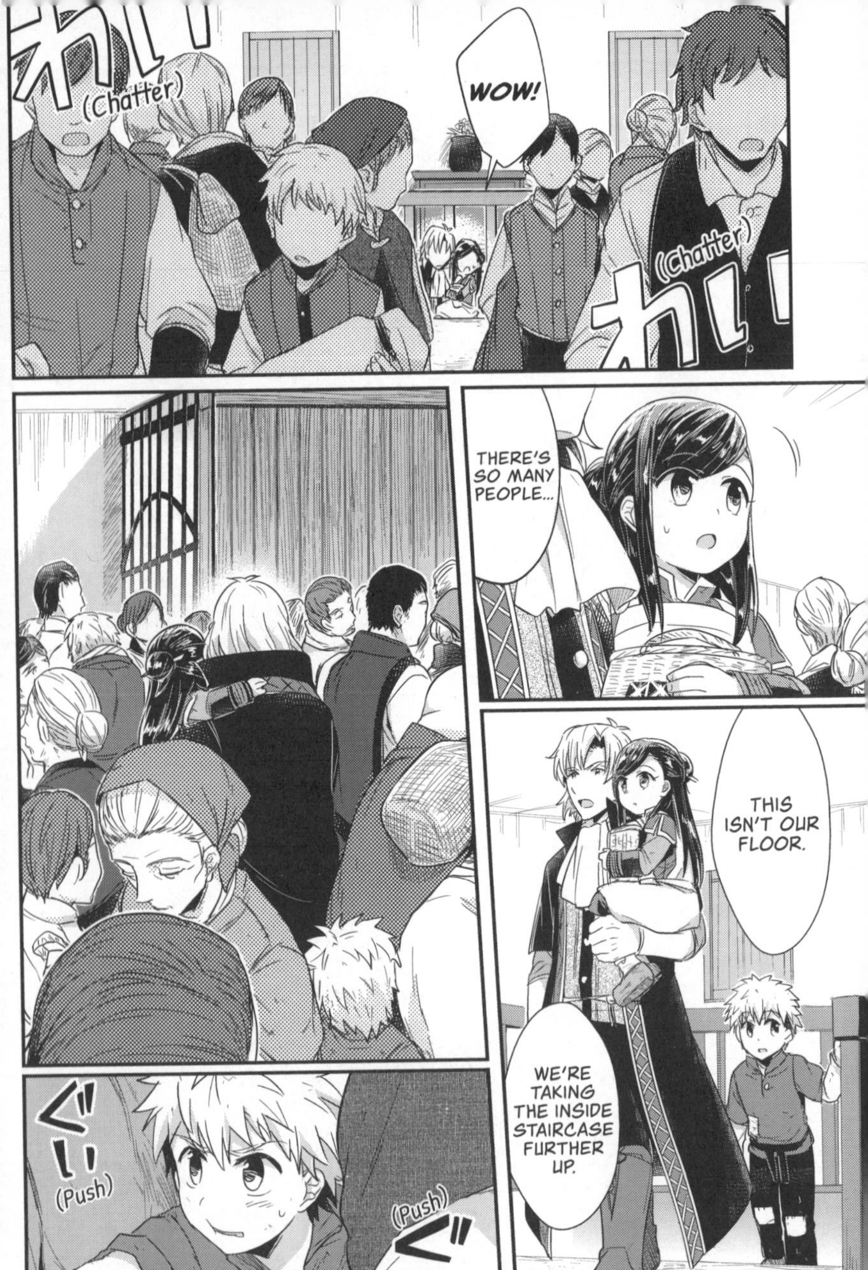
(Chatter)
WOW!
(Chatter)
THERE'S SO MANY PEOPLE...
THIS ISN'T OUR FLOOR.
WE'RE TAKING THE INSIDE STAIRCASE FURTHER UP.
(Push)
(Push)

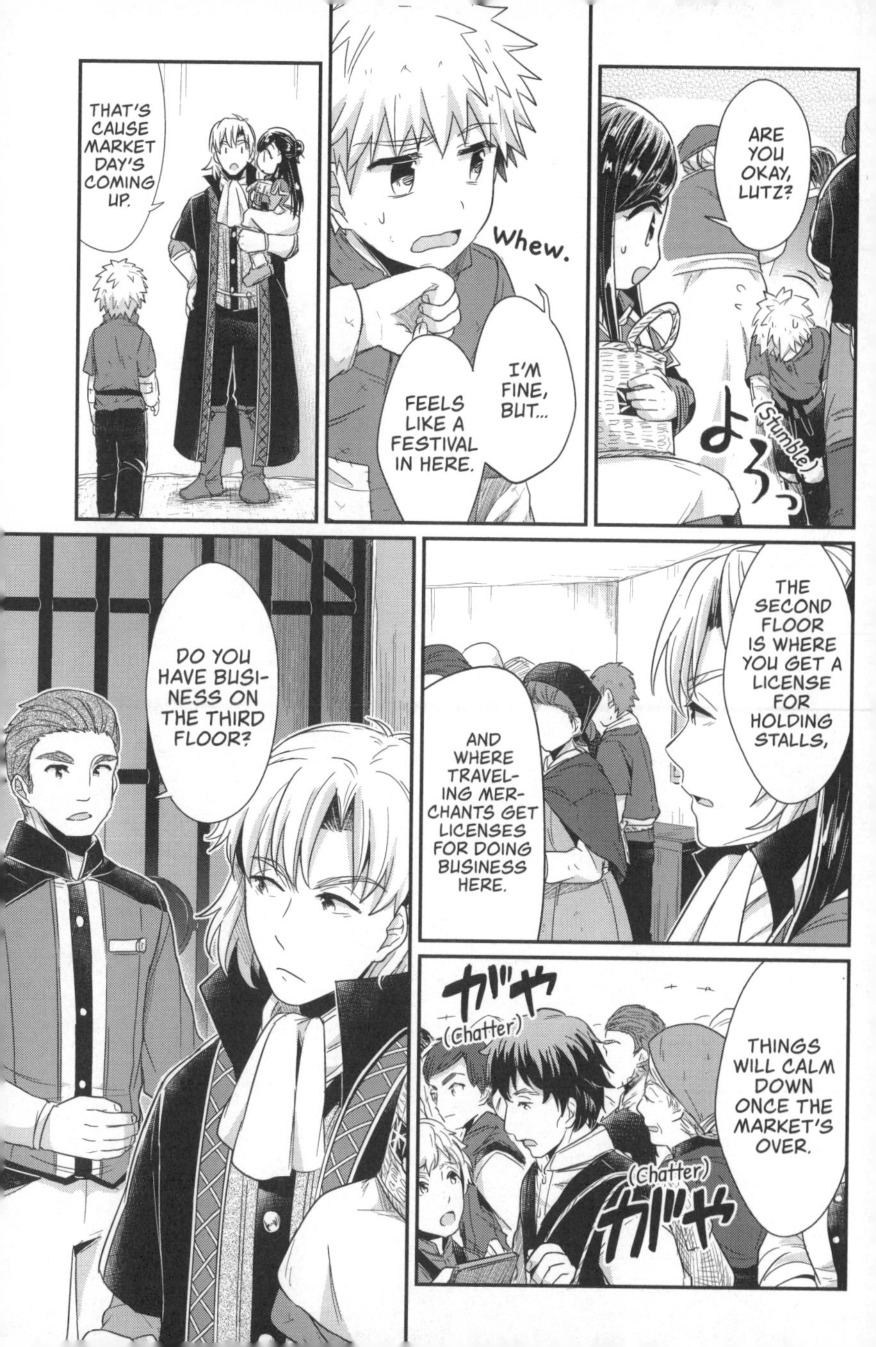
ARE YOU OKAY, LUTZ?
よろっ
(Stumble)
Whew.
I'M FINE, BUT...
FEELS LIKE A FESTIVAL IN HERE.
THAT'S CAUSE MARKET DAY'S COMING UP.
THE SECOND FLOOR IS WHERE YOU GET A LICENSE FOR HOLDING STALLS,
AND WHERE TRAVELING MERCHANTS GET LICENSES FOR DOING BUSINESS HERE.
ガヤ
(Chatter)
THINGS WILL CALM DOWN ONCE THE MARKET'S OVER.
(Chatter)
ガヤ
DO YOU HAVE BUSINESS ON THE THIRD FLOOR?

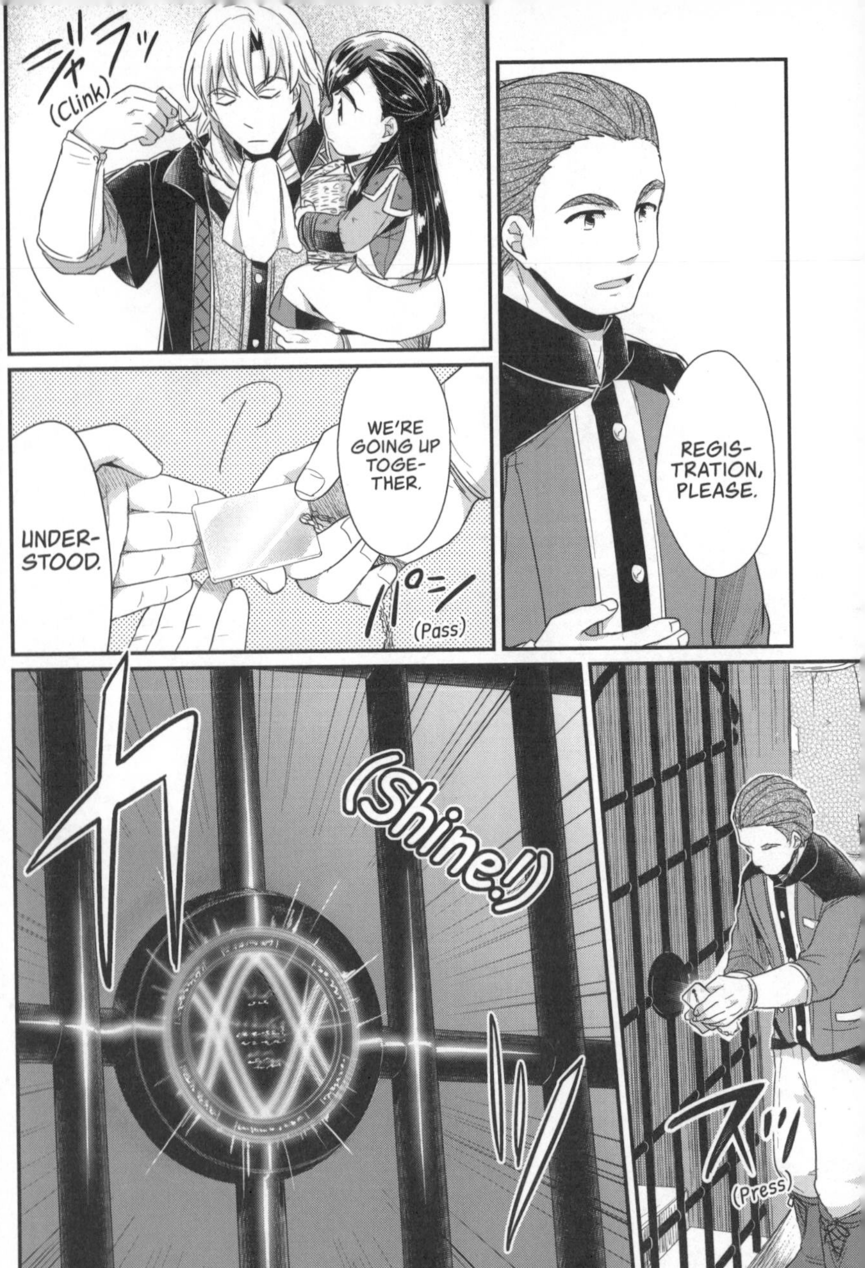
REGIS-TRATION, PLEASE.
ジャラッ
(Clink)
WE'RE GOING UP TOGE-THER.
UNDER-STOOD.
パッ
(Pass)
スッ
(Press)
カッ
(Shine!!)

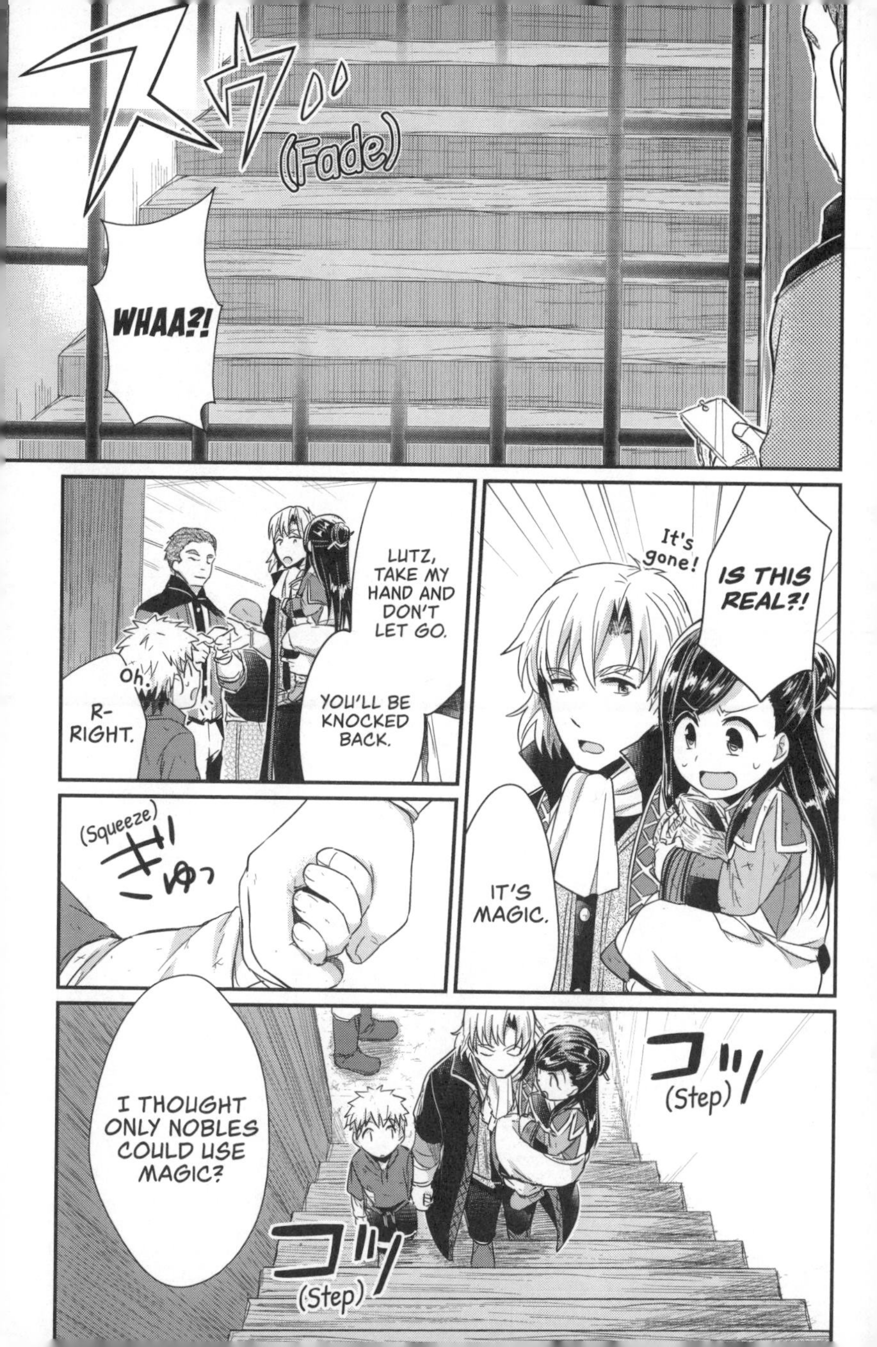
(Fade)
WHAA?!
It's gone!
IS THIS REAL?!
IT'S MAGIC.
LUTZ, TAKE MY HAND AND DON'T LET GO.
YOU'LL BE KNOCKED BACK.
Oh.
R-RIGHT.
ぎゅっ
(Squeeze)
コッ
(Step)
I THOUGHT ONLY NOBLES COULD USE MAGIC?
コッ
(Step)

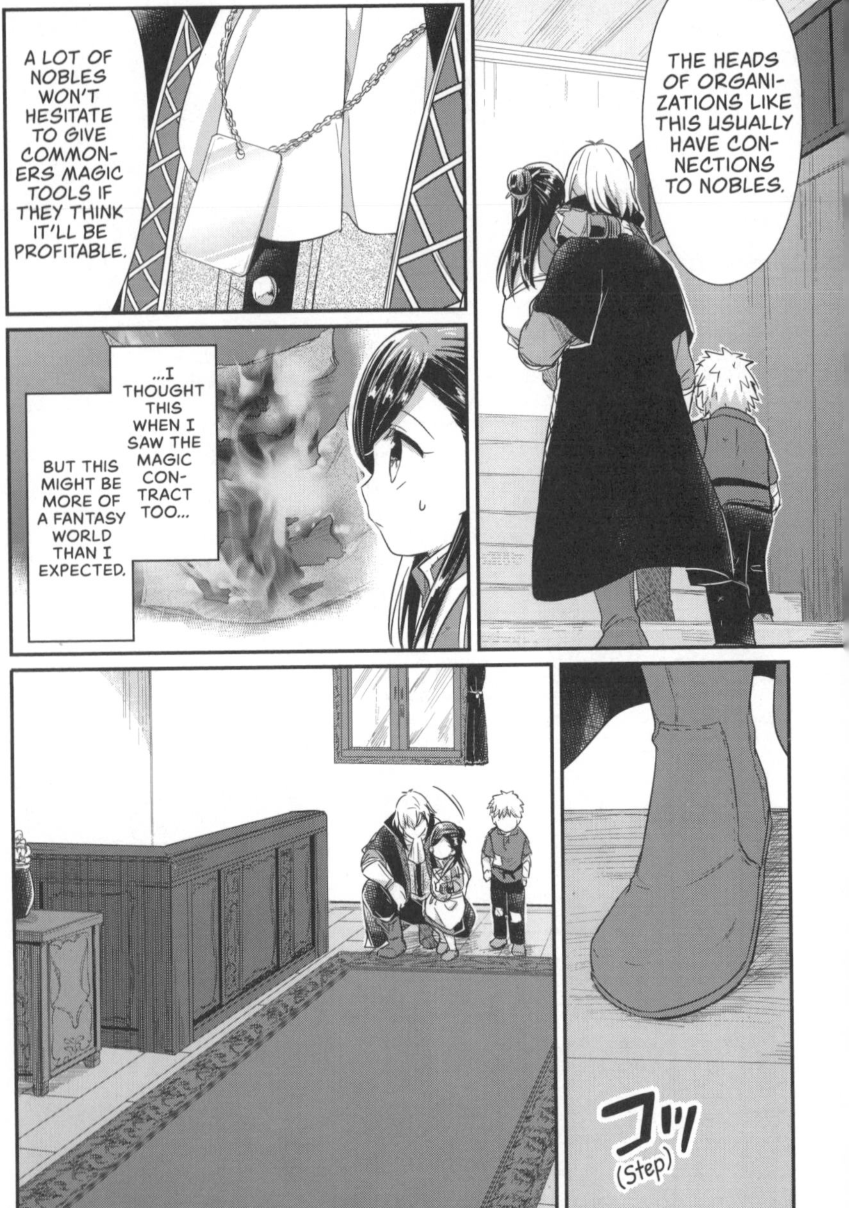
THE HEADS OF ORGANIZATIONS LIKE THIS USUALLY HAVE CONNECTIONS TO NOBLES.
A LOT OF NOBLES WON'T HESITATE TO GIVE COMMONERS MAGIC TOOLS IF THEY THINK IT'LL BE PROFITABLE.
...I THOUGHT THIS WHEN I SAW THE MAGIC CONTRACT TOO...
BUT THIS MIGHT BE MORE OF A FANTASY WORLD THAN I EXPECTED.
コッ
(Step)

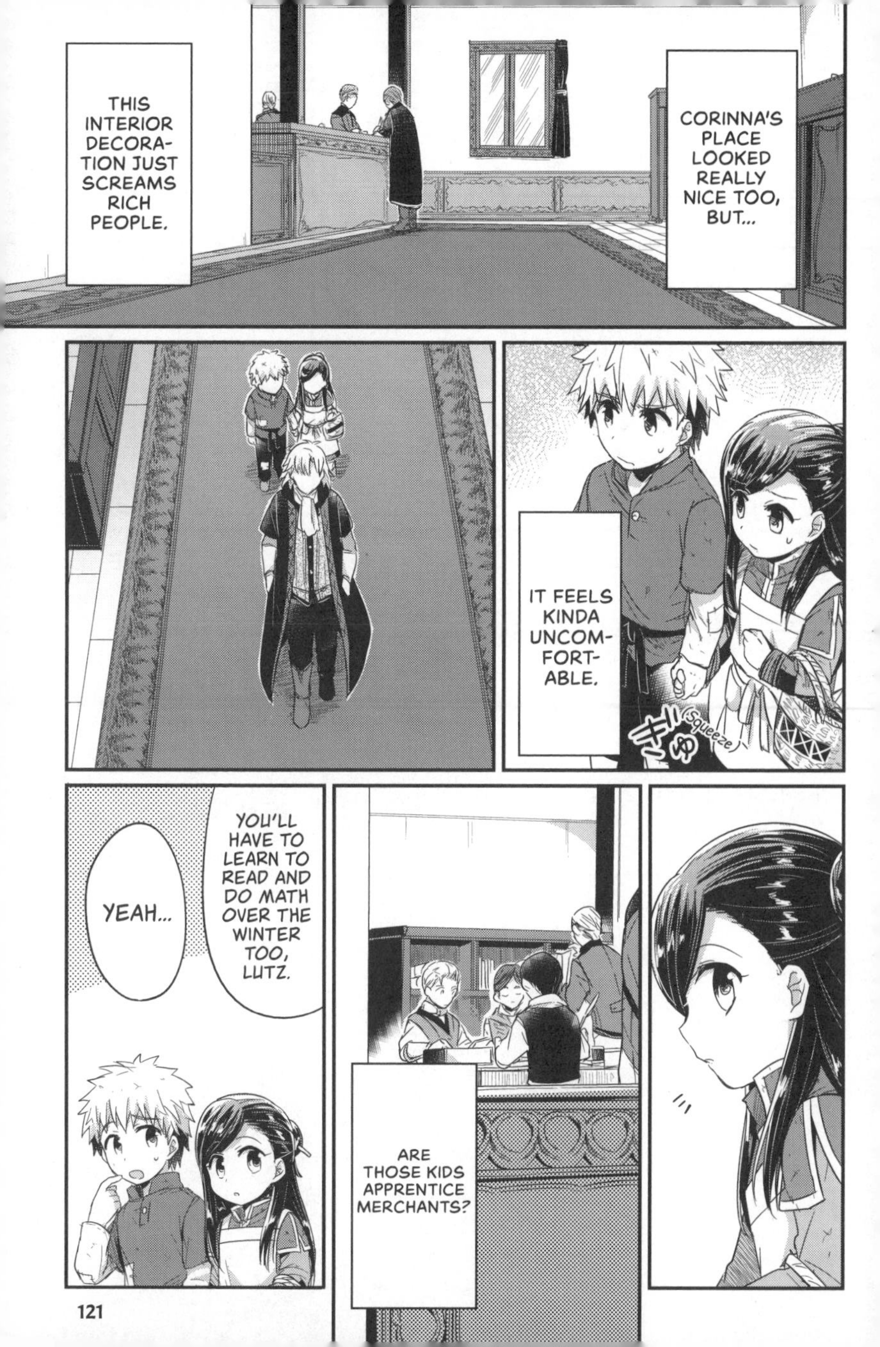
CORINNA'S PLACE LOOKED REALLY NICE TOO, BUT...
THIS INTERIOR DECORA-TION JUST SCREAMS RICH PEOPLE.
IT FEELS KINDA UNCOM-FORT-ABLE.
(Squeeze)
ARE THOSE KIDS APPRENTICE MERCHANTS?
YOU'LL HAVE TO LEARN TO READ AND DO MATH OVER THE WINTER TOO, LUTZ.
YEAH...

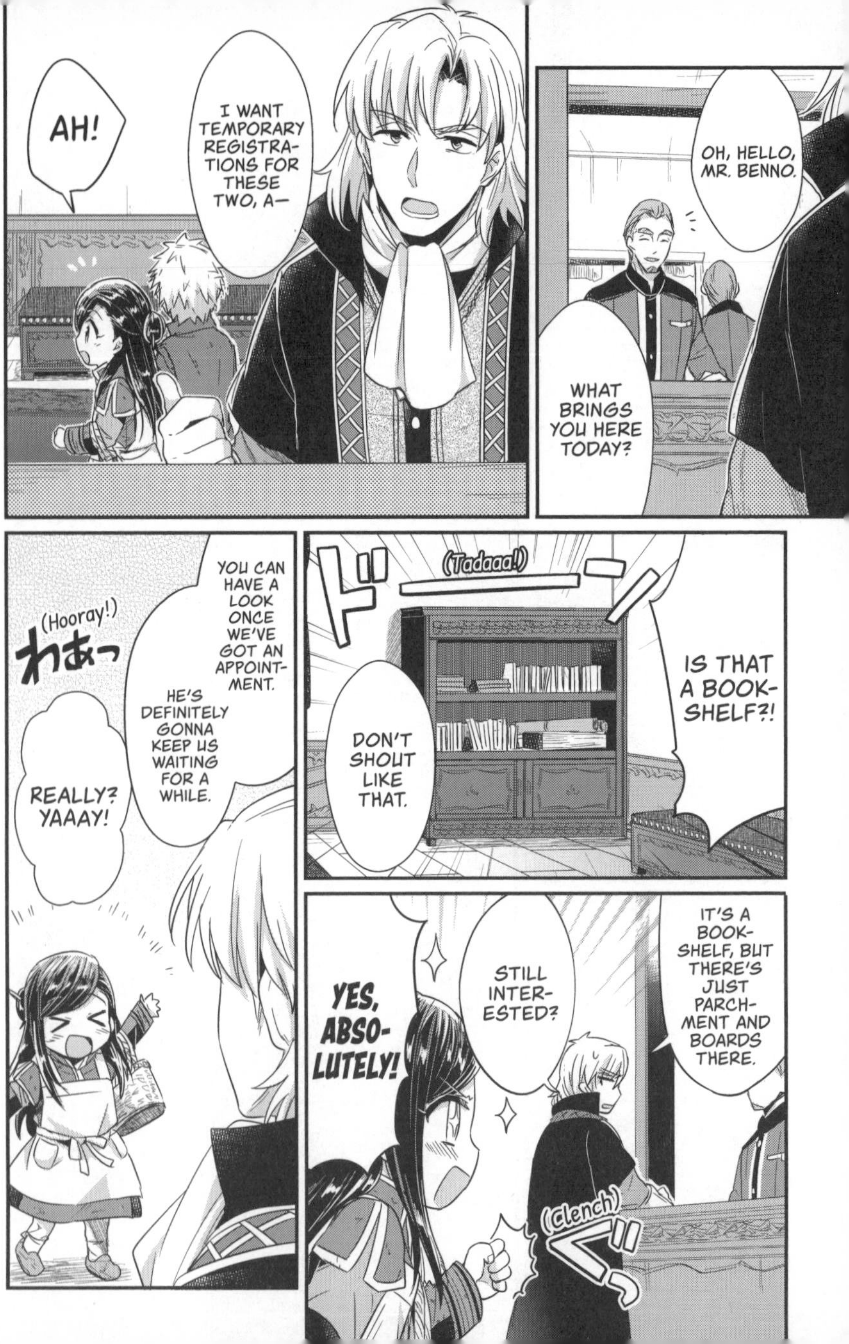
OH, HELLO, MR. BENNO.
WHAT BRINGS YOU HERE TODAY?
I WANT TEMPORARY REGISTRATIONS FOR THESE TWO, A—
AH!
IS THAT A BOOK-SHELF?!
ドーーー (Tadaaa!)
DON'T SHOUT LIKE THAT.
IT'S A BOOK-SHELF, BUT THERE'S JUST PARCHMENT AND BOARDS THERE.
STILL INTERESTED?
YES, ABSOLUTELY!
ぐっ (Clench)
YOU CAN HAVE A LOOK ONCE WE'VE GOT AN APPOINTMENT.
HE'S DEFINITELY GONNA KEEP US WAITING FOR A WHILE.
わあっ (Hooray!)
REALLY? YAAAY!

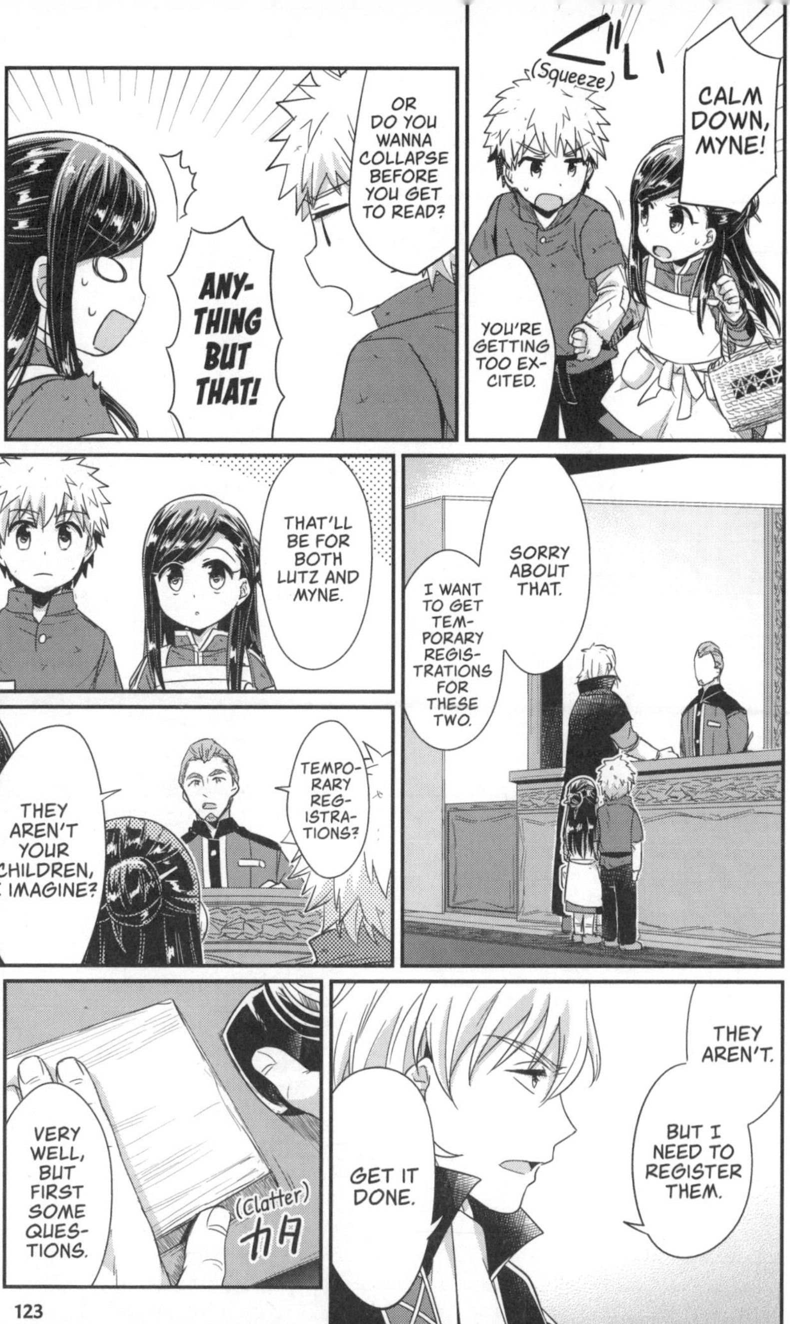
(Squeeze)
CALM DOWN, MYNE!
YOU'RE GETTING TOO EX-CITED.
OR DO YOU WANNA COLLAPSE BEFORE YOU GET TO READ?
ANY-THING BUT THAT!
SORRY ABOUT THAT.
I WANT TO GET TEM-PORARY REGIS-TRATIONS FOR THESE TWO.
THAT'LL BE FOR BOTH LUTZ AND MYNE.
TEMPO-RARY REG-ISTRA-TIONS?
THEY AREN'T YOUR CHILDREN, I IMAGINE?
THEY AREN'T.
BUT I NEED TO REGISTER THEM.
GET IT DONE.
VERY WELL, BUT FIRST SOME QUES-TIONS.
(Clatter)
カタ

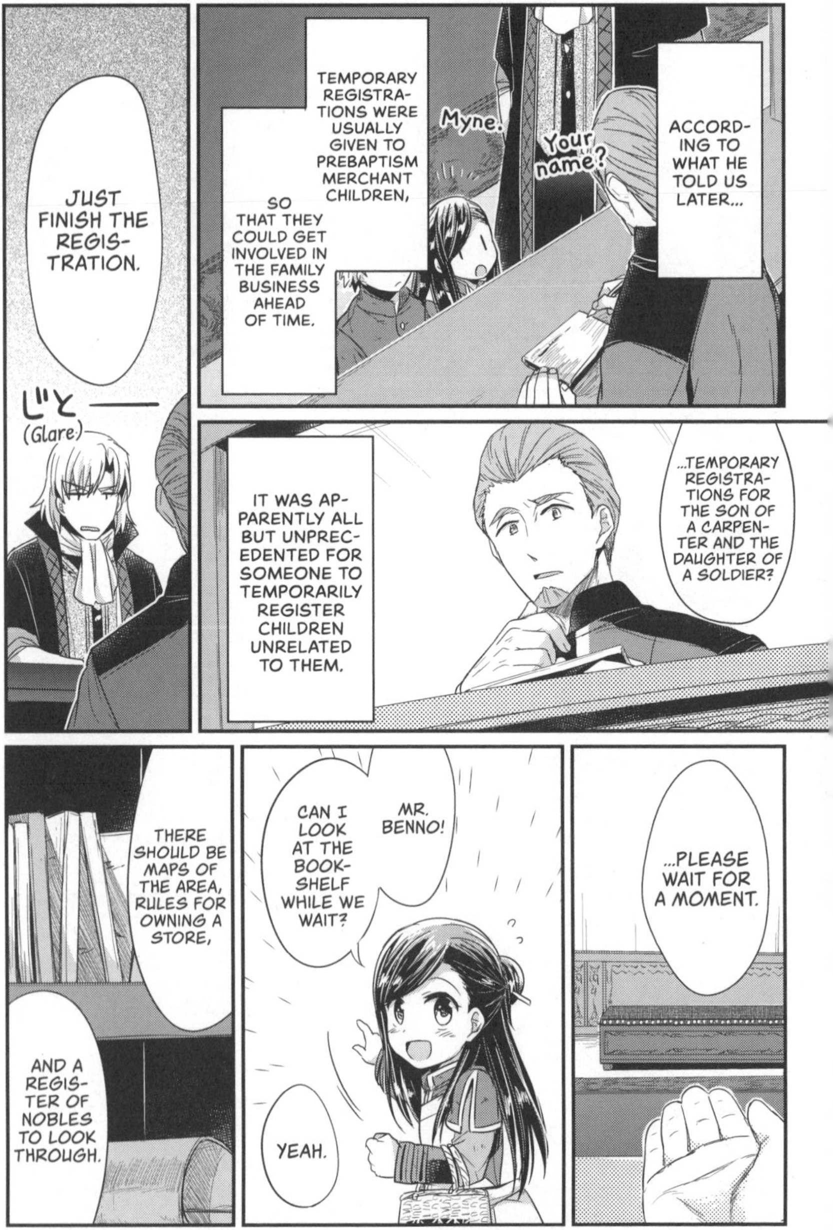
ACCORDING TO WHAT HE TOLD US LATER...
Your name?
Myne.
TEMPORARY REGISTRATIONS WERE USUALLY GIVEN TO PREBAPTISM MERCHANT CHILDREN,
SO THAT THEY COULD GET INVOLVED IN THE FAMILY BUSINESS AHEAD OF TIME.
...TEMPORARY REGISTRATIONS FOR THE SON OF A CARPENTER AND THE DAUGHTER OF A SOLDIER?
IT WAS APPARENTLY ALL BUT UNPRECEDENTED FOR SOMEONE TO TEMPORARILY REGISTER CHILDREN UNRELATED TO THEM.
JUST FINISH THE REGISTRATION.
じと—
(Glare)
...PLEASE WAIT FOR A MOMENT.
MR. BENNO!
CAN I LOOK AT THE BOOKSHELF WHILE WE WAIT?
YEAH.
THERE SHOULD BE MAPS OF THE AREA, RULES FOR OWNING A STORE,
AND A REGISTER OF NOBLES TO LOOK THROUGH.

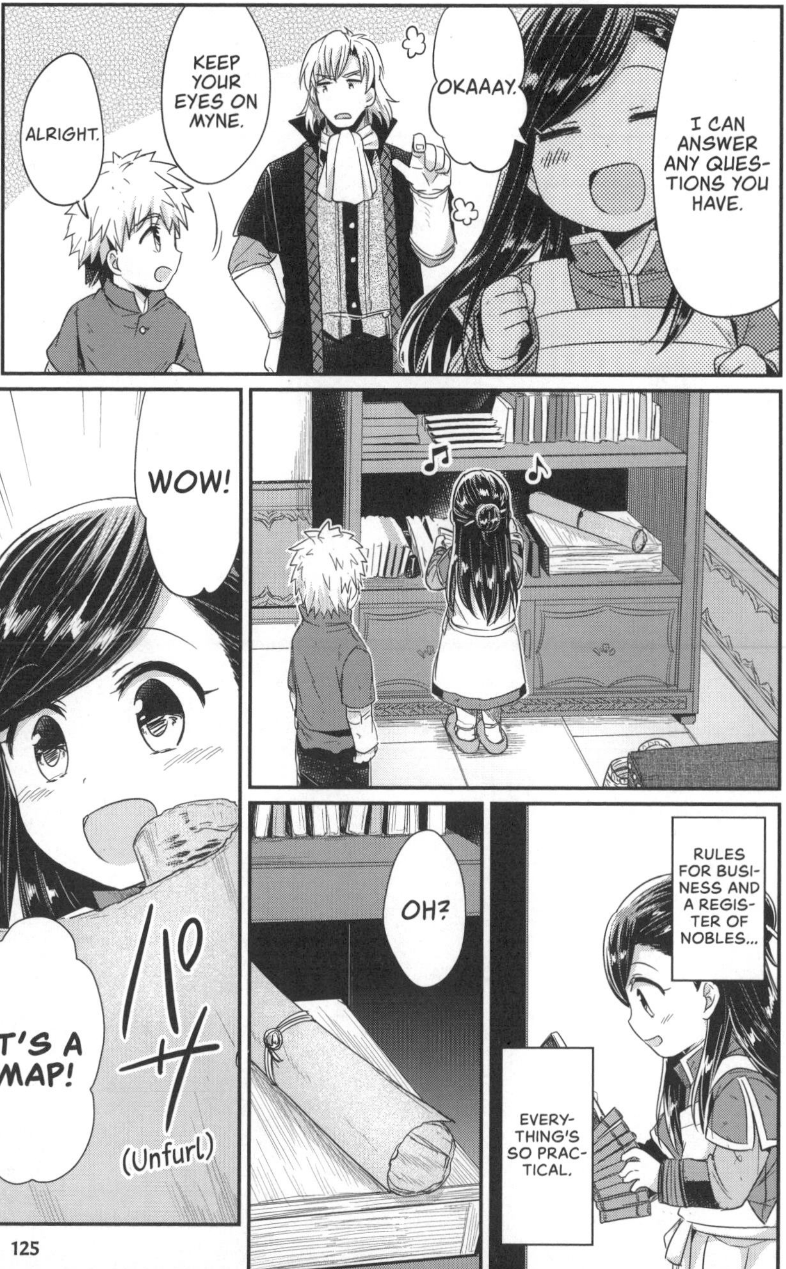
I CAN ANSWER ANY QUESTIONS YOU HAVE.
OKAAAY.
KEEP YOUR EYES ON MYNE.
ALRIGHT.
RULES FOR BUSINESS AND A REGISTER OF NOBLES...
EVERYTHING'S SO PRACTICAL.
OH?
WOW!
IT'S A MAP!
パッ
(Unfurl)

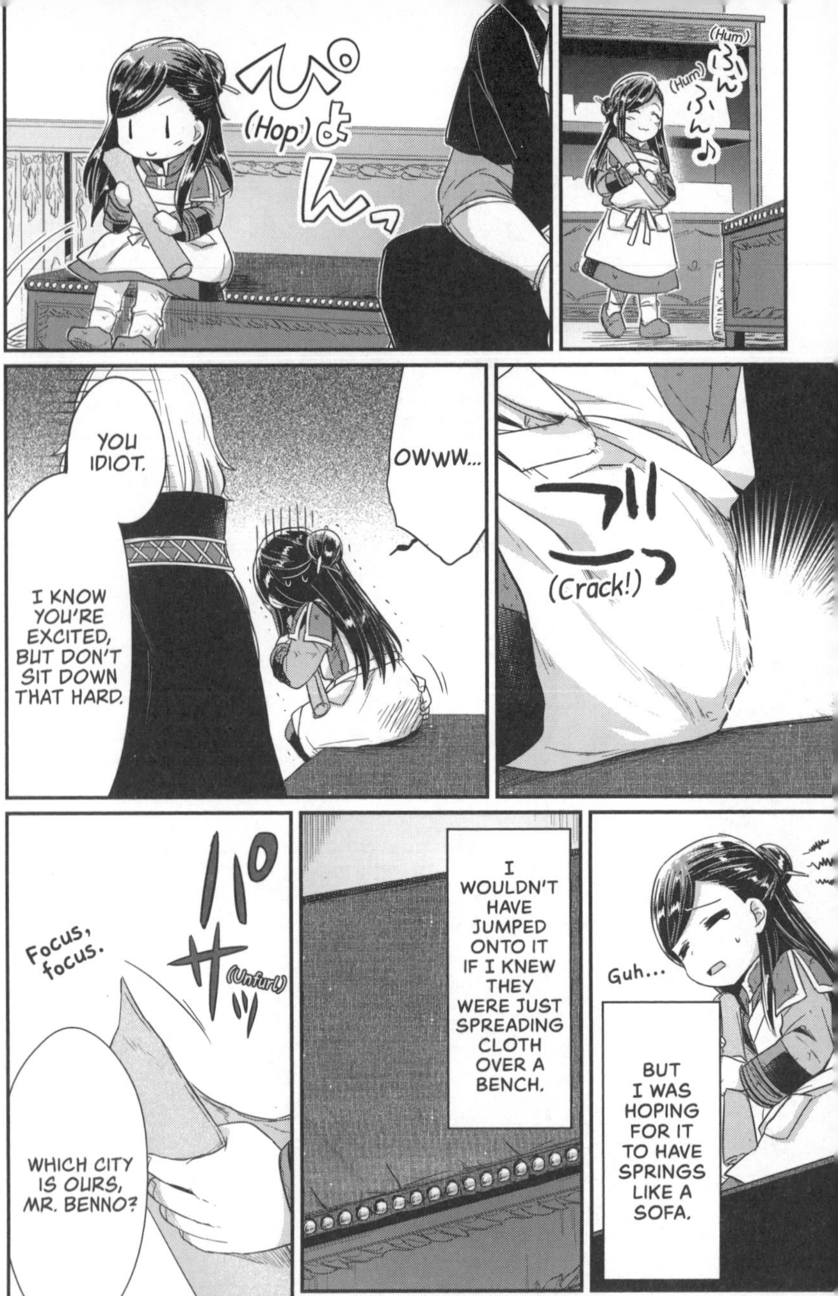

ふんふん♪
(Hum)
(Hum)
ぴょんっ
(Hop)
ゴッ
(Crack!)
OWWW...
YOU IDIOT.
I KNOW YOU'RE EXCITED, BUT DON'T SIT DOWN THAT HARD.
Guh...
BUT I WAS HOPING FOR IT TO HAVE SPRINGS LIKE A SOFA.
I WOULDN'T HAVE JUMPED ONTO IT IF I KNEW THEY WERE JUST SPREADING CLOTH OVER A BENCH.
Focus, focus.
パサッ
(Unfurl)
WHICH CITY IS OURS, MR. BENNO?

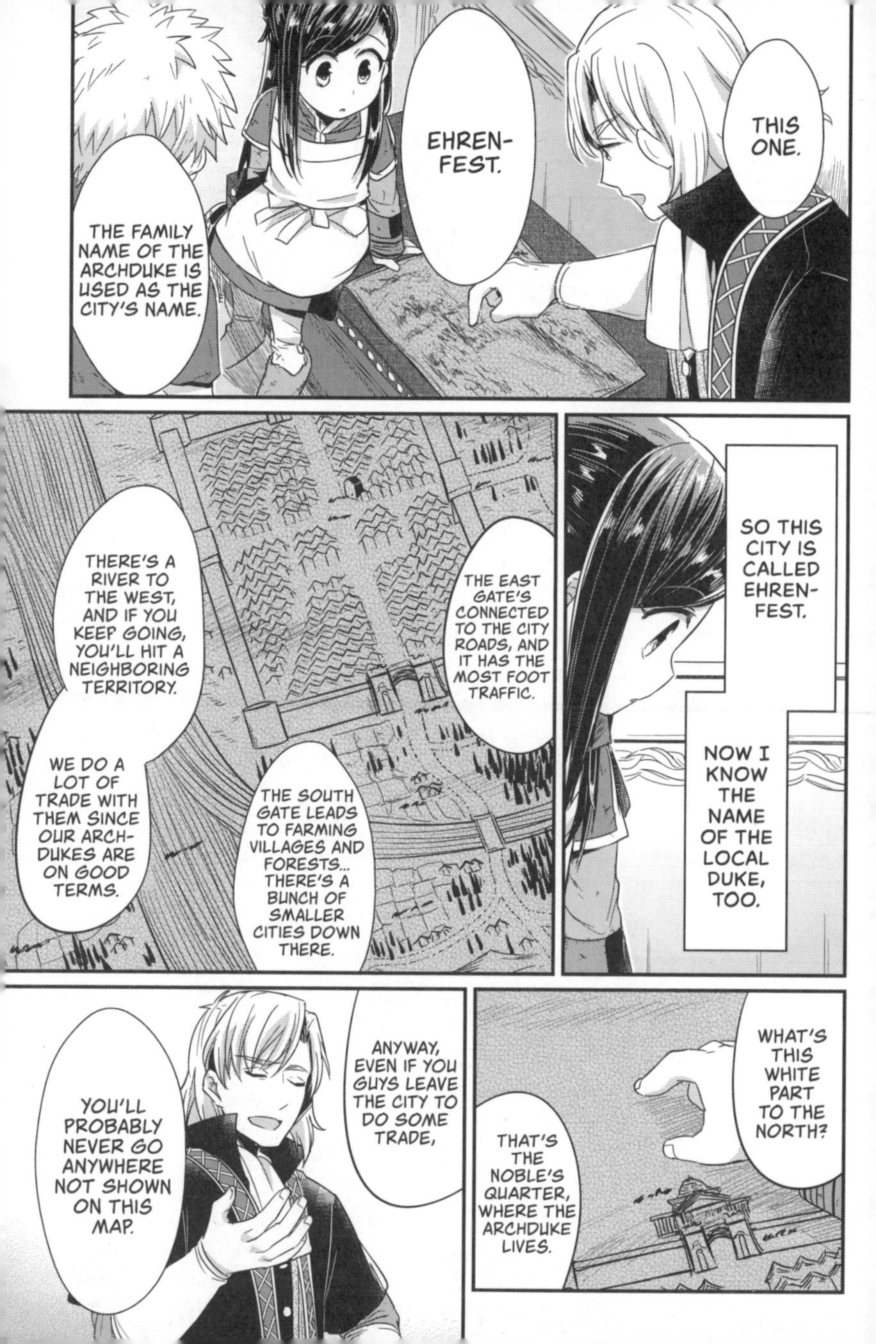
THIS ONE.
EHREN-FEST.
THE FAMILY NAME OF THE ARCHDUKE IS USED AS THE CITY'S NAME.
SO THIS CITY IS CALLED EHREN-FEST.
NOW I KNOW THE NAME OF THE LOCAL DUKE, TOO.
THE EAST GATE'S CONNECTED TO THE CITY ROADS, AND IT HAS THE MOST FOOT TRAFFIC.
THERE'S A RIVER TO THE WEST, AND IF YOU KEEP GOING, YOU'LL HIT A NEIGHBORING TERRITORY.
THE SOUTH GATE LEADS TO FARMING VILLAGES AND FORESTS... THERE'S A BUNCH OF SMALLER CITIES DOWN THERE.
WE DO A LOT OF TRADE WITH THEM SINCE OUR ARCH-DUKES ARE ON GOOD TERMS.
WHAT'S THIS WHITE PART TO THE NORTH?
THAT'S THE NOBLE'S QUARTER, WHERE THE ARCHDUKE LIVES.
ANYWAY, EVEN IF YOU GUYS LEAVE THE CITY TO DO SOME TRADE,
YOU'LL PROBABLY NEVER GO ANYWHERE NOT SHOWN ON THIS MAP.

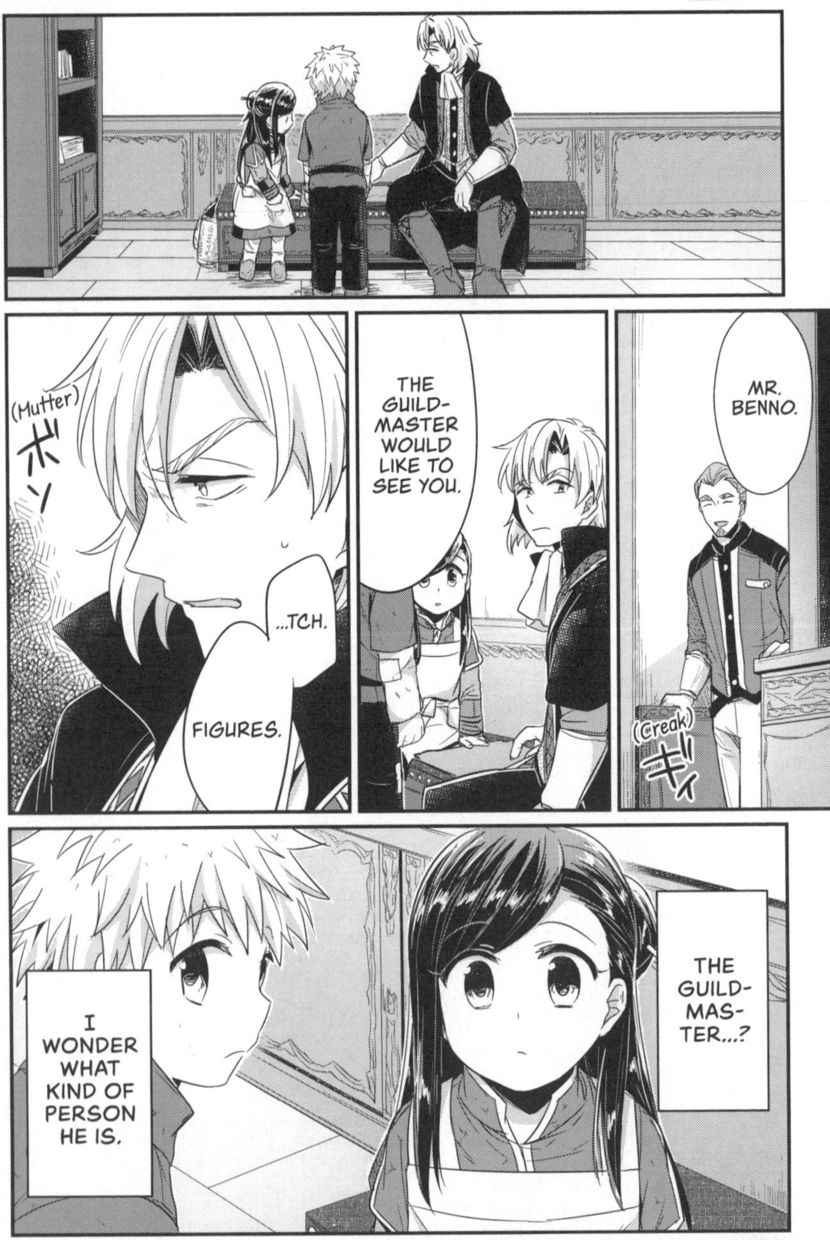
MR. BENNO.
(Creak)
ギィ
THE GUILD-MASTER WOULD LIKE TO SEE YOU.
(Mutter)
ボソ
...TCH.
FIGURES.
THE GUILD-MAS-TER...?
I WONDER WHAT KIND OF PERSON HE IS.

Ch.18: The Merchant's Guild End

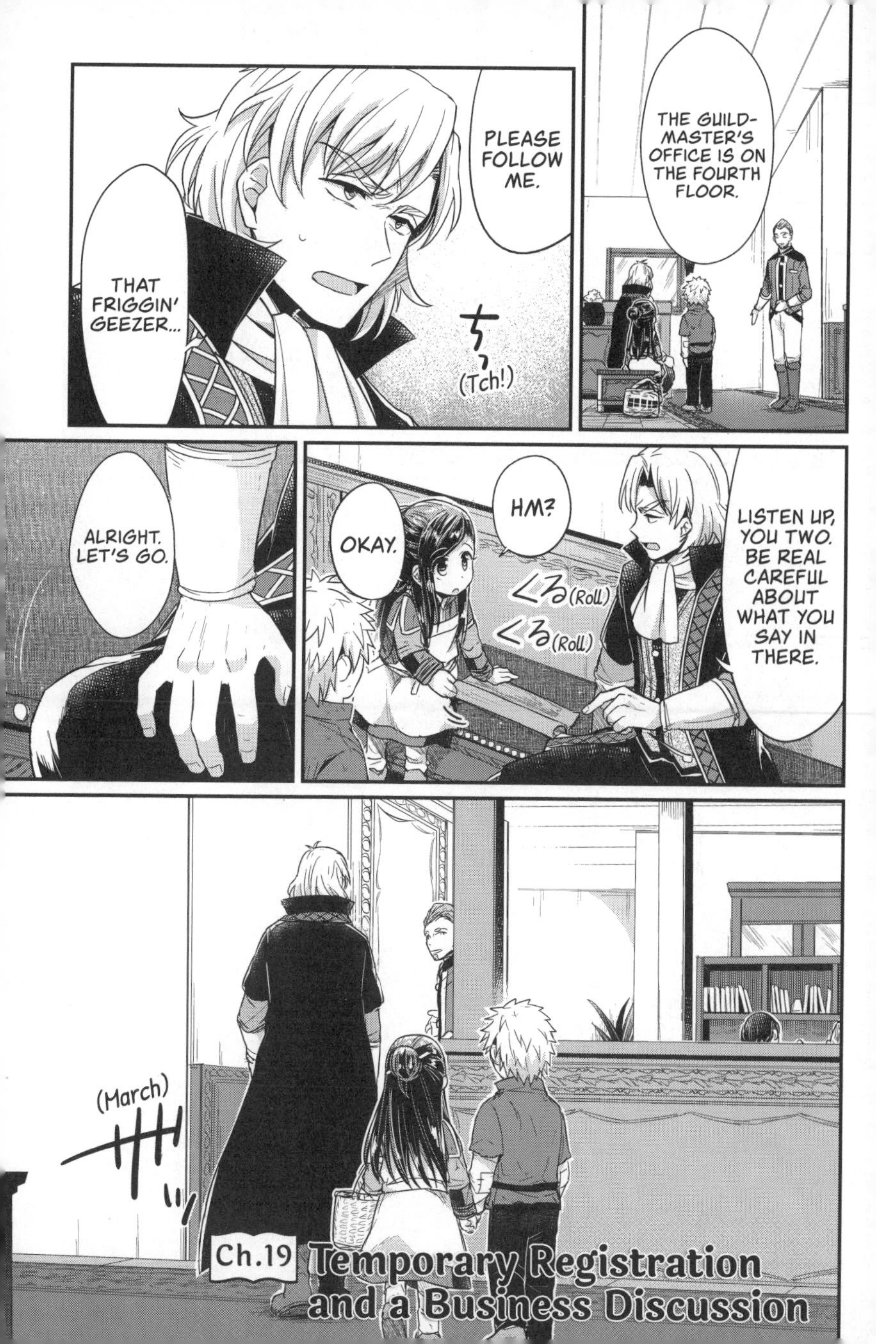
THE GUILD-MASTER'S OFFICE IS ON THE FOURTH FLOOR.
PLEASE FOLLOW ME.
THAT FRIGGIN' GEEZER...
ちっ (Tch!)
LISTEN UP, YOU TWO. BE REAL CAREFUL ABOUT WHAT YOU SAY IN THERE.
HM?
OKAY.
くる (Roll)
くる (Roll)
ALRIGHT. LET'S GO.
(March)
Ch.19 Temporary Registration and a Business Discussion

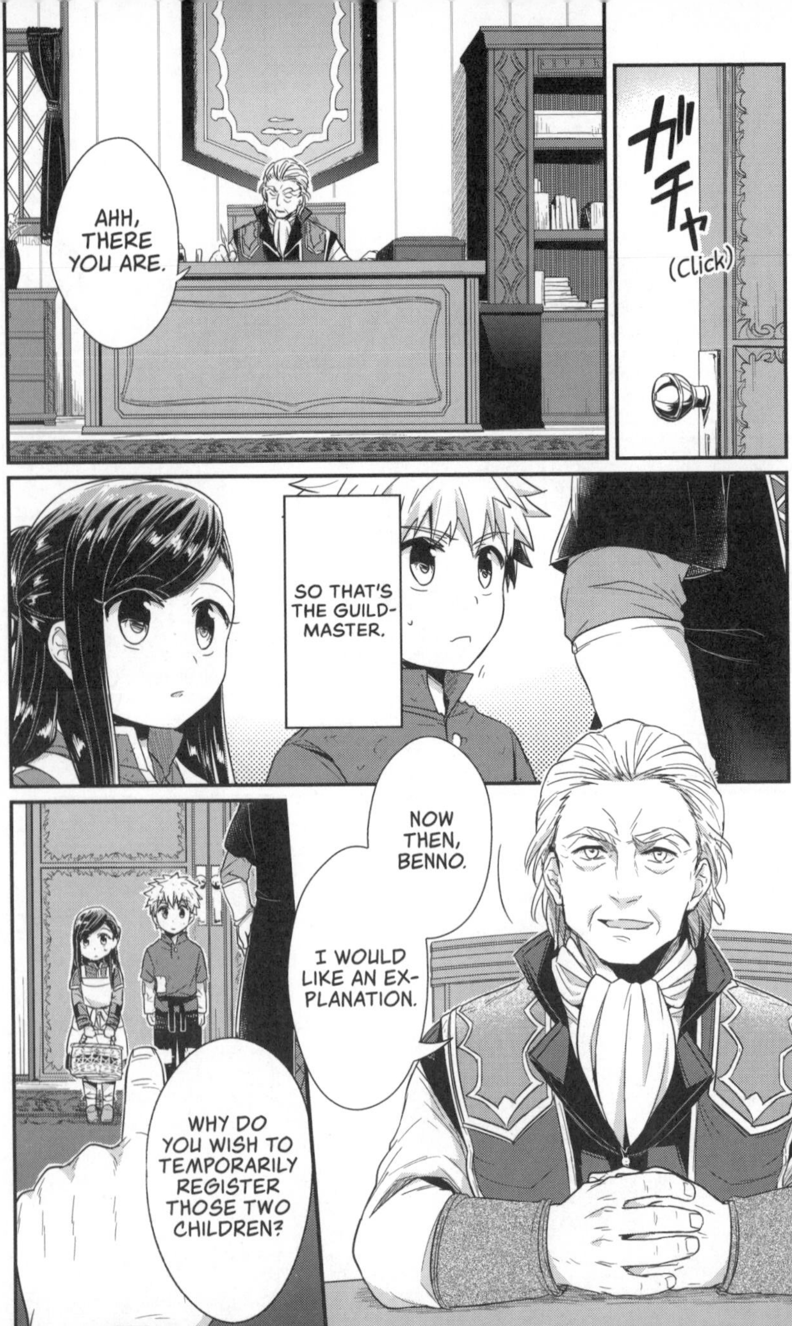
ガチャ
(Click)
AHH, THERE YOU ARE.
SO THAT'S THE GUILD-MASTER.
NOW THEN, BENNO.
I WOULD LIKE AN EX-PLANATION.
WHY DO YOU WISH TO TEMPORARILY REGISTER THOSE TWO CHILDREN?

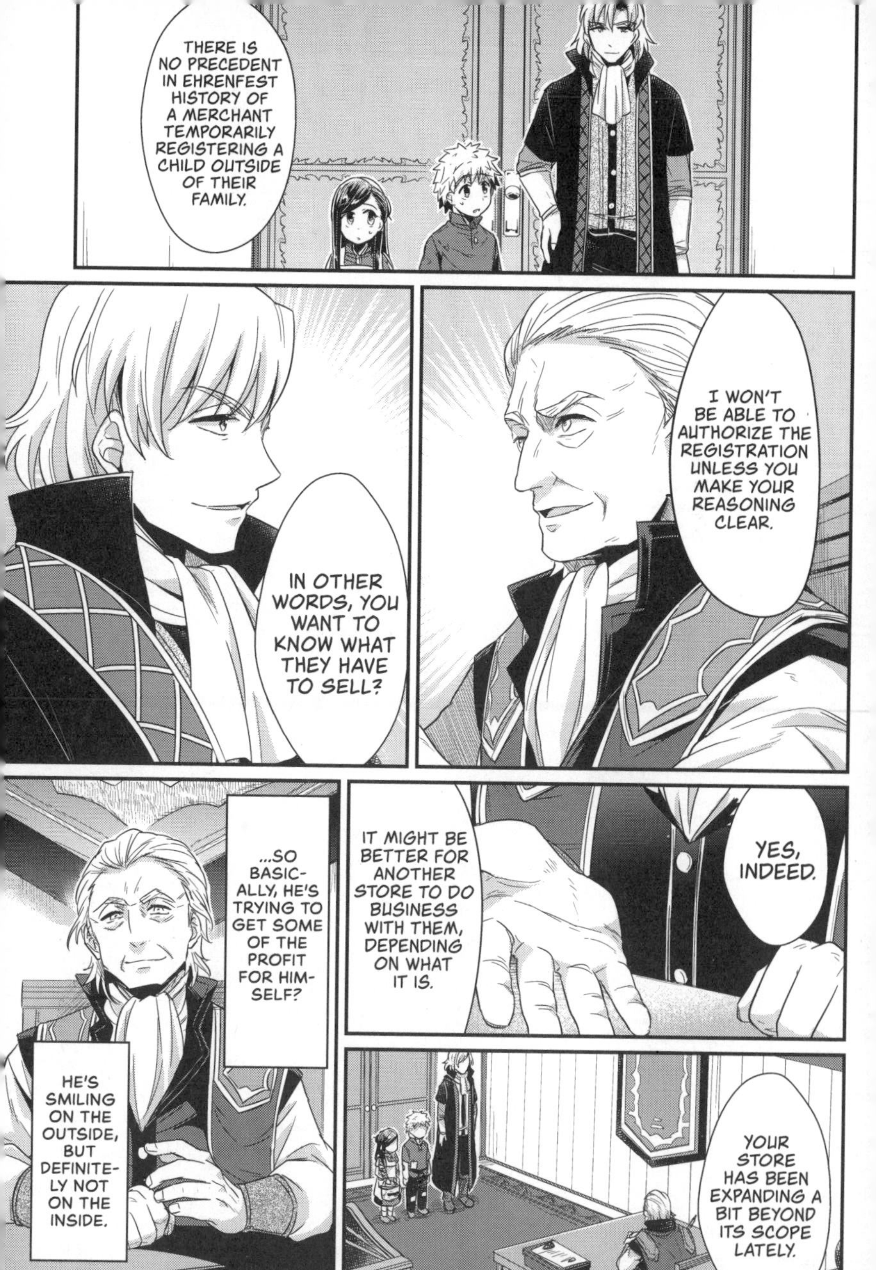
THERE IS NO PRECEDENT IN EHRENFEST HISTORY OF A MERCHANT TEMPORARILY REGISTERING A CHILD OUTSIDE OF THEIR FAMILY.
I WON'T BE ABLE TO AUTHORIZE THE REGISTRATION UNLESS YOU MAKE YOUR REASONING CLEAR.
IN OTHER WORDS, YOU WANT TO KNOW WHAT THEY HAVE TO SELL?
YES, INDEED.
IT MIGHT BE BETTER FOR ANOTHER STORE TO DO BUSINESS WITH THEM, DEPENDING ON WHAT IT IS.
YOUR STORE HAS BEEN EXPANDING A BIT BEYOND ITS SCOPE LATELY.
...SO BASIC-ALLY, HE'S TRYING TO GET SOME OF THE PROFIT FOR HIM-SELF?
HE'S SMILING ON THE OUTSIDE, BUT DEFINITE-LY NOT ON THE INSIDE.

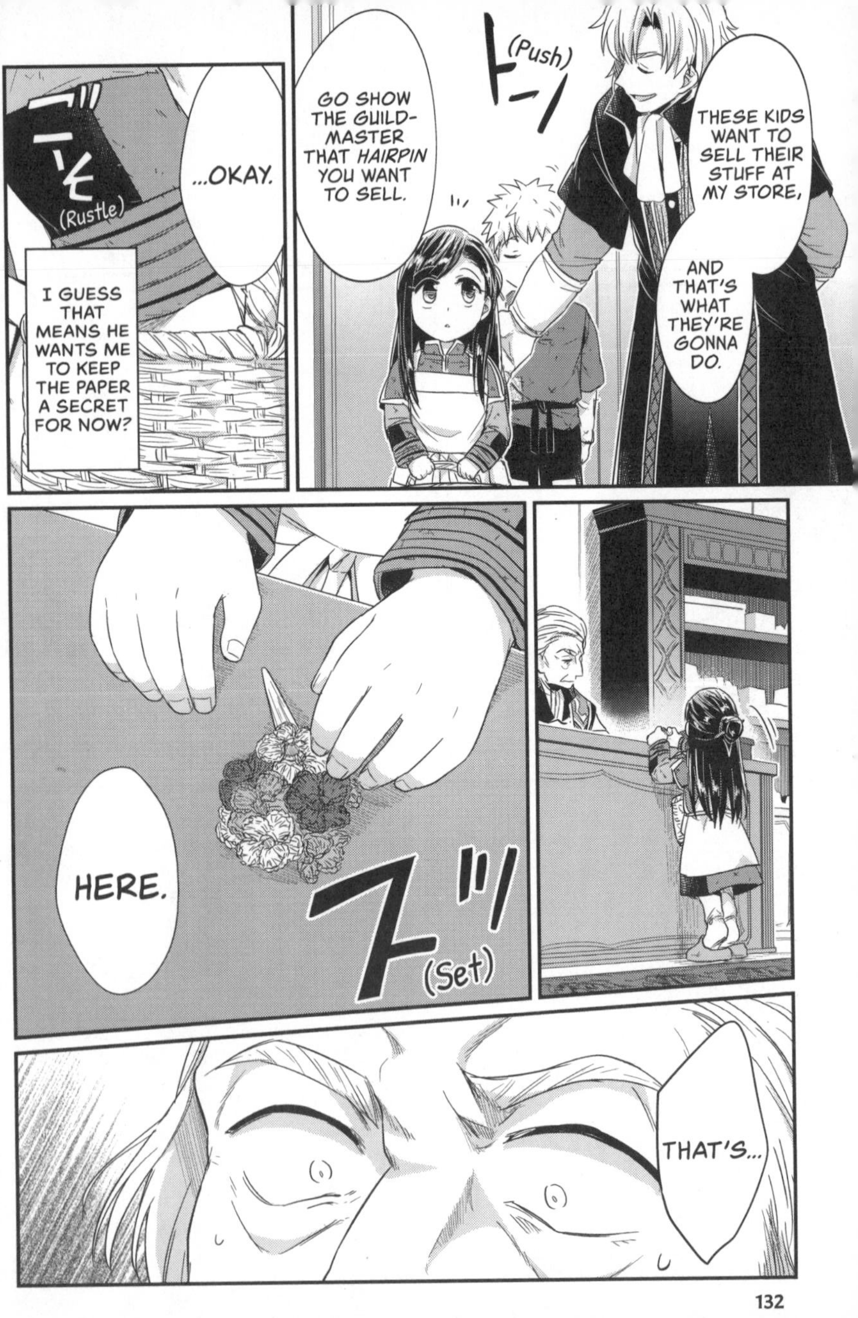
(Push)
THESE KIDS WANT TO SELL THEIR STUFF AT MY STORE,
AND THAT'S WHAT THEY'RE GONNA DO.
GO SHOW THE GUILD-MASTER THAT HAIRPIN YOU WANT TO SELL.
...OKAY.
(Rustle)
I GUESS THAT MEANS HE WANTS ME TO KEEP THE PAPER A SECRET FOR NOW?
HERE.
(Set)
THAT'S...

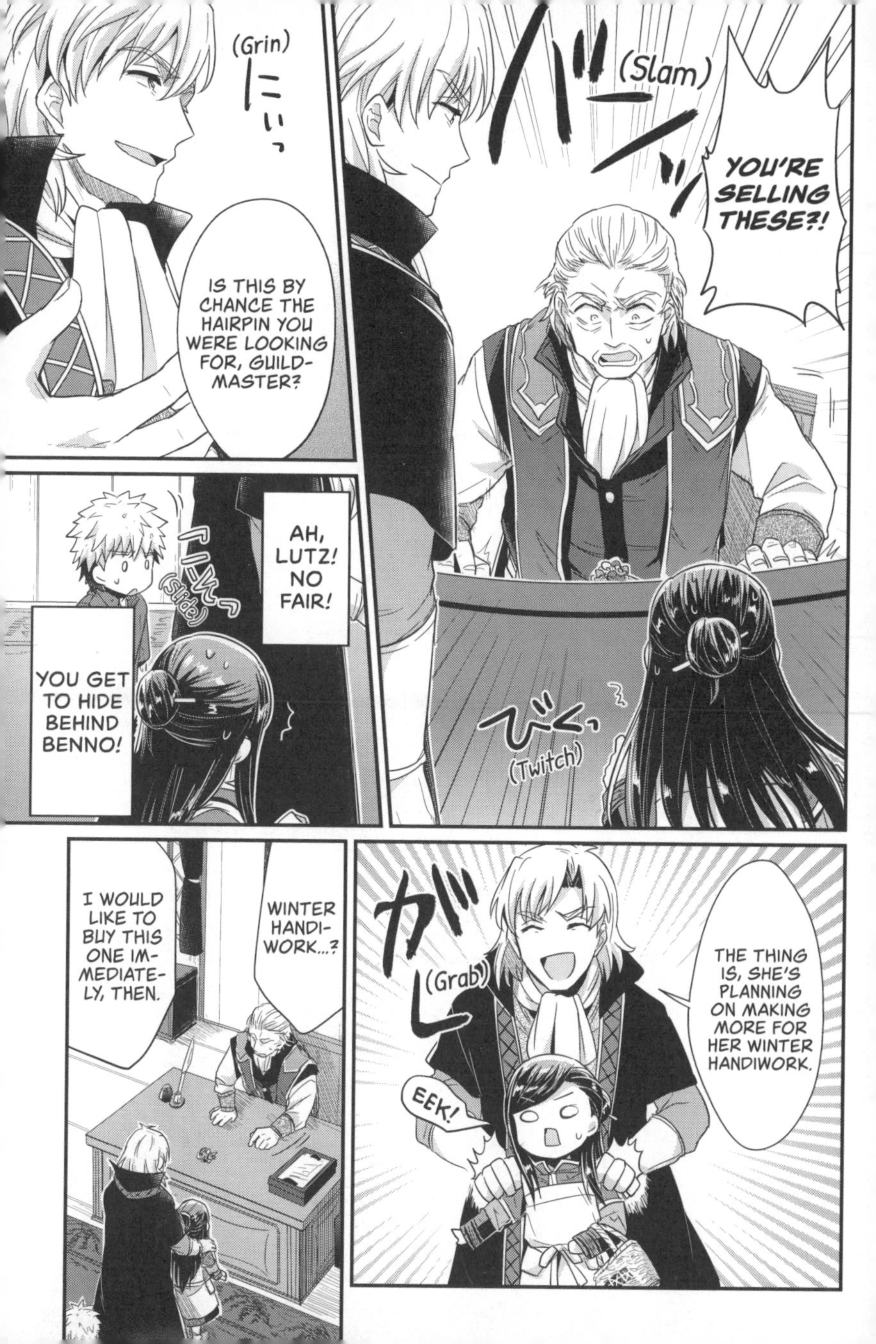

(Slam)
YOU'RE SELLING THESE?!
(Twitch)
(Grin)
IS THIS BY CHANCE THE HAIRPIN YOU WERE LOOKING FOR, GUILD-MASTER?
AH, LUTZ! NO FAIR!
(Slide)
YOU GET TO HIDE BEHIND BENNO!
(Grab)
THE THING IS, SHE'S PLANNING ON MAKING MORE FOR HER WINTER HANDIWORK.
EEK!
WINTER HANDI-WORK...?
I WOULD LIKE TO BUY THIS ONE IM-MEDIATE-LY, THEN.

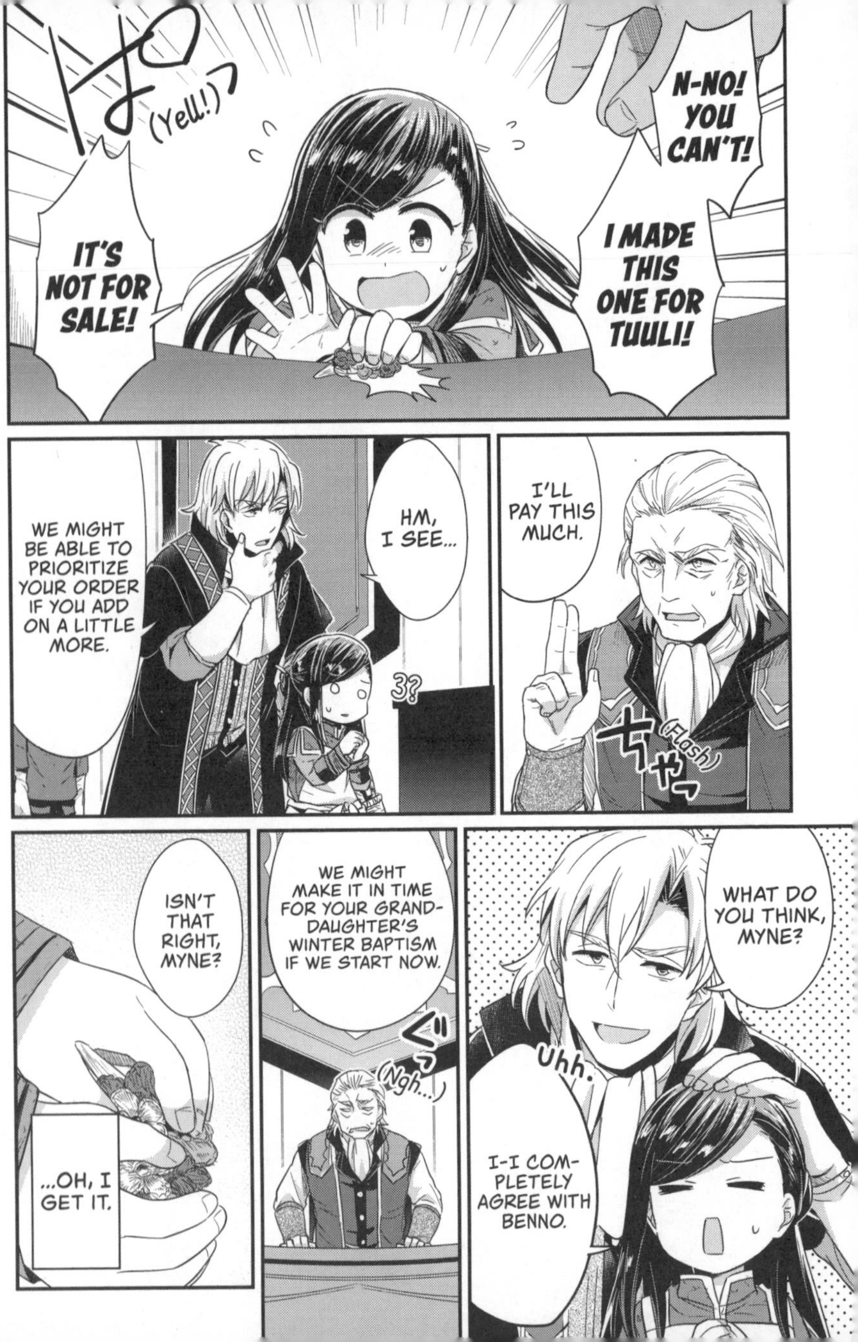
N-NO! YOU CAN'T!
(Yell!)
I MADE THIS ONE FOR TUULI!
IT'S NOT FOR SALE!
I'LL PAY THIS MUCH.
(Flash)
HM, I SEE...
3?
WE MIGHT BE ABLE TO PRIORITIZE YOUR ORDER IF YOU ADD ON A LITTLE MORE.
WHAT DO YOU THINK, MYNE?
Uhh.
I-I COMPLETELY AGREE WITH BENNO.
WE MIGHT MAKE IT IN TIME FOR YOUR GRAND-DAUGHTER'S WINTER BAPTISM IF WE START NOW.
(Ngh...)
ISN'T THAT RIGHT, MYNE?
...OH, I GET IT.

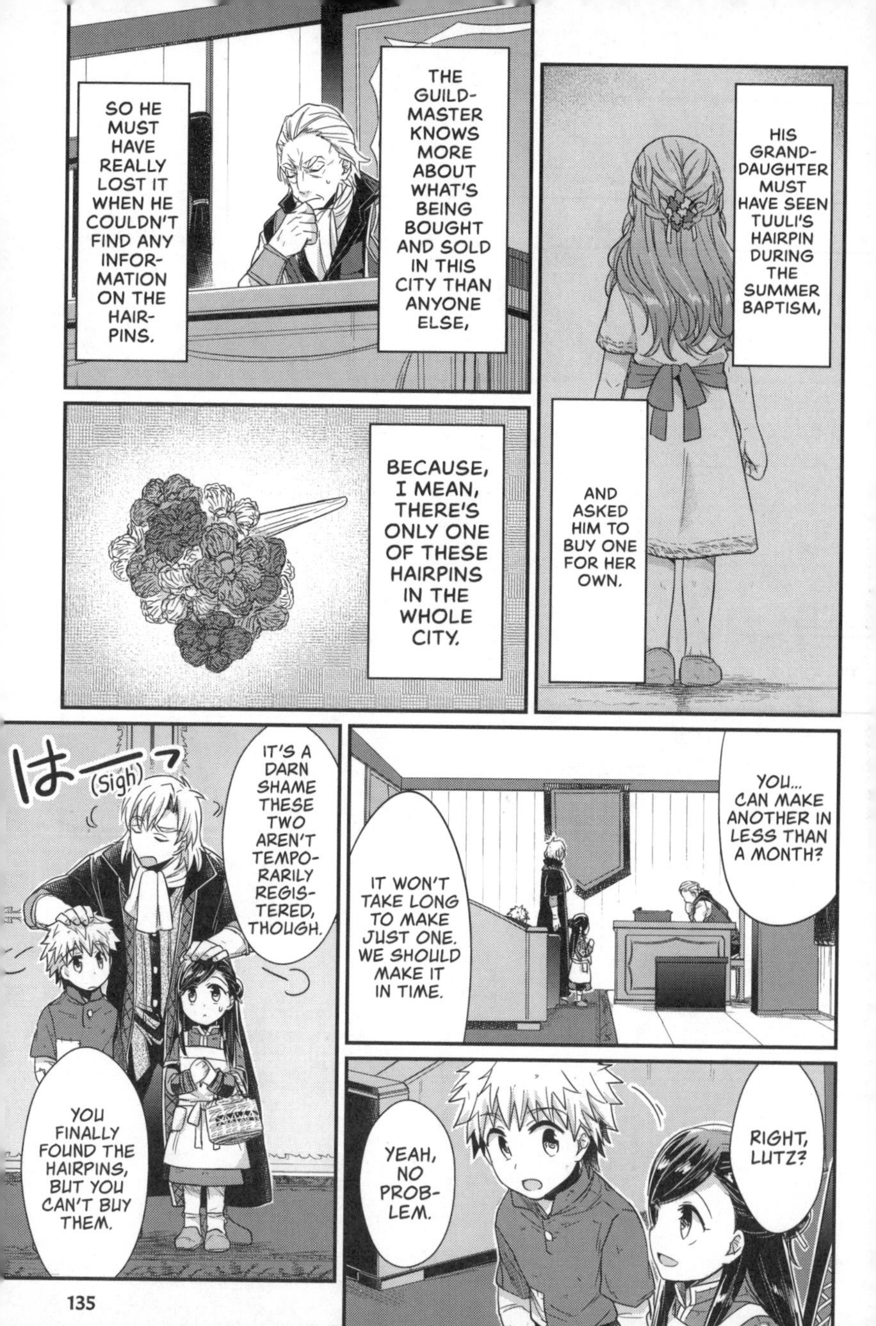
HIS GRAND-DAUGHTER MUST HAVE SEEN TUULI'S HAIRPIN DURING THE SUMMER BAPTISM,
AND ASKED HIM TO BUY ONE FOR HER OWN.
THE GUILD-MASTER KNOWS MORE ABOUT WHAT'S BEING BOUGHT AND SOLD IN THIS CITY THAN ANYONE ELSE,
SO HE MUST HAVE REALLY LOST IT WHEN HE COULDN'T FIND ANY INFOR-MATION ON THE HAIR-PINS.
BECAUSE, I MEAN, THERE'S ONLY ONE OF THESE HAIRPINS IN THE WHOLE CITY.
YOU... CAN MAKE ANOTHER IN LESS THAN A MONTH?
IT WON'T TAKE LONG TO MAKE JUST ONE. WE SHOULD MAKE IT IN TIME.
RIGHT, LUTZ?
YEAH, NO PROB-LEM.
はーっ
(Sigh)
IT'S A DARN SHAME THESE TWO AREN'T TEMPO-RARILY REGIS-TERED, THOUGH.
YOU FINALLY FOUND THE HAIRPINS, BUT YOU CAN'T BUY THEM.

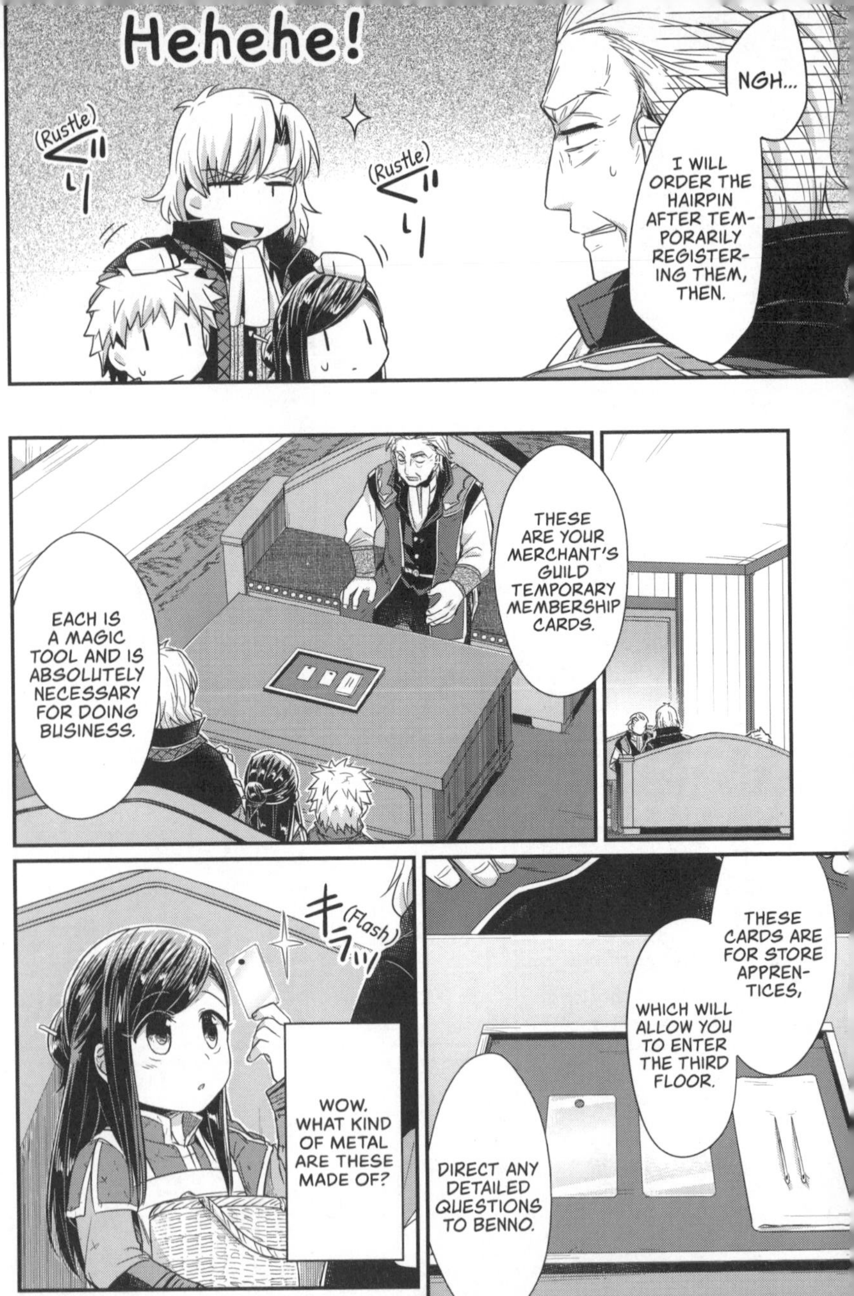
NGH...
I WILL ORDER THE HAIRPIN AFTER TEMPORARILY REGISTERING THEM, THEN.
Hehehe!
(Rustle)
(Rustle)
THESE ARE YOUR MERCHANT'S GUILD TEMPORARY MEMBERSHIP CARDS.
EACH IS A MAGIC TOOL AND IS ABSOLUTELY NECESSARY FOR DOING BUSINESS.
THESE CARDS ARE FOR STORE APPRENTICES,
WHICH WILL ALLOW YOU TO ENTER THE THIRD FLOOR.
DIRECT ANY DETAILED QUESTIONS TO BENNO.
(Flash)
WOW. WHAT KIND OF METAL ARE THESE MADE OF?

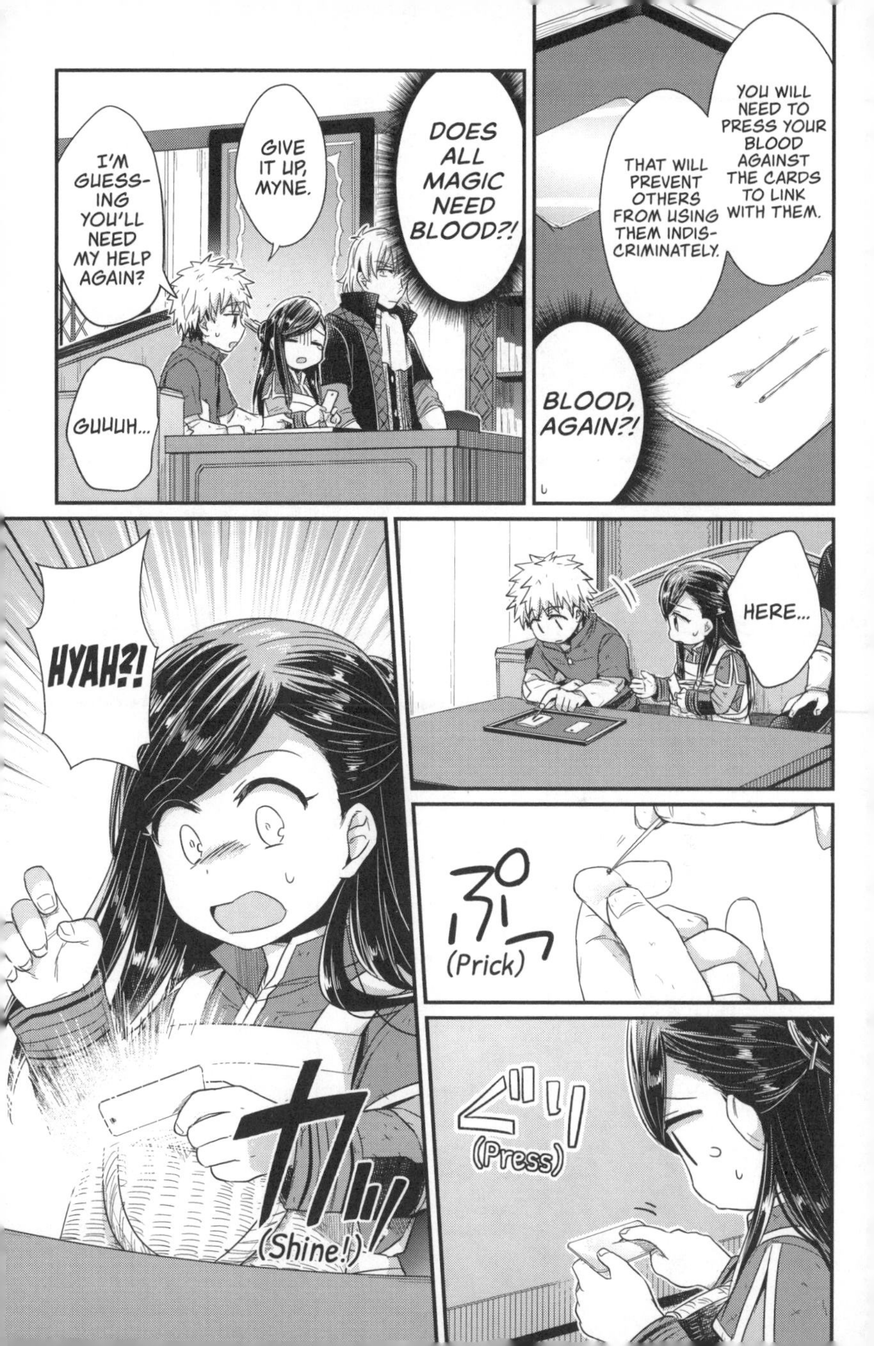
YOU WILL NEED TO PRESS YOUR BLOOD AGAINST THE CARDS TO LINK WITH THEM.
THAT WILL PREVENT OTHERS FROM USING THEM INDIS-CRIMINATELY.
BLOOD, AGAIN?!
DOES ALL MAGIC NEED BLOOD?!
GIVE IT UP, MYNE.
I'M GUESS-ING YOU'LL NEED MY HELP AGAIN?
GUUUH...
HERE...
(Prick)
(Press)
HYAH?!
(Shine!)

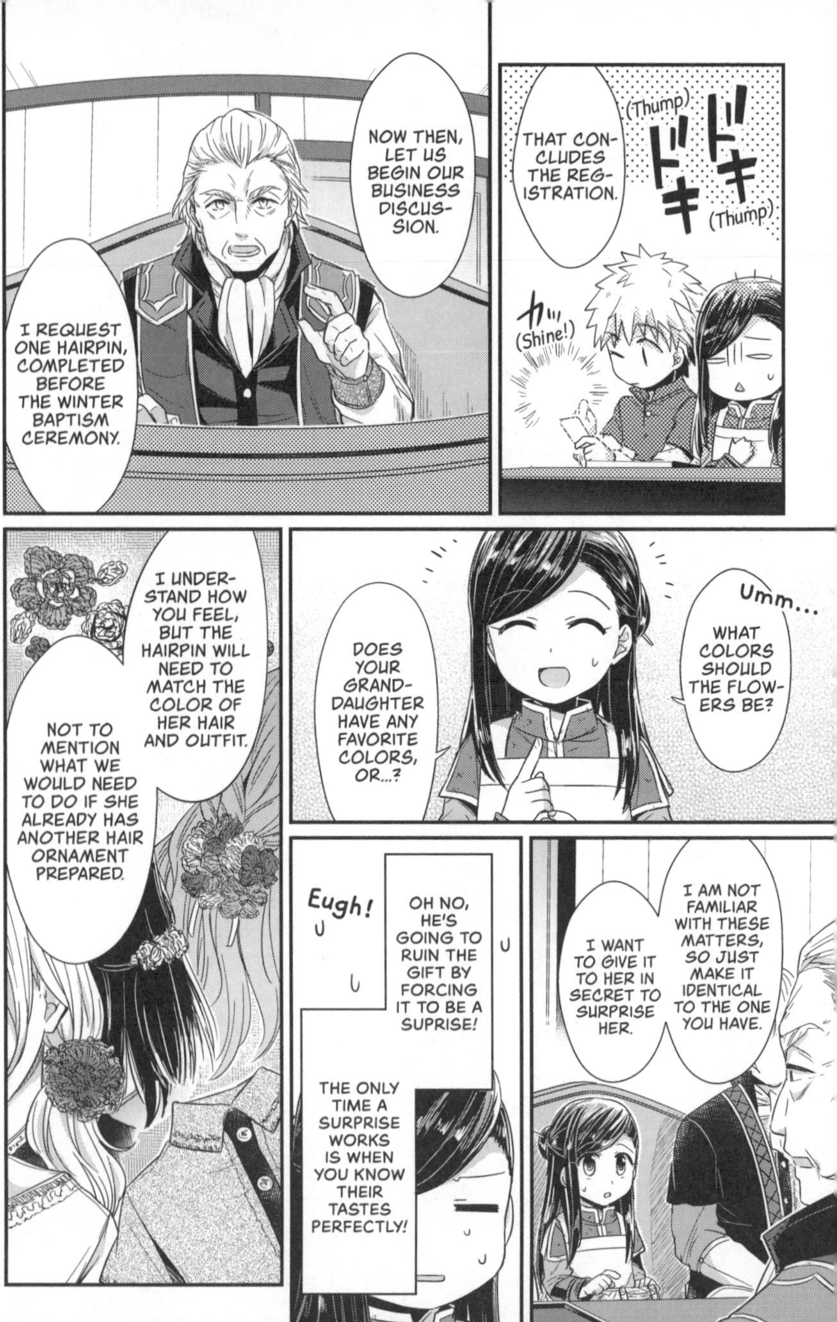

(Thump)
(Thump)
THAT CON-CLUDES THE REG-ISTRATION.
(Shine!)
NOW THEN, LET US BEGIN OUR BUSINESS DISCUS-SION.
I REQUEST ONE HAIRPIN, COMPLETED BEFORE THE WINTER BAPTISM CEREMONY.
Umm...
WHAT COLORS SHOULD THE FLOW-ERS BE?
DOES YOUR GRAND-DAUGHTER HAVE ANY FAVORITE COLORS, OR...?
I AM NOT FAMILIAR WITH THESE MATTERS, SO JUST MAKE IT IDENTICAL TO THE ONE YOU HAVE.
I WANT TO GIVE IT TO HER IN SECRET TO SURPRISE HER.
Eugh!
OH NO, HE'S GOING TO RUIN THE GIFT BY FORCING IT TO BE A SUPRISE!
THE ONLY TIME A SURPRISE WORKS IS WHEN YOU KNOW THEIR TASTES PERFECTLY!
I UNDER-STAND HOW YOU FEEL, BUT THE HAIRPIN WILL NEED TO MATCH THE COLOR OF HER HAIR AND OUTFIT.
NOT TO MENTION WHAT WE WOULD NEED TO DO IF SHE ALREADY HAS ANOTHER HAIR ORNAMENT PREPARED.

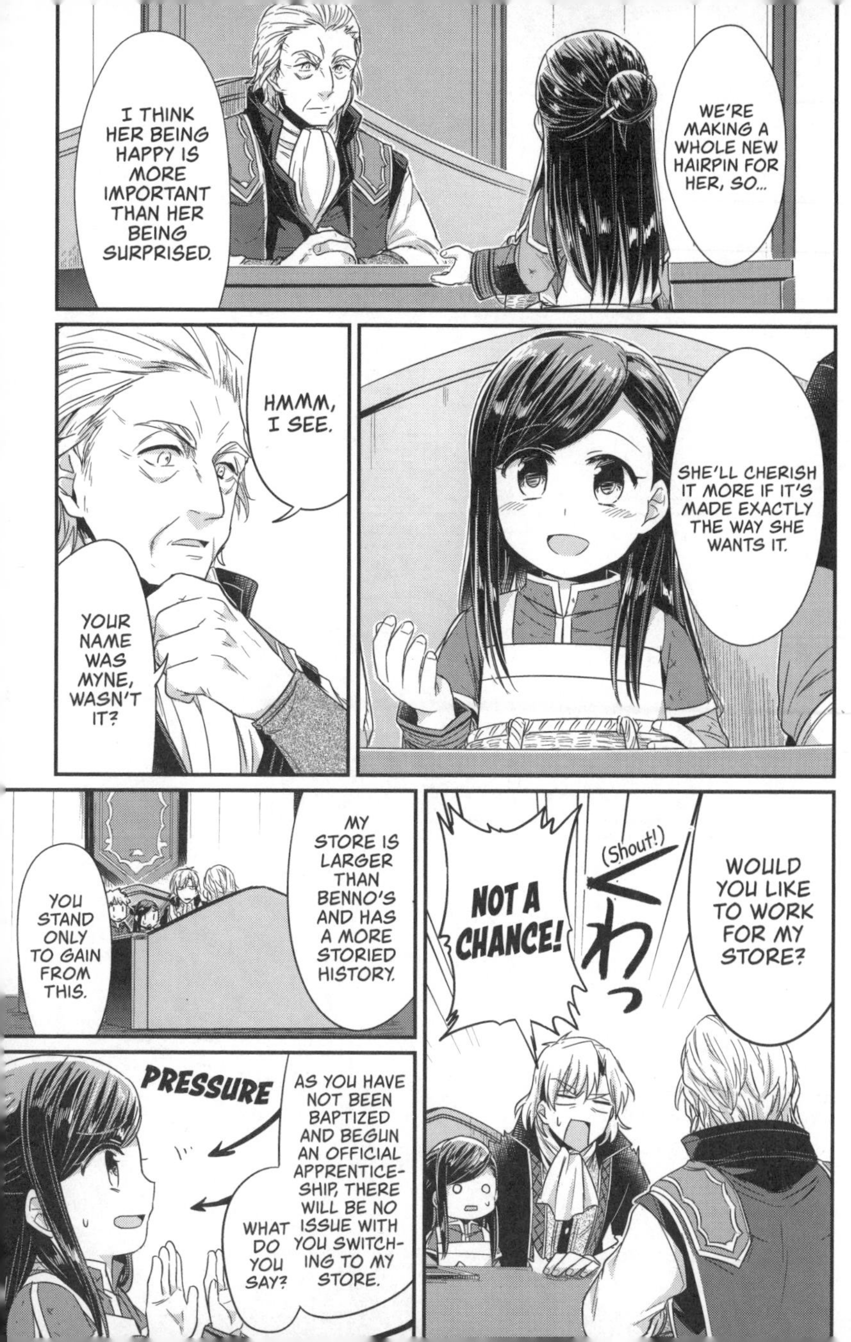
WE'RE MAKING A WHOLE NEW HAIRPIN FOR HER, SO...
I THINK HER BEING HAPPY IS MORE IMPORTANT THAN HER BEING SURPRISED.
SHE'LL CHERISH IT MORE IF IT'S MADE EXACTLY THE WAY SHE WANTS IT.
HMMM, I SEE.
YOUR NAME WAS MYNE, WASN'T IT?
WOULD YOU LIKE TO WORK FOR MY STORE?
(Shout!)
わっ
NOT A CHANCE!
MY STORE IS LARGER THAN BENNO'S AND HAS A MORE STORIED HISTORY.
YOU STAND ONLY TO GAIN FROM THIS.
AS YOU HAVE NOT BEEN BAPTIZED AND BEGUN AN OFFICIAL APPRENTICE-SHIP, THERE WILL BE NO ISSUE WITH YOU SWITCH-ING TO MY STORE.
WHAT DO YOU SAY?
PRESSURE

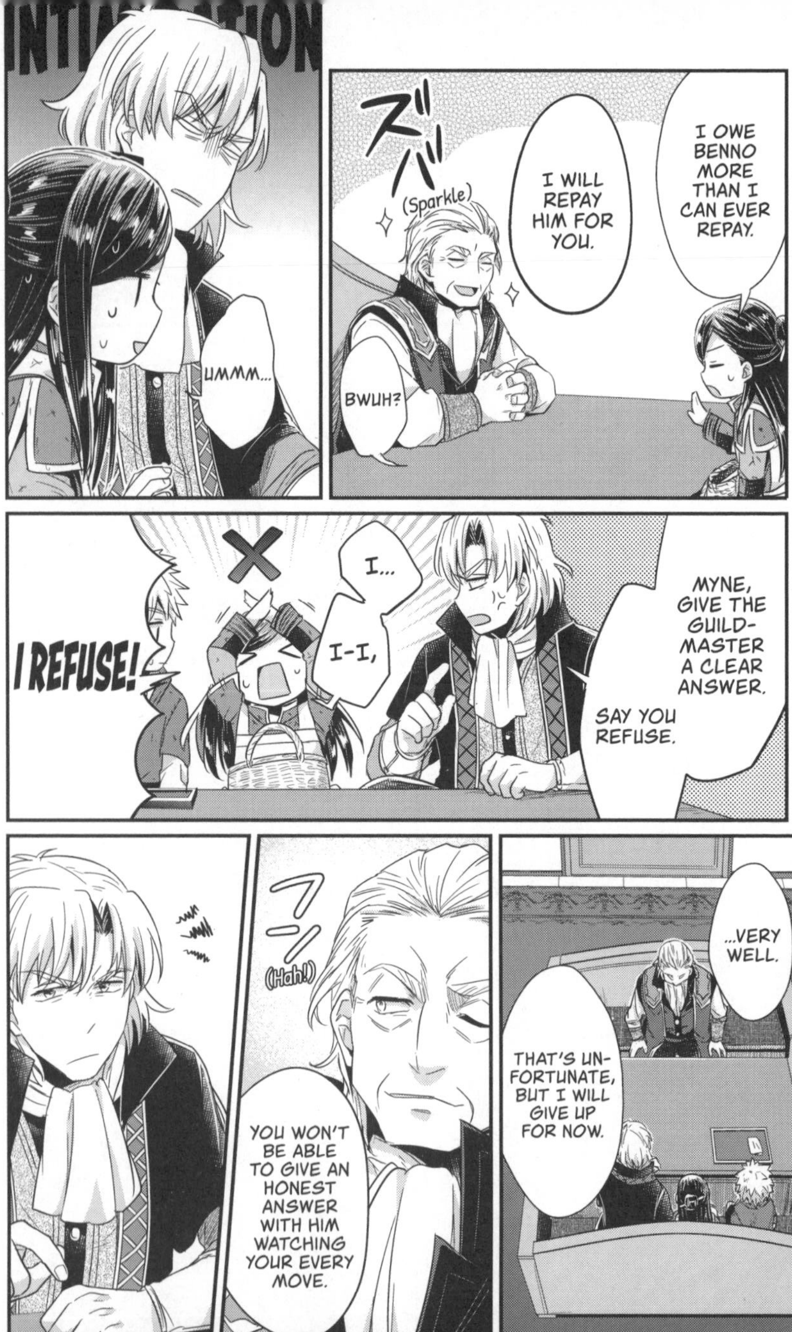
I OWE BENNO MORE THAN I CAN EVER REPAY.
I WILL REPAY HIM FOR YOU.
ズバ
(Sparkle)
BWUH?
UMMM...
MYNE, GIVE THE GUILD-MASTER A CLEAR ANSWER.
SAY YOU REFUSE.
I...
I-I,
I REFUSE!
...VERY WELL.
THAT'S UN-FORTUNATE, BUT I WILL GIVE UP FOR NOW.
フー
(Hah!)
YOU WON'T BE ABLE TO GIVE AN HONEST ANSWER WITH HIM WATCHING YOUR EVERY MOVE.

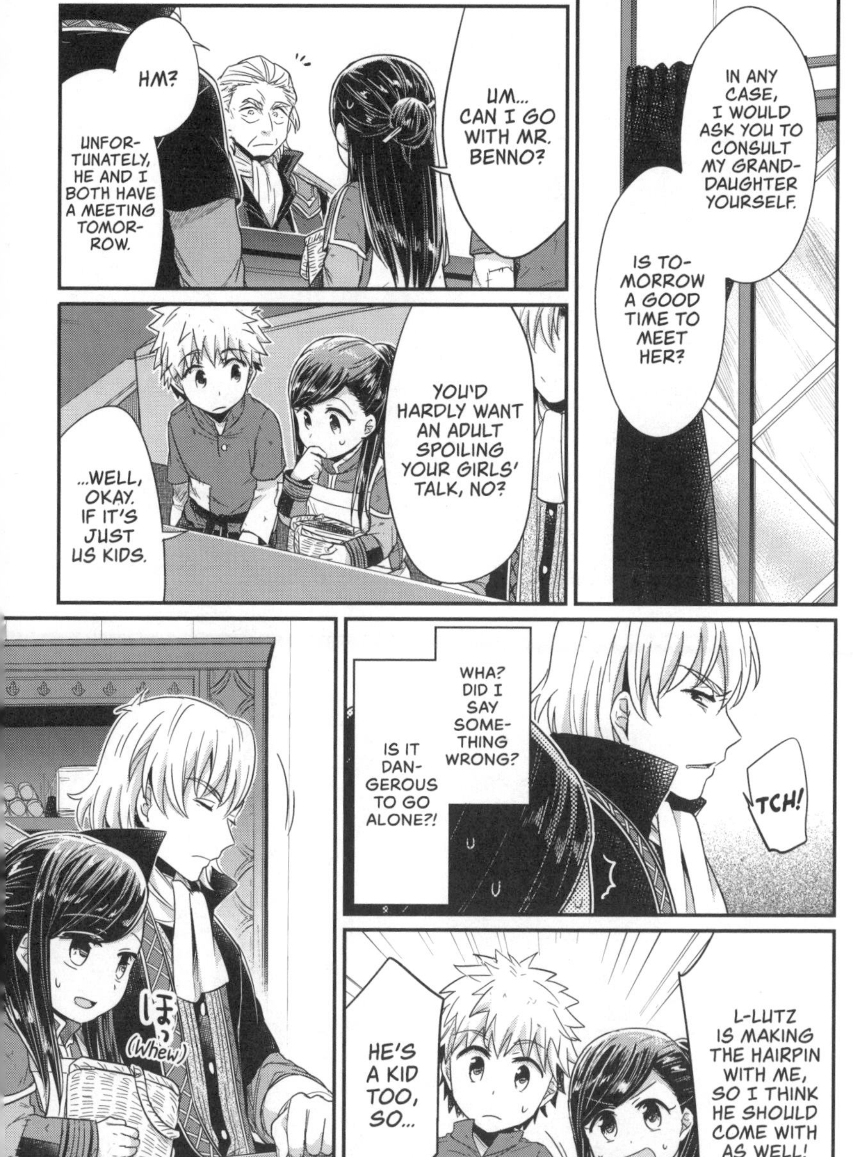
IN ANY CASE, I WOULD ASK YOU TO CONSULT MY GRAND-DAUGHTER YOURSELF.
IS TO-MORROW A GOOD TIME TO MEET HER?
UM... CAN I GO WITH MR. BENNO?
HM?
UNFOR-TUNATELY, HE AND I BOTH HAVE A MEETING TOMOR-ROW.
YOU'D HARDLY WANT AN ADULT SPOILING YOUR GIRLS' TALK, NO?
...WELL, OKAY. IF IT'S JUST US KIDS.
TCH!
WHA? DID I SAY SOME-THING WRONG?
IS IT DAN-GEROUS TO GO ALONE?!
L-LUTZ IS MAKING THE HAIRPIN WITH ME, SO I THINK HE SHOULD COME WITH AS WELL!
HE'S A KID TOO, SO...
ほっ
(Whew)

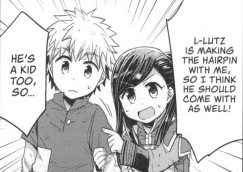

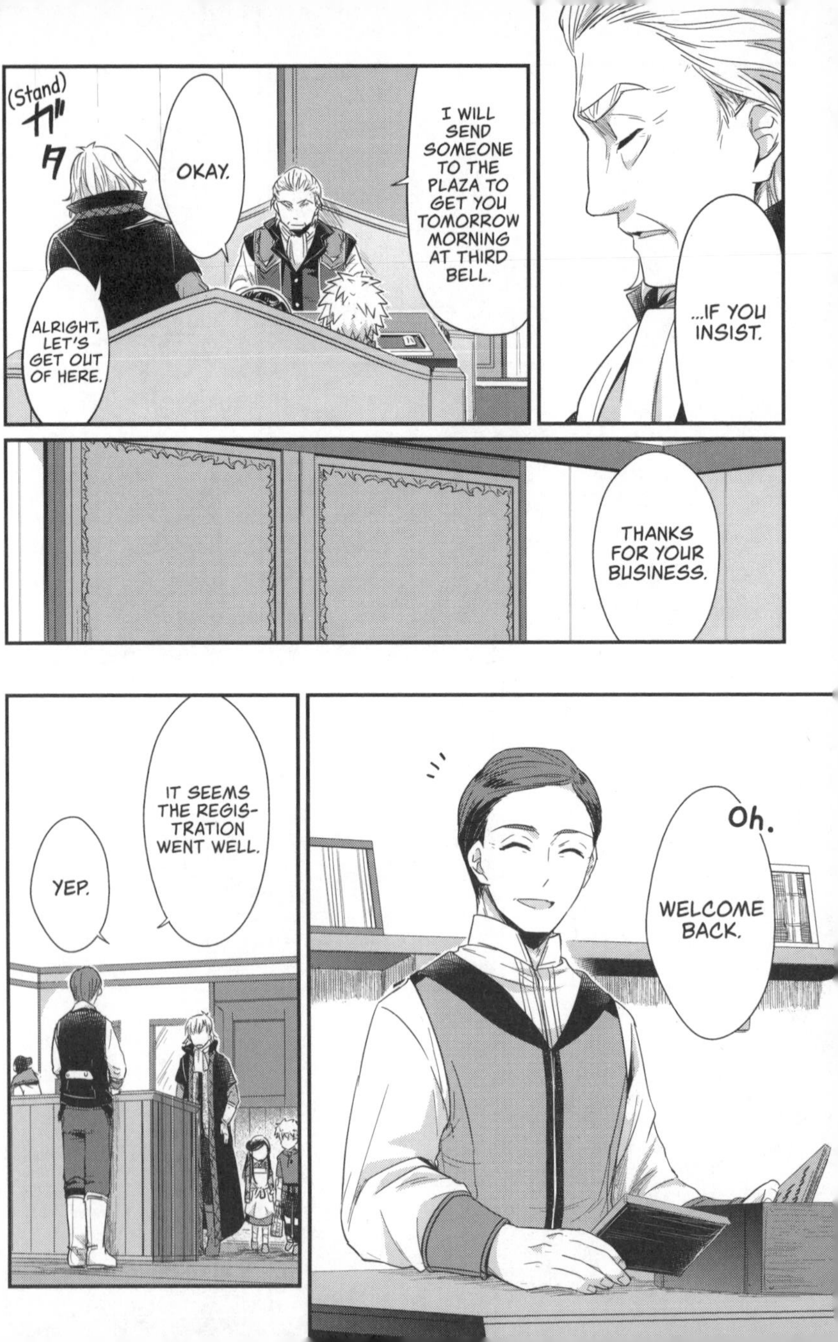
...IF YOU INSIST.
I WILL SEND SOMEONE TO THE PLAZA TO GET YOU TOMORROW MORNING AT THIRD BELL.
OKAY.
(Stand)
ガタ
ALRIGHT, LET'S GET OUT OF HERE.
THANKS FOR YOUR BUSINESS.
Oh.
WELCOME BACK.
IT SEEMS THE REGIS- TRATION WENT WELL.
YEP.

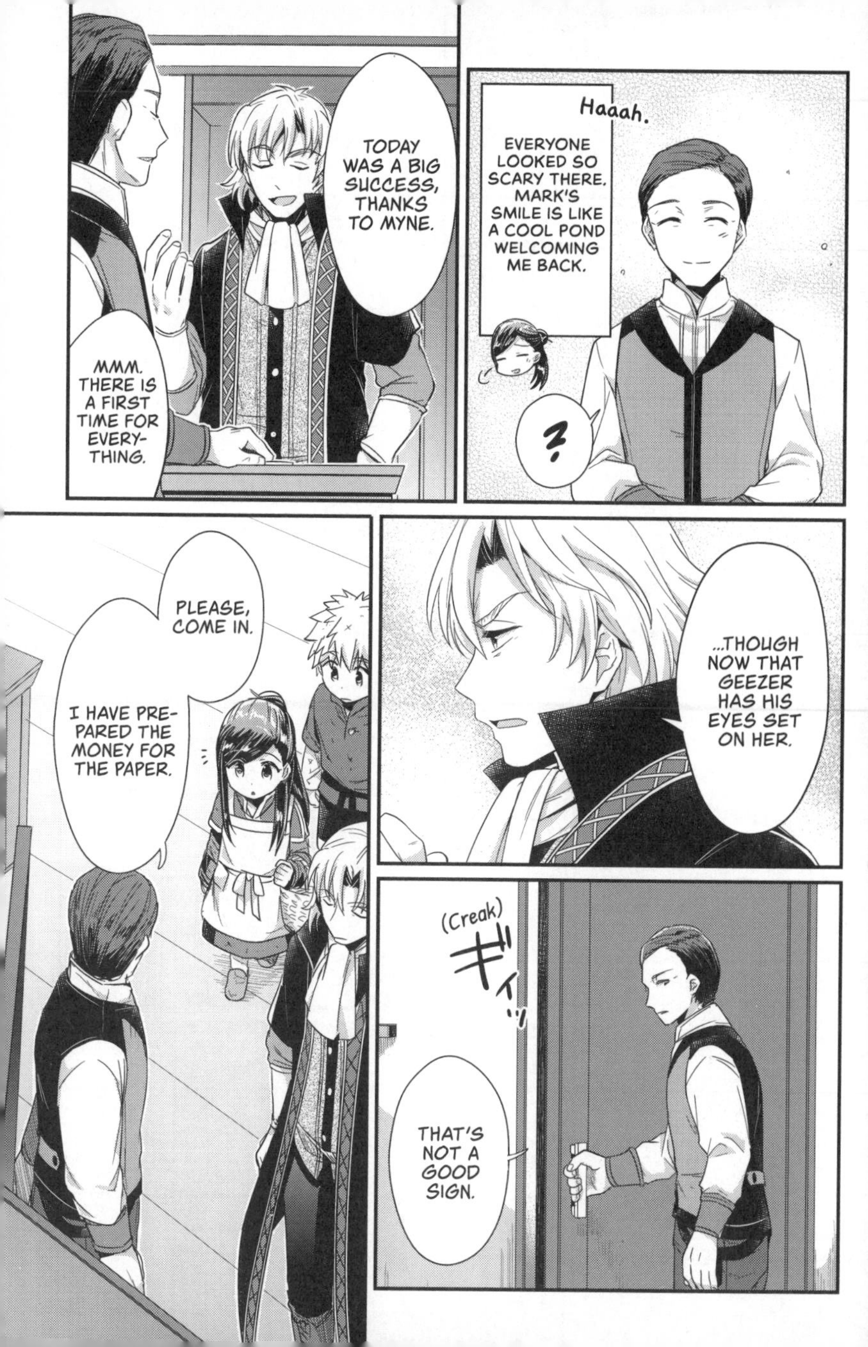
Haaah.
EVERYONE LOOKED SO SCARY THERE. MARK'S SMILE IS LIKE A COOL POND WELCOMING ME BACK.
?
TODAY WAS A BIG SUCCESS, THANKS TO MYNE.
MMM. THERE IS A FIRST TIME FOR EVERY-THING.
...THOUGH NOW THAT GEEZER HAS HIS EYES SET ON HER.
(Creak)
THAT'S NOT A GOOD SIGN.
PLEASE, COME IN.
I HAVE PRE-PARED THE MONEY FOR THE PAPER.

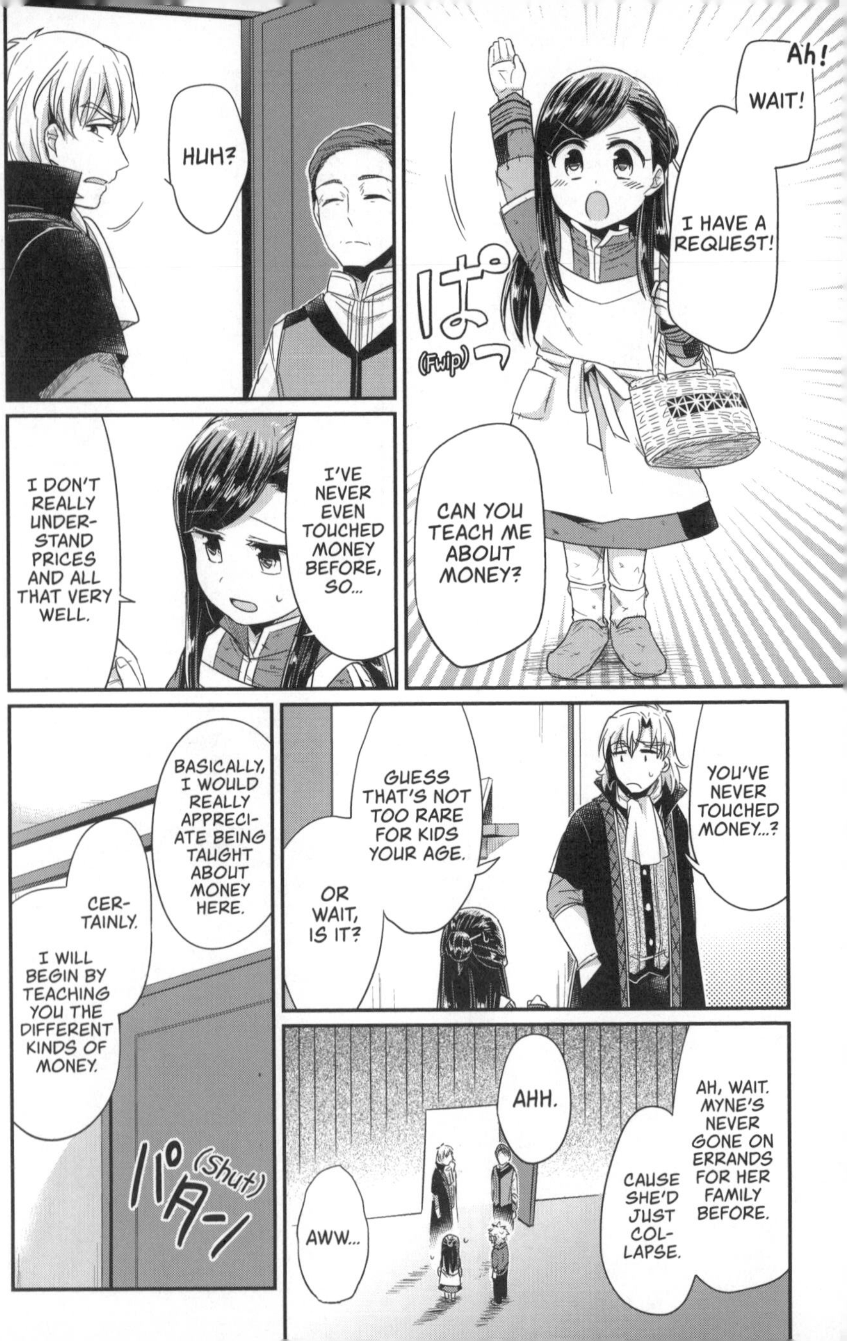
Ah!
WAIT!
I HAVE A REQUEST!
ぱっ
(Fwip)
CAN YOU TEACH ME ABOUT MONEY?
HUH?
I'VE NEVER EVEN TOUCHED MONEY BEFORE, SO...
I DON'T REALLY UNDERSTAND PRICES AND ALL THAT VERY WELL.
YOU'VE NEVER TOUCHED MONEY...?
GUESS THAT'S NOT TOO RARE FOR KIDS YOUR AGE.
OR WAIT, IS IT?
AH, WAIT. MYNE'S NEVER GONE ON ERRANDS FOR HER FAMILY BEFORE.
CAUSE SHE'D JUST COLLAPSE.
AHH.
AWW...
BASICALLY, I WOULD REALLY APPRECIATE BEING TAUGHT ABOUT MONEY HERE.
CERTAINLY.
I WILL BEGIN BY TEACHING YOU THE DIFFERENT KINDS OF MONEY.
パターン
(Shut)

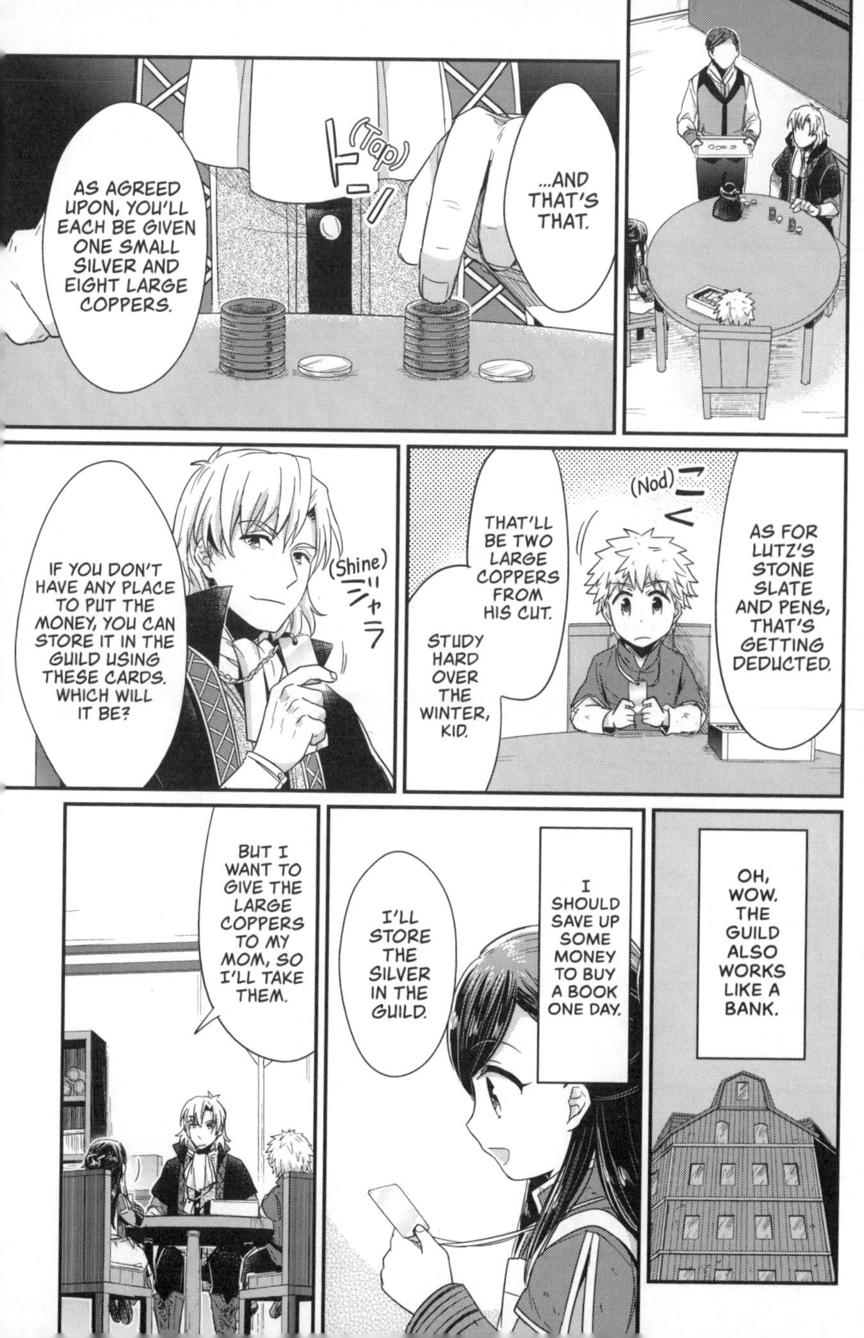
...AND THAT'S THAT.
(Tap)
AS AGREED UPON, YOU'LL EACH BE GIVEN ONE SMALL SILVER AND EIGHT LARGE COPPERS.
AS FOR LUTZ'S STONE SLATE AND PENS, THAT'S GETTING DEDUCTED.
(Nod)
THAT'LL BE TWO LARGE COPPERS FROM HIS CUT.
STUDY HARD OVER THE WINTER, KID.
(Shine)
IF YOU DON'T HAVE ANY PLACE TO PUT THE MONEY, YOU CAN STORE IT IN THE GUILD USING THESE CARDS. WHICH WILL IT BE?
OH, WOW. THE GUILD ALSO WORKS LIKE A BANK.
I SHOULD SAVE UP SOME MONEY TO BUY A BOOK ONE DAY.
I'LL STORE THE SILVER IN THE GUILD.
BUT I WANT TO GIVE THE LARGE COPPERS TO MY MOM, SO I'LL TAKE THEM.

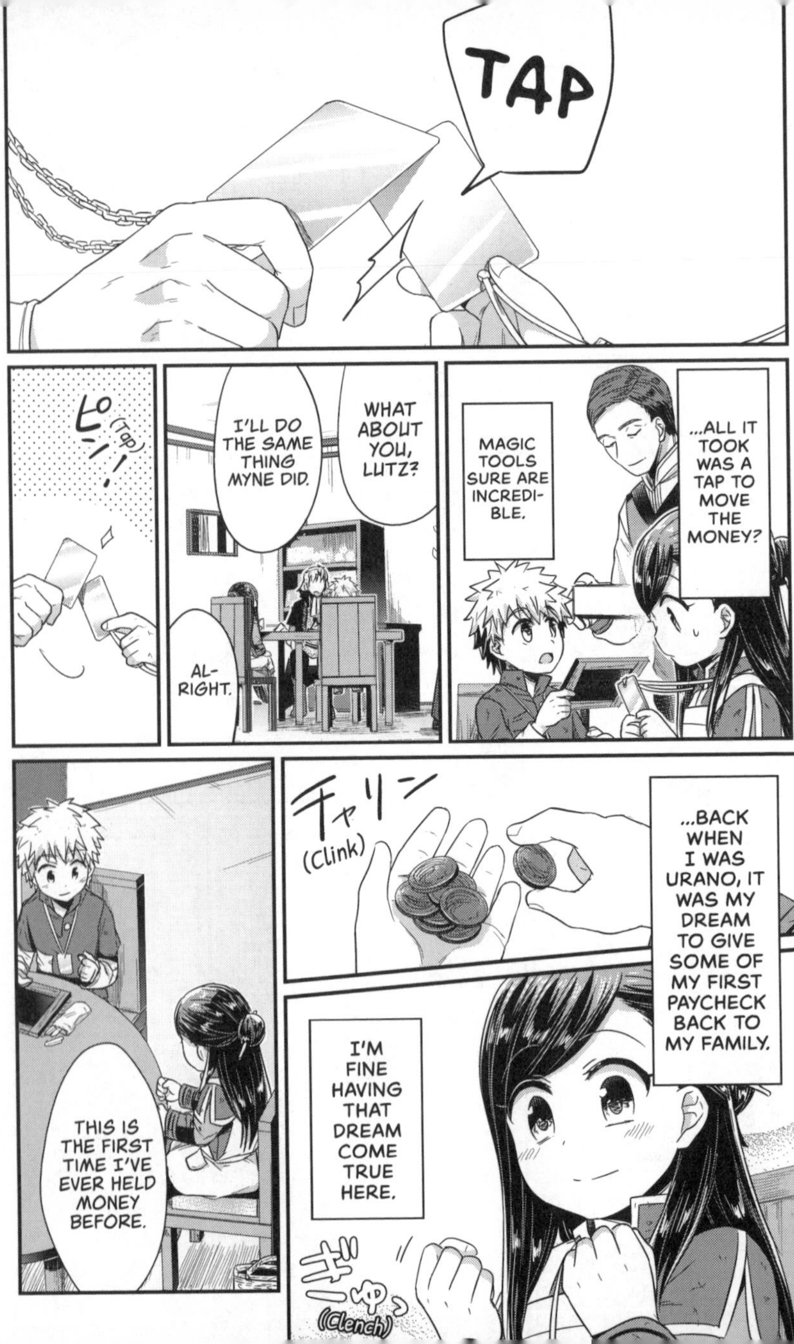
TAP
...ALL IT TOOK WAS A TAP TO MOVE THE MONEY?
MAGIC TOOLS SURE ARE INCREDIBLE.
WHAT ABOUT YOU, LUTZ?
I'LL DO THE SAME THING MYNE DID.
ALRIGHT.
ピッ
(Tap)
チャリン
(Clink)
...BACK WHEN I WAS URANO, IT WAS MY DREAM TO GIVE SOME OF MY FIRST PAYCHECK BACK TO MY FAMILY.
I'M FINE HAVING THAT DREAM COME TRUE HERE.
ぎゅっ
(Clench)
THIS IS THE FIRST TIME I'VE EVER HELD MONEY BEFORE.

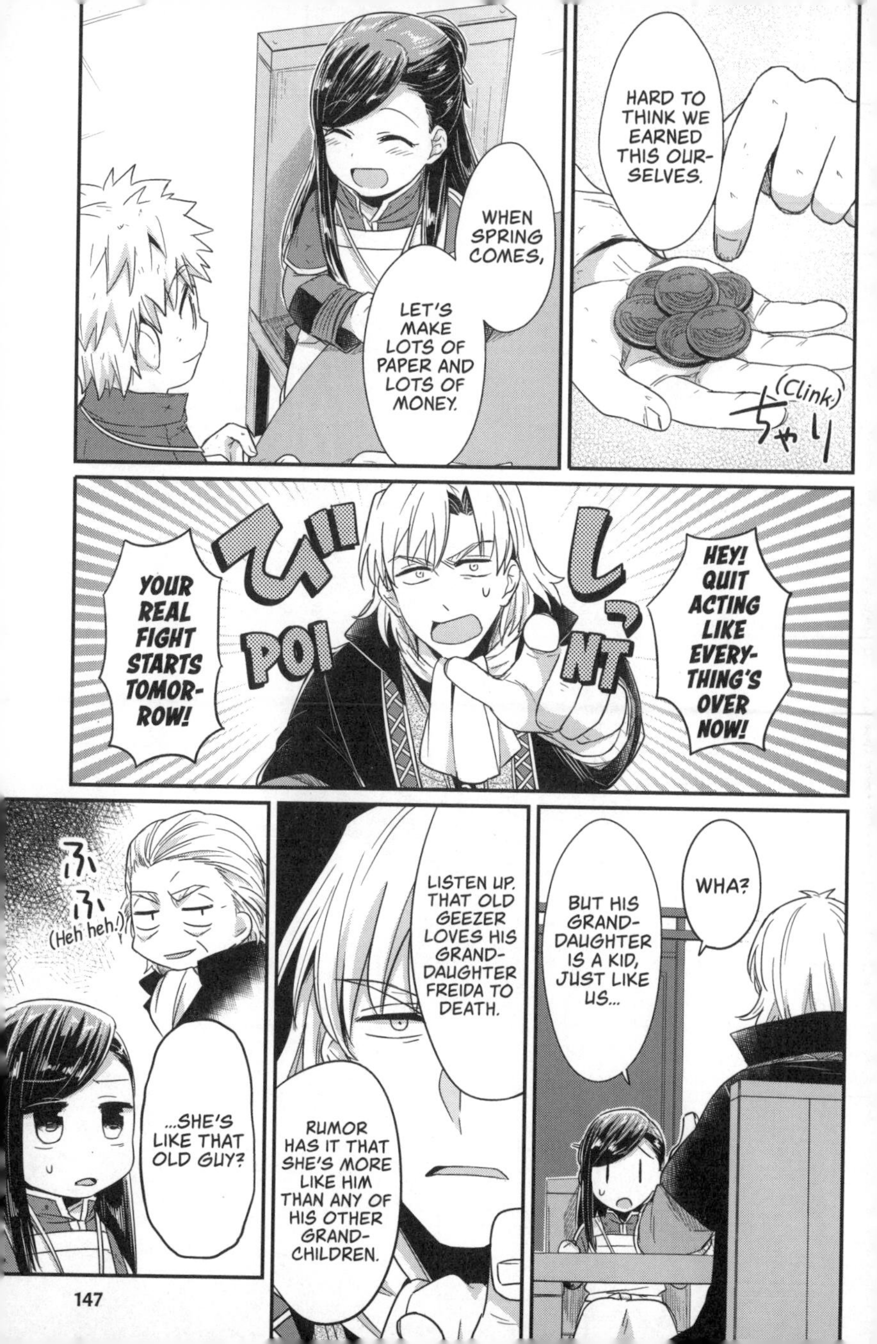
HARD TO THINK WE EARNED THIS OUR-SELVES.
(Clink)
ちゃり
WHEN SPRING COMES,
LET'S MAKE LOTS OF PAPER AND LOTS OF MONEY.
HEY! QUIT ACTING LIKE EVERY-THING'S OVER NOW!
びしっ
POINT
YOUR REAL FIGHT STARTS TOMOR-ROW!
WHA?
BUT HIS GRAND-DAUGHTER IS A KID, JUST LIKE US...
LISTEN UP. THAT OLD GEEZER LOVES HIS GRAND-DAUGHTER FREIDA TO DEATH.
RUMOR HAS IT THAT SHE'S MORE LIKE HIM THAN ANY OF HIS OTHER GRAND-CHILDREN.
ふふ
(Heh heh!)
...SHE'S LIKE THAT OLD GUY?

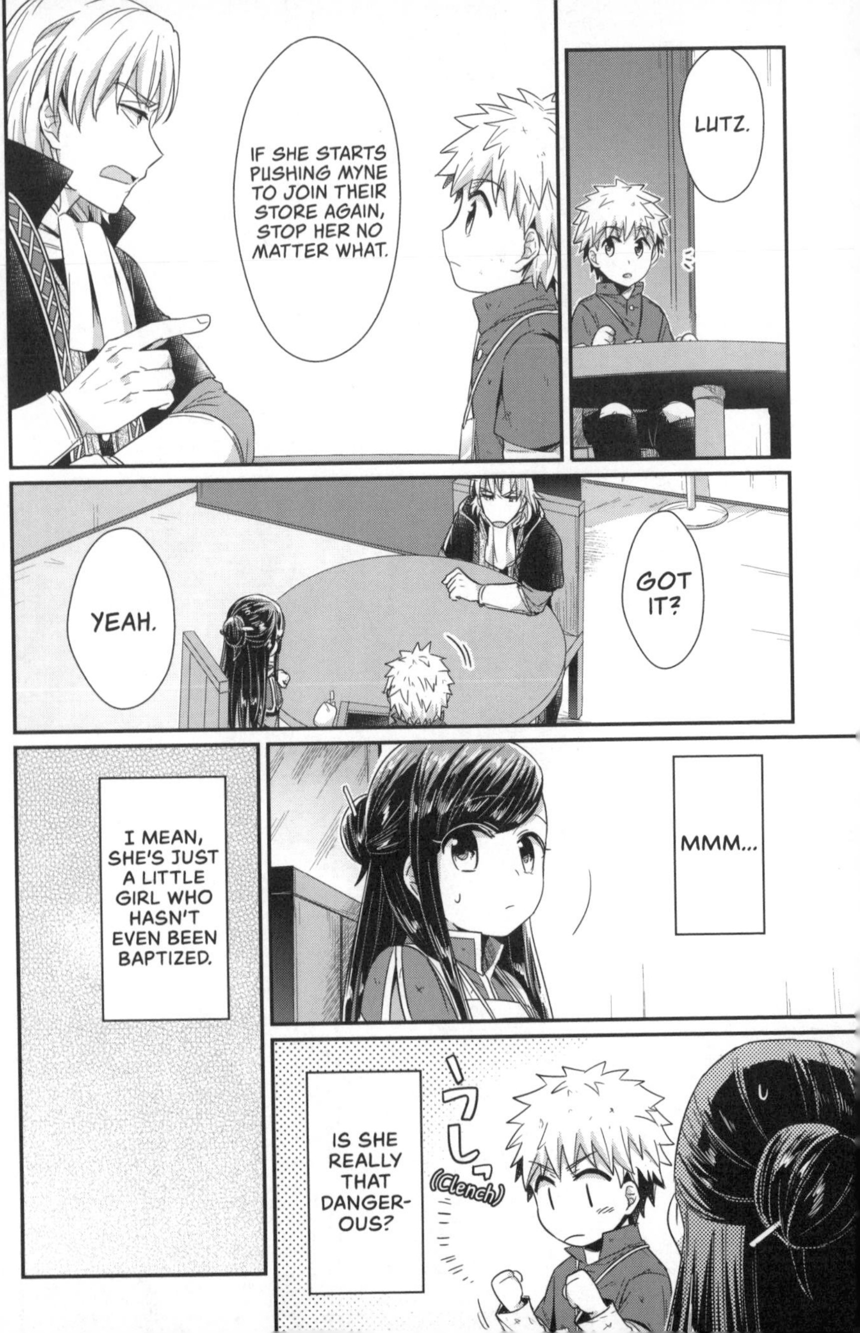
LUTZ.
IF SHE STARTS PUSHING MYNE TO JOIN THEIR STORE AGAIN, STOP HER NO MATTER WHAT.
GOT IT?
YEAH.
MMM...
(Clench)
IS SHE REALLY THAT DANGER-OUS?
I MEAN, SHE'S JUST A LITTLE GIRL WHO HASN'T EVEN BEEN BAPTIZED.

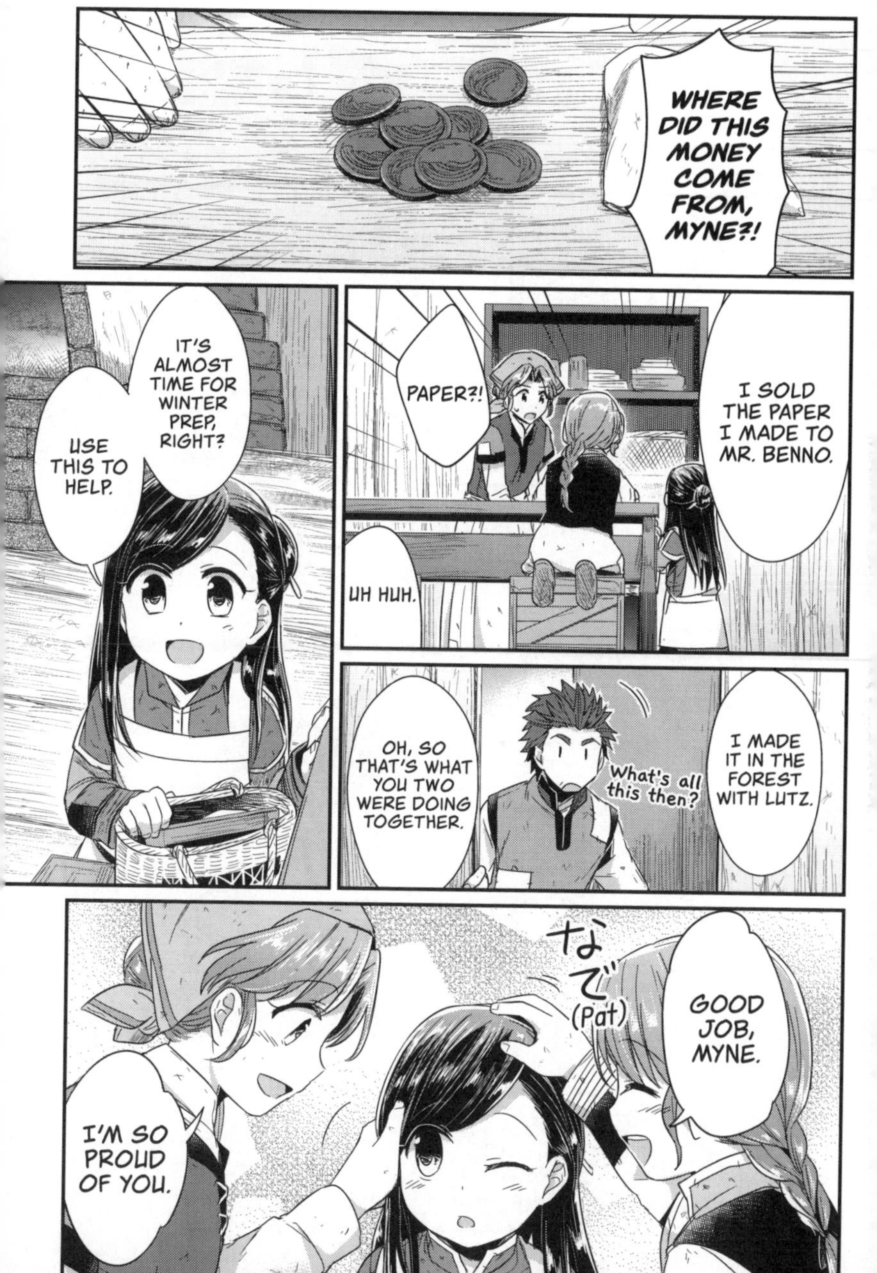
WHERE DID THIS MONEY COME FROM, MYNE?!
I SOLD THE PAPER I MADE TO MR. BENNO.
PAPER?!
UH HUH.
I MADE IT IN THE FOREST WITH LUTZ.
What's all this then?
OH, SO THAT'S WHAT YOU TWO WERE DOING TOGETHER.
IT'S ALMOST TIME FOR WINTER PREP, RIGHT?
USE THIS TO HELP.
GOOD JOB, MYNE.
なで
(Pat)
I'M SO PROUD OF YOU.

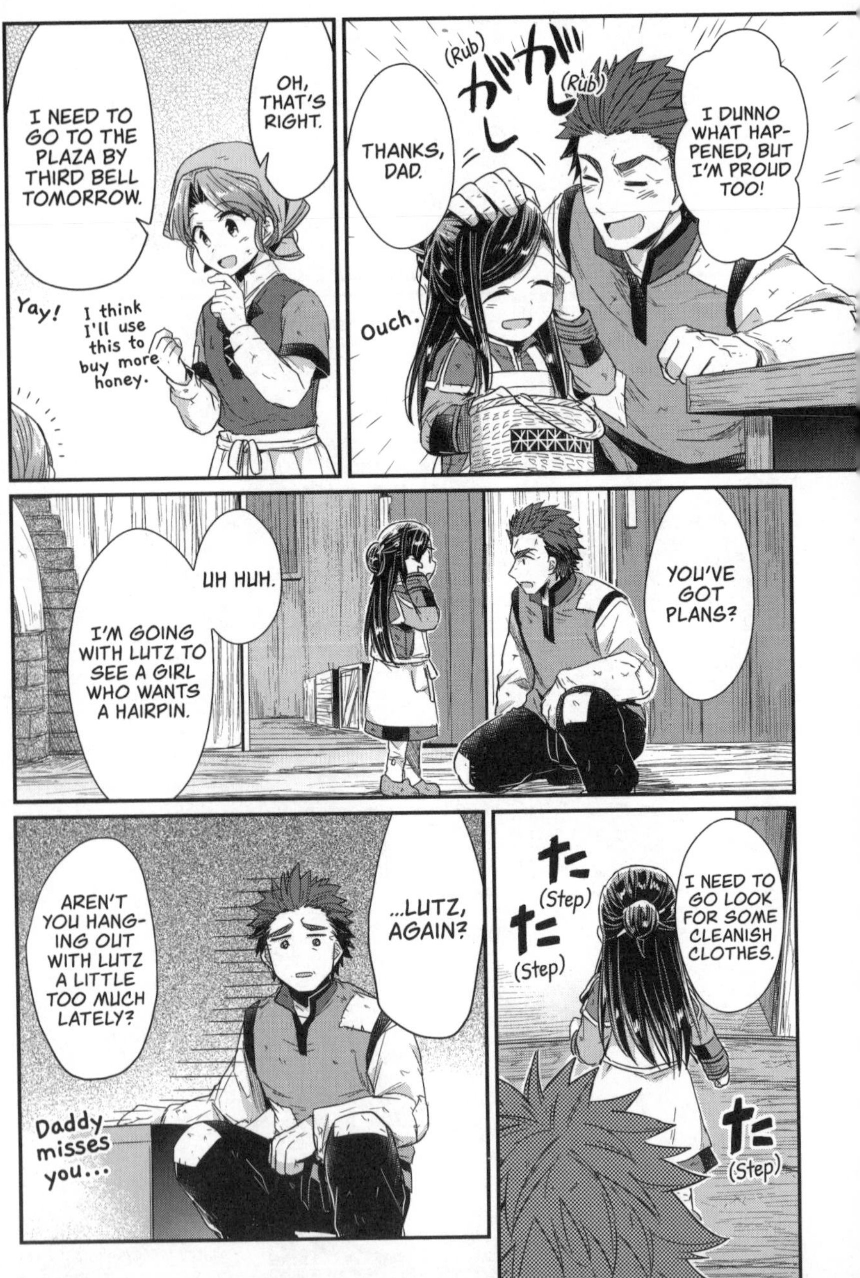
(Rub)
がしがし
(Rub)
I DUNNO WHAT HAP-PENED, BUT I'M PROUD TOO!
THANKS, DAD.
Ouch.
OH, THAT'S RIGHT.
I NEED TO GO TO THE PLAZA BY THIRD BELL TOMORROW.
Yay!
I think I'll use this to buy more honey.
YOU'VE GOT PLANS?
UH HUH.
I'M GOING WITH LUTZ TO SEE A GIRL WHO WANTS A HAIRPIN.
I NEED TO GO LOOK FOR SOME CLEANISH CLOTHES.
た (Step)
た (Step)
た (Step)
...LUTZ, AGAIN?
AREN'T YOU HANG-ING OUT WITH LUTZ A LITTLE TOO MUCH LATELY?
Daddy misses you...

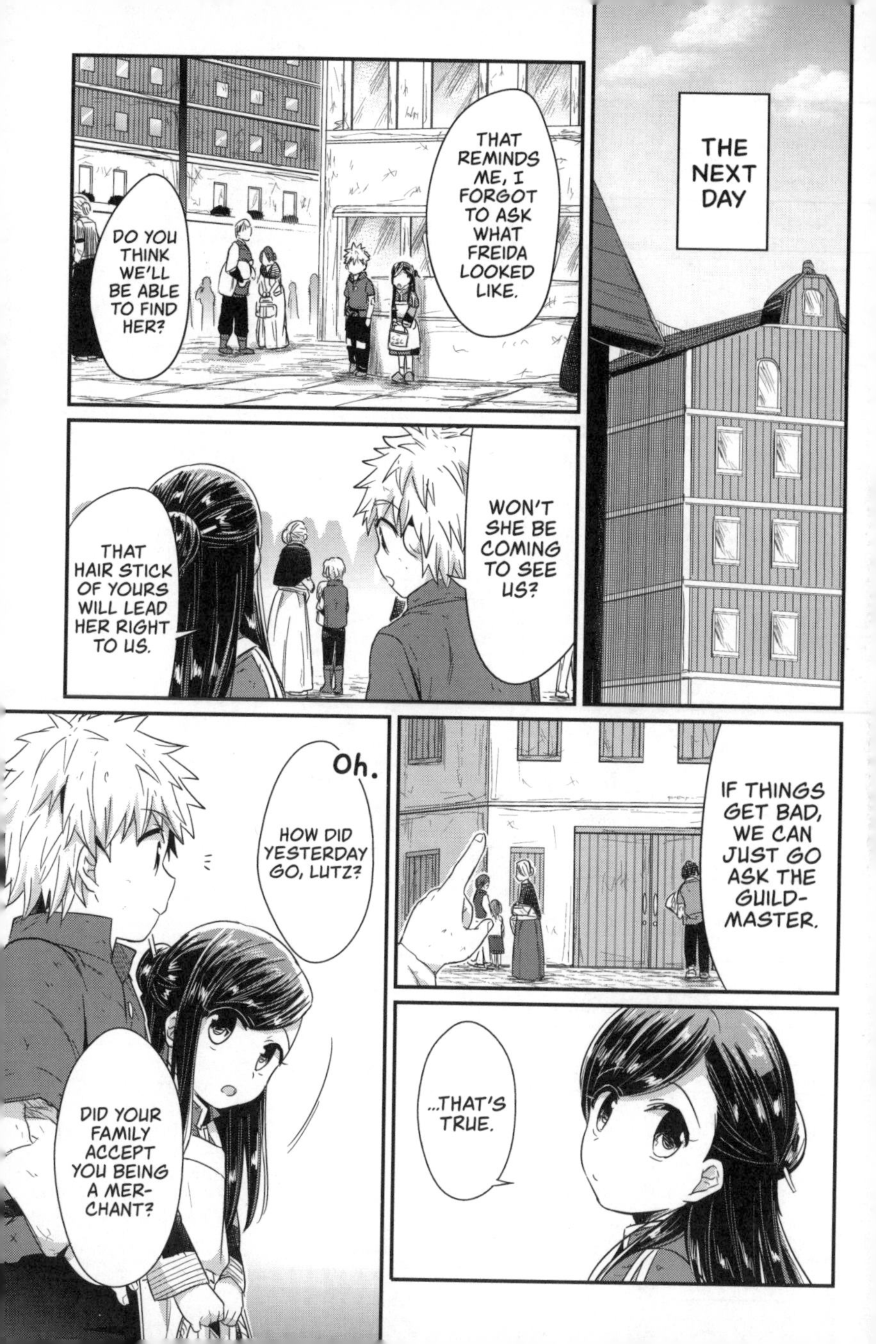
THE NEXT DAY
THAT REMINDS ME, I FORGOT TO ASK WHAT FREIDA LOOKED LIKE.
DO YOU THINK WE'LL BE ABLE TO FIND HER?
WON'T SHE BE COMING TO SEE US?
THAT HAIR STICK OF YOURS WILL LEAD HER RIGHT TO US.
IF THINGS GET BAD, WE CAN JUST GO ASK THE GUILD-MASTER.
...THAT'S TRUE.
Oh.
HOW DID YESTERDAY GO, LUTZ?
DID YOUR FAMILY ACCEPT YOU BEING A MER-CHANT?

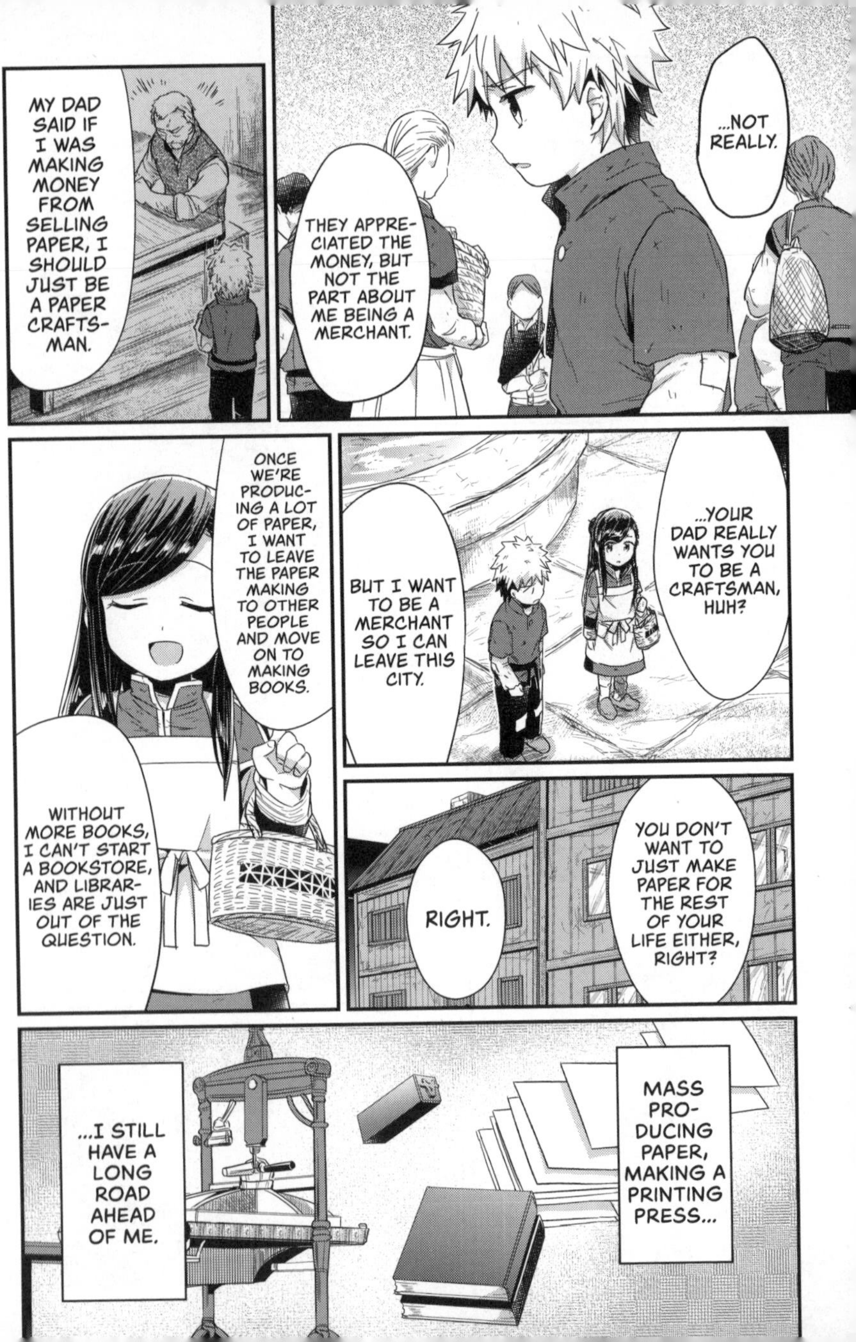
...NOT REALLY.
THEY APPRECIATED THE MONEY, BUT NOT THE PART ABOUT ME BEING A MERCHANT.
MY DAD SAID IF I WAS MAKING MONEY FROM SELLING PAPER, I SHOULD JUST BE A PAPER CRAFTSMAN.
...YOUR DAD REALLY WANTS YOU TO BE A CRAFTSMAN, HUH?
BUT I WANT TO BE A MERCHANT SO I CAN LEAVE THIS CITY.
YOU DON'T WANT TO JUST MAKE PAPER FOR THE REST OF YOUR LIFE EITHER, RIGHT?
RIGHT.
ONCE WE'RE PRODUCING A LOT OF PAPER, I WANT TO LEAVE THE PAPER MAKING TO OTHER PEOPLE AND MOVE ON TO MAKING BOOKS.
WITHOUT MORE BOOKS, I CAN'T START A BOOKSTORE, AND LIBRARIES ARE JUST OUT OF THE QUESTION.
MASS PRODUCING PAPER, MAKING A PRINTING PRESS...
...I STILL HAVE A LONG ROAD AHEAD OF ME.

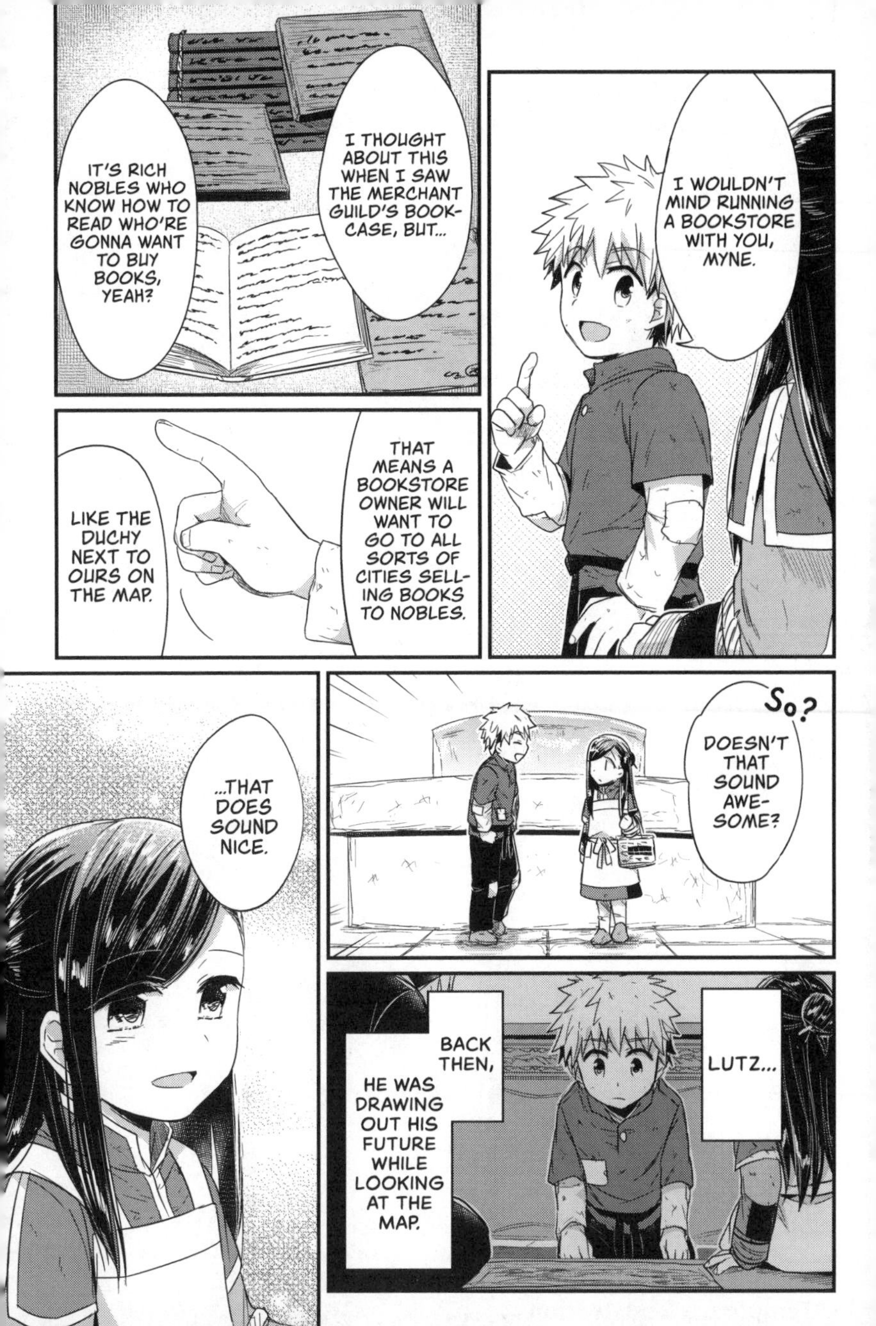
I WOULDN'T MIND RUNNING A BOOKSTORE WITH YOU, MYNE.
I THOUGHT ABOUT THIS WHEN I SAW THE MERCHANT GUILD'S BOOK-CASE, BUT...
IT'S RICH NOBLES WHO KNOW HOW TO READ WHO'RE GONNA WANT TO BUY BOOKS, YEAH?
THAT MEANS A BOOKSTORE OWNER WILL WANT TO GO TO ALL SORTS OF CITIES SELL-ING BOOKS TO NOBLES.
LIKE THE DUCHY NEXT TO OURS ON THE MAP.
So?
DOESN'T THAT SOUND AWE-SOME?
LUTZ...
BACK THEN, HE WAS DRAWING OUT HIS FUTURE WHILE LOOKING AT THE MAP.
...THAT DOES SOUND NICE.

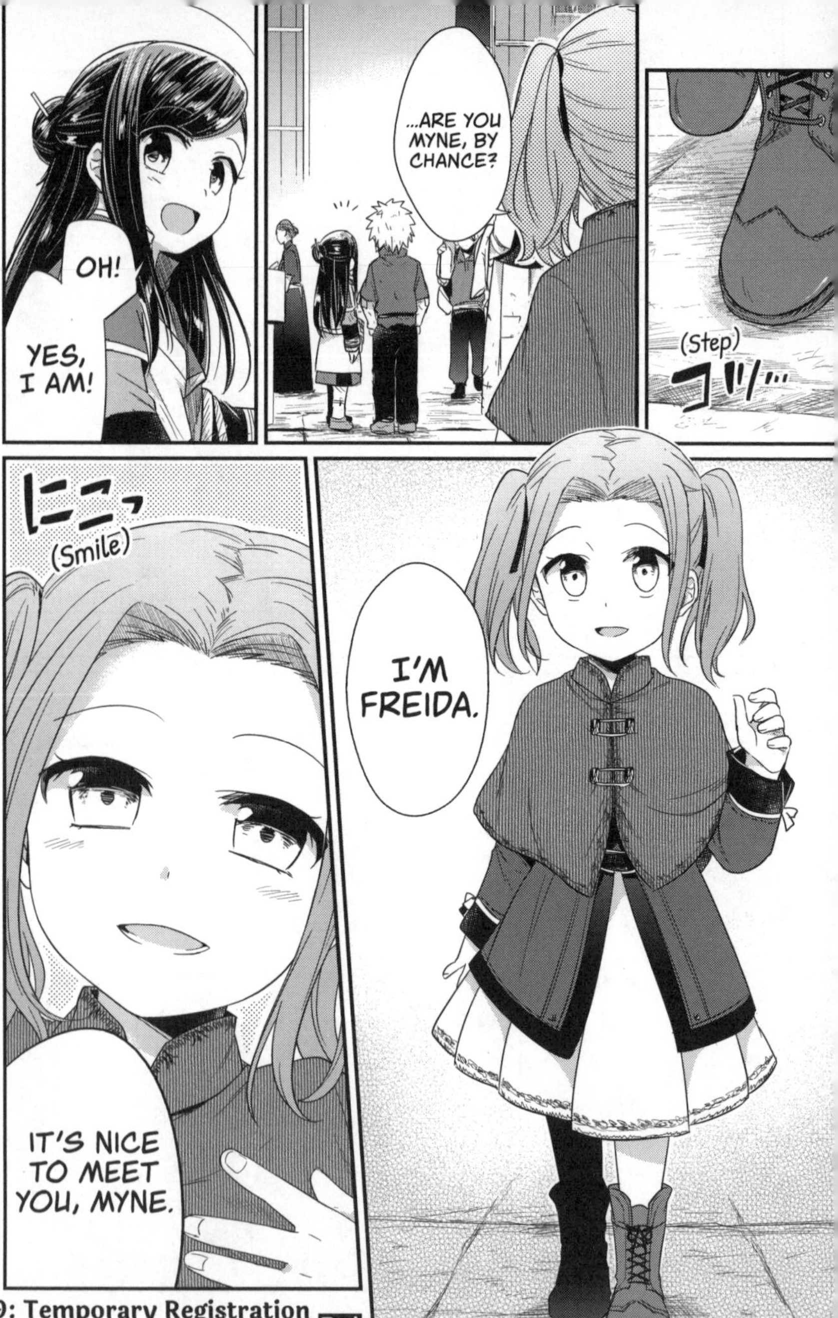
(Step)
コツ
...ARE YOU MYNE, BY CHANCE?
OH!
YES, I AM!
I'M FREIDA.
にこっ
(Smile)
IT'S NICE TO MEET YOU, MYNE.

.19: Temporary Registration and a Business Discussion End

ASCENDANCE
OF A
BOOKWORM
I'll do anything to
become a librarian!

Part 1 **If there aren't any
books, I'll just have
to make some!**

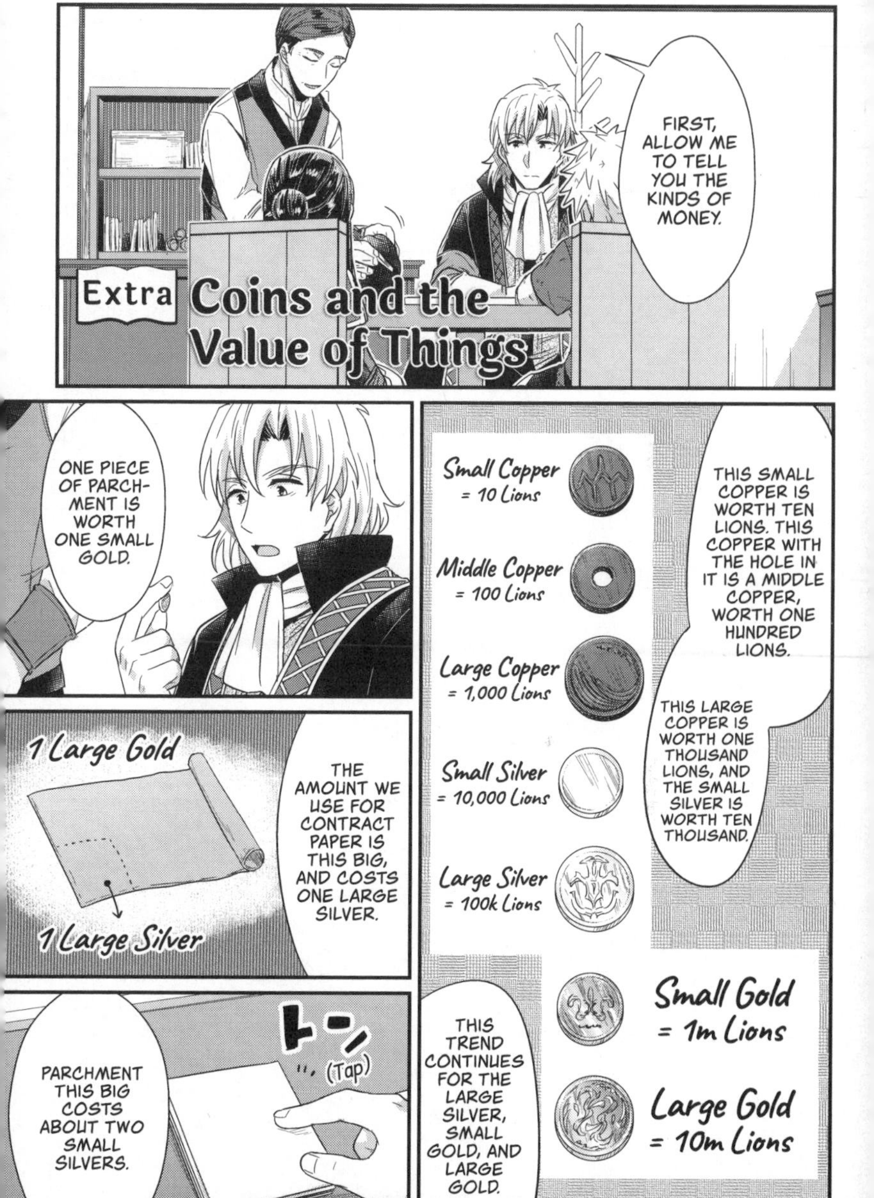
Extra Coins and the Value of Things
FIRST, ALLOW ME TO TELL YOU THE KINDS OF MONEY.
THIS SMALL COPPER IS WORTH TEN LIONS. THIS COPPER WITH THE HOLE IN IT IS A MIDDLE COPPER, WORTH ONE HUNDRED LIONS.
Small Copper = 10 Lions
Middle Copper = 100 Lions
THIS LARGE COPPER IS WORTH ONE THOUSAND LIONS, AND THE SMALL SILVER IS WORTH TEN THOUSAND.
Large Copper = 1,000 Lions
Small Silver = 10,000 Lions
Large Silver = 100k Lions
Small Gold = 1m Lions
THIS TREND CONTINUES FOR THE LARGE SILVER, SMALL GOLD, AND LARGE GOLD.
Large Gold = 10m Lions
ONE PIECE OF PARCHMENT IS WORTH ONE SMALL GOLD.
THE AMOUNT WE USE FOR CONTRACT PAPER IS THIS BIG, AND COSTS ONE LARGE SILVER.
1 Large Gold
1 Large Silver
(Tap)
PARCHMENT THIS BIG COSTS ABOUT TWO SMALL SILVERS.

*PRICES LOWER THAN TEN LIONS ARE HANDLED WITH BARTERING OF FOOD AND SMALL GOODS.

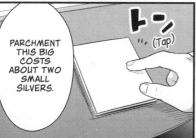

OH, AND DIDN'T DAD SAY SOMETHING LIKE...

ONE PIECE OF PARCHMENT WAS WORTH A MONTH OF HIS SALARY?

AS IF I'D BUY SOMETHING

THAT EXPENSIVE!

PARCHMENT THE SIZE OF A POSTCARD IS TWO SMALL SILVERS...?

WE'RE BASING THE PRICE OF YOUR PAPER ON THAT.

PARCHMENT REALLY IS EXPENSIVE HERE.

WE'LL TAKE THIRTY PERCENT OF THAT AS A HANDLING FEE.

HIGH QUALITY TROMBE PAPER WILL BE FOUR SMALL SILVERS.

VOLRIN PAPER WILL BE TWO SMALL SILVERS.

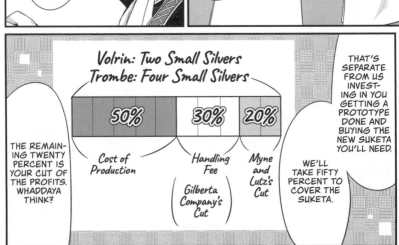

Volrin: Two Small Silvers
Trombe: Four Small Silvers

50%	30%	20%
Cost of Production	*Handling Fee*	*Myne and Lutz's Cut*
	Gilberta Company's Cut	

THE REMAINING TWENTY PERCENT IS YOUR CUT OF THE PROFITS. WHADDAYA THINK?

THAT'S SEPARATE FROM US INVESTING IN YOU GETTING A PROTOTYPE DONE AND BUYING THE NEW SUKETA YOU'LL NEED.

WE'LL TAKE FIFTY PERCENT TO COVER THE SUKETA.

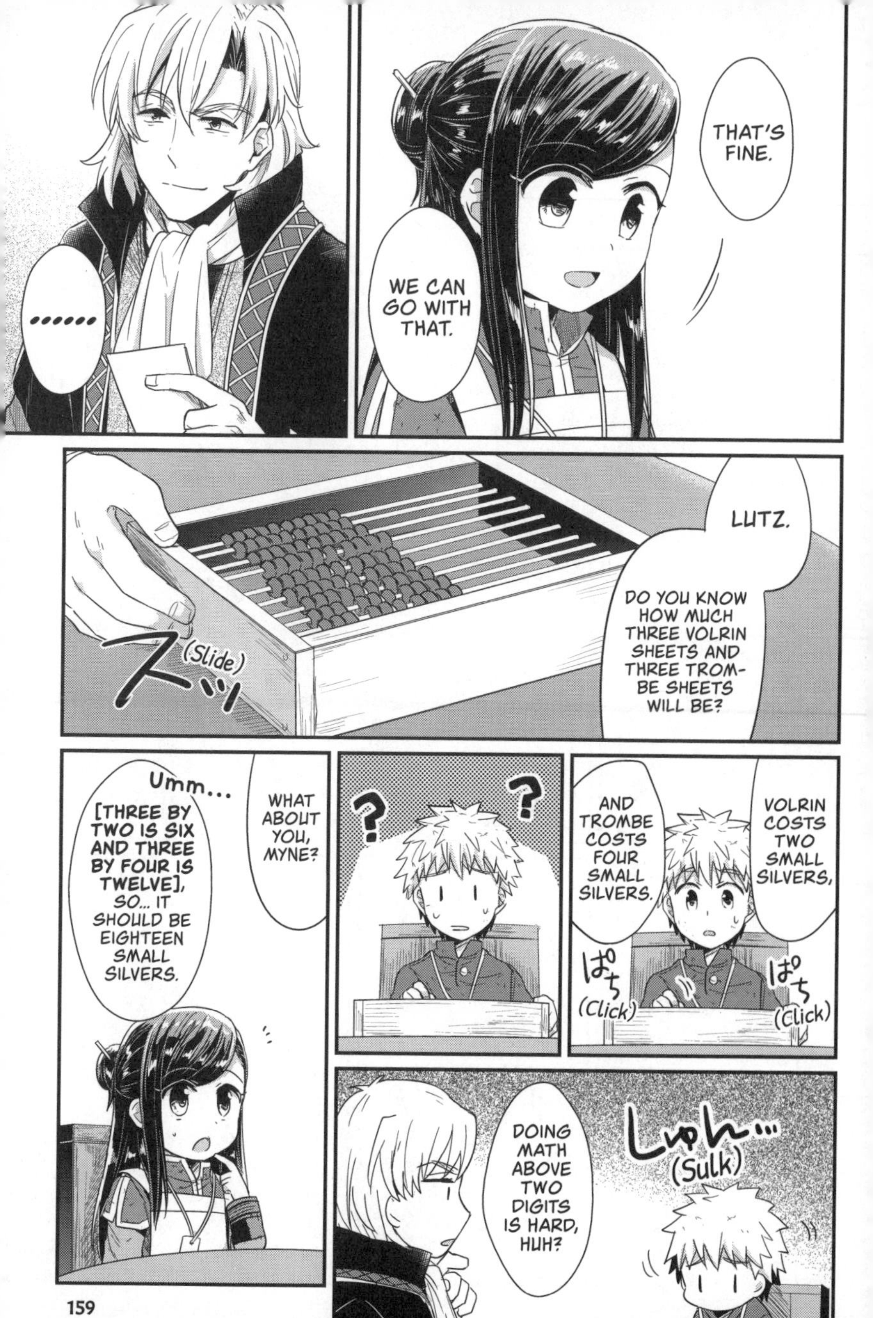
THAT'S FINE.
WE CAN GO WITH THAT.
......
LUTZ.
DO YOU KNOW HOW MUCH THREE VOLRIN SHEETS AND THREE TROM-BE SHEETS WILL BE?
(Slide)
VOLRIN COSTS TWO SMALL SILVERS,
AND TROMBE COSTS FOUR SMALL SILVERS.
(Click)
(Click)
?
?
DOING MATH ABOVE TWO DIGITS IS HARD, HUH?
(Sulk)
WHAT ABOUT YOU, MYNE?
Umm...
[THREE BY TWO IS SIX AND THREE BY FOUR IS TWELVE], SO... IT SHOULD BE EIGHTEEN SMALL SILVERS.

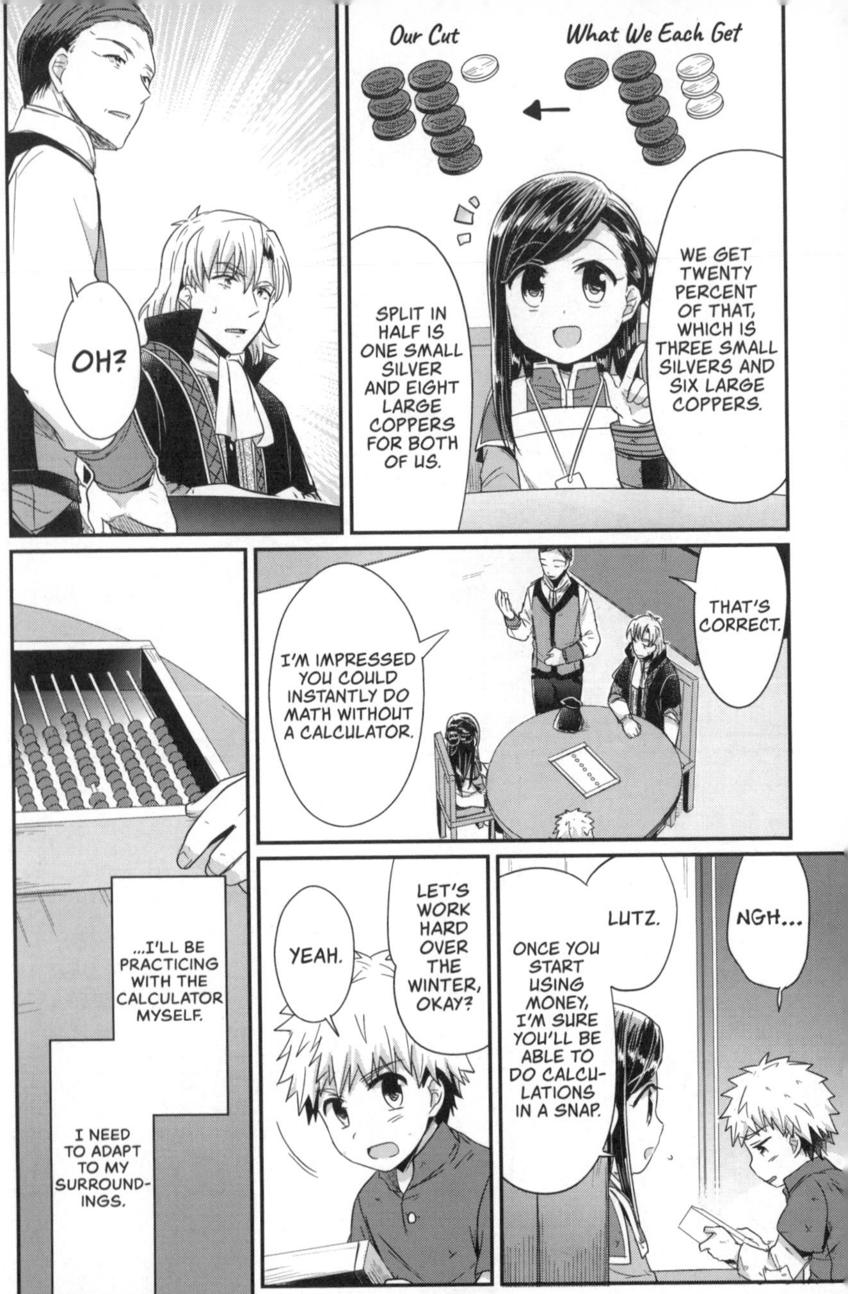
What We Each Get
Our Cut
WE GET TWENTY PERCENT OF THAT, WHICH IS THREE SMALL SILVERS AND SIX LARGE COPPERS.
SPLIT IN HALF IS ONE SMALL SILVER AND EIGHT LARGE COPPERS FOR BOTH OF US.
OH?
THAT'S CORRECT.
I'M IMPRESSED YOU COULD INSTANTLY DO MATH WITHOUT A CALCULATOR.
NGH...
LUTZ.
ONCE YOU START USING MONEY, I'M SURE YOU'LL BE ABLE TO DO CALCU-LATIONS IN A SNAP.
LET'S WORK HARD OVER THE WINTER, OKAY?
YEAH.
...I'LL BE PRACTICING WITH THE CALCULATOR MYSELF.
I NEED TO ADAPT TO MY SURROUND-INGS.

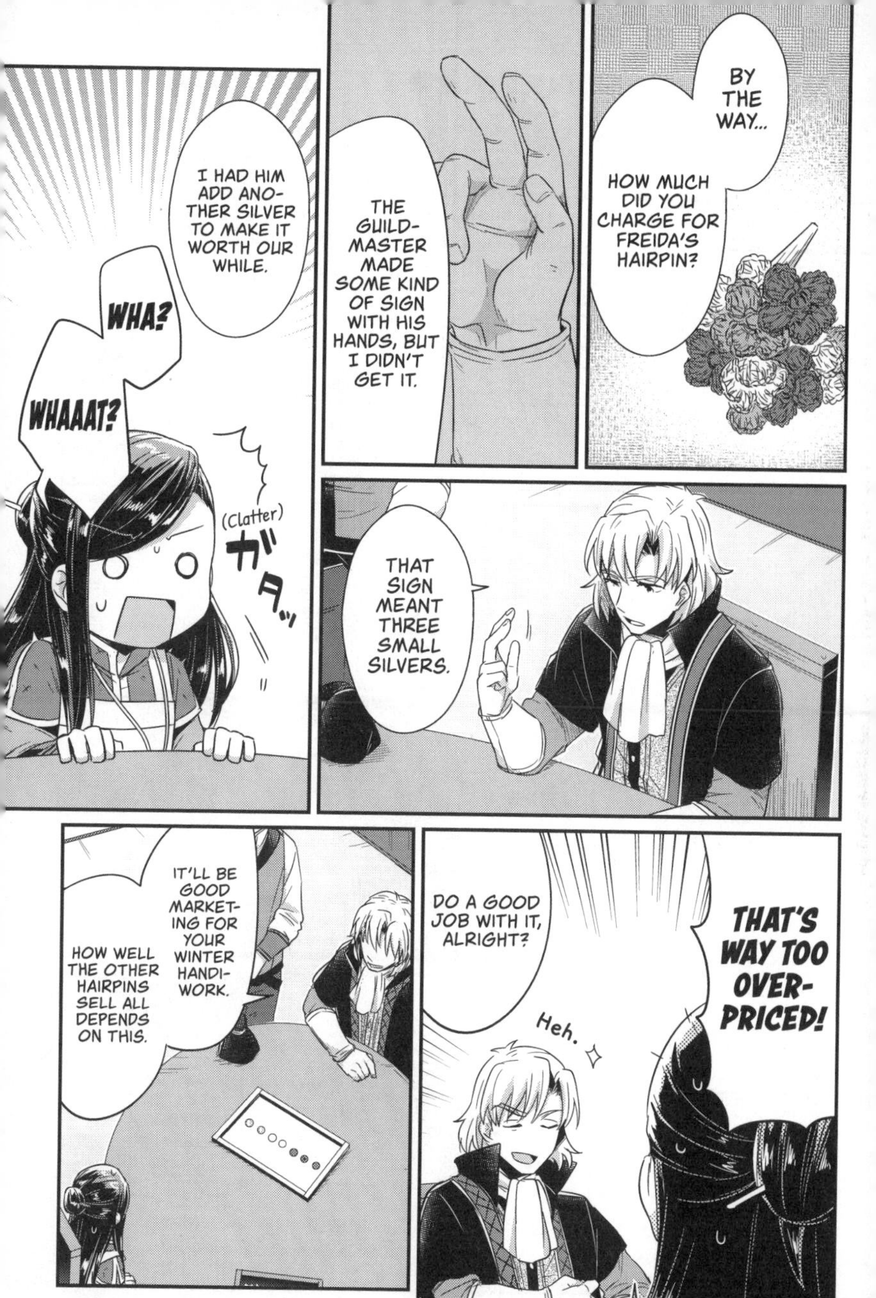
BY THE WAY...
HOW MUCH DID YOU CHARGE FOR FREIDA'S HAIRPIN?
THE GUILD-MASTER MADE SOME KIND OF SIGN WITH HIS HANDS, BUT I DIDN'T GET IT.
THAT SIGN MEANT THREE SMALL SILVERS.
I HAD HIM ADD ANO-THER SILVER TO MAKE IT WORTH OUR WHILE.
WHA?
WHAAAT?
(Clatter)
ガタッ
THAT'S WAY TOO OVER-PRICED!
DO A GOOD JOB WITH IT, ALRIGHT?
Heh.
IT'LL BE GOOD MARKET-ING FOR YOUR WINTER HANDI-WORK.
HOW WELL THE OTHER HAIRPINS SELL ALL DEPENDS ON THIS.

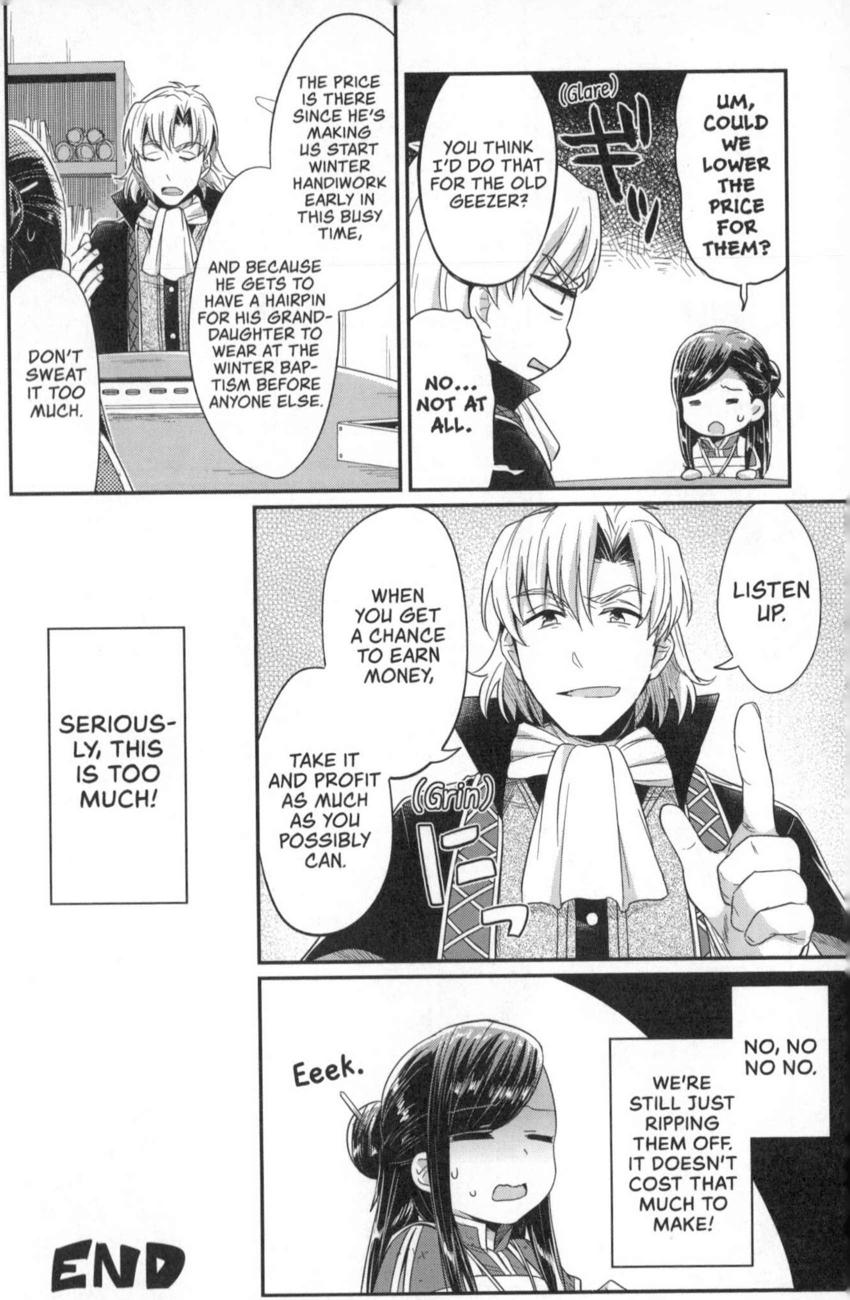
UM, COULD WE LOWER THE PRICE FOR THEM?
(Glare)
YOU THINK I'D DO THAT FOR THE OLD GEEZER?
NO... NOT AT ALL.
THE PRICE IS THERE SINCE HE'S MAKING US START WINTER HANDIWORK EARLY IN THIS BUSY TIME,
AND BECAUSE HE GETS TO HAVE A HAIRPIN FOR HIS GRAND-DAUGHTER TO WEAR AT THE WINTER BAP-TISM BEFORE ANYONE ELSE.
DON'T SWEAT IT TOO MUCH.
LISTEN UP.
WHEN YOU GET A CHANCE TO EARN MONEY,
TAKE IT AND PROFIT AS MUCH AS YOU POSSIBLY CAN.
(Grin)
SERIOUS-LY, THIS IS TOO MUCH!
NO, NO NO NO.
WE'RE STILL JUST RIPPING THEM OFF. IT DOESN'T COST THAT MUCH TO MAKE!
Eeek.
END

Zeg the Apprentice Craftsman

Zeg the Apprentice Craftsman

The sound of rustling terzini wood filled the room without pause. Ast, a senior apprentice, was good enough at weaving a type of wood called terzini into chairs that the foreman let him handle all the orders for terzini chairs—so good it was hard to think we were only three years apart in age.

The terzini chairs Ast was in the middle of making were often used in places where there was a lot of liquid, since terzini wood dried quickly after getting wet. Our own chairs tended to be used in the kitchens of restaurants, but those made in other workshops were used in the bathing rooms of nobles and the wealthy.

"Zeg, don't spend all day watching me. You need to get good at making baskets." The rustling of wood paused briefly while Ast called out to me. I shook myself awake and dropped my gaze down to my hands. There was a fancy basket made by some mystery person, and it was my job to recreate it.

Ast peeled off his leather gloves to take a break. He wiped his sweat and walked over to me, drinking from a leather flask as he looked down at my work. He then took the basket that the foreman had tossed my way and looked it over.

He was looking at it because the basket was so elaborately crafted that it stood out among all the hastily thrown together baskets made by women for over the winter. Quantity was more important than quality for winter handiwork, and it was unheard of for anyone to weave such elaborate designs that a craftsman would stop to buy one for his apprentices to learn to mimic. No craftsman in this area knew this way of weaving baskets, and everyone wondered who had made it.

"What do you think about it, Ast? The foreman said an amateur made it, but I dunno what kinda amateur could make something this fancy." Or to be honest, I just didn't want to think an amateur could make a more elaborately woven basket than me, an apprentice of a craftsman specializing in this kind of stuff. But Ast was firm in his reply.

"The foreman's right, this was made by an amateur. They're good at making the designs, but the actual weaving is way too loose, and they're not all equally tense. Whoever made this is probably pretty weak. They've gotta be an amateur. But if an amateur's making this, you've gotta surpass them if you want to get your next contract signed."

Apprentice contracts lasted three years and wouldn't get renewed if the foremand didn't approve of your skill level. Even moving to other workshops wouldn't be great since they wouldn't value your work. My contract was ending in just a year, so Ast's threat actually got me nervous. I needed to learn to make the kind of fancy basket that even a rich wife would like to buy so the foreman would renew my contract.

"Hey, Zeg. A customer came to see the foreman just now. Did you know who they were?" asked Ast, and I just shook my head with a "Nope." I wasn't experienced enough to deal with customers directly yet. I was told to go to the back as soon as anyone came inside. Sometimes I was allowed to deal with regulars we knew well, but never new customers or rich ones.

"It was a rich guy in a pretty sharp outfit with two kids wearing rags just like ours. Pretty weird," I told him.

"...Hm. Yeah, they sound pretty weird. Did the foreman leave with them?" he asked, and I nodded, telling him that they went to the thread store. Ast folded his arms and murmured, "Must be an order for something new."

"How can you tell that?"

"The foreman wouldn't need to leave the store if it's something we're used to making. He'd just send an apprentice out. Hopefully it'll be some new job that'll help our workshop stick out... Oh, sounds like the foreman's back. Let's get back to work. Try to focus a little better, Zeg." After glancing out the window, Ast went back to his table with a wave before putting on his leather gloves and picking up the terzini wood with a serious look on his face.

...One day, I'll be given serious work like Ast is, instead of just being sent out on chores and stuff.

"Foreman, I finished the basket. Could you take a look...?" I finished the basket and went to show it to the foreman, determined to show that I was better than some unknown amateur. I put extra focus on making all the folds equally tense and the like since Ast mentioned that as how he knew it was made by an amateur. I watched the foreman eagerly as he took it, hoping that he would approve of my work.

"Zeg, go to the thread store and get what I ordered."

...He's not even gonna comment on it?! Just more errands?!

Disappointed that he sent me on an errand before commenting on my work, I headed off for the thread store. The owner there knew me on sight since our store was close to his on

Craftsman's Alley and we used thread for many of our projects. I raced inside, entering the world of thread.

"Hey, I'm here to get the thread my foreman ordered. Where is it?"

"Zeg, huh? You should learn to be a little more polite. Keep talking like that, and he's never gonna let you do business with customers. Actually, is he even gonna renew your contract?" The store owner shook his head as he handed me the bundle of thread. Apparently I'd been rude enough for it to stick out that much to him.

"...My contract's ending in a year." As it stood, Ast was leagues better than me, and the foreman cared so little about the basket I busted my back to make that he sent me out on an errand before telling me what he thought about it. I slumped my shoulders sadly at how bad my situation was, and the store owner patted my shoulders.

"If you want to get your contract renewed, you've gotta have some skills that the workshop can't live without. This right here is your chance to get those. Put your all into working over the next year and you just might make it, kid."

"Huh? How is this my chance?"

"What, you don't know? This thread's crazy expensive cause it comes from spinnes, which're feybeasts. That means your workshop's gotten quite the valuable order. From the Gilberta Company, too."

"The Gilberta Company?"

"You don't know'm? It's a big store up in the north of town. I do business with'm since they deal with clothes 'n' such. But I've never had their right-hand man come over here himself. Hopefully this'll be an opportunity for us to get closer to'm too." The foreman started talking at length about how big of a store the Gilberta Company was and how important this job was to the foreman.

"...Alright, I get that the Gilberta Company's a big deal. But what's that got to do with me? He's not gonna give me work this important." I waved a pessimistic hand in the air, which made the store owned prod my forehead wth a finger.

"That's the problem with you! Always giving up so fast. This is the first time the foreman's making whatever this thing is. Watch him carefully and learn to make them too. If everything goes well, the Gilberta Company will come with orders for more. Whether you can make them or not then will change everything. You've gotta learn to make something Ast can't!"

"R-Right..."

Rubbing my forehead, I went back to the workshop and handed the foreman the spinne thread. Then, taking the thread store owner's advice to heart, I tried asking to help.

"Foreman, since I've finished the basket, can I help with this new job? You're gonna be making something with all this, right?" I pointed to a stack of cut bamboo to the side which the Gilberta Company had brought here. The foreman, still getting everything ready, blinked in surprise at my question before quickly returning to his usual surly expression and nodding.

"Alright. Slice the bamboo into strips this long," he said while handing me a thinly cut piece of bamboo. It was crooked with a diagonal tip and the surface was bumpy like it was covered in waves. I wasn't sure how long or thick he wanted me to cut it, either.

"...Foreman, how long is this thing? It's so crooked, I'm not sure how long it should be."

"Doesn't matter. Just decide on a length and make them all that long."

"Alright! How about the thickness? It's all bumpy on the front, should I just decide on whatever thickness looks good?" I asked, looking all over the bamboo stick. The foreman closed his eyes to think, then shook his head.

"Nah. Shave it down and make it as thin as the deepest groove."

I went and grabbed my tools, then sliced off the diagonal tip to set a standard length. I then started shaving down the bumpy surface.

"Man, these cuts are are pretty bad. I dunno who made these bamboo sticks, but they sure sucked at it. Feels like a kid who's never held a blade before cut'm." It was horrible work, even for amateurs. Not even comparable to the amateur that folded the basket. The foreman, hearing my murmur, let out a snort.

"That's what you get when an amateur kid who hasn't even been baptized does work. You weren't so much better when you first started your apprenticeship here."

I gave his observation a sharp frown while focusing on delicately cutting the bumpy bamboo flat, so flat that no amateur could hope to compare. Straight cuts that kept it horizontal and not diagonal. Cuts that would let me keep them all the same length and thickness.

"...How's this, foreman?" I showed him the first strip of bamboo I finished, the one I would be basing all the others on. Just finishing it alone was somehow enough to get me soaked in sweat.

He narrowed his eyes and looked it over carefully, evaluating my work so closely I couldn't help but swallow nervously for fear of what he would think.

"Not bad. Make more of them, just as long and thick as this one." The foreman had apparently finished his own work while I was cutting the example strip, and while giving me instructions he retied his gray hair behind his head. Once done, he sat down beside me and started making the same strips I was. He looked at the bamboo with a quiet expression, his hands unwavering and precise with every movement. He was leagues ahead of me and how long it took me to make just a single strip.

Gah...! I gotta get that good too!

"Calm down, Zeg. Unstable emotions lead to unstable blades." The foreman gave me a warning in a quiet voice, without his expression or quality of work changing for a second. I glanced at him. While working his eyes were scary sharp and much harsher than they usually were, but his flowing blade was as smooth as butter. He just quietly cut with a steady, repetitive rhythm.

I wanted to say something back, but I couldn't get the words out. My competitive feelings towards Ast and my fear for the upcoming contract renewal made it feel like my own soul was getting shaved down with each slice of the foreman's blade. For a moment I sat there, silently watching the foreman cut while a pleasant sound of cut wood filled the air.

"Zeg, move your hands, quietly." The foreman's stable, controlled tone of voice calmed me down somehow, and I picked my blade back up to get back to cutting. I worked slower than the foreman, but I took it seriously and made calm, delicate cuts that anyone could look at and recognize as the work of a professional.

My cutting was irregular at first, but over time the sound of me slicing wood began to match up with the foreman's regular rhythm.

"...Foreman, what are we gonna use these for?"

"Who knows. They said they wanted us to line up the bamboo strips and tie them together with strong thread to form a screen, but I don't know what they're gonna use it for," murmured the foreman while narrowing his eyes a bit to judge the length of the strip in his hand. The one I cut seemed to be good enough, as he put it to the side with the one he cut. They looked so similar to each other that I couldn't help but feel a burst of pride.

"I wanna learn to make these, screens. I feel like if I learn to make these I can really puff out my chest and say, 'I'm a real apprentice craftsman'... So, er..." I trailed off. The foreman blinked in surprise, then gave a little grin.

"Alright. Learn to make them. Dealing with spinne string isn't so easy, but... That basket you made was actually pretty good. As far as I'm concerned, you can call yourself a real apprentice craftsman now. You've earned it."

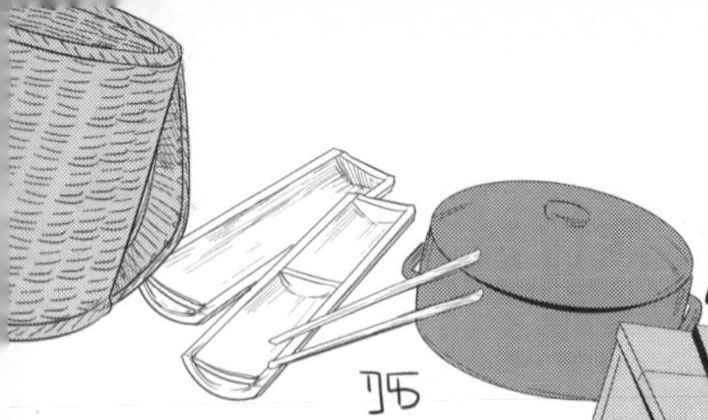

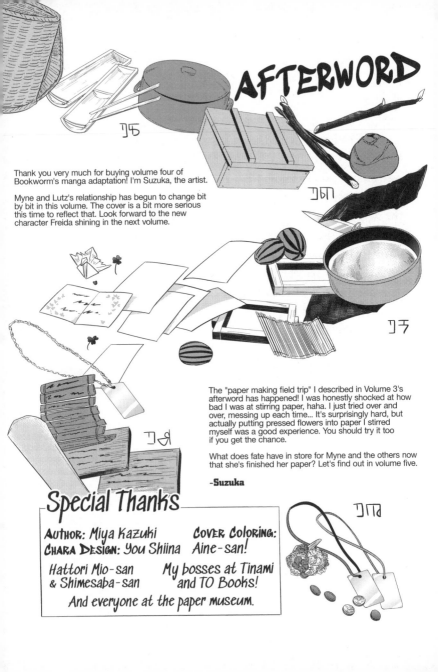

AFTERWORD

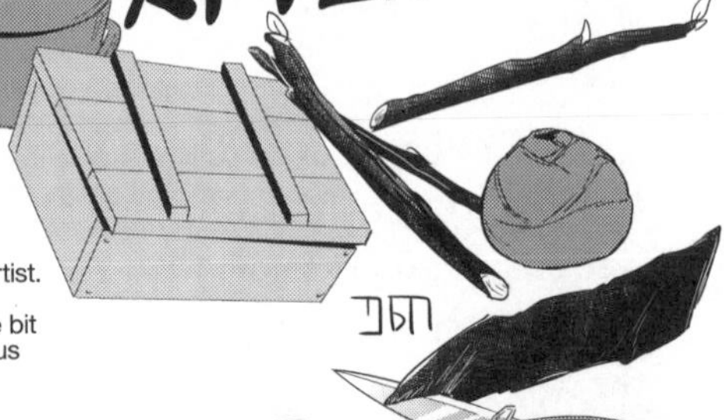

Thank you very much for buying volume four of Bookworm's manga adaptation! I'm Suzuka, the artist.

Myne and Lutz's relationship has begun to change bit by bit in this volume. The cover is a bit more serious this time to reflect that. Look forward to the new character Freida shining in the next volume.

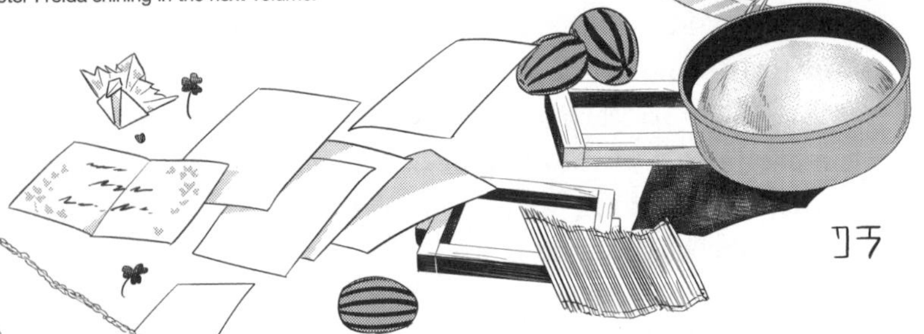

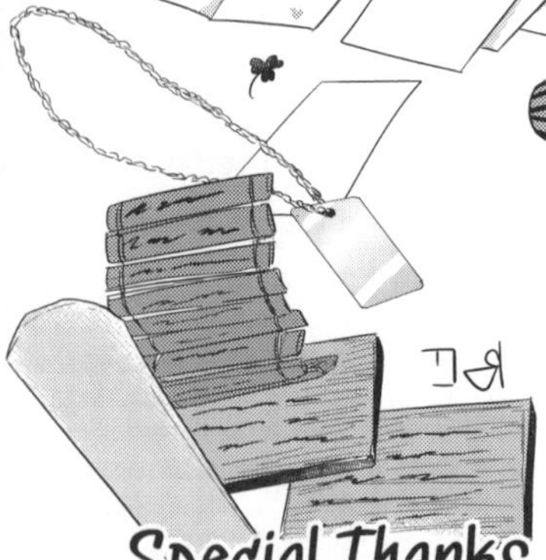

The "paper making field trip" I described in Volume 3's afterword has happened! I was honestly shocked at how bad I was at stirring paper, haha. I just tried over and over, messing up each time... It's surprisingly hard, but actually putting pressed flowers into paper I stirred myself was a good experience. You should try it too if you get the chance.

What does fate have in store for Myne and the others now that she's finished her paper? Let's find out in volume five.

-Suzuka

Special Thanks

Author: Miya Kazuki
Chara Design: You Shiina
Cover Coloring: Aine-san!

Hattori Mio-san & Shimesaba-san

My bosses at Tinami and TO Books!

And everyone at the paper museum.

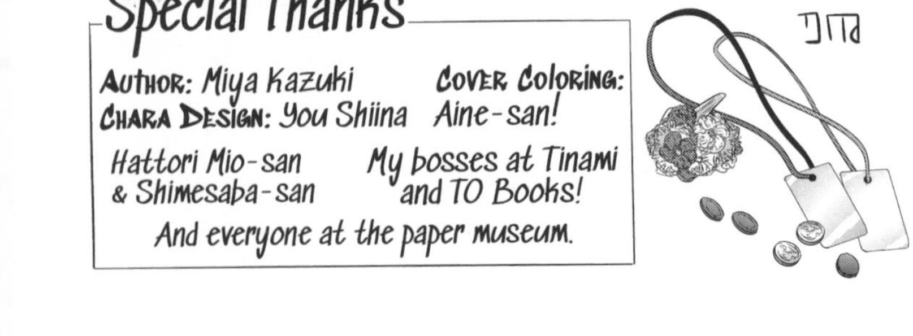

Afterword

To both those who are new to Bookworm and those who read the web novel or light novel: Thank you very much for reading Volume 4 of *Ascendance of a Bookworm*'s manga adaptation.

Myne and Lutz get more involved with the Gilberta Company to help their paper making, which expands the options available to them through the power of money. They go all over town buying things. Myne is so weak she rarely goes outside, so this led to her visiting places she had never been to before.

On top of that, these were shopping trips for book making. She's so prone to excitement that Lutz gets exhausted watching over her (haha). Still, it's nice that she could buy everything she wanted. Adults covering the investment allows her to proceed with paper making so fast, it's like all her past challenges and failures never happened at all. Benno is so generous with money. I love him!

Of course, Benno's doing all this with his eyes on the profit, but not even he expected Tuuli's hairpin to be pulled out of nowhere. Through that hairpin Myne meets the guildmaster of the Merchant's Guild and his grand-daughter, Freida. Both of them appeared in Volume 3's short story. Look forward to their future appearances.

I'm also moved by how detailed Suzuka-sama drew the city. It's very easy to tell how the wealthy north of the city is different from the south, where Myne lives. The buildings are bigger, the paving is better, the people dress better, and even the insides of buildings are decorated a lot differently from the south. Just compare the sights in this volume to the last volume.

Which reminds me. Suzuka-sama did the character designs for the logger and the craftsman. Both of them fit my descriptions perfectly. I actually like the craftsman quite a lot. Doesn't he look exactly like the kind of high-strung guy who does precise work?

Suzuka-sama's design for him was so perfect that I decided to write the short story for this volume from the perspective of his apprentice, Zeg. I was originally going to do it from the perspective of the thread store owner, but decided he could wait a bit, and thought more about who could best show how cool the craftsman is? And thus, Zeg was the natural choice.

Zeg doesn't appear in the original novels at all, but he grows a lot while performing the key role of making the screens (the "su" of the suketa) which are essential to paper making. Even though Myne's eyes never fall on him, he's a pillar that holds up the Gilberta Company's paper making efforts. Please enjoy a glimpse into a world that lives and breathes even without the protagonist around.

Miya Kazuki

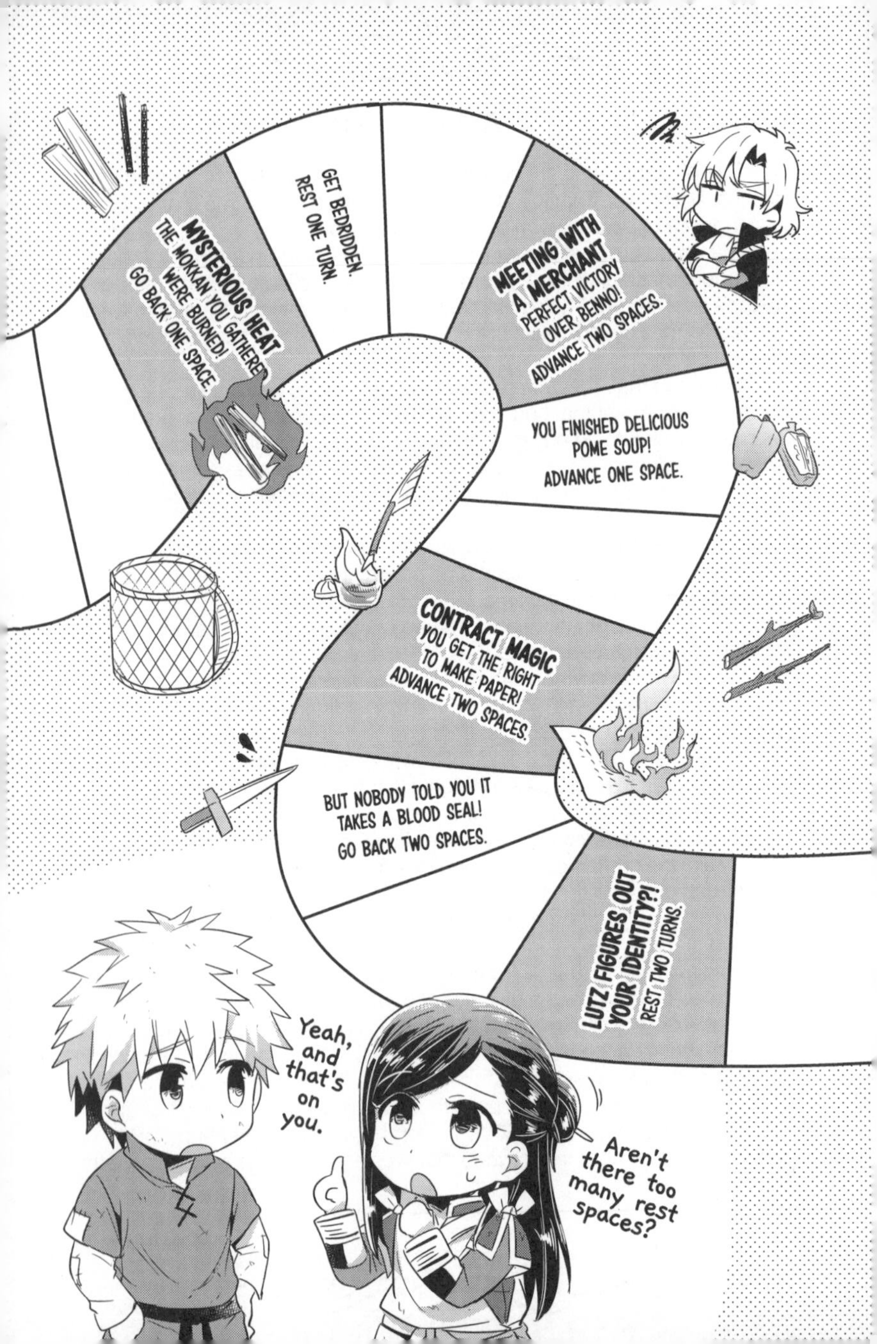
MYSTERIOUS HEAT
THE MOKKAN YOU GATHERED WERE BURNED!
GO BACK ONE SPACE.
GET BEDRIDDEN.
REST ONE TURN.
MEETING WITH A MERCHANT
PERFECT VICTORY OVER BENNO!
ADVANCE TWO SPACES.
YOU FINISHED DELICIOUS POME SOUP!
ADVANCE ONE SPACE.
CONTRACT MAGIC
YOU GET THE RIGHT TO MAKE PAPER!
ADVANCE TWO SPACES.
BUT NOBODY TOLD YOU IT TAKES A BLOOD SEAL!
GO BACK TWO SPACES.
LUTZ FIGURES OUT YOUR IDENTITY?!
REST TWO TURNS.
Aren't there too many rest spaces?
Yeah, and that's on you.

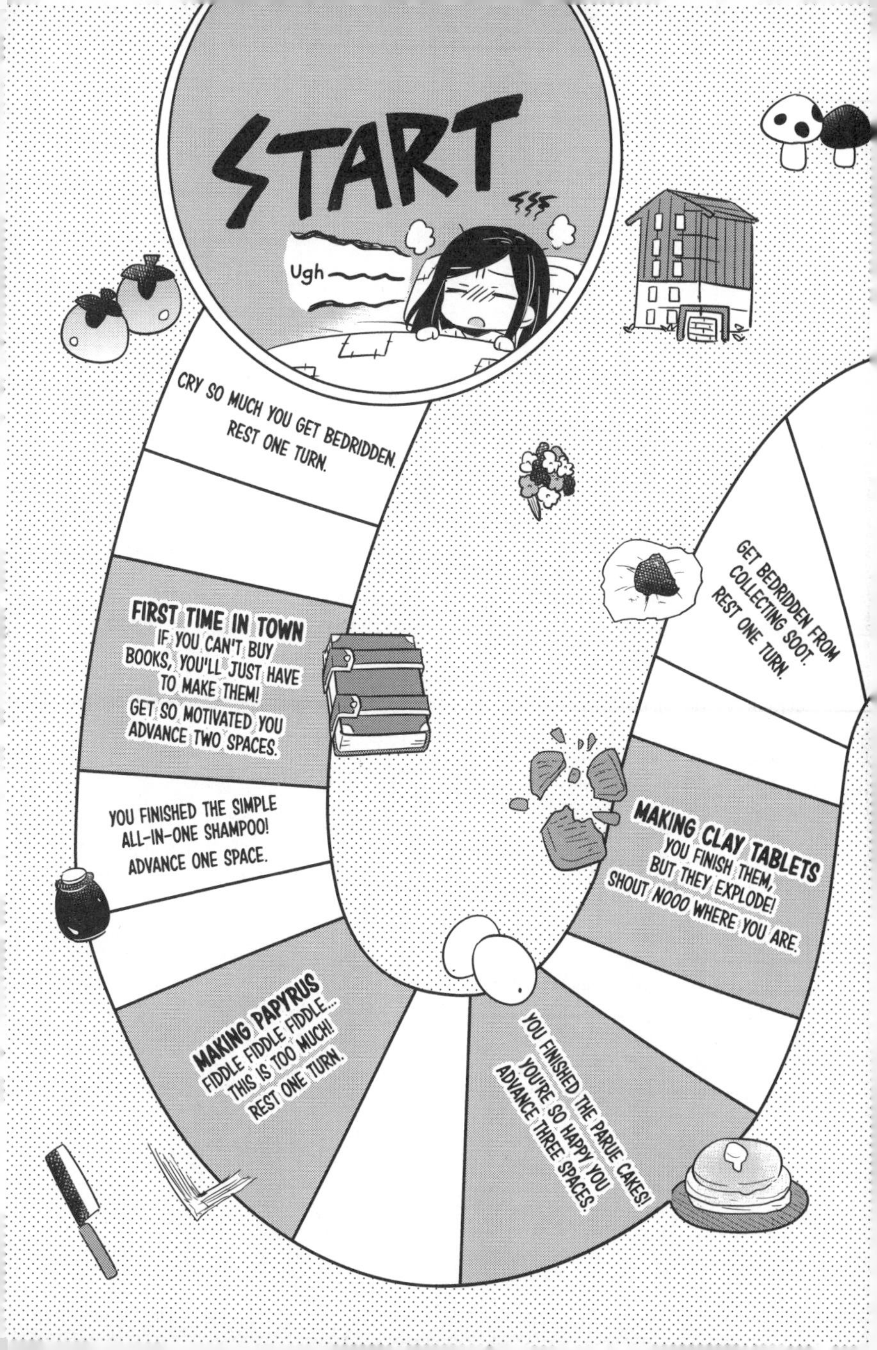
START
Ugh
CRY SO MUCH YOU GET BEDRIDDEN. REST ONE TURN.
FIRST TIME IN TOWN
IF YOU CAN'T BUY BOOKS, YOU'LL JUST HAVE TO MAKE THEM!
GET SO MOTIVATED YOU ADVANCE TWO SPACES.
YOU FINISHED THE SIMPLE ALL-IN-ONE SHAMPOO!
ADVANCE ONE SPACE.
MAKING PAPYRUS
FIDDLE FIDDLE FIDDLE... THIS IS TOO MUCH! REST ONE TURN.
YOU FINISHED THE PARUE CAKES!
YOU'RE SO HAPPY YOU ADVANCE THREE SPACES.
MAKING CLAY TABLETS
YOU FINISH THEM, BUT THEY EXPLODE!
SHOUT NOOO WHERE YOU ARE.
GET BEDRIDDEN FROM COLLECTING SOOT.
REST ONE TURN.

ASCENDANCE OF A BOOKWORM (MANGA) VOLUME 4
by Miya Kazuki (story) and Suzuka (artwork)
Original character designs by You Shiina

Translated by Carter "Quof" Collins
Edited by Aimee Zink
Lettered by Meiru

This book is a work of fiction. Names, characters, places, and incidents are the product of the author's imagination or are used fictitiously. Any resemblance to actual events, locales, or persons, living or dead, is coincidental.

First published in Japan in 2017 by TO Books, Tokyo.
Publication rights for this English edition arranged through TO Books, Tokyo.

President and Publisher: Samuel Pinansky
Managing Editor (Manga): J. Collis
Managing Translator: Kristi Fernandez
QA Manager: Hannah N. Carter
Marketing Manager: Stephanie Hii

ISBN: 978-1-7183-7253-5
Printed in Korea
First Printing: March 2021
10 9 8 7 6 5 4 3 2 1

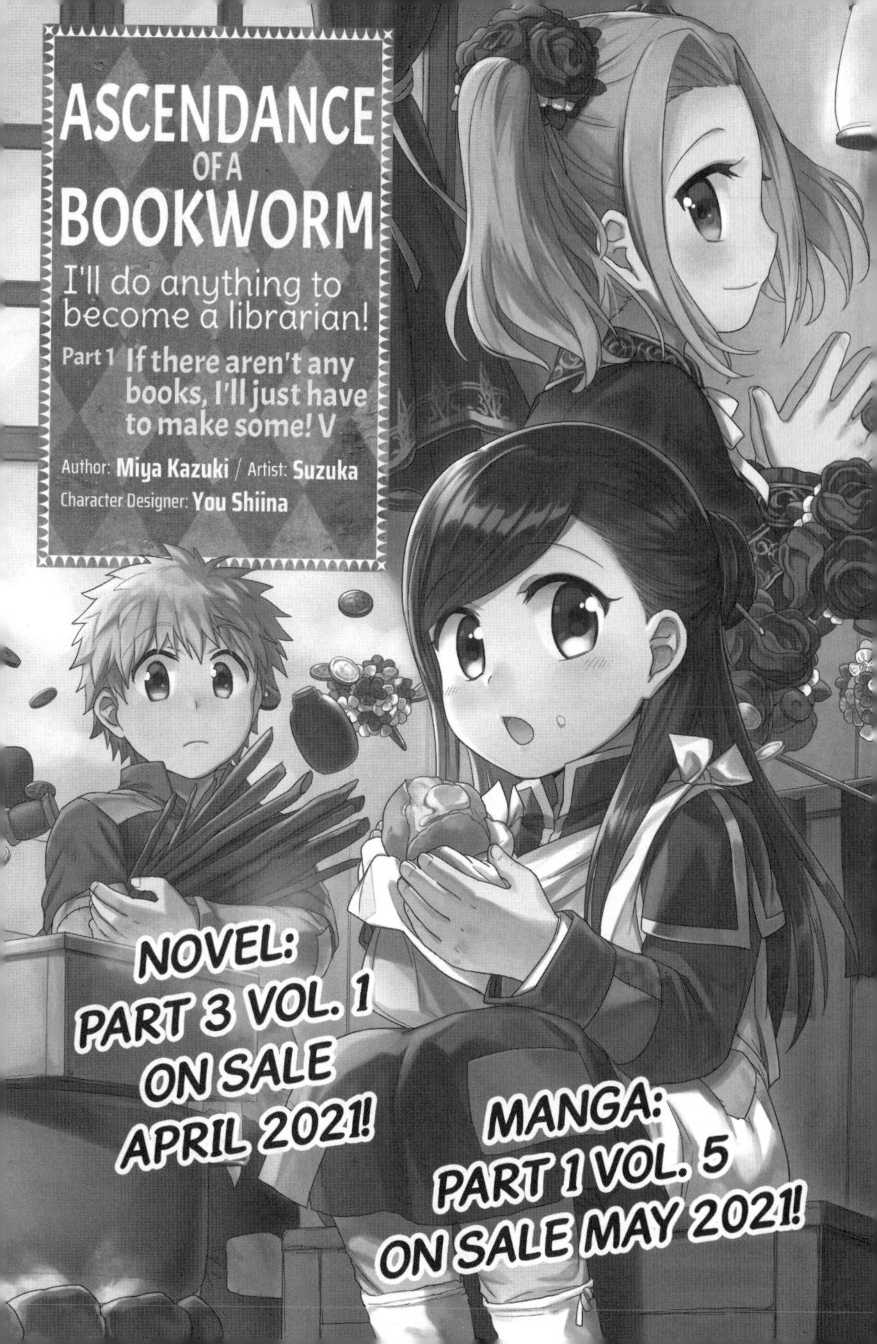

ASCENDANCE OF A BOOKWORM
I'll do anything to become a librarian!
Part 1 If there aren't any books, I'll just have to make some! V
Author: Miya Kazuki / Artist: Suzuka
Character Designer: You Shiina
NOVEL: PART 3 VOL. 1 ON SALE APRIL 2021!
MANGA: PART 1 VOL. 5 ON SALE MAY 2021!

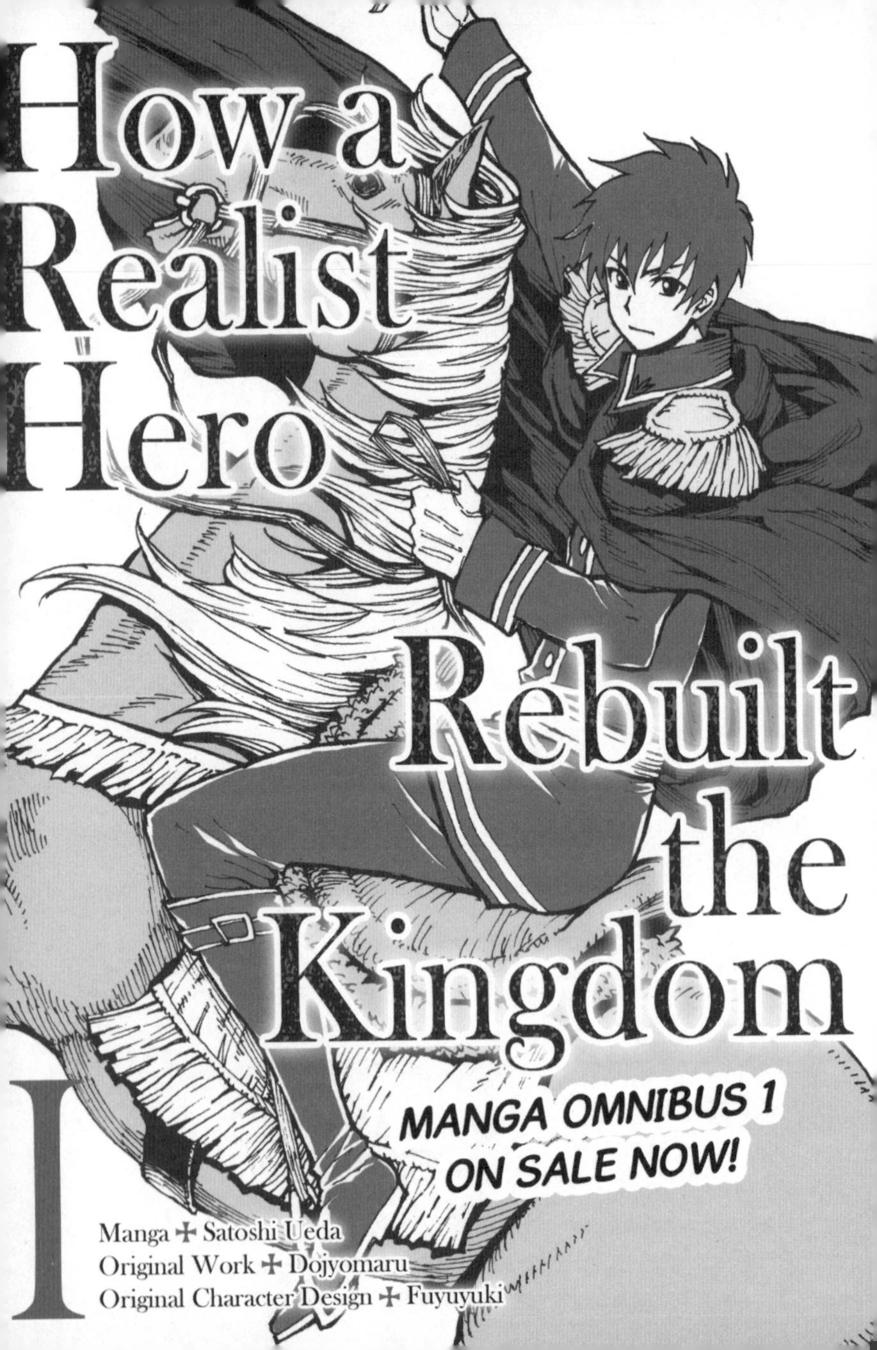
How a Realist Hero Rebuilt the Kingdom
I
MANGA OMNIBUS 1
ON SALE NOW!
Manga ✝ Satoshi Ueda
Original Work ✝ Dojyomaru
Original Character Design ✝ Fuyuyuki

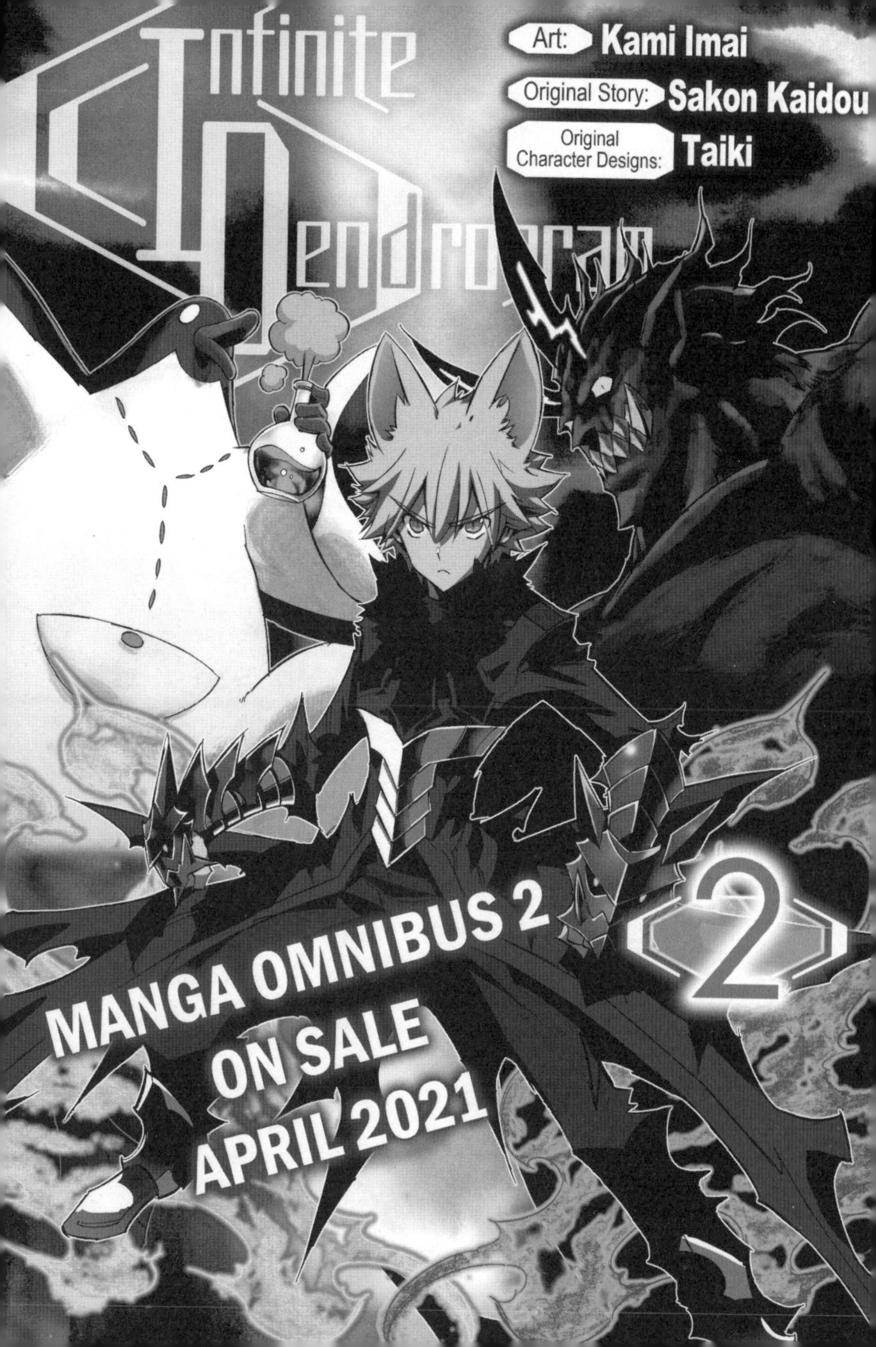

Infinite Dendrogram
Art: Kami Imai
Original Story: Sakon Kaidou
Original Character Designs: Taiki
2
MANGA OMNIBUS 2
ON SALE
APRIL 2021

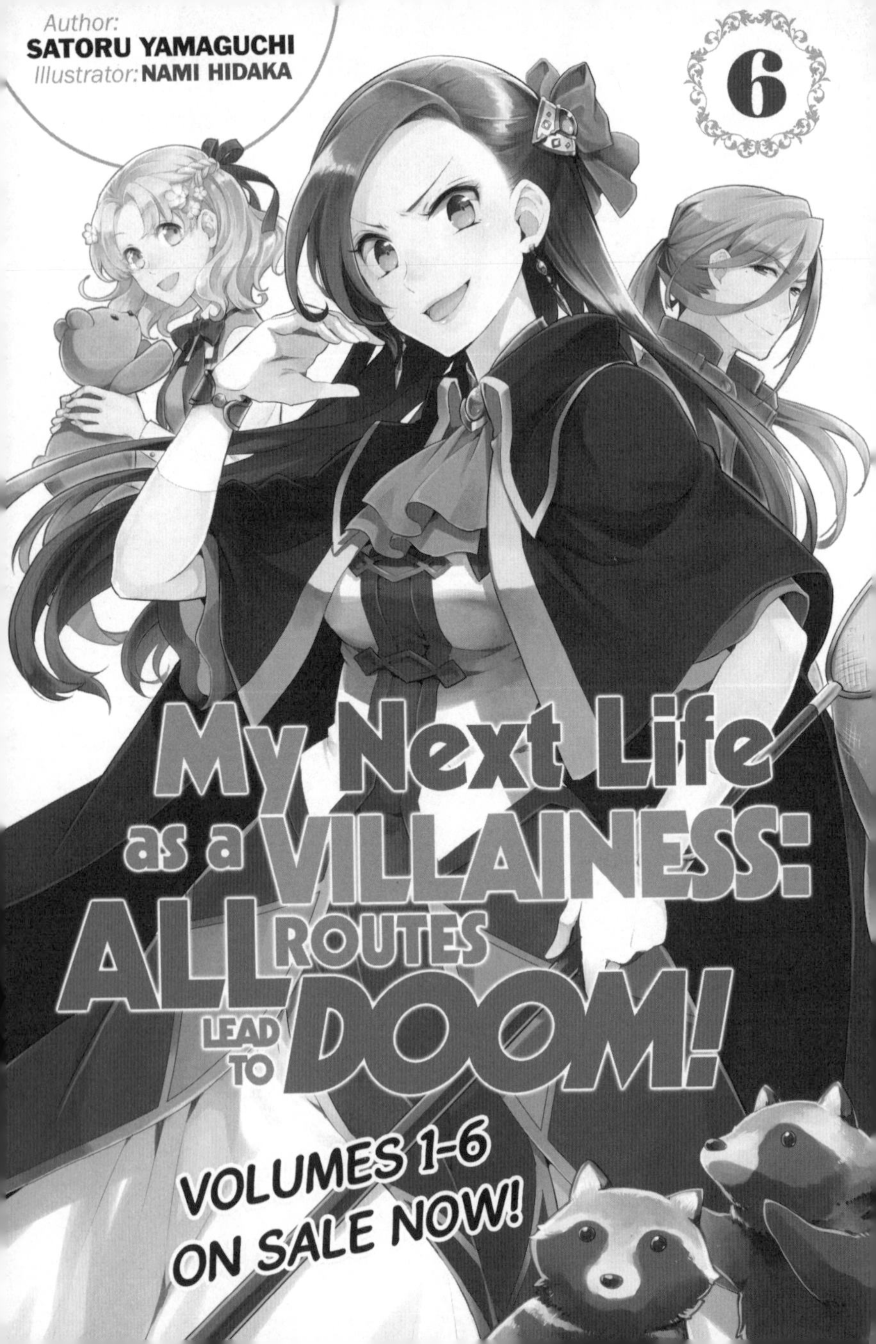
Author:
SATORU YAMAGUCHI
Illustrator: NAMI HIDAKA
6
My Next Life as a VILLAINESS: ALL ROUTES LEAD TO DOOM!
VOLUMES 1–6
ON SALE NOW!

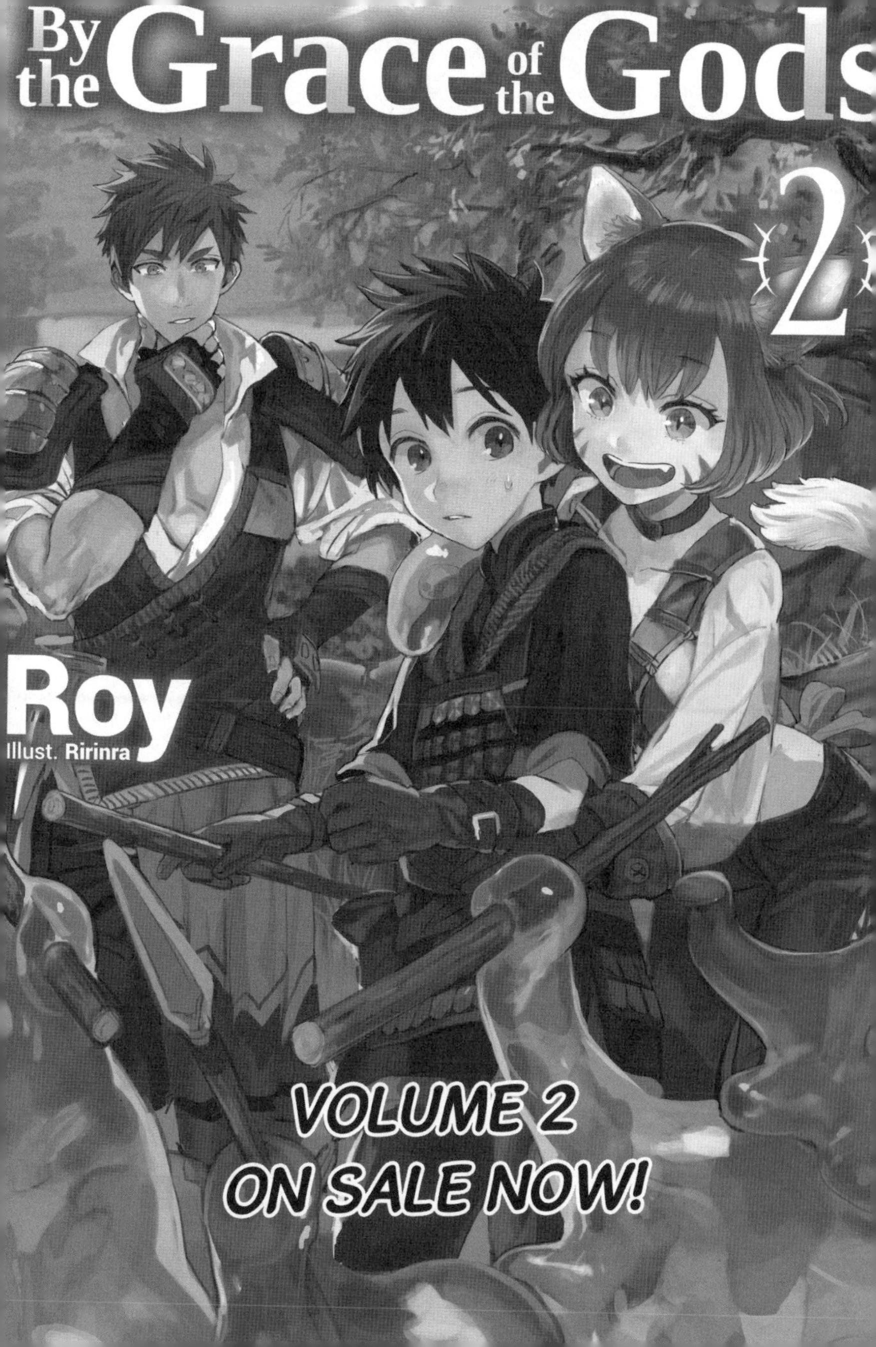

By the Grace of the Gods
2
Roy
Illust. Ririnra
VOLUME 2
ON SALE NOW!

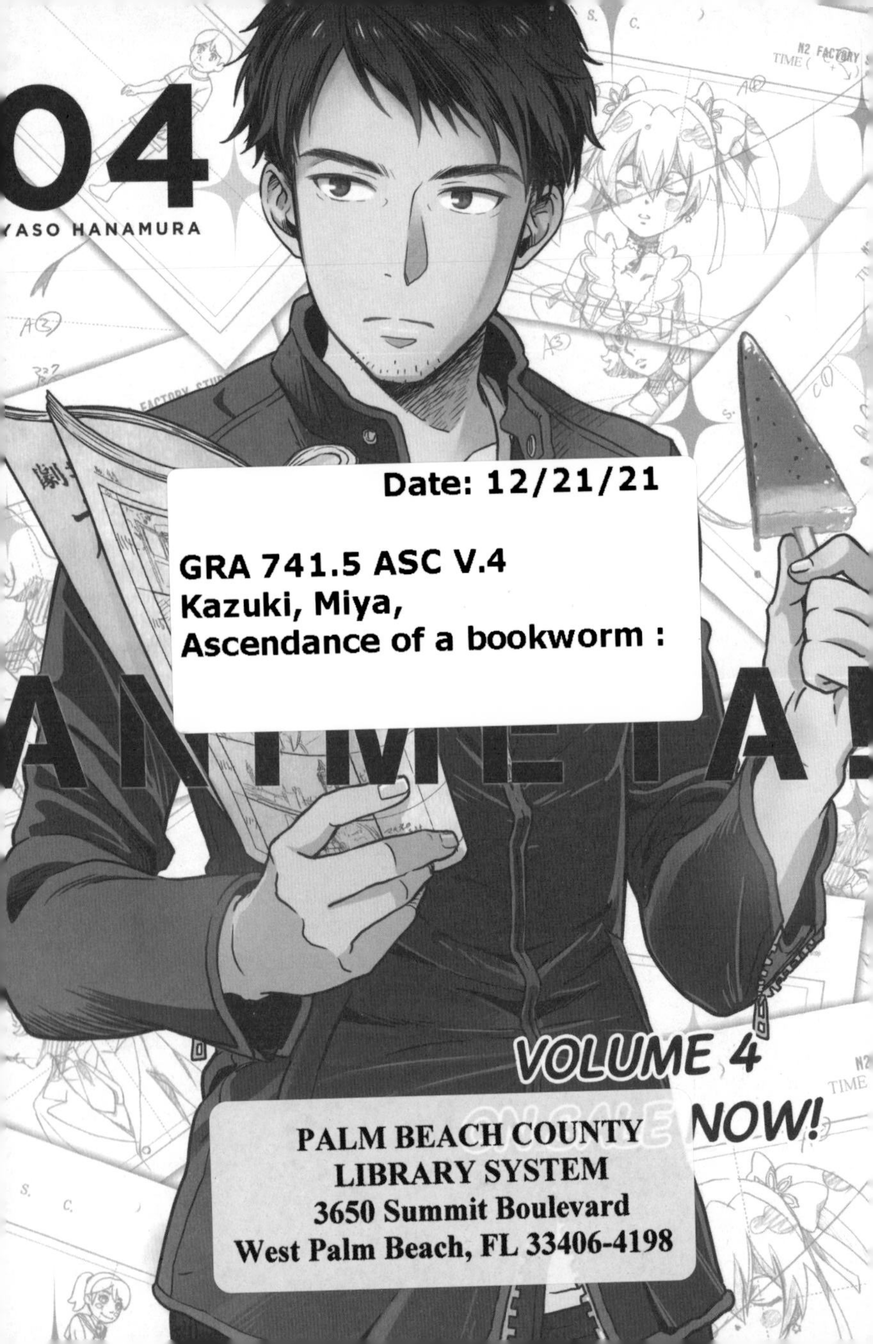
04
ASO HANAMURA
VOLUME 4
NOW!

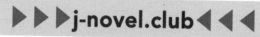

J-Novel Club Lineup

Ebook Releases Series List

A Lily Blooms in Another World
A Wild Last Boss Appeared!
Altina the Sword Princess
Amagi Brilliant Park
An Archdemon's Dilemma:
    How to Love Your Elf Bride
Arifureta Zero
Arifureta: From Commonplace
    to World's Strongest
Ascendance of a Bookworm
Beatless
Bibliophile Princess
Black Summoner
By the Grace of the Gods
Campfire Cooking in Another
    World with My Absurd Skill
Can Someone Please Explain
    What's Going On?!
Cooking with Wild Game
Crest of the Stars
Deathbound Duke's Daughter
Demon Lord, Retry!
Der Werwolf: The Annals of Veight
From Truant to Anime Screenwriter:
    My Path to "Anohana" and "The
    Anthem of the Heart"
Full Metal Panic!
Grimgar of Fantasy and Ash
Her Majesty's Swarm
Holmes of Kyoto
How a Realist Hero Rebuilt the
    Kingdom
How NOT to Summon a Demon
    Lord
I Refuse to Be Your Enemy!
I Saved Too Many Girls and Caused
    the Apocalypse
I Shall Survive Using Potions!
In Another World With My
    Smartphone
Infinite Dendrogram
Infinite Stratos
Invaders of the Rokujouma!?
Isekai Rebuilding Project
JK Haru is a Sex Worker in Another
    World
Kobold King
Kokoro Connect
Last and First Idol
Lazy Dungeon Master
Mapping: The Trash-Tier Skill That
    Got Me Into a Top-Tier Party

Middle-Aged Businessman, Arise in
    Another World!
Mixed Bathing in Another
    Dimension
Monster Tamer
My Big Sister Lives in a Fantasy
    World
My Instant Death Ability is So
    Overpowered, No One in This
    Other World Stands a Chance
    Against Me!
My Next Life as a Villainess: All
    Routes Lead to Doom!
Otherside Picnic
Outbreak Company
Outer Ragna
Record of Wortenia War
Seirei Gensouki: Spirit Chronicles
Sexiled: My Sexist Party Leader
    Kicked Me Out, So I Teamed Up
    With a Mythical Sorceress!
Slayers
Sorcerous Stabber Orphen:
    The Wayward Journey
Tearmoon Empire
Teogonia
The Bloodline
The Combat Butler and Automaton
    Waitress
The Economics of Prophecy
The Epic Tale of the Reincarnated
    Prince Herscherik
The Extraordinary, the Ordinary,
    and SOAP!
The Greatest Magicmaster's
    Retirement Plan
The Holy Knight's Dark Road
The Magic in this Other World is
    Too Far Behind!
The Master of Ragnarok & Blesser
    of Einherjar
The Sorcerer's Receptionist
The Tales of Marielle Clarac
The Underdog of the Eight Greater
    Tribes
The Unwanted Undead Adventurer
WATARU!!! The Hot-Blooded
    Fighting Teen & His Epic
    Adventures in a Fantasy World
    After Stopping a Truck with His
    Bare Hands!!

The White Cat's Revenge as
    Plotted from the Demon King's
    Lap
The World's Least Interesting
    Master Swordsman
Welcome to Japan, Ms. Elf!
When the Clock Strikes Z
Wild Times with a Fake Fake
    Princess

Manga Series:

A Very Fairy Apartment
An Archdemon's Dilemma:
    How to Love Your Elf Bride
Animeta!
Ascendance of a Bookworm
Bibliophile Princess
Black Summoner
Campfire Cooking in Another
    World with My Absurd Skill
Cooking with Wild Game
Demon Lord, Retry!
Discommunication
How a Realist Hero Rebuilt the
    Kingdom
I Love Yuri and I Got Bodyswapped
    with a Fujoshi!
I Shall Survive Using Potions!
Infinite Dendrogram
Mapping: The Trash-Tier Skill That
    Got Me Into a Top-Tier Party
Marginal Operation
Record of Wortenia War
Seirei Gensouki: Spirit Chronicles
Sorcerous Stabber Orphen:
    The Reckless Journey
Sorcerous Stabber Orphen:
    The Youthful Journey
Sweet Reincarnation
The Faraway Paladin
The Magic in this Other World is
    Too Far Behind!
The Master of Ragnarok & Blesser
    of Einherjar
The Tales of Marielle Clarac
The Unwanted Undead Adventurer

Keep an eye out at j-novel.club
for further new title
announcements!